HARCOURT

Math

Assessment Guide

Grade 3

Harcourt

Orlando Austin Chicago New York Toronto London San Diego

Visit *The Learning Site!*
www.harcourtschool.com

Printed in the United States of America

ISBN 0-15-336539-0

2 3 4 5 6 7 8 9 10 022 10 09 08 07 06 05 04

CONTENTS

TESTS

Assessment in Harcourt Math

Harcourt Math provides a wide range of assessment tools to measure student achievement before, during, and after instruction. These tools include:

- Entry Level Assessment
- Progress Monitoring
- Summative Evaluation
- Test Preparation

Entry Level Assessment

Inventory Tests—These tests, provided on pages AG1–AG8 in this *Assessment Guide*, may be administered at the beginning of the school year. This test evaluates the student's progress on the previous grade level's objectives.

Assessing Prior Knowledge ("Check What You Know")— This feature appears at the beginning of every chapter in the *Harcourt Math* Pupil Edition. It may be used before chapter instruction begins to determine whether students possess crucial prerequisite skills. Tools for intervention are provided.

Pretests—The Chapter Tests, Form A (multiple choice) or Form B (free response), may be used as pretests to measure what students already may have mastered before instruction begins. These tests are provided in this *Assessment Guide*.

Progress Monitoring

Daily Assessment—These point-of-use strategies allow you to continually adjust instruction so that all students are constantly progressing toward mastery of the grade-level objectives. These strategies appear in every lesson of the *Harcourt Math* Teacher's Edition, and include the Quick Review, Lesson Test Prep, and the Assess section of the lesson plan.

Intervention—While monitoring students' progress, you may determine that intervention is needed. The Intervention and Extension Resources page for each lesson in the Teacher's Edition suggests several options for meeting individual needs.

Student Self-Assessment—Students evaluate their own work through checklists, portfolios, and journals. Suggestions are provided in this *Assessment Guide*.

Summative Evaluation

Formal Assessment—Several options are provided to help the teacher determine whether students have achieved the goals defined by a given standard or set of standards. These options are provided at the end of each chapter and unit and at the end of the year. They include

Chapter Review/Test in the *Pupil Edition*
Chapter Tests in this *Assessment Guide*
Unit Tests in this *Assessment Guide*
Chapter Test Prep, in the *Pupil Edition*, for cumulative review

Performance Assessment—Two performance tasks for each unit are provided in the *Performance Assessment* book. Scoring rubrics and model papers are also provided in the *Performance Assessment* book. The tasks also appear in the *Pupil Edition* at the end of each unit.

Harcourt Assessment System—CD-ROM—This technology component provides the teacher with the opportunity to make and grade chapter and unit tests electronically. The tests may be customized to meet individual needs or to create standards-based tests from a bank of test items. A management system for generating reports is also included.

Test Preparation

Test Prep—To help students prepare for tests, the Lesson Test Prep, at the end of most lessons, provides items in standardized-test format. In addition, the Chapter Test Prep pages at the end of each chapter in the *Pupil Edition* provide practice in solving problems in a standardized test format. The Explain It questions provide students an opportunity to practice responding to written response questions of the type that may appear on a standardized test.

ASSESSMENT OPTIONS AT A GLANCE

ASSESSING PRIOR KNOWLEDGE

Check What You Know, *PE*
Inventory Test, Form A, *AG*
Inventory Test, Form B, *AG*

TEST PREPARATION

Chapter Test Prep, *PE*
Lesson Test Prep, *PE*
Study Guide and Review, *PE*
Explain It, *PE*

FORMAL ASSESSMENT

Chapter Review/Test, *PE*
Inventory Tests, *AG*
Pretest and Posttest Options
Chapter Test Form A, *AG*
Chapter Test Form B, *AG*
End-of-Year Tests, *AG*

Unit Test Form A, *AG*
Unit Test Form B, *AG*

Harcourt Assessment System—CD-ROM

DAILY ASSESSMENT

Quick Review, *PE*
Lesson Test Prep, *PE*
Number of the Day, *TE*
Problem of the Day, *TE*
Lesson Quiz, *TE*

PERFORMANCE ASSESSMENT

Performance Task A, *PA*
Performance Task B, *PA*

STUDENT SELF-ASSESSMENT

How Did Our Group Do?, *AG*
How Well Did I Work in My Group?, *AG*
How Did I Do?, *AG*
A Guide to My Math Portfolio, *AG*
Math Journal, *TE*

Key: AG=*Assessment Guide*, TE=*Teacher's Edition*, PE=*Pupil Edition*,
PA=*Performance Assessment*

PREPARING STUDENTS FOR SUCCESS

Assessing Prior Knowledge

Assessment of prior knowledge is essential to planning mathematics instruction and to ensure students' progress from what they already know to higher levels of learning. In *Harcourt Math*, each chapter begins with Check What You Know. This tool to assess prior knowledge can be used to determine whether students have the prerequisite skills to move on to the new skills and concepts of the subsequent chapter.

If students are found lacking in some skills or concepts, appropriate intervention strategies are suggested. The *Intervention • Skills* and *Intervention • Problem Solving* ancillaries provide additional options for intervention. The *Teacher's Edition* of the textbook provides references for reteaching, practice, and challenge activities as well as suggestions for reaching students with a wide variety of learning abilities.

Test Preparation

With increasing emphasis today on standardized tests, many students feel intimidated and nervous as testing time approaches. Whether they are facing teacher-made tests, program tests, or state-wide standardized tests, students will feel more confident with the test format and content if they know what to expect in advance.

Harcourt Math provides multiple opportunities for test preparation. At the end of most lessons there is a Lesson Test Prep, which provides items in a standardized-test format. Chapter Test Prep pages at the end of each chapter provide practice in problem solving presented in a standardized-test format. In the Student Handbook of the *Pupil Edition* there is a section on test-taking tips. Test-taking tips also appear in this *Assessment Guide* on pages AG l and AG li.

▶ FORMAL ASSESSMENT

Formal assessment in *Harcourt Math* consists of a series of reviews and tests that assess how well students understand concepts, perform skills, and solve problems related to program content. Information from these measures (along with information from other kinds of assessment) is needed to evaluate student achievement and to determine grades. Moreover, analysis of results can help determine whether additional practice or reteaching is needed.

Formal assessment in *Harcourt Math* includes the following measures:

- Inventory Tests, in this *Assessment Guide*
- Chapter Review/Tests, in the *Pupil Edition*
- Chapter Tests, in this *Assessment Guide*
- Unit Tests, in this *Assessment Guide*
- End-of-Year Tests, in this *Assessment Guide*

The **Inventory Tests** assess how well students have mastered the objectives from the previous grade level. There are two forms of Inventory Tests—multiple choice (Form A) and free response (Form B). Test results provide information about the kinds of review students may need to be successful in mathematics at the new grade level. The teacher may use the Inventory Test at the beginning of the school year or when a new student arrives in your class.

The **Chapter Review/Test** appears at the end of each chapter in the *Pupil Edition*. It can be used to determine whether there is a need for more instruction or practice. Discussion of responses can help correct misconceptions before students take the chapter test.

The **Chapter Tests** are available in two formats—multiple choice (Form A) and free response (Form B). Both forms assess the same content. The two different forms permit use of the measure as a pretest and a posttest or as two forms of the posttest.

The **Unit Tests**, in both Form A and Form B, follow the chapter tests in each unit. Unit tests assess skills and concepts from the preceding unit.

The **End-of-Year Tests** assess how well students have mastered the objectives in the grade level. There are two forms of End-of-Year Tests—multiple choice and free response. Test results may provide a teacher help in recommending a summer review program.

The **Answer Key** in this *Assessment Guide* provides reduced replications of the tests with answers. Two record forms are available for formal assessment—an Individual Record Form (starting on page AG xxviii) and a Class Record Form (starting on page AG xlvii).

Students may record their answers directly on the test sheets. However, for the multiple-choice tests, they may use the **Answer Sheet**, similar to the "bubble form" used for standardized tests. That sheet is located on page AG lii in this *Assessment Guide*.

▶ DAILY ASSESSMENT

Daily Assessment is embedded in daily instruction. Students are assessed as they learn and learn as they are assessed. First you observe and evaluate your students' work on an informal basis, and then you seek confirmation of those observations through other program assessments.

Harcourt Math offers the following resources to support informal assessment on a daily basis:

- Quick Review in the *Pupil Edition* on the first page of each lesson
- Lesson Test Prep in the *Pupil Edition* at the end of each skill lesson
- Number of the Day in the *Teacher's Edition* at the beginning of each lesson
- Problem of the Day in the *Teacher's Edition* at the beginning of each lesson
- Assess in the *Teacher's Edition* at the end of each lesson

Quick Review allows you to adjust instruction so that all students are progressing toward mastery of skills and concepts.

Lesson Test Prep provides review and practice for skills and concepts previously taught. Some of the items are written in a multiple-choice format.

Number of the Day and **Problem of the Day** kick off the lesson with problems that are relevant both to lesson content and the students' world. Their purpose is to get students thinking about the lesson topic and to provide you with insights about their ability to solve problems related to it. Class discussion may yield clues about students' readiness to learn a concept or skill emphasized in the lesson.

Assess in the Teacher's Edition at the end of each lesson includes three brief assessments: Discuss and Write—to probe students' grasp of the main lesson concept, and Lesson Quiz—a quick check of students' mastery of lesson skills.

Depending on what you learn from students' responses to lesson assessments, you may wish to use **Problem Solving, Reteach, Practice**, or **Challenge** copying masters before starting the next lesson.

▶ PERFORMANCE ASSESSMENT

Performance assessment can help reveal the thinking strategies students use to work through a problem. Students usually enjoy doing the performance tasks.

Harcourt Math offers the following assessment measures, scoring instruments, and teacher observation checklists for evaluating student performance.

- Unit Performance Assessments and Scoring Rubrics, in the *Performance Assessment* book
- Project Scoring Rubric in this *Assessment Guide*
- Portfolio Evaluation in this *Assessment Guide*
- Problem Solving Think Along Response Sheets and Scoring Guides in this *Assessment Guide*

The **Performance Assessment** book includes two tasks per unit. These tasks can help you assess students' ability to use what they have learned to solve everyday problems. The students work on extended-response items similar to those on many state assessments. For more information see the *Performance Assessment* book.

The **Project Scoring Rubric** can be used to evaluate an individual or group project. This rubric can be especially useful in evaluating the Problem Solving Project that appears in the *Teacher's Edition* at the beginning of every chapter. The project is an open-ended, problem-solving task that may involve activities such as gathering data, constructing a data table or graph, writing a report, building a model, or creating a simulation.

The **Problem Solving Think Along** is a performance assessment that is designed around the problem-solving method used in *Harcourt Math*. You may use either the Oral Response or Written Response form to evaluate the students. For more information see pages AG xxii–AG xxvi.

Portfolios can also be used to assess students' mathematics performance. For more information, see pages AG xviii–AG xxi.

▶ STUDENT SELF-ASSESSMENT

Research shows that self-assessment can have significant positive effects on students' learning. To achieve these effects, students must be challenged to reflect on their work and to monitor, analyze, and control their learning. Their ability to evaluate their behaviors and to monitor them grows with their experience in self-assessment.

Harcourt Math offers the following self-assessment tools:

- Math Journal, ideas for journal writing found in the *Teacher's Edition*
- Group Project Evaluation Sheet
- Individual Group Member Evaluation Sheet
- End-of-Chapter Individual Survey Sheet

The **Math Journal** is a collection of student writings that may communicate feelings, ideas, and explanations as well as responses to open-ended problems. It is an important evaluation tool in math even though it is not graded. Use the journal to gain insights about student growth that you cannot obtain from other assessments. Look for journal icons in your *Teacher's Edition* for suggested journal-writing activities.

The **Group Project Evaluation Sheet** ("How Did Our Group Do?") is designed to assess and build up group self-assessment skills. The Individual Group Member Evaluation ("How Well Did I Work in My Group?") helps the student evaluate his or her own behavior in and contributions to the group.

The **End-of-Chapter Survey** ("How Did I Do?") leads students to reflect on what they have learned and how they learned it. Use it to help students learn more about their own capabilities and develop confidence.

Discuss directions for completing each checklist or survey with the students. Tell them there are no "right" responses to the items. Talk over reasons for various responses.

Project Scoring Rubric

Check the indicators that describe a student's or group's performance on a project.
Use the check marks to help determine the individual's or group's overall score.

Score 3 Indicators: The student/group

_____ makes outstanding use of resources.

_____ shows thorough understanding of content.

_____ demonstrates outstanding grasp of mathematics skills.

_____ displays strong decision-making/problem-solving skills.

_____ exhibits exceptional insight/creativity.

_____ communicates ideas clearly and effectively.

Score 2 Indicators: The student/group

_____ makes good use of resources.

_____ shows adequate understanding of content.

_____ demonstrates good grasp of mathematics skills.

_____ displays adequate decision-making/problem-solving skills.

_____ exhibits reasonable insight/creativity.

_____ communicates most ideas clearly and effectively.

Score 1 Indicators: The student/group

_____ makes limited use of resources.

_____ shows partial understanding of content.

_____ demonstrates limited grasp of mathematics skills.

_____ displays weak decision-making/problem-solving skills.

_____ exhibits limited insight/creativity.

_____ communicates some ideas clearly and effectively.

Score 0 Indicators: The student/group

_____ makes little or no use of resources.

_____ fails to show understanding of content.

_____ demonstrates little or no grasp of mathematics skills.

_____ does not display decision-making/problem-solving skills.

_____ does not exhibit insight/creativity.

_____ has difficulty communicating ideas clearly and effectively.

Overall score for the project. _____

Comments: _____

_____

How Did Our Group Do?

Discuss the question. Then circle the score your group thinks it earned.

	SCORE		
How well did our group	**Great Job**	**Good Job**	**Could Do Better**
1. share ideas?	3	2	1
2. plan what to do?	3	2	1
3. carry out plans?	3	2	1
4. share the work?	3	2	1
5. solve group problems without seeking help?	3	2	1
6. make use of resources?	3	2	1
7. record information and check for accuracy?	3	2	1
8. show understanding of math ideas?	3	2	1
9. demonstrate creativity and critical thinking?	3	2	1
10. solve the project problem?	3	2	1

Write your group's answer to each question.

11. What did our group do best? _____

_____

_____

12. How can we help our group do better? _____

_____

_____

Name _____ Date _____

Project _____

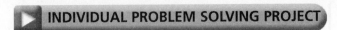

How Well Did I Work in My Group?

Circle **yes** if you agree. Circle **no** if you disagree.

1. I shared my ideas with my group.   yes   no

2. I listened to the ideas of others in my group.   yes   no

3. I was able to ask questions of my group.   yes   no

4. I encouraged others in my group to share their ideas.   yes   no

5. I was able to discuss opposite ideas with my group.   yes   no

6. I helped my group plan and make decisions.   yes   no

7. I did my fair share of the group's work.   yes   no

8. I understood the problem my group worked on.   yes   no

9. I understood the solution to the problem my group
   worked on.   yes   no

10. I can explain to others the problem my group
    worked on and its solution.   yes   no

How Did I Do?

Write your response.

1. I thought the lessons in this chapter were

   _____

2. The lesson I enjoyed the most was

   _____

3. Something that I still need to work on is

   _____

4. One thing that I think I did a great job on was

   _____

5. I would like to learn more about

   _____

6. Something I understand now that I did not understand before these lessons is

   _____

7. I think I might use the math I learned in these lessons to

   _____

8. The amount of effort I put into these lessons was

   _____

   (very little   some   a lot)

▶ PORTFOLIO ASSESSMENT

A portfolio is a collection of each student's work gathered over an extended period of time. A portfolio illustrates the growth, talents, achievements, and reflections of the learner and provides a means for the teacher to assess the student's performance and progress.

Building a Portfolio

There are many opportunities to collect students' work throughout the year as you use *Harcourt Math*. Suggested portfolio items are found throughout the *Teacher's Edition*. Give students the opportunity to select some work samples to be included in the portfolio.

- Provide a folder for each student with the student's name clearly marked.
- Explain to students that throughout the year they will save some of their work in the folder. Sometimes it will be their individual work; sometimes it will be group reports and projects or completed checklists.
- Have students complete "A Guide to My Math Portfolio" several times during the year.

Evaluating a Portfolio

The following points made with regular portfolio evaluation will encourage growth in self-evaluation:

- Discuss the contents of the portfolio as you examine it with each student.
- Encourage and reward students by emphasizing growth, original thinking, and completion of tasks.
- Reinforce and adjust instruction of the broad goals you want to accomplish as you evaluate the portfolios.
- Examine each portfolio on the basis of individual growth rather than in comparison with other portfolios.
- Use the Portfolio Evaluation sheet for your comments.
- Share the portfolios with families during conferences or send the portfolio, including the Family Response form, home with the students.

A Guide to My Math Portfolio

What Is in My Portfolio	What I Learned
1.	
2.	
3.	
4.	
5.	

I organized my portfolio this way because _____

_____

_____

Name _____

Date _____

Evaluating Performance	Evidence and Comments
1. What mathematical understandings are demonstrated?	_____ _____ _____
2. What skills are demonstrated?	_____ _____ _____
3. What approaches to problem solving and critical thinking are evident?	_____ _____ _____
4. What work habits and attitudes are demonstrated?	_____ _____ _____

Summary of Portfolio Assessment

For This Review			Since Last Review		
Excellent	Good	Fair	Improving	About the Same	Not as Good

Date _____

Dear Family,

    This is your child's math portfolio. It contains work samples that your child and I have selected to show how his or her abilities in math have grown. Your child can explain what each sample shows.

    Please look over the portfolio with your child and write a few comments in the blank space at the bottom of this sheet about what you have seen. Your child has been asked to bring the portfolio with your comments included back to school.

    Thank you for helping your child evaluate his or her portfolio and for taking pride in the work he or she has done. Your interest and support is important to your child's success in school.

Sincerely,

_____
(Teacher)

- -

Response to Portfolio:

_____
(Family member)

▶ ASSESSING PROBLEM SOLVING

Assessing a student's ability to solve problems involves more than checking the student's answer. It involves looking at how students process information and how they work at solving problems. The problem-solving method used in *Harcourt Math*—Understand, Plan, Solve, and Check—guides the student's thinking process and provides a structure within which the student can work toward a solution. The following instruments can help you assess students' problem-solving abilities:

- Think Along, Oral Response Form   p. AG xxiii
  (copy master)
- Oral Response Scoring Guide   p. AG xxiv
- Think Along, Written Response Form   p. AG xxv
  (copy master)
- Written Response Scoring Guide   p. AG xxvi

The **Oral Response Form** (page AG xxiii) can be used by a student or a group as a self-questioning instrument or as a guide for working through a problem. It can also be an interview instrument the teacher can use to assess students' problem-solving skills.

The analytic **Scoring Guide for Oral Responses** (page AG xxiv) has a criterion score for each section. It may be used to evaluate the oral presentation of an individual or group.

The **Written Response Form** (page AG xxv) provides a recording sheet for a student or group to record their responses as they work through each section of the problem-solving process.

The analytic **Scoring Guide for Written Responses** (page AG xxvi), which gives a criterion score for each section, will help you pinpoint the parts of the problem-solving process in which your students need more instruction.

Problem-Solving Think Along:
Oral Response Form

Solving problems is a thinking process. Asking yourself questions as you work through the steps in solving a problem can help guide your thinking. These questions will help you understand the problem, plan how to solve it, solve it, and then look back and check your solution. These questions will also help you think about other ways to solve the problem.

Understand

1. What is the problem about?

2. What is the question?

3. What information is given in the problem?

Plan

4. What problem-solving strategies might I try to help me solve the problem?

5. What is my estimated answer?

Solve

6. How can I solve the problem?

7. How can I state my answer in a complete sentence?

Check

8. How do I know whether my answer is reasonable?

9. How else might I have solved this problem?

Name _____

Date _____

Problem-Solving Think Along:
Scoring Guide • Oral Responses

Understand   *Criterion Score 4/6*   *Pupil Score* _____

_____ **1.** *Restate the problem in his or her own words.*
- 2 points   Complete problem restatement given.
- 1 point   Incomplete problem restatement.
- 0 points   No restatement given.

_____ **2.** *Identify the question.*
- 2 points   Complete problem restatement of the question given.
- 1 point   Incomplete problem restatement of the question given.
- 0 points   No restatement of the question given.

_____ **3.** *State list of information needed to solve the problem.*
- 2 points   Complete list given.
- 1 point   Incomplete list given.
- 0 points   No list given.

Plan   *Criterion Score 3/4*   *Pupil Score* _____

_____ **1.** *State one or more strategies that might help solve the problem.*
- 2 points   One or more useful strategies given.
- 1 point   One or more strategies given but are poor choices.
- 0 points   No strategies given.

_____ **2.** *State reasonable estimated answer.*
- 2 points   Reasonable estimate given.
- 1 point   Unreasonable estimate given.
- 0 points   No estimated answer given.

Solve   *Criterion Score 3/4*   *Pupil Score* _____

_____ **1.** *Describe a solution method that correctly represents the information in the problem.*
- 2 points   Correct solution method given.
- 1 point   Incorrect solution method given.
- 0 points   No solution method given.

_____ **2.** *State correct answer in complete sentence.*
- 2 points   Complete sentence given; answer to question is correct.
- 1 point   Sentence given does not answer the question correctly.
- 0 points   No sentence given.

Check   *Criterion Score 3/4*   *Pupil Score* _____

_____ **1.** *State sentence explaining why the answer is reasonable.*
- 2 points   Complete and correct explanation given.
- 1 point   Sentence given with incomplete or incorrect reason.
- 0 points   No solution method given.

_____ **2.** *Describe another strategy that could have been used to solve the problem.*
- 2 points   Another useful strategy described.
- 1 point   Another strategy described, but strategy is a poor choice.
- 0 points   No other strategy described.

TOTAL 13/18   *Pupil Score* _____

Problem Solving

Understand

1. Retell the problem in your own words. _____

_____

_____

_____

2. Restate the question as a fill-in-the-blank sentence. _____

_____

3. List the information needed to solve the problem. _____

_____

Plan

4. List one or more problem-solving strategies that you can use. _____

_____

5. Predict what your answer will be. _____

_____

Solve

6. Show how you solved the problem. _____

_____

7. Write your answer in a complete sentence. _____

_____

Check

8. Tell how you know your answer is reasonable. _____

_____

9. Describe another way you could have solved the problem. _____

_____

Problem-Solving Think Along:
Scoring Guide • Written Responses

Understand

Indicator 1:
Student restates the problem in his or her own words.

Criterion Score 4/6
Scoring:
2 points Complete problem restatement written.
1 point Incomplete problem restatement written.
0 points No restatement written.

Indicator 2:
Student restates the question as a fill-in-the-blank statement.

2 points Correct restatement of the question.
1 point Incorrect or incomplete restatement.
0 points No restatement written.

Indicator 3:
Student writes a complete list of the information needed to solve the problem.

2 points Complete list made.
1 point Incomplete list made.
0 points No list made.

Plan

Indicator 1:
Student lists one or more problem-solving strategies that might be helpful in solving the problem.

Criterion Score 3/4
Scoring:
2 points One or more useful strategies listed.
1 point One or more strategies listed, but strategies are poor choices.
0 points No strategies listed.

Indicator 2:
Student gives a reasonable estimated answer.

2 points Reasonable estimate given.
1 point Unreasonable estimate given.
0 points No estimated answer given.

Solve

Indicator 1:
Student shows a solution method that correctly represents the information in the problem.

Criterion Score 3/4
Scoring:
2 points Correct solution method written.
1 point Incorrect solution method written.
0 points No solution method written.

Indicator 2:
Student writes a complete sentence giving the correct answer.

2 points Sentence has correct answer and completely answers the question.
1 point Sentence has an incorrect numerical answer or does not answer the question.
0 points No sentence written.

Check

Indicator 1:
Student writes a sentence explaining why the answer is reasonable.

Criterion Score 3/4
Scoring:
2 points Gives a complete and correct explanation.
1 point Gives an incomplete or incorrect reason.
0 points No sentence written.

Indicator 2:
Student describes another strategy that could have been used to solve the problem.

2 points Another useful strategy described.
1 point Another strategy described, but it is a poor choice.
0 points No other strategy described.

TOTAL 13/18

MANAGEMENT FORMS

This *Assessment Guide* contains two types of forms to help you manage your record keeping and evaluate students in various types of assessment. On the following pages (AG xxviii–AG xlvi) you will find Individual Record Forms that contain all of the Learning Goals for the grade level, divided by unit. After each Learning Goal are correlations to the items in Form A and Form B of the Chapter Tests. Criterion scores for each Learning Goal are given. The form provides a place to enter a single student's scores on formal tests and to indicate the objectives he or she has met. A list of review options is also included. The options include lessons in the *Pupil Edition* and *Teacher's Edition*, and activities in the Workbooks that you can assign to the student who is in need of additional practice.

The Class Record Form (pages AG xlvii–AG xlix) makes it possible to record the test scores of an entire class on a single form.

Individual Record Form

Grade 3 • Unit 1 Understand Numbers and Operations

Student Name _____

Test	Chapter 1	Chapter 2	Chapter 3	Unit 1 Test
Form A				
Form B				

	GOALS AND LESSONS ASSESSED		CHAPTER TEST FORM A/B				UNIT 1 TEST FORM A/B				REVIEW
Goal #	Learning Goal	PE/TE Lessons	Test Items	Criterion Score	Student's Score Form A	Form B	Test Items	Criterion Score	Student's Score Form A	Form B	Workbooks P, R, C, PS
1A	To write addition and subtraction facts by using fact families	1.1	1-4	3/4			6, 19	2/2			1.1
1B	To identify and write missing addends	1.2	5-8	3/4			8, 25	2/2			1.2
1C	To write sums of 2 or 3 addends by using addition strategies such as the Order, Zero, and Grouping Properties of Addition	1.3	9–11	2/3			18, 27	2/2			1.3
1D	To write sums and differences of two-digit numbers with and without regrouping	1.4 1.5	12, 14, 15, 18 13, 16, 17	5/7			9, 32 12, 23	3/4			1.4 1.5
1E	To solve problems by using an appropriate skill such as *choose the operation*	1.6	19, 20	2/2			3	1/1			1.6
2A	To identify even and odd numbers	2.1	1, 4, 10, 15	3/4			13, 30	2/2			2.1
2B	To read, write and identify the value of whole numbers through 9,999	2.2 2.3	3, 7, 13, 19 2, 9, 12, 14, 18	6/9			21, 24 7, 29	3/4			2.2 2.3
2C	To solve problems by using an appropriate strategy such as *use logical reasoning*	2.4	8, 20	2/2			28	1/1			2.4
2D	To identify, extend, develop, and use number patterns	2.5	6, 16	2/2			4	1/1			2.5
2E	To read, write and identify the value of whole numbers through 999,999	2.6	5, 11, 17	2/3			2, 10, 20	2/3			2.6

CHAPTER 1 — rows 1A–1E
CHAPTER 2 — rows 2A–2E

Goal #	Learning Goal	PE/TE Lessons	Test Items	Criterion Score	Student's Score Form A	Student's Score Form B	Test Items	Criterion Score	Student's Score Form A	Student's Score Form B	Workbooks P, R, C, PS
3A	To compare and order numbers to 999,999 using appropriate strategies	3.1 3.2 3.3	2, 4, 6 10, 14, 18 3, 7, 8	6/9			5, 11 17, 22 1	3/5			3.1 3.2 3.3
3B	To solve problems using an appropriate strategy such as *use a bar graph*	3.4	15–17	2/3			14, 15	2/2			3.4
3C	To round numbers to the nearest 10, 100, and 1,000	3.5 3.6	1, 11, 13, 19 5, 9, 12, 20	5/8			31, 33 16, 26	3/4			3.5 3.6

CHAPTER 3

KEY: **P**-Practice, **R**-Reteach, **C**-Challenge, **PS**-Problem Solving

Individual Record Form

Individual Record Form

Grade 3 • Unit 2 **Addition, Subtraction, Money, and Time**

Student Name ______________________

Test	Chapter 4	Chapter 5	Chapter 6	Chapter 7	Unit 2 Test
Form A					
Form B					

	GOALS AND LESSONS ASSESSED			CHAPTER TEST FORM A/B				UNIT 2 TEST FORM A/B				REVIEW
	Goal #	**Learning Goal**	**PE/TE Lessons**	**Test Items**	**Criterion Score**	**Student's Score**		**Test Items**	**Criterion Score**	**Student's Score**		**Workbooks**
						Form A	**Form B**			**Form A**	**Form B**	**P, R, C, PS**
CHAPTER 4	4A	To write estimates and sums of two- to four-digit numbers with and without regrouping	4.1 4.3 4.5	1–4 5–9 13–17	10/14			28 15, 16 8	3/4			4.1 4.3 4.5
	4B	To solve problems by using an appropriate strategy such as *predict and test*	4.4	10–12	2/3			7	1/1			4.4
	4C	To write expressions and complete number sentences using addition or subtraction	4.6	18–20	2/3			14, 19	2/2			4.6
CHAPTER 5	5A	To write estimates and differences of two- to four-digit numbers with and without regrouping	5.1 5.3 5.4	1–6 7–11 12–16	11/16			25 13, 23, 26 4	3/5			5.1 5.3 5.4
	5B	To solve problems using an appropriate skill such as *estimate or exact answer*	5.6	17–20	3/4							5.6

Goal #	Learning Goal	PE/TE Lessons	Test Items	Criterion Score	Student's Score Form A	Student's Score Form B	Test Items	Criterion Score	Student's Score Form A	Student's Score Form B	Workbooks P, R, C, PS
6A	To count amounts of coins and bills and to write equivalent or greater amounts	6.1 6.3	1, 6, 10, 11, 13, 16, 19 2, 8, 20	7/10			9, 33 6, 27	3/4			6.1 6.3
6B	To write sums and differences of amounts of money and to make change by counting on	6.4 6.5	3, 7, 15, 18 5, 9, 12, 17	5/8			1, 10, 17 18, 24, 30	4/6			6.4 6.5
6C	To solve problems by using an appropriate strategy such as *make a table*	6.2	4, 14	2/2			5	1/1			6.2
7A	To identify the time of day	7.1 7.2	1, 3, 7, 8 5, 6	4/6			31–32 20	2/3			7.1 7.2
7B	To write elapsed times	7.3	2, 4, 9, 10	3/4			29	1/1			7.3
7C	To use a schedule and a calendar	7.4 7.5	14–16 11–13	4/6			21, 22 11, 12	3/4			7.4 7.5
7D	To solve problems by using an appropriate skill such as *sequence events*	7.6	17–20	3/4			2, 3	2/2			7.6

CHAPTER 6 · CHAPTER 7

KEY: **P**-Practice, **R**-Reteach, **C**-Challenge, **PS**-Problem Solving

Individual Record Form

Individual Record Form

Grade 3 • Unit 3 Multiplication Concepts and Facts

Student Name _____

INDIVIDUAL RECORD FORM

Test	Chapter 8	Chapter 9	Chapter 10	Chapter 11	Unit 3 Test
Form A					
Form B					

			CHAPTER TEST FORM A/B				UNIT 3 TEST FORM A/B				REVIEW
Goal #	**Learning Goal**	**PE/TE Lessons**	**Test Items**	**Criterion Score**	**Student's Score Form A**	**Form B**	**Test Items**	**Criterion Score**	**Student's Score Form A**	**Form B**	**Workbooks P, R, C, PS**
8A	To connect multiplication sentences with addition sentences, and to draw arrays to represent multiplication sentences	8.1 8.3	1, 18 3, 10, 15, 20	4/6			33 27	2/2			8.1 8.3
8B	To write multiplication facts with factors 2 and 5 using a variety of formats and strategies	8.2	2, 6, 8, 11, 12, 16	4/6			15, 18	2/2			8.2
8C	To write multiplication facts with the factor 3, and to write products by using the Order Property of Multiplication	8.4	4, 9, 13, 14, 19	3/5			2, 10	2/2			8.4
8D	To solve problems by using an appropriate skill such as *evaluate too much/too little information*	8.5	5, 7, 17	2/3			7, 23	2/2			8.5
9A	To write multiplication facts with factors 0, 1, and 4 using a variety of formats and strategies	9.1 9.2 9.4	2, 4, 10, 18 1, 6, 9,17 7, 12, 15	7/11			26, 30 11 14	3/4			9.1 9.2 9.4
9B	To identify and write missing factors	9.5	3, 11, 14, 16, 20	3/5			1, 22, 29	2/3			9.5
9C	To solve problems by using an appropriate strategy such as *find a number pattern*	9.3	5, 8, 13, 19	3/4			9, 17	2/2			9.3

CHAPTER 8 — CHAPTER 9

GOALS AND LESSONS ASSESSED

Goal #	Learning Goal	PE/TE Lessons	Test Items	Criterion Score	Student's Score Form A	Student's Score Form B	Test Items	Criterion Score	Student's Score Form A	Student's Score Form B	Workbooks P, R, C, PS
10A	To write multiplication facts with factors 6, 7, and 8 using a variety of formats and strategies	10.1 10.2 10.4 10.5	3, 5, 6, 10, 12 8, 13, 14, 17 1, 7, 9, 15, 16 2, 4, 11	12/17			5, 31 3 12, 25, 28	4/6			10.1 10.2 10.4 10.5
10B	To solve problems by using an appropriate strategy such as *use a pictograph*	10.3	18–20	2/3			6	1/1			10.3
11A	To write multiplication facts with factors 9 and 10 using a variety of formats and strategies	11.1	1, 12, 17, 19	3/4			19, 32	2/2			11.1
11B	To identify and write the rule for a linear pattern, and to extend the pattern and solve problems by using the rule	11.2	3, 4, 9, 10, 15	3/5			4, 24	2/2			11.2
11C	To write products of 2 or 3 factors by using multiplication properties such as the Identity, Zero, Commutative, Associative, and Distributive Properties to solve problems	11.3 11.4	2, 16, 20 5–8	3/5			8, 13 16	2/3			11.3 11.4
11D	To solve problems by using an appropriate skill such as *solve multistep problems*	11.5	11, 13, 14, 18	3/4			20, 21	2/2			11.5

CHAPTER 10 · CHAPTER 11

KEY: **P**-Practice, **R**-Reteach, **C**-Challenge, **PS**-Problem Solving

Individual Record Form

Individual Record Form

Grade 3 • Unit 4 Division Concepts and Facts

Student Name _____

INDIVIDUAL RECORD FORM

Test	Chapter 12	Chapter 13	Chapter 14	Unit 4 Test
Form A				
Form B				

GOALS AND LESSONS ASSESSED / CHAPTER TEST FORM A/B / UNIT 4 TEST FORM A/B / REVIEW

Goal #	Learning Goal	PE/TE Lessons	Test Items	Criterion Score	Student's Score Form A	Form B	Test Items	Criterion Score	Student's Score Form A	Form B	Workbooks P, R, C, PS
CHAPTER 12											
12A	To model the meaning of division	12.1	1–3	2/3			1	1/1			12.1
12B	To relate division to subtraction	12.2	4–8	3/5			2	1/1			12.2
12C	To write division facts by using multiplication facts and fact families	12.3 12.4	9–13 14–17	6/9			3–5 6–7	3/5			12.3 12.4
12D	To solve problems by using an appropriate strategy such as *write a number sentence*	12.5	18–20	2/3			8, 9	2/2			12.5
CHAPTER 13											
13A	To write division facts with divisors of 2, 5, 3, and 4, and to understand the special properties of 0 and 1 in division	13.1 13.2 13.3	1–4 5–9 10–12	8/12			10–12 13–14 15–16	5/7			13.1 13.2 13.3
13B	To write expressions and complete number sentences by using addition, subtraction, multiplication, or division	13.4	13–16	3/4			17–19	2/3			13.4
13C	To solve problems by using an appropriate skill such as *choose the operation*	13.5	17–20	3/4			20	1/1			13.5

Goal #	Learning Goal	PE/TE Lessons	Test Items	Criterion Score	Student's Score Form A	Student's Score Form B	Test Items	Criterion Score	Student's Score Form A	Student's Score Form B	Workbooks P, R, C, PS
14A	To write division facts with divisors of 6, 7, 8, 9, and 10	14.1 14.2 14.3	1–5 6–10 11–13	9/13			21–23 24–25 26–27	5/7			14.1 14.2 14.3
14B	To write the unit or total cost of multiple items	14.4	14–16	2/3			28–30	2/3			14.4
14C	To solve problems by using an appropriate strategy such as *work backward*	14.5	17–20	3/4			31–33	2/3			14.5

CHAPTER 14

KEY: **P**-Practice, **R**-Reteach, **C**-Challenge, **PS**-Problem Solving

Individual Record Form

Grade 3 • Unit 5 Data and Measurement

Student Name _____

Test	Chapter 15	Chapter 16	Chapter 17	Chapter 18	Unit 5 Test
Form A					
Form B					

GOALS AND LESSONS ASSESSED

			CHAPTER TEST FORM A/B					UNIT 5 TEST FORM A/B				REVIEW
Goal #	Learning Goal	PE/TE Lessons	Test Items	Criterion Score	Student's Score Form A	Form B	Test Items	Criterion Score	Student's Score Form A	Form B	Workbooks P, R, C, PS
CHAPTER 15 15A	To collect, record, and classify data	15.1 15.2 15.3	1–3 4–7 8–10	7/10			1, 2 3, 4 5	3/5			15.1 15.2 15.3
15B	To solve problems by using an appropriate strategy such as *make a table*	15.4	11, 12	2/2			6	1/1			15.4
15C	To read and interpret data from a survey and in a line plot; to find the range, mode and median of the data	15.5 15.6	13–16 17–20	5/8			7, 8 9, 10	3/4			15.5 15.6
CHAPTER 16 16A	To solve problems by using an appropriate strategy such as *make a graph*	16.1	1–4	3/4			11, 12	2/2			16.1
16B	To read, interpret, and draw bar graphs	16.2 16.3	5–7 8–11	5/7			13, 14	2/2			16.2 16.3
16C	To locate points on a grid	16.4	12–15	3/4			15, 16	2/2			16.4
16D	To read and interpret line graphs	16.5	16–18	2/3			17, 18	2/2			16.5

Student Name ______________________

Unit 5 (continued)

Chapter	Goal #	Learning Goal	PE/TE Lessons	Test Items	Criterion Score	Student's Score Form A	Student's Score Form B	Test Items	Criterion Score	Student's Score Form A	Student's Score Form B	Workbooks P, R, C, PS
CHAPTER 17	17A	To estimate and measure length, distance, capacity, and weight using appropriate customary units	17.1 17.2 17.3 17.4	1–3 4–7 8–10 11–13	9/13			19 20 21 22	3/4			17.1 17.2 17.3 17.4
	17B	To use a variety of methods to convert units within the customary system of measurement	17.5	14–17	3/4			23, 24	2/2			17.5
	17C	To solve problems by using an appropriate skill such as *estimate or measure*	17.6	18–20	2/3			25	1/1			17.6
CHAPTER 18	18A	To estimate and measure length by using metric units	18.1	1–4	3/4			26, 27	2/2			18.1
	18B	To solve problems by using an appropriate strategy such as *make a table*	18.2	5–8	3/4			28, 29	2/2			18.2
	18C	To estimate and measure capacity and mass using metric units	18.3 18.4	9–12 13–16	5/8			30 31	2/2			18.3 18.4
	18D	To estimate and measure temperature by using metric and customary units	18.5	17–20	3/4			32, 33	2/2			18.5

KEY: **P**-Practice, **R**-Reteach, **C**-Challenge, **PS**-Problem Solving

Individual Record Form

Grade 3 • Unit 6 Geometry

Student Name _____

Test	Chapter 19	Chapter 20	Chapter 21	Chapter 22	Unit 6 Test
Form A					
Form B					

GOALS AND LESSONS ASSESSED / CHAPTER TEST FORM A/B / UNIT 6 TEST FORM A/B / REVIEW

			CHAPTER TEST FORM A/B				UNIT 6 TEST FORM A/B				REVIEW
Goal #	Learning Goal	PE/TE Lessons	Test Items	Criterion Score	Student's Score Form A	Form B	Test Items	Criterion Score	Student's Score Form A	Form B	Workbooks P, R, C, PS
19A	To identify and compare lines, line segments, line relationships, rays, and angles	19.1 19.2	1–4 5–7	5/7			1, 2 3, 4	3/4			19.1 19.2
19B	To identify, describe, and classify polygons, triangles, and quadrilaterals	19.3 19.4 19.5	8, 9 10–13 14–16	6/9			5, 6 7–9 10, 11	5/7			19.3 19.4 19.5
19C	To solve problems by using an appropriate strategy such as *draw a diagram*	19.6	17, 18	2/2			12	1/1			19.6
20A	To identify and draw congruent and similar figures, lines of symmetry, and transformations of polygons	20.1 20.2 20.3 20.4	1–3 4–6 7–9 10–12	8/12			13, 14 15 16 17, 18	4/6			20.1 20.2 20.3 20.4
20B	To solve problems by using an appropriate strategy such as *make a model*	20.5	13, 14	2/2			19, 20	2/2			20.5

CHAPTER 19 — rows 19A, 19B, 19C
CHAPTER 20 — rows 20A, 20B

Goal #	Learning Goal	PE/TE Lessons	Test Items	Criterion Score	Student's Score Form A	Form B	Test Items	Criterion Score	Student's Score Form A	Form B	Workbooks P, R, C, PS
21A	To identify solid figures and their properties and relationships with plane figures	21.1 21.2	1–5 6–8	5/8			21, 22 23, 24	3/4			21.1 21.2
21B	To combine plane figures to form patterns	21.3	9–12	3/4			25	1/1			21.3
21C	To draw polygons using line segments	21.4	13–16	3/4			26	1/1			21.4
21D	To solve problems by using an appropriate skill such as *identify relationships*	21.5	17, 18	2/2			27	1/1			21.5
22A	To estimate and measure perimeter and area using nonstandard and standard units	22.1 22.2	1–6 7–10	7/10			28, 29 30	2/3			22.1 22.2
22B	To solve problems by using an appropriate skill such as *make generalizations*	22.3	11–14	3/4			31	1/1			22.3
22C	To estimate volume using nonstandard and standard units	22.4	15–20	4/6			32, 33	2/2			22.4

CHAPTER 21 CHAPTER 22

KEY: **P**-Practice, **R**-Reteach, **C**-Challenge, **PS**-Problem Solving

Individual Record Form

Grade 3 • Unit 7 Patterns and Probability

Student Name _____

Test	Chapter 23	Chapter 24	Unit 7 Test
Form A			
Form B			

GOALS AND LESSONS ASSESSED

CHAPTER TEST FORM A/B

Goal #	Learning Goal	PE/TE Lessons	Test Items	Criterion Score	Student's Score Form A	Student's Score Form B
23A	To describe, extend, and create geometric, visual, and number patterns, and to identify missing parts in patterns	23.1 23.2 23.3 23.4	1–4 5–8 9–12 13–16	11/16		
23B	To solve problems by using an appropriate strategy such as *find a pattern*	23.5	17–20	3/4		

UNIT 7 TEST FORM A/B

REVIEW

Test Items	Criterion Score	Student's Score Form A	Student's Score Form B	Workbooks P, R, C, PS
1, 2 3, 4 5–7 8, 9	6/9			23.1 23.2 23.3 23.4
10, 11	2/2			23.5

CHAPTER 23

Goal #	Learning Goal	PE/TE Lessons	Test Items	Criterion Score	Student's Score Form A	Student's Score Form B	Test Items	Criterion Score	Student's Score Form A	Student's Score Form B	Workbooks P, R, C, PS
24A	To identify, predict, summarize, and record combinations and outcomes of events and experiments	24.1 24.2 24.3 24.4 24.5	1–2 3–5 6, 7, 10, 11 8, 9 12–14	10/14			12 13–15 16–18 19, 20 21, 22	7/11			24.1 24.2 24.3 24.4 24.5
24B	To solve problems by using an appropriate strategy such as *make a list*	24.6	15–18	3/4			23, 24	2/2			24.6

CHAPTER 24

KEY: **P**-Practice, **R**-Reteach, **C**-Challenge, **PS**-Problem Solving

Individual Record Form

Individual Record Form

Grade 3 • Unit 8 Fractions and Decimals

Student Name _____

Test	Chapter 25	Chapter 26	Chapter 27	Chapter 28	Unit 8 Test
Form A					
Form B					

GOALS AND LESSONS ASSESSED / CHAPTER TEST FORM A/B / UNIT 8 TEST FORM A/B / REVIEW

Goal #	Learning Goal	PE/TE Lessons	Test Items	Criterion Score	Student's Score Form A	Form B	Test Items	Criterion Score	Student's Score Form A	Form B	Workbooks P, R, C, PS
25A	To identify and write fractions for parts of a whole or for parts of a group	25.1 25.2	1, 2 3–6	4/6			1 2	2/2			25.1 25.2
25B	To write equivalent fractions	25.3	7, 8	2/2			3, 5	2/2			25.3
25C	To compare and order fractions	25.4	9–12	3/4			6, 7	2/2			25.4
25D	To solve problems by using an appropriate strategy such as *make a model*	25.5	13, 14	2/2			9, 11	2/2			25.5
25E	To read and write mixed numbers	25.6	15, 16	2/2			12	1/1			25.6
26A	To find sums of like fractions	26.1 26.2	1–5 6–8	5/8			13, 14 15, 16	3/4			26.1 26.2
26B	To find differences of like fractions	26.3 26.4	9–12 13–16	5/8			17, 18 19, 20	3/4			26.3 26.4
26C	To solve problems by using an appropriate skill such as *reasonable answers*	26.5	17–20	3/4			21	1/1			26.5

CHAPTER 25   CHAPTER 26

Goal #	Learning Goal	PE/TE Lessons	Test Items	Criterion Score	Student's Score Form A	Student's Score Form B	Test Items	Criterion Score	Student's Score Form A	Student's Score Form B	Workbooks P, R, C, PS
27A	To use models and place value charts to read and write decimals	27.1 27.4	1, 2 10–13	3/5			22, 23 26	2/2			27.1 27.4
27B	To write fractions as decimals and decimals as fractions	27.2 27.3	3–5 6–9	7/11			24 25	2/3			27.2 27.3
27C	To compare and order decimals	27.5	14, 19, 20	2/3			27	1/1			27.5
27D	To solve problems by using an appropriate skill such as *too much/too little information*	27.6	15–18	3/4			28, 29	2/2			27.6
28A	To write amounts of money as fractions and decimals of a dollar	28.1 28.2	1–4 5–9	6/9			30, 31 32	2/3			28.1 28.2
28B	To find sums and differences of decimals and money amounts	28.3	10–16	5/7			4, 8	2/2			28.3
28C	To solve problems by using an appropriate strategy such as *solve a simpler problem*	28.4	17–20	3/4			10, 33	2/2			28.4

CHAPTER 27 (27A–27D) · CHAPTER 28 (28A–28C)

KEY: **P**-Practice, **R**-Reteach, **C**-Challenge, **PS**-Problem Solving

Individual Record Form

Individual Record Form

Grade 3 • Unit 9 Multiply and Divide by 1– Digit Numbers

Student Name _____

Test	Chapter 29	Chapter 30	Unit 9 Test
Form A			
Form B			

GOALS AND LESSONS ASSESSED			CHAPTER TEST FORM A/B					UNIT 9 TEST FORM A/B					REVIEW
		PE/TE	Test	Criterion	Student's Score		Test	Criterion	Student's Score		Workbooks
Goal #	Learning Goal	Lessons	Items	Score	Form A	Form B	Items	Score	Form A	Form B	P, R, C, PS
29A	To multiply two- and three-digit numbers by one-digit numbers	29.1 29.2 29.4	1–5 6–10 15–20	11/16			1–3 4–6 10–12	6/9			29.1 29.2 29.4
29B	To solve problems by using an appropriate skill such as *choose the operation*	29.3	11–14	3/4			7–9	2/3			29.3

CHAPTER 29

Individual Record Form

Goal #	Learning Goal	PE/TE Lessons	Test Items	Criterion Score	Student's Score		Test Items	Criterion Score	Student's Score		Workbooks P, R, C, PS
					Form A	Form B			Form A	Form B	
30A	To divide two-digit dividends by one-digit divisors and write the solution	30.1 30.2	1–5 6–9	6/9			13–15 16–18	4/6			30.1 30.2
30B	To solve problems by using an appropriate skill such as *interpret the remainder*	30.3	10–14	3/5			19–21	2/3			30.3
30C	To divide three-digit dividends by one-digit divisors	30.4	15, 16, 19, 20	3/4			22–24	2/3			30.4
30D	To estimate or write quotients by using basic facts	30.5	17, 18	2/2			25–28	3/4			30.5

CHAPTER 30

KEY: **P**-Practice, **R**-Reteach, **C**-Challenge, **PS**-Problem Solving

Test	EOY Test
Form A	
Form B	

Individual Record Form

Grade 3 • End of Year Test

Student Name _____

Test Items	Learning Goal	PE/TE Lessons
1	2B	2.3
2	3A	3.2
3	4C	4.6
4	5A	5.3
5	6A	6.1
6	6B	6.5
7	7C	7.4
8	8B	8.2
9	8C	8.4
10 11	9A	9.1 9.2
12	10A	10.2
13	10B	10.3
14	11B	11.2
15	11D	11.5
16	12C	12.3
17	14A	14.1
18	23A	23.3

Test Items	Learning Goal	PE/TE Lessons
19, 20	16B	16.2
21	17A	17.2
22 23	19B	19.4 19.5
24	21A	21.1
25	22B	22.3
26	22C	22.4
27	24A	24.3
28	24B	24.6
29	25C	25.4
30	26A	26.2
31	26B	26.4
32	27B	27.2
33	27C	27.5
34	28B	28.3
35	29B	29.3
36	30B	30.3

Formal Assessment

Class Record Form

CHAPTER TESTS

School												
Teacher												
NAMES	Date											

Formal Assessment

Class Record Form

UNIT TESTS

School												
Teacher												
NAMES	Date											

Formal Assessment

Class Record Form

INVENTORY/END OF YEAR TESTS

School												
Teacher												
NAMES	Date											

▶ Test-Taking Tips

Being a good test taker is like being a good problem solver. When you answer test questions, you are solving problems. Remember to **UNDERSTAND, PLAN, SOLVE,** and **CHECK**.

Understand

Read the problem.
- Look for math terms and recall their meanings.
- Reread the problem and think about the question.
- Use the details in the problem and the question.
- Each word is important. Missing a word or reading it incorrectly could cause you to get the wrong answer.
- Pay attention to words that are in **bold** type, all CAPITAL letters, or *italics*.
- Some other words to look for are <u>round</u>, <u>about</u>, <u>only</u>, <u>best</u>, or <u>least to greatest</u>.

Plan

Think about how you can solve the problem.
- Can you solve the problem with the information given?
- Pictures, charts, tables, and graphs may have the information you need.
- Sometimes you may need to remember some information that is not given.
- Sometimes the answer choices have information to help you solve the problem.
- You may need to write a number sentence and solve it to answer the question.
- Some problems have two steps or more.
- In some problems you may need to look at relationships instead of computing an answer.
- If the path to the solution isn't clear, choose a problem-solving strategy.
- Use the strategy you chose to solve the problem.

Follow your plan, working logically and carefully.
- Estimate your answer. Look for unreasonable answer choices.
- Use reasoning to find the most likely choices.
- Make sure you solved all the steps needed to answer the problem.
- If your answer does not match one of the answer choices, check the numbers you used. Then check your computation.

Solve the problem.

- If your answer still does not match one of the choices, look for another form of the number such as decimals instead of fractions.
- If answer choices are given as pictures, look at each one by itself while you cover the other three.
- If you do not see your answer and the answer choices include NOT HERE, make sure your work is correct and then mark NOT HERE.
- Read answer choices that are statements and relate them to the problem one by one.
- Change your plan if it isn't working. You may need to try a different strategy.

Check

Take time to catch your mistakes.

- Be sure you answered the question asked.
- Check that your answer fits the information in the problem.
- Check for important words you may have missed.
- Be sure you used all the information you needed.
- Check your computation by using a different method.
- Draw a picture when you are unsure of your answer.

Don't forget!

Before the Test	During the Test
• Listen to the teacher's directions and read the instructions.	• Work quickly but carefully. If you are unsure how to answer a question, leave it blank and return to it later.
• Write down the ending time if the test is timed.	
• Know where and how to mark your answers.	• If you cannot finish on time, look over the questions that are left. Answer the easiest ones first. Then go back to the others.
• Know whether you should write on the test page or use scratch paper.	
• Ask any questions you have before the test begins.	• Fill in each answer space carefully and completely. Erase completely if you change an answer. Erase any stray marks.

Name _____ Date _____

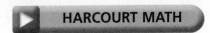

Test Answer Sheet

Test Title _____

1. Ⓐ Ⓑ Ⓒ Ⓓ
2. Ⓕ Ⓖ Ⓗ Ⓙ
3. Ⓐ Ⓑ Ⓒ Ⓓ
4. Ⓕ Ⓖ Ⓗ Ⓙ
5. Ⓐ Ⓑ Ⓒ Ⓓ

6. Ⓕ Ⓖ Ⓗ Ⓙ
7. Ⓐ Ⓑ Ⓒ Ⓓ
8. Ⓕ Ⓖ Ⓗ Ⓙ
9. Ⓐ Ⓑ Ⓒ Ⓓ
10. Ⓕ Ⓖ Ⓗ Ⓙ

11. Ⓐ Ⓑ Ⓒ Ⓓ
12. Ⓕ Ⓖ Ⓗ Ⓙ
13. Ⓐ Ⓑ Ⓒ Ⓓ
14. Ⓕ Ⓖ Ⓗ Ⓙ
15. Ⓐ Ⓑ Ⓒ Ⓓ

16. Ⓕ Ⓖ Ⓗ Ⓙ
17. Ⓐ Ⓑ Ⓒ Ⓓ
18. Ⓕ Ⓖ Ⓗ Ⓙ
19. Ⓐ Ⓑ Ⓒ Ⓓ
20. Ⓕ Ⓖ Ⓗ Ⓙ

21. Ⓐ Ⓑ Ⓒ Ⓓ
22. Ⓕ Ⓖ Ⓗ Ⓙ
23. Ⓐ Ⓑ Ⓒ Ⓓ
24. Ⓕ Ⓖ Ⓗ Ⓙ
25. Ⓐ Ⓑ Ⓒ Ⓓ

26. Ⓕ Ⓖ Ⓗ Ⓙ
27. Ⓐ Ⓑ Ⓒ Ⓓ
28. Ⓕ Ⓖ Ⓗ Ⓙ
29. Ⓐ Ⓑ Ⓒ Ⓓ
30. Ⓕ Ⓖ Ⓗ Ⓙ

31. Ⓐ Ⓑ Ⓒ Ⓓ
32. Ⓕ Ⓖ Ⓗ Ⓙ
33. Ⓐ Ⓑ Ⓒ Ⓓ
34. Ⓕ Ⓖ Ⓗ Ⓙ
35. Ⓐ Ⓑ Ⓒ Ⓓ

36. Ⓕ Ⓖ Ⓗ Ⓙ
37. Ⓐ Ⓑ Ⓒ Ⓓ
38. Ⓕ Ⓖ Ⓗ Ⓙ
39. Ⓐ Ⓑ Ⓒ Ⓓ
40. Ⓕ Ⓖ Ⓗ Ⓙ

41. Ⓐ Ⓑ Ⓒ Ⓓ
42. Ⓕ Ⓖ Ⓗ Ⓙ
43. Ⓐ Ⓑ Ⓒ Ⓓ
44. Ⓕ Ⓖ Ⓗ Ⓙ
45. Ⓐ Ⓑ Ⓒ Ⓓ

46. Ⓕ Ⓖ Ⓗ Ⓙ
47. Ⓐ Ⓑ Ⓒ Ⓓ
48. Ⓕ Ⓖ Ⓗ Ⓙ
49. Ⓐ Ⓑ Ⓒ Ⓓ
50. Ⓕ Ⓖ Ⓗ Ⓙ

Choose the correct answer.

1. What is the value of the underlined digit?

$$\underline{7}6$$

A 70 **B** 60 **C** 7 **D** 7

2. Which is NOT a way to show 84?

F 8 tens 4 ones

G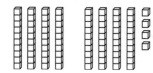

H 40 + 8

J

tens	ones
8	4

Use the tally table for 3–4.

Kira's Group's Favorite Fruit	
Fruit	Tally
apple	I
peach	IIII
pear	II
watermelon	⌖

3. Which fruit did the most children choose in Kira's group?

A apple **C** pear
B peach **D** watermelon

4. Predict which fruit the most children in Kira's class would choose.

F apple **H** pear
G peach **J** watermelon

Use the pictograph for 5–6.

Favorite Sea Creature	
whale	🐬🐬🐬🐬
dolphin	🐬🐬🐬🐬🐬
shark	🐬🐬
octopus	🐬🐬🐬

Key: Each 🐬 stands for 2 children

5. How many children chose the shark?

A 2 **B** 4 **C** 6 **D** 8

6. Which sea creature did the most children choose?

F whale **H** dolphin
G shark **J** octopus

7. Which belongs in the fact family for this set of numbers?

7   8   15

A 7 + 7 = 14
B 7 + 8 = 15
C 8 − 7 = 1
D 15 − 5 = 10

8. Solve these related problems.

15 − 8 = ■

■ + 8 = 15

F 8   **H** 6
G 7   **J** 5

Go On ▶

9. Choose how many tens and ones.

tens	ones

A 2 tens 8 ones
B 7 tens 0 ones
C 7 tens 2 ones
D 8 tens 2 ones

10. 46
   + 38

F 74   H 84
G 76   J 86

11. 38
   + 25

A 54   C 63
B 59   D 64

12. How many tens and ones are left?

65 − 9 = ▦

F 4 tens 6 ones
G 5 tens 5 ones
H 5 tens 6 ones
J 5 tens 7 ones

13. Dana had 47 stickers. She gave 9 stickers to Dawn. How many stickers does Dana have left?

A 38   B 37   C 28   D 27

14. Matt has 22 dimes. Laurel gives him 13 more dimes. How many dimes does Matt have altogether?

F 25   G 28   H 35   J 37

15. 58
   − 29

A 28   C 30
B 29   D 31

16. 73
   − 48

F 27   H 25
G 26   J 24

17. 26
     25
   + 29

A 85   C 80
B 81   D 70

18. 57
   − 38

F 30   H 25
G 29   J 19

19. Lizzie bought gloves for $4.49 and lunch for $3.57. She had $9.50 when she began. How much money does she have left?

A $1.40   C $2.44
B $1.44   D $2.46

Go On ▶

AG2 Assessment Guide

Form A • Multiple Choice

20. Choose the total amount.

F 99¢ **G** 92¢ **H** 89¢ **J** 72¢

21. What time is it?

A quarter past 9
B quarter to 9
C half past 9
D quarter to 3

For question 22, use the chart.

701	702	703	704	705	706	707	708	709	710
711	712	713	714	715	716	717	718	719	720
721	722	723	724	725	726	727	728	729	730
731	732	733	734	735	736	737	738	739	740
741	742	743	744	745	746	747	748	749	750

22. Choose the next number in the pattern.

F 750   **H** 754
G 752   **J** 756

23. Divide 26 bananas into groups of 7.

A 3 groups 5 left over
B 4 groups 5 left over
C 5 groups 1 left over
D 5 groups 3 left over

Use the calendar for 24.

NOVEMBER						
S	M	T	W	T	F	S
	1	2	3	4	5	6
7	8	9	10	11	12	13
14	15	16	17	18	19	20
21	22	23	24	25	26	27
28	29	30				

24. Mark has a hockey game one week before November 25. What is the date of the hockey game?

F November 30
G November 27
H November 18

25. Is pulling a 🜄 from the bag **more likely** or **less likely**?

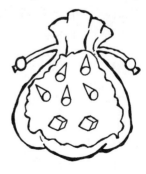

A more likely **B** less likely

Go On ▶

Form A • Multiple Choice   **Assessment Guide   AG3**

26. Choose the solid figure you can use to draw the shapes.

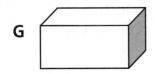

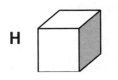

F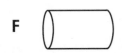

G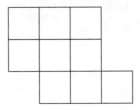

H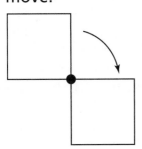

27. Choose the word that names the move.

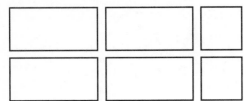

A turn **B** flip **C** slide

28. Find the pattern unit. Then choose what comes next.

F ☐⬤

G ☐⬤⬤

H ⬤⬤☐

J ⬤☐⬤

29. Predict the area. Then count the units to check.

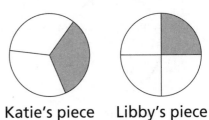

A 6 units   **C** 8 units
B 7 units   **D** 9 units

30. There are two pumpkin pies.
Katie gets $\frac{1}{3}$ of one pie.
Libby gets $\frac{1}{4}$ of the other pie.
Who gets the larger piece?

Katie's piece   Libby's piece

F Katie   **G** Libby

31. Choose the value of the underlined digit.

7<u>4</u>3

A 400   **B** 40   **C** 43

32. Choose <, >, or =.

354 ⬤ 354

F <   **G** >   **H** =

Stop

Write the correct answer.

1. What is the value of the underlined digit?

<u>9</u>3

_____

2. Which is NOT a way to show the number 47? Circle it.

7 tens 4 ones

tens	ones
4	7

tens	ones

40 + 7

Use the tally table for 3–4.

Owen's Group's Favorite Pet	
Pet	**Tally**
cat	II
dog	III
hamster	IIII
fish	IIII

3. Which pet did the most students choose in Owen's group?

_____

4. Predict which pet the most students in Owen's class would choose.

_____

Use the pictograph for 5–6.

Ways to Travel	
cars	
buses	
trains	
planes	

Key: Each   stands for 2 choices.

5. How many students chose trains?

_____

6. Which way to travel did the **least** students choose?

_____

7. Which belongs in the fact family for this set of numbers? Circle it.

3   8   11

4 + 4 = 8   11 − 8 = 3

11 + 8 = 19   8 − 3 = 5

Go On

8. Solve these related problems.

$10 - 7 =$ _____

_____ $+ 7 = 10$

9. Write how many tens and ones.

tens	ones

_____ tens _____ ones

10.   47
        + 36

11.   59
        + 37

12. How many tens and ones are left?

$85 - 7 =$ ▪

_____ tens _____ ones

13. Tori has 21 walnuts. She gives 6 walnuts to Alma. How many walnuts does Tori have left?

_____ walnuts

14. Sam has 55 baseball cards. Luke gives him 17 more cards. How many baseball cards does Sam have altogether?

_____ baseball cards

15.   87
        − 58

16.   48
        − 39

17.   21
           19
        + 48

18.   84
        − 26

Go On ▶

19. Lori spent $3.24 to buy a birthday card. Then her mother gave her $3.75. Lori had $7.50 when she began. How much money does Lori have now?

_____

20. Write the total amount.

_____

21. What time is it?

_____ : _____

Use the chart for question 22.

901	902	903	904	905	906	907	908	909	910
911	912	913	914	915	916	917	918	919	920
921	922	923	924	925	926	927	928	929	930
931	932	933	934	935	936	937	938	939	940
941	942	943	944	945	946	947	948	949	950

22. Write the next number in the pattern.

_____

23. Divide 23 apples into groups of 8.

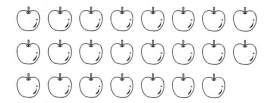

_____ groups _____ left over

Use the calendar for 24.

FEBRUARY						
S	M	T	W	T	F	S
						1
2	3	4	5	6	7	8
9	10	11	12	13	14	15
16	17	18	19	20	21	22
23	24	25	26	27	28	

24. Miranda's birthday is two weeks after Valentine's Day. Valentine's Day is February 14. When is Miranda's birthday?

_____

Go On ►

25. Is pulling a △ from the bag **more likely** or **less likely**?

more likely   less likely

26. Circle the solid figure you can use to draw the shapes.

27. Write the word that names the move.

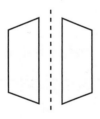

_____

28. Circle the pattern unit. Then draw what comes next.

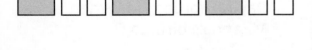

_____

29. Write the area of the figure.

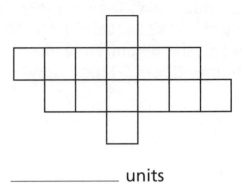

_____ units

30. There are 2 sheets of art paper.

Jesse gets $\frac{1}{2}$ of one sheet.

Alan gets $\frac{1}{5}$ of the other sheet. Who gets the larger piece?

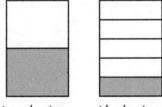

Jesse's piece   Alan's piece

_____

31. Write the value of the underlined digit.

$\underline{7}15$

_____

32. Write <, >, or = in the ◯.

694 ◯ 469

Stop

Choose the correct answer.

1. $7 - 4 = 3$, so $4 + 3 = \blacksquare$

  A 1   **C** 4
  B 3   **D** 7

2. $2 + 8 = 10$, so $10 - 2 = \blacksquare$

  F 2   **H** 10
  G 8   **J** 12

3. $7 + 4 = 11$, so $11 - \blacksquare = 7$

  A 4   **C** 11
  B 10   **D** 18

4. What fact is part of the fact family 5, 9, and 14?

  F $9 - 4 = 5$
  G $14 + 5 = 19$
  H $9 - 5 = 4$
  J $5 + 9 = 14$

For 5–7, find the missing addend.

5. $6 + \blacksquare = 12$

  A 6   **C** 12
  B 7   **D** 16

6. $\blacksquare + 4 = 13$

  F 3   **H** 10
  G 9   **J** 15

7. $8 + \blacksquare = 11$

  A 1   **C** 4
  B 3   **D** 7

8. I am a number less than 50. My tens digit is 2 more than my ones digit. My ones digit is 1. What number am I?

  F 13   **H** 31
  G 21   **J** 32

For 9–11, use the correct property to solve.

9. $8 + 0 = \blacksquare$

  A 0   **C** 8
  B 1   **D** 16

10. $(3 + 8) + 5 = \blacksquare$

  F $(7 + 3) + 5$
  G $(5 + 3) + 5$
  H $5 + (8 + 5)$
  J $3 + (8 + 5)$

`Go On` ▶

11. 2 + 5 = 5 + ■ ?

   A 0   **C** 2
   B 1   **D** 7

For 12–14, find the sum.

12. 27
    + 36

   F 63   **H** 78
   G 73   **J** 513

13. 77
    + 39

   A 1,016   **C** 106
   B 116   **D** 38

14. 95
    + 56

   F 39   **H** 151
   G 141   **J** 1,411

15. Beau has 32 stickers. His sister has 26. How many stickers do they have altogether?

   A 6   **C** 56
   B 14   **D** 58

For 16–17, find the difference.

16. 48
    − 19

   F 21   **H** 31
   G 29   **J** 67

17. 83
    − 56

   A 129   **C** 30
   B 37   **D** 27

18. There were 64 monkeys at the zoo. Susan saw 33 monkeys climbing in the trees. The rest of the monkeys were eating. How many monkeys were eating?

   F 21   **H** 37
   G 31   **J** 97

For 19–20, choose the operation to solve. Then solve.

19. Jamal collected 48 stamps. Peter collected 39 stamps. How many more stamps did Jamal collect than Peter?

   A addition, 87
   B addition, 77
   C subtraction, 19
   D subtraction, 9

20. There were 28 singers in the school chorus last year. There are 15 more singers in the chorus this year. How many singers are in the chorus this year?

   F addition, 43
   G addition, 53
   H subtraction, 32
   J subtraction, 13

Stop

Write the correct answer.

1. $6 + 9 = 15$, so $15 - \blacksquare = 9$

_____

2. $18 - 9 = 9$, so $9 + 9 = \blacksquare$

_____

3. $4 + 2 = 6$, so $6 - 2 = \blacksquare$

_____

4. Write a fact that is part of the fact family for 3, 9, and 12.

_____

For 5–7, find the missing addend.

5. $7 + \blacksquare = 9$

_____

6. $\blacksquare + 9 = 14$

_____

7. $5 + \blacksquare = 12$

_____

8. I am a number less than 50. My tens digit is 3 more than my ones digit. My ones digit is 0. What number am I?

_____

For 9–11, use the correct property to solve.

9. $1 + 0 = \blacksquare$

_____

10. $(2 + 4) + 9 = \blacksquare$

_____

Go On ▶

11. $9 + 4 = 4 + \blacksquare$?

_____

For 12–14, find the sum.

12.   35
        $+ 48$

_____

13.   89
        $+ 44$

_____

14.   57
        $+ 19$

_____

15. Laurie spent 25 minutes playing softball on Saturday and 35 minutes playing softball on Sunday. How many minutes did she spend playing softball altogether?

_____

16.   64
        $- 38$

_____

17.   71
        $- 63$

_____

18. Mrs. Stokes has 14 pens and pencils on her desk. If 8 are pens, how many are pencils?

_____

For 19–20, choose the operation to solve. Then solve.

19. Tyra made 37 free throws during basketball practice. Lin made 18 free throws. How many more free throws did Tyra make than Lin?

_____

20. The recycling center collected 76 pounds of plastic last week. This week it collected 15 more pounds than last week. How many pounds of plastic were collected at the recycling center this week?

_____

Stop

Choose the correct answer.

1. What number is **odd**?

   A 18   C 66
   B 47   D 94

2. What is the value of the 5 in 4,572?

   F 5   H 500
   G 50   J 5,000

3. What is 345 written in expanded form?

   A 300 + 40 + 5
   B 30 + 45
   C 34 + 5
   D 3 + 4 + 5

4. What number is **even**?

   F 133   H 358
   G 247   J 581

5. What is the value of the 8 in 683,472?

   A 800
   B 8,000
   C 80,000
   D 800,000

6. Predict the next number in the pattern.

   33, 37, 41, 45, _____

   F 47   H 51
   G 49   J 59

7. What is 700 + 50 + 8 written in standard form?

   A 7,508   C 758
   B 7,058   D 20

8. Jesse modeled 133 with base-ten blocks. He used 1 hundred and 2 tens. How many ones did he use?

   F 33   H 13
   G 23   J 3

9. What is 8,734 written in expanded form?

   A 87 + 34
   B 800 + 734
   C 800 + 70 + 34
   D 8,000 + 700 + 30 + 4

10. Which number is **odd**?

   F 244   H 658
   G 401   J 972

   Go On

11. What is 18,329 written in expanded form?

   A 10,000 + 8,000 + 300 + 20 + 9
   B 18,000 + 3,000 + 29
   C 1,800 + 300 + 20 + 9
   D 1 + 8 + 3 + 2 + 9

12. What is four thousand, six hundred five written in standard form?

   F 4,065   H 4,650
   G 4,605   J 46,005

13. What is eight hundred seventy-two written in standard form?

   A 80,072   C 8,072
   B 8,702   D 872

14. What number completes the number sentence?

   8,000 + 400 + ■ + 5 = 8,425

   F 2,000   H 20
   G 25   J 2

15. Jenny skip-counts by threes. She says, "3, 6, 9, 12." What numbers should Jenny say next?

   A 15, 18, 21   C 16, 18, 21
   B 16, 17, 18   D 20, 25, 30

16. The code to a safe is a number pattern that skip-counts by hundreds. The first number is 432. The second number is 532. The third number is 632. What is the fourth number of the code?

   F 732   H 832
   G 782   J 1,632

17. What is two hundred fifty-five thousand, four hundred eight written in standard form?

   A 255,408   C 255,048
   B 255,084   D 25,548

18. What is the greatest 4-digit number that can be written using 3,8,5, and 6?

   F 8,653   H 8,563
   G 8,635   J 8,536

19. What is the greatest 3-digit number that can be written using 5, 7, and 2?

   A 257   C 725
   B 572   D 752

20. Brittany made a model using base-ten blocks. She used 4 hundreds, 17 tens, and 6 ones. What number did she model?

   F 476   H 516
   G 486   J 576

Stop

Write the correct answer.

1. Is 33 **even** or **odd**?

_____

2. Write the value of the 3 in the number 2,385.

_____

3. Write 471 in expanded form.

_____

4. Is 326 **even** or **odd**?

_____

5. Write the value of the 5 in 752,034.

_____

6. Predict the next number in the pattern.

46, 49, 52, 55,

_____

7. Write this number in standard form.

300 + 20 + 8

_____

8. Luke modeled 354 with base-ten blocks. He used 2 hundreds and 4 ones. How many tens did he use?

_____

9. Write 9,256 in expanded form.

_____

10. Circle the **even** number.

392

491

763

807

Go On ▶

Name _____

11. Write 14,752 in expanded form.

_____

12. Write five thousand, eight hundred two in standard form.

_____

13. Write two hundred sixty-four in standard form.

_____

14. Write the number that completes the number sentence.

$5{,}000 + 300 + \underline{\hspace{1cm}} + 2 = 5{,}372$

15. Peggy skip-counted by twos. She said, "4, 6, 8, 10." Write the next three numbers.

_____ , _____ , _____

16. Rachel made a number pattern that skip-counts by tens. The first number is 791. The second number is 801. The third number is 811. What is the fourth number of her pattern?

_____

17. Write four hundred thirty-seven thousand, six hundred four in standard form.

_____

18. Write the **greatest** 4-digit number possible using 2, 5, 9, and 4.

_____

19. Write the **greatest** 3-digit number possible using 0, 6, and 2.

_____

20. Toby made a model using base-ten blocks. He used 2 hundreds, 7 tens, and 23 ones. What number did he model?

_____

Stop

Form B • Free Response

Choose the correct answer.

1. What is 585 rounded to the nearest hundred?

   A 600   **C** 580
   B 590   **D** 500

2. Choose a benchmark of 10, 100, 500, or 1,000 to ESTIMATE the number of players on a hockey team.

   F 1,000   **H** 100
   G 500   **J** 10

3. Which group of numbers is in order from **least** to **greatest**?

   A 5,592; 5,583; 4,785
   B 5,583; 5,592; 4,785
   C 4,785; 5,592; 5,583
   D 4,785; 5,583; 5,592

4. Which number is **greater than** 7,560?

   F 7,559   **H** 7,000
   G 7,060   **J** 7,801

5. What is 14,781 rounded to the nearest thousand?

   A 15,000   **C** 14,000
   B 14,700   **D** 10,000

6. Choose a benchmark of 10, 50, 100, or 1,000 to ESTIMATE the number of peanuts in a large bag.

   F 10   **H** 100
   G 50   **J** 1,000

7. Which group of numbers is in order from **least** to **greatest**?

   A 737,869; 733,457; 825,789
   B 737,869; 825,789; 733,457
   C 825,789; 733,457; 737,869
   D 733,457; 737,869; 825,789

8. Which group of numbers is in order from **greatest** to **least**?

   F 38,621; 38,479; 38,512
   G 38,621; 38,512; 38,479
   H 38,512; 38,479; 38,621
   J 38,479; 38,512; 38,621

9. What is 7,356 rounded to the nearest thousand?

   A 8,000   **C** 7,300
   B 7,400   **D** 7,000

10. What is the **greatest** place-value position in which the digits of 8,451 and 8,579 are different?

   F ones   **H** hundreds
   G tens   **J** thousands

11. What is 355 rounded to the nearest ten?

   A 300   **C** 360
   B 350   **D** 400

12. The height of Grand Teton is 13,766 ft. What is this number rounded to the nearest thousand?

   F 14,000   **H** 13,600
   G 13,700   **J** 10,000

Go On ▶

13. What is 7,642 rounded to the nearest hundred?

A 8,000   C 7,640
B 7,700   D 7,600

14. Which is a true statement?

F 4,895 > 4,871
G 4,356 < 3,789
H 389 > 398
J 861 < 816

For 15–17, use the bar graph.

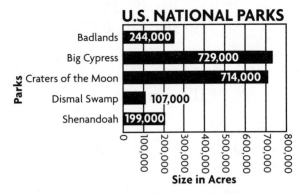

U.S. NATIONAL PARKS

Badlands 244,000
Big Cypress 729,000
Craters of the Moon 714,000
Dismal Swamp 107,000
Shenandoah 199,000

Parks

Size in Acres

15. Which two national parks are **smaller** than Badlands?

A Big Cypress and Shenandoah
B Dismal Swamp and Big Cypress
C Craters of the Moon and Shenandoah
D Shenandoah and Dismal Swamp

16. Which two parks have areas **greater than** 300,000 acres?

F Big Cypress and Badlands
G Dismal Swamp and Big Cypress
H Big Cypress and Craters of the Moon
J Badlands and Dismal Swamp

17. Which lists these parks in order from **least** to **greatest**?

A Dismal Swamp, Shenandoah, Badlands
B Big Cypress, Craters of the Moon, Badlands
C Shenandoah, Dismal Swamp, Badlands
D Badlands, Shenandoah, Dismal Swamp

18. Which number is **less than** 383,064?

F 383,064   H 384,000
G 383,100   J 383,060

For 19–20, use the table.

BASEBALL GAME ATTENDANCE	
Day	Number of People
Friday	8,749
Saturday	9,322
Sunday	4,886

19. To the nearest hundred, how many people attended the baseball game on Friday?

A 9,000   C 8,700
B 8,750   D 8,000

20. To the nearest thousand, how many people attended the games on Saturday and Sunday altogether?

F 10,000   H 14,000
G 13,000   J 15,000

Stop

Write the correct answer.

1. **Round** 639 **to the nearest hundred.**

_____

2. Circle a benchmark to ESTIMATE the number of players on a baseball team.

        10   100   500

3. Write the numbers 4,481; 3,539; and 4,492 in order from **least** to **greatest.**

_____ ; _____ ; _____

4. Circle the number **greater than** 6,380.

   6,372   6,384   6,299

5. **Round** 23,603 **to the nearest thousand.**

_____

6. Circle a benchmark to ESTIMATE the number of pages in a photo album.

        5   50   500

7. Write the numbers 647,729; 747,538; and 647,810 in order from **least** to **greatest.**

_____ ; _____ ; _____

8. Write the numbers 24,039; 23,507; and 24,258 in order from **greatest** to **least.**

_____ ; _____ ; _____

9. Round 8,206 to the nearest thousand.

_____

10. Circle the name of the **greatest** place-value position in which 5,398 and 5,379 are different.

    Ones   Tens

    Hundreds   Thousands

11. **Round** 659 **to the nearest ten.**

_____

12. There were 12,499 people at a football game. **Round** this number **to the nearest thousand.**

_____

Go On ►

13. **Round** 5,362 **to the nearest hundred**.

_____

14. Compare the numbers. Write <, >, or = in the ◯.

2,533 ◯ 2,542

For 15–17, use the bar graph.

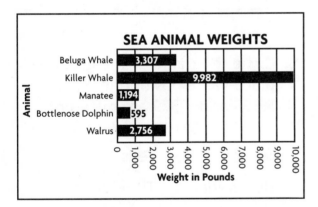

15. Circle the three sea animals that weigh **less than** the beluga whale.

killer whale, manatee, walrus

bottlenose dolphin, walrus, killer whale

walrus, killer whale, bottlenose dolphin

manatee, bottlenose dolphin, walrus

16. Which sea animal is **heavier than** a manatee, but **lighter than** a beluga whale?

_____

17. Which sea animal from this chart weighs the most?

_____

18. Circle the number **less than** 894,057.

894,108   894,049   904,039

For 19–20, use the table.

| NEWSPAPER RECYCLING ||
Day	Pounds of Paper
Monday	1,650
Wednesday	1,049
Friday	1,670

19. To the **nearest hundred**, how many pounds of paper were collected on Monday?

_____ pounds

20. To the **nearest thousand**, how many pounds of paper were collected on Monday and Wednesday altogether?

_____ pounds

Stop

Name _____

Choose the correct answer.

1. Which group of numbers is in order from **greatest** to **least**?

- **A** 243,918; 242,927; 243,876
- **B** 242,927; 243,876; 243,918
- **C** 243,876; 242,927; 243,918
- **D** 243,918; 243,876; 242,927

2. What is the value of the 4 in 248,216?

- **F** 400
- **G** 4,000
- **H** 40,000
- **J** 400,000

3. At 3:00 there were 67 skaters in the park. By 7:00 there were 92 skaters. Which number sentence would help you find how many more skaters were in the park at 7:00 than at 3:00?

- **A** $92 - 67 = \blacksquare$
- **B** $92 + 67 = \blacksquare$
- **C** $92 - 24 = \blacksquare$
- **D** $67 + 92 = \blacksquare$

4. Predict the next number in the pattern.

438, 441, 444, 447, $\blacksquare$

- **F** 449
- **G** 450
- **H** 451
- **J** 453

5. Use the benchmark to estimate the number of flowers in the garden.

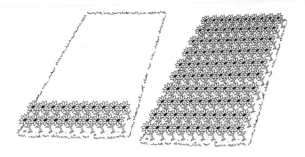

20 flowers   ___?___ flowers

- **A** 10
- **B** 25
- **C** 100
- **D** 500

6. Which subtraction fact is in the same fact family as $8 + 6 = 14$?

- **F** $14 - 9 = 5$
- **G** $8 - 6 = 2$
- **H** $14 - 8 = 6$
- **J** $8 - 5 = 3$

7. $3,000 + 700 + 3 = \blacksquare$

- **A** 3,730
- **B** 3,703
- **C** 3,073
- **D** 3,037

8. $9 + \blacksquare = 14$

- **F** 5
- **G** 7
- **H** 9
- **J** 23

Go On ►

Form A • Multiple Choice

9. 73 + 67 = ■

   A 6
   B 34
   C 140
   D 150

10. What is the value of the 2
    in 867,281?

   F 2   **H** 2,000
   G 200   **J** 20,000

11. Use the benchmark to estimate
    the number of marbles in Jar B.

   A   B

   5 marbles   _?_ marbles

   A about 5   **C** about 20
   B about 10   **D** about 100

12. 54 − 37 = ■

   F 13   **H** 23
   G 17   **J** 91

13. Which number is **even**?

   A 45   **C** 72
   B 33   **D** 81

For 14–15, use the bar graph.

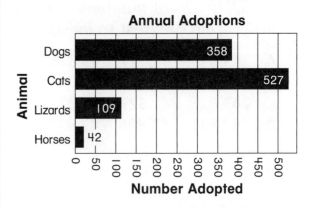

14. Which animal was adopted **more
    than** lizards, but **less than** cats?

   F horses   **H** dogs
   G cats   **J** lizards

15. Which two animals were
    adopted most often?

   A cats and dogs
   B cats and horses
   C lizards and horses
   D horses and cats

16. What is 8,524 **rounded to the
    nearest thousand**?

   F 7,000
   G 8,000
   H 8,500
   J 9,000

17. What is the **greatest** place-value
    position in which the digits of
    5,456 and 5,179 are different?

   A ones   **C** hundreds
   B tens   **D** thousands

   `Go On ▶`

18. Which property of addition is shown by $1 + 0 = \blacksquare$?

   F   Zero Property of Addition
   G   Order Property of Addition
   H   Grouping Property of Addition

19. Which addition fact is in the same fact family as $18 - 9 = 9$?

   A $18 + 9 = 27$
   B $6 + 6 = 12$
   C $9 + 9 = 18$
   D $10 + 8 = 18$

20. What is three hundred thirty-two thousand, twelve written in standard form?

   F   32,012   H   303,212
   G   302,021   J   332,012

21. $700 + 90 + 1 = \blacksquare$

   A   7,910
   B   7,901
   C   7,091
   D   791

22. Which number is **greater than** 457,950 but **less than** 458,950?

   F   457,850   H   458,962
   G   458,430   J   459,750

23. There are 73 students in the school band. 56 students play a wind instrument. How many students do NOT play a wind instrument?

   A   17
   B   23
   C   29
   D   129

24. What is 735 written in expanded form?

   F $700 + 35$
   G $700 + 30 + 5$
   H $70 + 35$
   J $7 + 3 + 5$

25. Billy had 7 video games. His brother gave Billy some games. Billy now has 15 video games. How many video games did Billy's brother give him?

   A   7
   B   8
   C   21
   D   22

Go On

Form A • Multiple Choice

Assessment Guide   AG23

26. What is 3,692 **rounded to the nearest thousand**?

    F 1,000
    G 3,000
    H 3,700
    J 4,000

27. Which number completes this number sentence?

$$\blacksquare + 2 = 2$$

    A 4
    B 2
    C 1
    D 0

28. I am a 3-digit number. The sum of my digits is 4. I have the same number of hundreds and ones. My middle digit is NOT a zero. Which number am I?

    F 112
    G 121
    H 211
    J 400

29. How many hundreds are in 5,000?

    A 5
    B 15
    C 50
    D 500

30. What types of numbers are 12, 46, 74, and 98?

    F odd
    G even
    H both odd and even
    J neither odd or even

31. What is 572 **rounded to the nearest hundred**?

    A 500
    B 570
    C 580
    D 600

32. There are 43 third grade students and 48 fourth grade students at Tanglewood Elementary. How many third and fourth grade students are there altogether?

    F 5
    G 81
    H 85
    J 91

33. What is 883 rounded to the nearest ten?

    A 900
    B 880
    C 830
    D 800

Stop

Write the correct answer.

1. Circle the numbers that are in order from **greatest** to **least**.

873,938; 873,398; 872,498

872,498; 873,398; 873,938

873,398; 872,498; 873,938

873,398; 873,938; 872,498

2. Write the value of the 8 in 383,451.

_____

3. There are 87 fish in a small tank and 94 fish in a larger tank. Write a number sentence that shows how to find how many more fish were in the larger tank.

_____

4. Write the next number in the pattern.

870, 860, 850, 840, ■

_____

5. Use the benchmark to estimate the number of pictures on the bulletin board. Circle the number.

 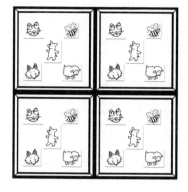

5 pictures   ___?___ pictures

     5   20   100

6. Write a subtraction fact that is in the same fact family as $7 + 4 = 11$.

_____

7. Write $9,000 + 30 + 1$ in standard form.

_____

8. Write the missing number.

$7 + ■ = 16$

_____

Go On ▶

9. Add.

$$76 + 36 = \blacksquare$$

_____

10. Write the value of the 4 in 704,852.

_____

11. Use the benchmark to estimate the number of CDs on the rack. Circle the number.

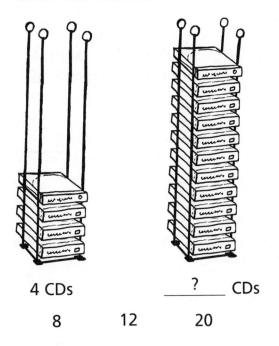

4 CDs   _____ CDs
                          ?

8   12   20

12. Subtract.

$$47 - 8 = \blacksquare$$

_____

13. Write whether 48 is **odd** or **even**.

_____

For 14–15, use the bar graph.

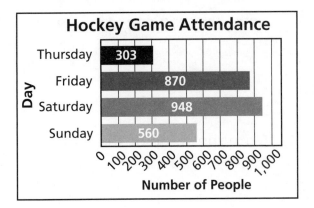

Hockey Game Attendance

Day	
Thursday	303
Friday	870
Saturday	948
Sunday	560

0 100 200 300 400 500 600 700 800 900 1,000
Number of People

14. Which day had more people attending than Friday?

_____

15. Which two days had the most people attending the hockey games?

_____ and _____

16. Round 5,239 to the nearest thousand.

_____

Go On ▶

17. Write the greatest place-value position in which the digits of 25,610 and 26,634 are different.

_____ place

18. Circle the property of addition that is shown by the following:

$(1 + 9) + 3 = 1 + (9 + 3)$

Grouping Property of Addition

Order Property of Addition

Zero Property of Addition

19. Write the addition fact that is in the same fact family as $12 - 6 = 6$.

_____

20. Write four hundred twenty-two thousand, fifteen in standard form.

_____

21. Write $2,000 + 700 + 50$ in standard form.

_____

22. Which number is **greater than** 744,838 but **less than** 745,838?

745,938   754,938

744,938   754,389

23. In the museum there are 96 paintings and 57 statues. How many more paintings than statues are there in the museum?

_____

24. Write 682 in expanded form.

_____

25. In the morning there were 8 cows in the field. Later in the day there were 14 cows in the field. How many more cows were in the field in the afternoon?

_____

Go On

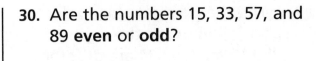
26. Round 34,720 to the nearest thousand.

_____

27. Write the missing number.

$$\blacksquare + 7 = 7$$

_____

28. I am a 2-digit number. The sum of my digits is 12. My tens digit is 4 more than my ones digit. What number am I?

_____

29. How many 100s are in 4,000?

_____

30. Are the numbers 15, 33, 57, and 89 **even** or **odd**?

_____

31. Round 480 to the nearest hundred.

_____

32. Natalie counted 32 tomatoes and 29 cucumbers in her garden. How many tomatoes and cucumbers were there in all?

_____

33. Round 752 to the nearest ten.

_____

Stop

Choose the correct answer.

1. **Round to the nearest ten** to ESTIMATE the sum.

   235
   + 552

   A 700
   B 780
   C 790
   D 800

2. Which two numbers have a sum that is about 800?

   F 243 and 489
   G 243 and 702
   H 325 and 489
   J 325 and 243

3. Which two numbers have a sum that is about 6,000?

   A 4,289 and 1,802
   B 3,457 and 3,821
   C 2,056 and 4,902
   D 1,723 and 5,625

4. Use **front–end estimation** to ESTIMATE the sum.

   408
   + 354

   F 600
   G 700
   H 800
   J 900

5. 3,524
   + 106

   A 3,520
   B 3,620
   C 3,630
   D 3,720

6. 315
   + 576

   F 881
   G 891
   H 981
   J 8,811

7. $3.50
   + $5.75

   A $8.25
   B $8.45
   C $8.55
   D $9.25

8. 229
   148
   + 356

   F 913
   G 733
   H 725
   J 713

9. 4,623
   + 2,947

   A 7,581
   B 7,580
   C 7,570
   D 7,560

10. The sum of two numbers is 35. Their difference is 9. What are the numbers?

    F 15 and 20
    G 15 and 24
    H 22 and 13
    J 18 and 17

Go On ▶

11. Joel has 210 baseball and football cards. He has 50 more baseball cards than football cards. How many of each does he have?

   A 130 baseball and 80 football
   B 120 baseball and 70 football
   C 110 baseball and 60 football
   D 80 baseball and 130 football

12. A parking lot has 85 cars and trucks in it. There are 17 more trucks than cars. How many of each are there?

   F 17 cars and 68 trucks
   G 23 cars and 62 trucks
   H 34 cars and 51 trucks
   J 40 cars and 45 trucks

13. $5,629 + 3,782 = \blacksquare$

   A 9,411   C 8,311
   B 9,402   D 8,301

14. $\$25.83 + \$65.27 = \blacksquare$

   F $91.10   H $80.10
   G $90.10   J $80.00

15. Gina has $34.75. She earns $15.95. How much money does she have in all?

   A $40.70   C $49.70
   B $49.60   D $50.70

16. $5,781 + 2,653 = \blacksquare$

   F 7,334   H 8,334
   G 7,434   J 8,434

17. A high school has 1,523 students. Another high school has 2,079 students. How many students are there in the two schools altogether?

   A 3,692   C 3,593
   B 3,602   D 3,592

18. José has 85 more colored pencils than pens. He has 49 pens. Which expression shows how many colored pencils he has?

   F $85 - 49$ H $85 + 85$
   G $49 + 85$ J $49 + 49$

19. A store has 24 blue, 49 white, 18 red, and 33 black shirts. Which expression can be used to find how many more white than red shirts there are?

   A $49 + 18$ C $33 - 18$
   B $49 - 18$ D $49 - 24$

20. What is the missing number?

   $$205 + \blacksquare = 430$$

   F 635   H 225
   G 235   J 175

Stop

Write the correct answer.

1. Round to the nearest ten to ESTIMATE the sum.

357
+ 539

_____

2. Circle the two numbers whose sum is about 700.

536 and 108

392 and 276

3. Circle the two numbers whose sum is about 7,000.

3,682 and 2,857

2,360 and 5,892

4. Use **front–end estimation** to ESTIMATE the sum.

218
+ 443

_____

5. 1,789
     +   203

6. 468
     + 329

7. $4.50
     + $3.89

8. 325
      248
     + 196

9. 5,739
     + 1,620

10. The sum of two numbers is 28. Their difference is 2. What are the numbers?

_____ and _____

Go On ▶

Form B • Free Response

Assessment Guide   AG31

11. Lauren has collected 150 nickels and dimes. She has 70 more nickels than dimes. How many of each does she have?

_____ nickels and _____ dimes

12. There are 40 people at a picnic. There are 4 more children than adults. How many of each are there?

_____ adults and _____ children

13. $6,533 + 2,677 =$ _____

14. $\$16.86 + \$14.39 =$ _____

15. Mike has $46.85. He earns $18.75. How much money does he have in all?

_____

16. $3,693 + 1,895 =$ _____

17. A library has 1,478 books. Another library has 3,256 books. How many books do the two libraries have altogether?

_____ books

18. Darin counted 46 more cars than trucks in a parking lot. There were 29 trucks. Write an expression that shows how many cars were in the parking lot.

_____

19. A bike shop has 8 red, 5 blue, 12 black, and 9 white bikes. Write an expression that shows how many more black bikes than red bikes there are.

_____

20. What is the missing number?

$306 +$ _____ $= 450$

Stop

Choose the correct answer.

1. Which two numbers have a difference that is about 300?

A 871 and 495
B 839 and 272
C 710 and 482
D 792 and 546

2. Round to the nearest hundred to ESTIMATE the difference.

$$\begin{array}{r} 5,679 \\ -\ 4,458 \\ \hline \end{array}$$

F 200   **H** 1,200
G 1,100   **J** 1,300

3. Laura watched 618 minutes of TV in May and 389 minutes in June. About how many more minutes of TV did she watch in May than in June?

A 600   **C** 200
B 400   **D** 100

4. Use **front–end estimation** to ESTIMATE the difference.

4,727 – 1,283

F 6,000   **H** 4,000
G 5,000   **J** 3,000

5. Round to the nearest ten to ESTIMATE the sum.

$$\begin{array}{r} 329 \\ +\ 544 \\ \hline \end{array}$$

A 800   **C** 870
B 850   **D** 880

6. Round to the nearest dollar to ESTIMATE the difference.

$$\begin{array}{r} \$7.28 \\ -\ \$4.80 \\ \hline \end{array}$$

F $2.00   **H** $3.00
G $2.50   **J** $12.00

7.
$$\begin{array}{r} 562 \\ -\ 288 \\ \hline \end{array}$$

A 274   **C** 386
B 326   **D** 850

8. 606 – 311 = ■

F 315   **H** 295
G 305   **J** 285

9.
$$\begin{array}{r} \$8.74 \\ -\ \$2.75 \\ \hline \end{array}$$

A $5.99   **C** $6.09
B $6.01   **D** $6.79

10.
$$\begin{array}{r} 900 \\ -\ 126 \\ \hline \end{array}$$

F 764   **H** 864
G 774   **J** 884

Go On

11. Joe has 24 CDs, 208 stickers, and 134 trading cards. How many more stickers than trading cards does he have?

   A 342   C 110
   B 184   D 74

12.   6,000
    − 3,859

                   F 2,140
                   G 2,141
                   H 3,251
                   J 3,859

13. 5,246 − 789 = ■
                   A 4,457
                   B 4,547
                   C 5,447
                   D 5,543

14.   5,668
    −   792

                   F 4,876
                   G 4,966
                   H 5,876
                   J 5,976

15. Mr. Gomez traveled 5,389 miles last year. Mr. Burton traveled 7,912 miles. How many more miles did Mr. Burton travel than Mr. Gomez?

   A 2,517   C 2,673
   B 2,523   D 2,677

16. Kayla lives 2,379 miles away from her grandparents. Marcus lives 1,480 miles away from his grandparents. How much farther from her grandparents does Kayla live than Marcus?

   F 1,299 miles H 899 miles
   G 1,119 miles J 859 miles

17. A restaurant will serve pancakes to 25 adults and 13 children. Each person will eat 2 pancakes. About how many pancakes should the cook make?

   A 50   C 80
   B 60   D 100

18. A store sells pens for $1.29 and paper for $1.49. Margo has $5.00. How much money will she have left if she buys paper?

   F $3.51   H $4.81
   G $4.61   J $6.49

For 19–20, use this information.
Tasha's dad spent $35.06 at the grocery store. Tasha's mom spent $47.50 at the hardware store.

19. Which expression can you use to show how much money Tasha's mom and dad spent in all?

   A $35.06 + $35.06
   B $35.06 + $47.50
   C $47.50 − $35.06
   D $47.50 + $47.50

20. How much money did Tasha's mom and dad spend in all?

   F $12.44   H $82.56
   G $70.12   J $95.00

Stop

Write the correct answer.

1. Circle the two numbers whose difference is about 200.

    571 and 308

    425 and 216

2. **Round to the nearest hundred** to ESTIMATE the difference.

    4,221
    − 3,449

    _____

3. Martin collected 129 pounds of paper for recycling in March and 288 pounds in April. About how many more pounds did he collect in April than in March?

    about _____ pounds

4. Use **front–end estimation** to ESTIMATE the difference.

    3,829 − 1,346

    _____

5. **Round to the nearest ten** to ESTIMATE the difference.

    373
    − 89

    _____

6. **Round to the nearest dollar** to ESTIMATE the difference.

    $8.32
    − $3.97

    _____

7.   621
      − 454

8. 508 − 133 = _____

9. $7.63
     − $3.64

10.   800
      − 334

11. A nursery has 202 evergreens, 56 vines, and 129 roses. How many more evergreens than roses does the nursery have?

_____ evergreens

12. $\begin{array}{r} 5,000 \\ -\ 2,412 \\ \hline \end{array}$

13. $4,325 - 537 =$ _____

14. $\begin{array}{r} 6,486 \\ -\ 663 \\ \hline \end{array}$

15. Jay flew 2,573 miles in an airplane to visit his cousins. Jody flew 1,175 miles to visit her cousins. How many more miles did Jay fly than Jody?

_____ miles

16. Find the difference between 5,285 and 3,492.

_____

17. A third-grade class is planning a family picnic for 22 students and 37 adults. Each person will drink 2 sodas at the picnic. About how many sodas will they need?

about _____ sodas

18. A deli sells roast beef sandwiches for $2.79 and ham sandwiches for $2.99.

Linda has $5.00. How much money will she have left if she buys a ham sandwich?

_____

For 19–20, use this information.

Kai's sister spent $19.08 at the sporting goods store. Kai's brother spent $52.66 at the art supplies store.

19. Write an expression you can use to show how much money Kai's brother and sister spent in all.

_____

20. How much money did Kai's brother and sister spend in all?

_____

Stop

Choose the correct answer.

1. Which is an equivalent set for $0.89?

   A 8 dimes, 2 nickels
   B 7 dimes, 5 nickels
   C 3 quarters, 1 dime, 4 pennies
   D 3 quarters, 1 nickel, 4 pennies

2. Which is the **greatest** amount of money?

   F 3 quarters, 6 dimes, 4 nickels
   G 3 quarters, 7 dimes, 4 nickels
   H 4 quarters, 7 dimes
   J 5 quarters, 2 dimes, 8 pennies

3. A soda costs $0.86. Darren pays with a $1 bill. Which set of coins should he get in change?

   A 2 dimes
   B 1 dime, 1 nickel
   C 1 dime, 1 nickel, 4 pennies
   D 1 dime, 4 pennies

4. Make a table to find how many ways you can make $0.30.

   F 4   H 6
   G 5   J more than 6

5. $5.37 + $4.72 = ■

   A $10.09
   B $9.45
   C $9.09
   D $9.00

6. Which is an equivalent set for $1.32?

   F one $1 bill, 1 quarter
   G one $1 bill, 3 dimes, 2 pennies
   H one $1 bill, 6 nickels
   J one $1 bill, 2 dimes

7. Andre spent $2.36. He gave the clerk a $5 bill. How much change should he get?

   A $2.64   C $3.36
   B $2.74   D $3.74

8. Which is the **greatest** amount of money?

   F two $1 bills, 10 nickels
   G two $1 bills, 5 dimes, 4 nickels
   H two $1 bills, 6 dimes
   J two $1 bills, 3 quarters

9. $8.34 − $5.65 = ■

   A $2.69
   B $2.71
   C $2.79
   D $3.31

10. Kamar has 2 quarters, 4 dimes, and 3 nickels. How many ways can he pay for a can of juice that costs $0.55?

   F 2   H 4
   G 3   J 5

Go On

11. Which is an **equivalent** set for $3.55?

   A three $1 bills, 5 dimes
   B three $1 bills, 5 nickels
   C three $1 bills, 2 quarters,
     1 nickel
   D three $1 bills, 2 quarters

12. Joan has $2.68 and Bob has $4.97. How much money do they have in all?

   F $2.29   H $7.55
   G $6.55   J $7.65

13. Pat has 3 quarters and 5 dimes. Marc has 2 quarters and 7 dimes. Sue has 5 quarters. Tim has 3 quarters and 5 nickels. Which two people have the same amount of money?

   A Pat and Marc
   B Pat and Sue
   C Marc and Sue
   D Tim and Marc

14. Make a table to find how many ways you can make $0.18.

   F 10   H 2
   G 6   J 1

15. A box of soap costs $4.65. Jean pays with a $5 bill. Which set of coins should she get in change?

   A 1 quarter, 3 nickels
   B 1 quarter, 5 pennies
   C 1 quarter, 1 dime
   D 1 quarter, 2 dimes

16. What amount of money is equivalent to four $1 bills, 1 quarter, and 4 pennies?

   F $4.39   H $4.29
   G $4.34   J $4.24

17. Kim spends $6.79. Amy spends $9.33. How much more money does Amy spend than Kim?

   A $2.46   C $3.54
   B $2.54   D $3.56

18. Kay bought a sandwich for $2.45. She paid for it with three $1 bills. Which set of coins should she get in change?

   F 2 quarters, 1 nickel
   G 4 dimes, 1 nickel
   H 2 quarters, 4 nickels
   J 2 quarters, 1 dime

19. Tao has 5 quarters, 2 dimes, 3 nickels, and 8 pennies. How many different sets of coins could he use to make $1.22?

   A 10   C 4
   B 8   D 1

20. Lynne has one $1 bill, 2 quarters, and 3 dimes. Leo has 5 quarters and 8 nickels. Meg has 6 quarters and 4 dimes. Jan has 2 quarters and 9 dimes. Who has the **greatest** amount of money?

   F Lynne   H Leo
   G Meg   J Jan

Stop

Form A • Multiple Choice

Write the correct answer.

1. Circle the set of coins that is **equivalent** to $0.68.

2 quarters, 1 nickel,
2 pennies

OR

2 quarters, 1 dime,
1 nickel, 3 pennies

2. Circle the amount that is **greater**.

3 quarters, 1 dime

OR

2 quarters, 2 dimes,
2 nickels

3. A notebook costs $0.78. You pay with a $1 bill. What coins should you get in change?

_____ dimes _____ pennies

4. Make a table to find how many ways you can make $0.12.

_____ ways

5. $4.58 + $5.61= _____

6. Circle the set of bills and coins that is equivalent to $1.26.

One $1 bill,
1 quarter, 1 penny

OR

One $1 bill, 1 dime,
6 pennies

7. Kendra bought a book for $3.26. She paid with a $5 bill. How much change should she get?

_____

8. Circle the amount that is **greater**.

Two $1 bills, 2 quarters,
3 nickels

OR

Two $1 bills, 1 quarter,
3 dimes

9. $9.27 − $6.48 = _____

10. Donna has 3 quarters, 2 dimes, and 6 pennies. She buys an orange drink for $0.65. How many quarters, dimes, and pennies could she use to make $0.65?

_____ quarters _____ dime

_____ pennies

Go On ▶

11. Circle the set that is **equivalent** to $2.45.

> Two $1 bills, 1 quarter,
> 2 nickels
>
> OR
>
> Two $1 bills, 4 dimes,
> 1 nickel

12. Kate has $3.29 and Joey has $4.09. How much money do they have in all?

_____

13. Rodney has 2 quarters and 6 dimes. Don has 4 quarters and 5 nickels. Pat has 5 quarters. Which two people have the same amount of money?

_____ and _____

14. Make a table to find how many ways you can make $0.15.

_____ ways

15. Kathy buys a box of fabric softener for $4.20. She pays with a $5 bill. What coins should she get in change?

_____ quarters _____ nickels

16. Make a set of $1 bills, quarters, and pennies that is **equivalent** to $3.53.

_____ $1 bills _____ quarters

_____ pennies

17. Jason saves $7.28. Carla saves $9.12. How much more money does Carla save than Jason?

_____

18. Calvin buys a notebook for $3.29. He pays with four $1 bills. How many of each coin should he get in change?

_____ quarters _____ dimes

_____ pennies

19. Ryan has 6 quarters, 3 dimes, 2 nickels and 4 pennies. How many different sets of coins could he use to make $1.50?

_____ sets

20. Joann has two $1 bills and 3 dimes. Peter has 6 quarters and 2 dimes. Who has the **greater** amount of money?

_____

`Stop`

Choose the correct answer.

1. What time does the clock show?

   A 2:14
   B 3:14
   C 3:46
   D 4:14

2. School starts at 8:00 A.M. After 3 hours and 35 minutes it is time for lunch. What time is lunch?

   F 10:25 A.M.   H 11:05 A.M.
   G 10:35 A.M.   J 11:35 A.M.

3. What time does the clock show?

   A 7:23
   B 5:36
   C 4:36
   D 4:33

4. Find the elapsed time from 8:15 P.M. to 8:45 P.M.

   F 15 minutes H 30 minutes
   G 20 minutes J 45 minutes

5. Which of these activities would you **most likely** do at 3:00 A.M.?

   A sleep   C play outside
   B go shopping D eat lunch

6. The clock shows when school starts. At what time does school start?

   F 7:25 A.M.
   G 7:30 A.M.
   H 7:35 A.M.
   J 8:25 A.M.

For 7–8, use this clock.

7. What time does the clock show?

   A 11:07   C 10:07
   B 10:53   D 9:53

8. What is another way to read the time?

   F 7 minutes before 10
   G 7 minutes after 10
   H 53 minutes before 11
   J 30 minutes before 10

9. A movie began at 8:05 P.M. and ended at 10:00 P.M. How long was the movie?

   A 2 hours
   B 1 hour 55 minutes
   C 1 hour 50 minutes
   D 1 hour 40 minutes

10. Ken started piano practice at 4:45 P.M. He practiced for 1 hour 30 minutes. At what time did he stop practicing?

   F 6:15 P.M.   H 5:45 P.M.
   G 6:00 P.M.   J 5:00 P.M.

For 11–13, use this calendar.

APRIL						
Sun	Mon	Tue	Wed	Thu	Fri	Sat
	1	2	3	4	5	6
7	8	9	10	11	12	13
14	15	16	17	18	19	20
21	22	23	24	25	26	27
28	29	30				

11. The sun was shining every day from April 3 to April 24. How many weeks of sun were there?

   A 1   B 2   C 3   D 4

Go On

12. Practice is Monday through Friday and begins on April 1. It ends on April 26. How many days of practice are there?

    F 28 **G** 20 **H** 12 **J** 11

13. Spring softball practice begins on April 5 and lasts for 2 weeks and 3 days. When does practice end?

    A April 19 **C** April 23
    B April 22 **D** April 24

For 14–16, use this schedule.

APPOINTMENT SCHEDULE	
Person	Time
May	8:00 A.M.–9:00 A.M.
Peg	9:00 A.M.–9:45 A.M.
Jon	9:45 A.M.–10:45 A.M.
Sue	9:45 A.M.–11:10 A.M.

14. Which person's appointment is 45 minutes long?

    F May **H** Jon
    G Peg **J** Sue

15. Which person's appointment ends at 9:00 A.M.?

    A May **C** Jon
    B Peg **D** Sue

16. Who has the longest appointment?

    F May **H** Jon
    G Peg **J** Sue

For 17–20, use the table. You may want to draw a time line to help.

YEAR OF STATEHOOD	
State	Year
Florida	1845
Idaho	1890
Indiana	1816
Oklahoma	1907
Virginia	1788
Hawaii	1959

17. Which became a state before Indiana?

    A Idaho **C** Oklahoma
    B Florida **D** Virginia

18. Which became a state between Idaho and Hawaii?

    F Indiana **H** Oklahoma
    G Florida **J** Virginia

19. Wisconsin became a state in 1848. Between which two states should Wisconsin appear on a time line?

    A Florida and Idaho
    B Indiana and Florida
    C Virginia and Florida
    D Idaho and Oklahoma

20. New Mexico became a state in 1912. Which became a state five years before New Mexico?

    F Hawaii **H** Indiana
    G Idaho **J** Oklahoma

    Stop

Name _____

Write the correct answer.

1. What time does the clock show?

_____ : _____

2. A soccer game begins at 6:00 P.M. After 2 hours and 10 minutes the game ends. What time does the game end? Circle A.M. or P.M.

_____ : _____   A.M.
P.M.

3. What time does the clock show?

_____ : _____

4. Find the elapsed time from 3:30 P.M. to 3:45 P.M.

_____ minutes

5. Circle the activity that would **most likely** happen at 9:00 A.M.

go to bed for the night

start school day

6. The clock shows the time the amusement park closes. What time does the amusement park close? Circle A.M. or P.M.

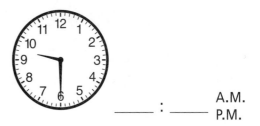

_____ : _____   A.M.
P.M.

For 7–8, use this clock.

7. What time does the clock show?

_____ : _____

8. Circle another way to read the time.

12 minutes after 8

12 minutes before 9

9. A play began at 7:30 P.M. and ended at 8:50 P.M. How long was the play?

_____ hour(s) _____ minute(s)

10. Mac went outside to play with his friends at 3:30 P.M. He played for 1 hour and 45 minutes and went inside. What time did he go inside? Circle A.M. or P.M.

_____ : _____   A.M.
P.M.

Go On ▶

Form B • Free Response

For 11–13, use this calendar.

11. Practice for the winter play is Monday through Friday and begins on January 14. It ends on January 29. How many days of practice are there?

JANUARY						
S	M	T	W	T	F	S
		1	2	3	4	5
6	7	8	9	10	11	12
13	14	15	16	17	18	19
20	21	22	23	24	25	26
27	28	29	30	31		

_____ days

12. It rained every day from January 3 to January 17. How many weeks did it rain?

_____ weeks

13. Fred's father goes out of town for 1 week and 4 days on January 7. When will he return?

_____

For 14–16, use this schedule.

FIELD TRIP SCHEDULE	
Activity	Time
Drive to zoo	9:45 A.M.–10:15 A.M.
Unload busses	10:15 A.M.–10:30 A.M.
See animals	10:30 A.M.–Noon
Lunch	Noon–1:00 P.M.
Watch movie	1:00 P.M.–1:45 P.M.

14. Which activity is 45 minutes?

_____

15. Which activity ends at 10:15?

_____

16. Which activity is the longest?

_____

For 17–20, use the table. You may want to draw a time line to help.

YEAR ELECTED	
President	Year
Lincoln	1860
Kennedy	1960
Carter	1976
Jackson	1828
Taft	1908
Reagan	1980

17. Who was a President of the United States before Lincoln?

_____

18. Who was a President between Kennedy and Reagan?

_____

19. James Garfield was elected President in 1880. Between which two presidents should Garfield appear on a time line?

_____ and _____

20. John Quincy Adams was elected President in 1824. Who was elected four years later?

Stop

Form B • Free Response

Choose the correct answer.

1. A sandwich costs $4.19. Walt pays with a $5 bill. Which set of coins should he get in change?

    A 3 quarters, 1 nickel, 1 penny
    B 3 quarters, 1 nickel
    C 3 quarters, 1 penny
    D 2 quarters, 4 dimes

For 2–3, use the chart. You may want to draw a time line to help.

YEAR OF BIRTH	
Family Member	**Year**
Felix	1987
Mom	1962
Crystal	1996
Uncle Clayton	1971
Dad	1964

Crystal wrote down the years that some of her family members were born.

2. Who was born 23 years before Felix?

    F Mom   H Uncle Clayton
    G Crystal   J Dad

3. Aunt Dafina was born in 1973. Between which two family members should Aunt Dafina appear on a time line?

    A Mom and Dad
    B Uncle Clayton and Felix
    C Mom and Uncle Clayton
    D Felix and Crystal

4. 3,000
   − 1,488

    F 2,612
    G 2,512
    H 2,488
    J 1,512

5. Make a table to find how many different equivalent sets can be made with a value of $0.20.

    A 1   C 3
    B 2   D more than 4

6. Karen has 1 quarter and 3 dimes. Dan has 5 dimes. Who has **more** money?

    F Karen   G Dan

7. The sum of two numbers is 29. Their difference is 3. What are the numbers?

    A 14 and 15
    B 13 and 16
    C 12 and 17
    D 12 and 15

8. $34.51
   + $12.69

    F $46.10
    G $47.10
    H $47.20
    J $57.20

Go On ▶

Form A • Multiple Choice

9. Which is an equivalent set of coins for $0.63?

   A 2 quarters, 1 nickel, 3 pennies
   B 2 quarters, 1 dime, 3 pennies
   C 5 dimes, 3 pennies
   D 4 dimes, 3 nickels, 3 pennies

10. Nicole buys a sandwich for $3.79. She pays with a $5 bill. How much change should she get?

   F $2.21   H $1.21
   G $1.79   J $1.09

For 11–12, use this calendar.

OCTOBER						
S	M	T	W	T	F	S
			1	2	3	4
5	6	7	8	9	10	11
12	13	14	15	16	17	18
19	20	21	22	23	24	25
26	27	28	29	30	31	

11. An art show starts on October 7 and ends on October 25. How many days long is the art show?

   A 14 days   C 19 days
   B 15 days   D 25 days

12. Peggy will move to a new house in 2 weeks. Today is October 2. When will she move?

   F October 14
   G October 16
   H October 18
   J October 19

13.   847
    − 568

   A 279
   B 315
   C 321
   D 339

14. Maria has 23 more dolls than stuffed animals. She has 18 stuffed animals. Which expression shows how many dolls she has?

   F 18 + 23
   G 18 + 18
   H 23 − 18
   J 23 + 23

15. Mark spent $2.75 on Monday and $4.80 on Tuesday. How much did Mark spend in all?

   A $2.05
   B $5.16
   C $6.55
   D $7.55

16. $618 + 199 = \blacksquare$

   F 861
   G 817
   H 771
   J 717

Go On

17. Jake buys an apple for $0.35. He pays with a $1 bill. What change should he get?

   A   1 quarter, 3 dimes
   B   1 quarter, 3 dimes, 1 nickel
   C   2 quarters, 1 nickel
   D   2 quarters, 1 dime, 1 nickel

18. Sue has $5.19 and Megan has $8.58. How much more money does Megan have than Sue?

   F $3.49   H $3.39
   G $3.41   J $2.39

19. Which number sentence is true?

   A   752 − 147 = 615
   B   208 + 32 + 9 = 249
   C   501 − 88 = 589
   D   630 + 219 = 839

20. The clock shows the time reading class begins. What time does reading class begin?

   F   3:50 A.M.   H   10:15 A.M.
   G   3:50 P.M.   J   10:15 P.M.

For 21–22, use this schedule.

MUSIC LESSONS	
Instrument	Time
Piano	2:00 P.M.–2:40 P.M.
Flute	2:45 P.M.–3:25 P.M.
Tuba	3:25 P.M.–4:00 P.M.
Clarinet	4:00 P.M.–5:00 P.M.

21. Which lesson is one hour long?

   A   piano   C   tuba
   B   flute   D   clarinet

22. Which lessons last the same amount of time?

   F   piano and flute
   G   piano and tuba
   H   flute and tuba
   J   tuba and clarinet

23. $9.21
      − $5.77
      ─────────
                  A $3.44
                  B $4.54
                  C $4.56
                  D $4.98

24. $3.78 + $6.49 = ■

                  F $10.27
                  G $9.27
                  H $9.17
                  J $9.07

Go On

25. Use **front–end estimation** to ESTIMATE the difference.

927 − 688

A 300   **C** 100
B 200   **D** 60

26. 822 − 374 = ■

F 448
G 458
H 549
J 552

27. Which is the **least** amount of money?

A 6 dimes, 1 nickel
B 3 quarters, 1 dime
C 3 quarters, 1 nickel, 1 penny
D 2 quarters, 3 dimes

28. **Round to the nearest hundred** to ESTIMATE the sum.

294
+ 632

F 700
G 800
H 900
J 1000

29. What is the elapsed time from 6:45 A.M. to 7:30 A.M.?

A 15 minutes
B 30 minutes
C 45 minutes
D 50 minutes

30. $7.15 − $4.29 = ■

F $2.86
G $3.14
H $3.86
J $3.96

For 31–32, use this clock.

31. What time does the clock show?

A 8:42   **C** 7:42
B 8:32   **D** 7:35

32. What is another way to read the time?

F 42 minutes before 8
G 18 minutes before 8
H 18 minutes after 8
J 15 minutes before 9

33. Which is an equivalent set for $2.26?

A two $1 bills, 2 dimes, 1 nickel
B one $1 bill, 2 dimes, 1 nickel, 1 penny
C 4 quarters, 2 dimes, 6 pennies
D two $1 bills, 2 dimes, 6 pennies

Stop

Write the correct answer.

1. Phil buys a pair of sunglasses for $3.69. He pays with a $5 bill. How much change should he get?

_____

For 2–3, use the chart. You may want to draw a time line to help.

YEAR OF BIRTH	
Family Member	**Year**
Uncle Mihir	1948
Jeevan	1997
Mom	1963
Sushila	1991
Dad	1961

Jeevan wrote down the years that some of his family members were born.

2. Who was born 36 years before Jeevan?

_____

3. Aunt Vajra was born in 1952. Between which two family members should Aunt Vajra appear on a time line?

_____ and _____

4.   6,000
    − 3,561
   _____

5. Make a table to show how many different equivalent sets can be made with a value of $0.17.

_____ sets

6. Jill has 3 quarters and 2 dimes. Jamie has 2 quarters, 2 dimes, and 3 nickels. Who has **less** money?

_____

7. The sum of two numbers is 26. Their difference is 4. What are the numbers?

_____ and _____

8. $56.24
    + $14.87
   _____

Go On ▶

9. Circle the set of coins with a value of $0.80.

     2 quarters, 2 dimes

            OR

     3 quarters, 1 nickel

10. Maggie buys a brush for $4.18. She pays with a $5 bill. How much change should she get?

_____

For 11–13, use this calendar.

APRIL						
S	M	T	W	T	F	S
					1	2
3	4	5	6	7	8	9
10	11	12	13	14	15	16
17	18	19	20	21	22	23
24	25	26	27	28	29	30

11. Softball practice ends 4 weeks after April 2. On what date does softball practice end?

_____

12. Today is April 3. The science test is in 1 week and 2 days. Write the date of the science test.

_____

13.   621
     $-$ 256

14. Paul has 15 more action figures than he has cars. He has 8 cars. Write an expression to show how many action figures he has.

_____

15. A coloring book costs $2.89. A box of colored pencils costs $1.79. How much do the items cost in all?

_____

16.   589
     $+$ 236

17. A large can of tomato juice costs $0.79. Joey pays with a $1 bill. Circle the change he should get.

     2 dimes, 1 penny

            OR

     3 dimes, 1 penny

Go On

18. Judy has $7.25. Katie has $8.45. How much more money does Katie have than Judy?

_____

19. Circle the number sentence that is true.

$$782 - 359 = 427$$

$$307 + 45 + 8 = 360$$

20. Write the time shown on the clock.

_____

For 21–22, use this schedule.

LIBRARY STORY TIME	
Group	**Time (A.M.)**
Ages 3–4	9:00–9:20
Ages 5–6	9:20–9:50
Ages 7–8	9:50–10:20
Ages 9–10	10:20–11:00

21. Which group's story time lasts 40 minutes?

Ages _____

22. Which two groups' story times last for the same amount of time?

Ages _____

and

Ages _____

23. $7.31
       $- 3.46

24. $4.52 + $5.86 = _____

25. Use **front–end estimation** to ESTIMATE the difference.

$$783 - 512 = $$ _____

26. $936 - 457 = $ _____

Go On ▶

27. Circle the **least** amount of money.

2 quarters, 2 dimes, 1 nickel

OR

3 quarters, 1 dime

28. Round to the nearest hundred to ESTIMATE the sum.

$$\begin{array}{r} 287 \\ + 516 \\ \hline \end{array}$$

_____

29. Write the elapsed time from 5:45 P.M. to 6:15 P.M.

_____ minutes

30. $5.21 − $2.32 = _____

For 31–32, use this clock.

31. Write the time.

_____

32. Circle another way to read the time.

5 minutes after 4

OR

5 minutes before 4

33. Circle the equivalent set for $3.35.

Three $1 bills, 1 quarter, 1 nickel

OR

Three $1 bills, 3 dimes, 1 nickel

Stop

Choose the correct answer.

1. Which number sentence matches the problem?

$$7 + 7 + 7 = 21$$

  A $20 + 1 = 21$
  B $3 \times 7 = 21$
  C $7 \times 7 = 49$
  D $14 + 14 = 28$

2. What are the factors in the number sentence $5 \times 8 = 40$?

  F 5 and 40   **H** 8 and 40
  G 5 and 8   **J** 4 and 0

3. Which multiplication sentence matches the array?

  A $2 + 8 = 10$
  B $2 \times 8 = 16$
  C $8 + 8 = 16$
  D $2 \times 2 = 4$

4. $3 \times 9 = \blacksquare$

  F 12   **H** 27
  G 18   **J** 39

5. Tom and Kelli walked to the store in 15 minutes. At the store they bought 2 candy bars. How much did they spend in all?

  A $30
  B $17
  C 30 minutes
  D Too little information

6.

4 groups of 5 equals $\blacksquare$

  F 9   **H** 20
  G 14   **J** 45

7. Soccer practice lasts for 2 hours, 3 nights a week. Izumi also spends 4 hours playing basketball. How many hours does he practice soccer in a week?

  A 5
  B 6
  C 10
  D Too little information

8. $\begin{array}{r} 9 \\ \times\ 2 \\ \hline \end{array}$ **F** 29
                G 18
                H 16
                J 11

9. What is the missing factor?

$$7 \times 3 = \blacksquare \times 7$$

  A 6   **C** 4
  B 5   **D** 3

10.

$$5 \times 2 = \blacksquare$$

  F 7   **H** 20
  G 10   **J** 25

11. Lisa bought 2 packages of pencils. There are 6 pencils in each package. How many pencils did Lisa buy?

  A 4   **C** 12
  B 8   **D** 26

12. There are 5 snack bars in each package. Each package costs $2.00. How many bars are in 4 packages?

  F 9
  G 11
  H 20
  J 22

13. There are 6 apples in a box. If Ben buys 3 boxes, how many apples will he buy?

  A 18   **C** 6
  B 9   **D** 3

14. Doug bought 3 packages of socks. There are 4 pairs of socks in each package. How many pairs of socks did he buy?

  F 3   **H** 7
  G 4   **J** 12

15. ■ rows of ■ = ■

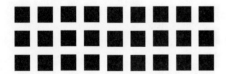

  A 3 rows of 9 = 27
  B 3 rows of 9 = 39
  C 2 rows of 8 = 28
  D 2 rows of 9 = 29

16. Marta has 5 pairs of shoes. How many shoes does she have?

  F 5   **H** 10
  G 7   **J** 25

17. It takes 2 eggs to make each cake. A box of cake mix costs $0.79. Teri needs to make 4 cakes. How many eggs will she need?

  A 2
  B 6
  C 8
  D Too little information

18. Which number sentence is another way to find $3 \times 5 = 15$?

  F $5 + 5 + 5 = 15$
  G $7 + 8 = 15$
  H $3 \times 3 = 9$
  J $5 \times 5 = 15$

19. Margo spends 3 hours each day, 7 days a week practicing ice-skating. How many hours does she spend ice-skating in one week?

  A 7   **C** 14
  B 10   **D** 21

20. $6 \times 5 = $ ■

  F 14   **H** 30
  G 24   **J** 68

Stop

Write the correct answer.

1. Write a multiplication sentence that matches the problem.

$$3 + 3 + 3 + 3 + 3 = 15$$

_____ × _____ = _____

2. What are the factors in the number sentence $4 \times 2 = 8$?

_____ and _____

3. Complete the multiplication sentence that matches the array.

$2 \times$ _____ = _____

4. $3 \times 6 =$ _____

5. Write whether the problem has **too much, too little,** or **the right amount** of information. Solve if you can.

Richard has 2 books of stamps. He bought 10 new stamps. How much did the stamps cost?

_____

6.

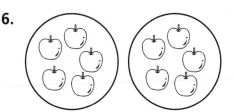

2 groups of 5 equals _____

7. Write whether the problem has **too much, too little,** or **the right amount** of information. Solve if you can.

Mary performed in a 2-hour play 4 nights last week. She spent 7 hours ice-skating. How many hours did she perform in the play last week?

_____

8.   8
      $\times\,2$
      ———

9. What is the missing factor?

$8 \times 3 =$ _____ $\times 8$

10.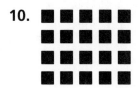

$4 \times 5 =$ _____

Go On ➡

11. Ron bought 2 boxes of muffins. There are 9 muffins in each box. How many muffins did he buy?

_____ muffins

12. There are 5 green peppers in each bag. A bag costs $2.00. How many peppers are in 3 bags?

_____ peppers

13. Glasses come in cartons of 8. If Joe buys 3 cartons, how many glasses will he buy?

_____ glasses

14. There are 3 flowers in each pot. You buy 2 pots. How many flowers will you have?

_____ flowers

15.

5 rows of _____ = _____

16. Greta has 5 packages of balloons. Each package has 8 balloons in it. How many balloons does Greta have?

_____ balloons

17. Write whether the problem has **too much**, **too little**, or **the right amount** of information. Solve if you can.

There are 4 bags of crackers inside each box. Joe buys 2 boxes. How many bags of crackers does he have?

_____

18. Circle the number sentence that is another way to find $2 \times 7 = 14$.

$7 + 7 = 14$ $\qquad$ $4 + 10 = 14$

19. Larry has 3 boxes with 3 toy cars in each box. How many cars does he have?

_____ cars

20.

$4 \times 3 =$ _____

Stop

Choose the correct answer.

1.
$$\begin{array}{r} 1 \\ \times\, 4 \\ \hline \end{array}$$

A 1   **C** 4
B 3   **D** 5

2. $8 \times 1 = \blacksquare$

F 0   **H** 8
G 1   **J** 9

3. What is the missing factor?

$$5 \times \blacksquare = 25$$

A 2   **C** 4
B 3   **D** 5

4. $6 \times 1 = \blacksquare$

F 7   **H** 5
G 6   **J** 0

5. What are the next 3 numbers in the pattern?

5, 7, 9, 11, _____, _____, _____

A 12, 14, 16
B 13, 15, 17
C 14, 17, 20
D 15, 19, 23

6. What is the product of 4 and 7?

F 3   **H** 28
G 11   **J** 47

7. Amy made 4 cups of hot chocolate. She put 4 small marshmallows in each cup. How many marshmallows did she use?

A 20   **C** 12
B 16   **D** 8

8. Jill is thinking of a number pattern. The first four numbers in her pattern are 5, 10, 15, and 20. What is a rule for her pattern?

F multiply by 2
G add 5
H subtract 4
J add 10

9. A classroom has 6 rows with 4 desks in each row. How many desks are in the room?

A 24   **C** 12
B 20   **D** 10

10. What is the product of 0 and 8?

F 0   **H** 8
G 4   **J** 12

Go On

11. When 8 is multiplied by a number, the answer is 24. What is the number?

A 2   C 4
B 3   D 5

12. Each package of pens contains 3 blue and 5 black pens. How many pens are in 4 packages?

F 12   H 23
G 17   J 32

13. Abby is thinking of a number pattern. Her pattern starts with 8, 14, 20, 26, and 32. Which number doesn't fit the pattern if it continues?

A 56   C 50
B 52   D 44

14. $9 \times \blacksquare = 0$

F 0   H 9
G 1   J 90

15. Eric has 4 nickels. Each nickel is worth 5 cents. How much money does Eric have?

A 4¢   C 9¢
B 5¢   D 20¢

16. The product of 2 and another factor is 18. Which number sentence could be used to find the missing factor?

F $2 + \blacksquare = 18$
G $2 \times \blacksquare = 18$
H $18 - \blacksquare = 2$
J $\blacksquare - 2 = 18$

17. There are 4 apartments in each building. How many apartments are there in 9 buildings?

A 5   C 18
B 13   D 36

18. Phil's mom buys 5 boxes of cereal. Each box should have 1 prize in it. Phil found 0 prizes in each box. How many prizes did he get?

F 6   H 4
G 5   J 0

19. Josh's number pattern starts with 38, 36, 37, 35, 36, 34, and 35. What are the next 3 numbers in the number pattern?

A 36, 35, 37
B 33, 34, 32
C 34, 36, 35
D 31, 32, 29

20. A number multiplied by 4 equals 12. What is the number?

F 2   H 8
G 3   J 16

Stop

Write the correct answer.

1. $\begin{array}{r} 6 \\ \times\ 4 \\ \hline \end{array}$

2. $6 \times 1 =$ _____

3. Write the missing factor.

    $4 \times$ _____ $= 16$

4. $8 \times 1 =$ _____

5. Write the next 3 numbers in the pattern.

6, 9, 12, 15, _____, _____, _____

6. Write the product of 4 and 5.

_____

7. Andrea is planting tulips. She plants 4 bulbs in each hole. She dug 7 holes. How many bulbs does she need?

_____ bulbs

8. Karen is thinking of a number pattern. The first four numbers in her pattern are 20, 17, 14, and 11. What is a rule for her pattern?

_____

9. Jim arranges his model planes in 4 rows with 3 planes in each row. How many model planes does he have?

_____ planes

10. What is the product of 0 and 3?

_____

11. When 5 is multiplied by another factor, the answer is 10. What is the other factor?

_____

Go On

12. John bought 4 bags of bagels. Each bag contains 8 bagels. How many bagels did he buy in all?

_____ bagels

13. Alex is thinking of a number pattern. His pattern is 5, 9, 13, 17, and 21. Circle the number that doesn't fit in the pattern if it continues.

26   33   37

14. $8 \times$ _____ $= 0$

15. Bruce has 4 boxes. He puts 1 car in each box. How many cars does he have in all?

_____ cars

16. The product of 3 and another factor is 15. Circle the number sentence that could be used to find the missing factor.

$3 + \blacksquare = 15$

$3 \times \blacksquare = 15$

17. There are 9 cookies on each tray. How many cookies are there on 4 trays?

_____ cookies

18. A store gave free bags to its customers. Some of the bags had a prize inside. Chris opened 6 bags. Each bag had 0 prizes inside. How many prizes did Chris find?

_____ prizes

19. Paul's number pattern is 34, 32, 29, 27, 24 and 22. What are the next three numbers in the pattern?

_____, _____, _____

20. A number multiplied by 5 equals 25. What is the number?

_____

Stop

Choose the correct answer.

1. $2 \times 7 = \blacksquare$

A 5   C 14
B 9   D 27

2. Which of the following is true?

F $7 \times 3 > 4 \times 6$
G $7 \times 5 < 6 \times 5$
H $8 \times 4 = 7 \times 6$
J $3 \times 8 = 4 \times 6$

3. What is the missing factor?

$$5 \times \blacksquare = 30$$

A 6   C 4
B 5   D 3

4. Which symbol makes the following true?

$$7 \times 7 \; \bullet \; 6 \times 8$$

F $<$ G $>$ H $=$

5. Keith's father works 6 days each week. How many days does his father work in 7 weeks?

A 13   C 42
B 21   D 67

6.
$$\begin{array}{r} 9 \\ \times 6 \\ \hline \end{array}$$

F 48
G 54
H 56
J 63

7. Steve bought 7 boxes of cupcakes. There were 4 cupcakes in each box. Twelve cupcakes had white icing and the rest had chocolate icing. How many had chocolate icing?

A 13   C 20
B 16   D 28

8. What is the product of 8 and 9?

F 1   H 72
G 17   J 89

9. What number completes the number sentence?

$$3 \times \blacksquare = 20 + 1$$

A 10   C 8
B 9   D 7

10. The product of two factors is 54. One of the factors is 6. What is the other factor?

F 6   H 8
G 7   J 9

Go On ➡

11. Emily has 2 jobs. At one job she works 6 hours each day, 3 days a week. At her other job she works 8 hours each day, 2 days a week. How many hours does she work in one week?

   A 36   C 30
   B 34   D 28

12. Each bicycle has 2 wheels. What expression shows how many wheels there are on 6 bicycles?

   F $2 + 6$
   G $6 - 2$
   H 6×2
   J 6×6

13. There are 4 small pizzas in each box. Mrs. Owens buys 8 boxes. How many pizzas will she have?

   A 4   C 24
   B 12   D 32

14. Danny has 48 plants to arrange in his garden. He wants 6 rows with the same number of plants in each row. How many plants should be in each row?

   F 9   H 7
   G 8   J 6

15. Each roll of ribbon has 9 yards on it. Megan needs 63 yards. How many rolls should she buy in order to have enough?

   A 7   C 5
   B 6   D 4

16. Each week, Nate goes to school 5 days and spends 2 days at home. How many days does he spend at school in 7 weeks?

   F 14   H 35
   G 17   J 49

17. Cheryl was playing a math game. The answer was 40. Which of these could have been the problem?

   A $8 \times 6 = $ ■   C $7 \times 6 = $ ■
   B $8 \times 5 = $ ■   D $7 \times 5 = $ ■

For 18–20, use the pictograph.

FAVORITE PLACES TO VISIT	
City Park	🚗
Lake	🚗 🚗 🚗
Mountains	🚗 🚗 🚗
Amusement Park	🚗 🚗 🚗 🚗 🚗
Zoo	🚗 🚗 🚗 🚗
Nature Trail	🚗 🚗

Key: Each 🚗 = 4 votes.

18. How many more votes did the lake receive than the nature trail?

   F 1   H 4
   G 2   J 10

19. How many people altogether voted for the amusement park and the zoo?

   A 32   C 36
   B 34   D 40

20. Which three numbers represented on the pictograph are multiples of 4?

   F 4, 8, 10   H 8, 14, 16
   G 8, 10, 16   J 8, 12, 20

Stop

Write the correct answer.

1. $3 \times 7 =$ _____

2. Compare. Write $<$, $>$, or $=$ in the $\bigcirc$.

   $3 \times 6 \bigcirc 2 \times 7$

3. What is the missing factor?

   $6 \times$ _____ $= 24$

4. Compare. Write $<$, $>$, or $=$ in the $\bigcirc$.

   $7 \times 6 \bigcirc 6 \times 8$

5. Carl has 6 pages of stickers. Each page holds 6 stickers. How many stickers does he have?

   _____ stickers

6. $\begin{array}{r} 5 \\ \times 6 \\ \hline \end{array}$

7. Kim bought 7 packages of pens. There were 5 pens in each package. Twenty pens were red and the rest were blue. How many blue pens were there?

   _____ blue pens

8. What is the product of 8 and 5?

   _____

9. Complete.

   $7 \times$ _____ $= 2 + 5$

10. The product of two factors is 12. One of the factors is 6. What is the other factor?

    _____

11. Alex bought 6 containers of flowers. There were 4 flowers in each container. He also bought 8 containers that had 2 flowers in each container. How many flowers did he buy in all?

    _____ flowers

    Go On ▶

12. There are 3 apples in each box. Circle the expression that shows how many apples there are in 6 boxes.

3×2 6×3

13. Kyle buys 8 packages of hamburger patties. Each package contains 4 patties. How many hamburger patties does he buy?

_____ hamburger patties

14. Danielle has 24 CDs to arrange. She wants 8 CDs on each shelf. How many shelves will she need?

_____ shelves

15. Each roll of wrapping paper is 7 feet long. How many feet of wrapping paper are there on 4 of these rolls?

_____ feet

16. There are 7 days in a week. How many days are there in 8 weeks?

_____ days

17. Molly was playing a math game. The answer was 64. Circle the problem with that answer.

8×8 8×9

For 18–20, use the pictograph.

AMUSEMENT PARK RIDES SEATING CAPACITY	
Roller Coaster	👤👤👤👤👤👤👤
Spider	👤👤👤👤
Raging River	👤👤👤👤
Water Plunge	👤👤
Merry-Go-Round	👤👤👤👤👤👤
Flying Carpet	👤

Key: Each 👤 = 4 seats.

18. How many more people can ride the Spider compared to the Flying Carpet?

_____

19. Janet's class has 22 students. Which rides have enough seats for everyone in her class?

_____

_____

20. Zach is waiting in line to ride the Raging River ride. There are 34 people in front of him. How many times will the seats fill up before he gets on the ride?

_____

Stop

Choose the correct answer.

1. What is the missing factor?

$$■ \times 9 = 54$$

A 8   C 6
B 7   D 5

2. Find the product.

$$3 \times (5 \times 2) = ■$$

F 56   H 13
G 30   J 10

3. What is the rule for the table?

Packages	1	2	3	4	5	6
Flowers	6	12	18	24	30	36

A Multiply the number of packages by 6.
B Add 5 to the number of packages.
C Subtract 5 from the number of flowers.
D Multiply the number of packages by 5.

4. What is the rule for the table?

Weeks	1	2	3	4	5	6
Days	7	14	21	28	35	42

F Multiply the number of days by 7.
G Add 6 to the number of weeks.
H Multiply the number of weeks by 7.
J Subtract 6 from the number of days.

For 5–6, find the missing number for each _____.

5. $2 \times (4 \times 3) = ($ _____ $\times 4) \times 3$

A 2   C 4
B 3   D 12

6. $7 \times$ _____ $= 8 \times 7$

F 1   H 8
G 4   J 56

For 7–8, tell what property you would use to find the product.

7. 1×8

A Associative Property
B Identity Property
C Distributive Property
D Commutative Property

8. 9×4

F Associative Property
G Identity Property
H Zero Property
J Distributive Property

For 9–10, use this table.

Packages	1	2	3	4	5	6
Cupcakes	2	4	6	■	■	■

9. Which numbers complete the table?

A 7, 8, 9   C 12, 14, 16
B 8, 10, 12   D 9, 12, 15

10. Suppose you had 16 cupcakes. How many packages would you have?

F 7   H 9
G 8   J 10

Go On ▶

11. Ellen has $35. A pair of sunglasses sells for $7. A hair bow sells for $2. She buys 2 pairs of sunglasses and 4 hair bows. How much money does she have left?

A $3   C $8
B $7   D $13

12. The product of a number and 8 is 72. What is the number?

F 9   H 64
G 10   J 80

13. There are 4 cupcakes in each box. Each cupcake has 1 cherry on top. Crystal buys 5 boxes of cupcakes. How many cherries are there?

A 9   C 20
B 10   D 24

14. Adult tickets cost $3 each. Student tickets cost $2 each. How much will 5 adult tickets and 10 student tickets cost?

F $35   H $50
G $40   J $56

15. Which numbers complete the table?

Octopuses	3	4	5	6	7	8
Arms	24	32	40	■	■	■

A 44, 48, 52
B 45, 50, 55
C 46, 52, 58
D 48, 56, 64

16. Find the product.

$$(3 \times 3) \times 9 = \blacksquare$$

F 27   H 80
G 71   J 81

17. Which symbol makes the number sentence true?

$$18 + 15 \bullet 3 \times 10$$

A >   B <   C =

18. Kate had 50 stickers. She gave 15 away on Monday and 24 on Tuesday. How many stickers does she have left?

F 11   H 59
G 21   J 81

19. A nickel has the same value as 5 pennies. John has 9 nickels. How many pennies would this be?

A 14   C 45
B 40   D 50

20. A restaurant sells roast beef sandwiches for $5 each. There are 2 sandwiches in a bag. Which expression shows how much it would cost to buy 4 bags?

F $(2 \times 5) \times 4$
G $(4 + 2) \times 5$
H $4 + (2 \times 5)$
J $4 \times (2 + 5)$

Stop

Write the correct answer.

1. Write the missing factor.

_____ $\times\ 9 = 36$

2. Find the product.

$4 \times (3 \times 1) =$ _____

3. Circle the rule for the table.

Flowers	2	3	4	5	6
Petals	10	15	20	25	30

Multiply the flowers by 5.

Add 8 to flowers.

4. Write a rule to find the number of pennies.

Dimes	1	2	3	4	5
Pennies	10	20	30	40	50

_____

_____

5. Write the missing number.

$4 \times 6 = (4 \times$ _____$) + (4 \times 1)$

6. Write the missing number.

$4 \times (3 \times 7) = ($_____$\times\ 3) \times 7$

For 7–8, write the property you would use to find the product.

7. $7 \times (5 \times 3)$

_____

8. 8×6

_____

For 9–10, use this table.

Packages	2	3	4	5	6	7
Markers	8	12	16	■	■	■

9. Complete the table.

_____, _____, _____

10. Suppose you have 32 markers. How many packages would you have?

_____ packages

Go On ▶

11. Kelly has $40. A pair of socks costs $2. A notebook costs $3. She buys 3 pairs of socks and 4 notebooks. How much money does she have left?

_____

12. The product of two factors is 45. One of the factors is 5. What is the other factor?

_____

13. Evan gave each of his 2 friends 2 packages of sports cards. Each package contains 5 cards. How many cards did he give away?

_____ cards

14. Large balls cost $5 each and small balls cost $2 each. How much would 4 large balls and 6 small balls cost?

_____

15. Complete the table.

Teams	1	2	3	4	5	6
Players	9	18	27	■	■	■

_____, _____, _____

16. Find the product.

$(4 \times 2) \times 8 =$ _____

17. Compare. Write $<$, $>$, or $=$ in the $\bigcirc$.

$13 + 17 \bigcirc 4 \times 10$

18. Joel found 35 seashells. He gave his mother 10 and his grandmother 8. How many seashells does he have left?

_____ seashells

19. A dime has the same value as 10 pennies. Bob has 9 dimes. How many pennies would this be?

_____ pennies

20. Mrs. Gomez has 2 children. Each child needs 3 notebooks. The notebooks cost $2 each. Write an expression to show how much it will cost Mrs. Gomez to buy the notebooks.

_____ $\times$ _____ $\times$ _____

Stop

Form B • Free Response

Choose the correct answer.

1. The product of 3 and another factor is 15. What is the other factor?

   A 18
   B 12
   C 5
   D 4

2. $\begin{array}{r} 8 \\ \times\ 3 \\ \hline \end{array}$

   F 11
   G 16
   H 21
   J 24

3. Which is true?

   A $8 \times 5 < 7 \times 6$
   B $8 \times 3 = 7 \times 4$
   C $7 \times 4 = 5 \times 6$
   D $6 \times 4 > 8 \times 4$

4. What is a rule for this table?

Box	1	2	3	4	5
Glasses	4	8	12	16	20

   F Add 4 to the number of boxes.
   G Add 3 to the number of boxes.
   H Subtract 3 from the number of glasses.
   J Multiply the number of boxes by 4.

5. Each school van seats 6 students. If there are 9 school vans, how many students can ride in the vans?

   A 3
   B 15
   C 54
   D 58

For 6, use the pictograph.

WAYS TO TRAVEL	
Plane	☺ ☺ ☺ ☺ ☺
Car	☺ ☺ ☺
Train	☺ ☺ ☺ ☺
Boat	☺

Key: Each ☺ = 3 votes.

6. How many more people prefer to travel by train than by boat?

   F 12
   G 9
   H 6
   J 3

7. Matt and Jackie have 3 dogs and 2 cats. They went shopping for pet food. How much would 2 bags of pet food cost?

   A $4
   B $5
   C $10
   D Too little information

Go On

8. Three friends each wear 2 bracelets on each of their wrists. Which expression shows how to find how many bracelets they are wearing in all?

   F $(2 + 3) + 2$
   G $(2 \times 3) + 3$
   H $(2 \times 2) \times 3$
   J $3 \times (2 + 1)$

9. What are the next 3 numbers in the pattern?

   9, 12, 15, 18, ▪, ▪, ▪

   A 19, 20, 21
   B 21, 24, 27
   C 22, 26, 30
   D 23, 28, 33

10. What is the missing factor?

   $3 \times 4 = 4 \times$ ▪

   F 3
   G 4
   H 5
   J 6

11. What is the product of 4 and 5?

   A 1
   B 9
   C 20
   D 45

12. What symbol makes this true?

   8×4 ● 7×5

   F <   G >   H =

13. $8 \times (4 \times 1) =$ ▪

   A 13
   B 32
   C 40
   D 64

14. What symbol makes this true?

   5×0 ● 7×1

   F <   G >   H =

15. There are 5 bananas in each bunch. Taylor buys 2 bunches. How many bananas does she buy?

   A 3
   B 7
   C 10
   D 12

16. Which property would you use to find the product of 5×1?

   F Identity Property
   G Zero Property
   H Distributive Property
   J Associative Property

Go On

17. Jeff is thinking of a number pattern. The first four numbers are 7, 11, 15, and 19. What is a rule for his pattern?

A Add 4.
B Subtract 5.
C Add 3.
D Multiply by 2.

18.　 4
　　 × 2
　　　　　　 F 2
　　　　　　 G 4
　　　　　　 H 6
　　　　　　 J 8

19. ■ = 10 × 9

A 19　　　　**C** 90
B 60　　　　**D** 109

20. Diane has 2 packages of socks. Each package contains 2 pairs of white socks, 1 pair of blue socks, and 1 pair of pink socks. How many pairs of socks does she have in all?

F 10 pairs of socks
G 8 pairs of socks
H 6 pairs of socks
J 4 pairs of socks

21. An adult's dinner costs $7. A child's dinner costs $4. How much would it cost for 2 adults and 3 children to eat dinner?

A $34　　　**C** $26
B $29　　　**D** $16

22. What is the missing factor?

■ × 6 = 30

F 4　　　　**H** 6
G 5　　　　**J** 7

23. Mr. Bloom works 8 hours each day, 5 days a week. It takes him 1 hour to get to work. How many hours does he work each week?

A 13 hours
B 40 hours
C 45 hours
D Too little information

24. Which numbers complete the table?

Tables	1	2	3	4	5	6
Legs	3	6	9	■	■	■

F 10, 11, 12
G 11, 14, 17
H 12, 15, 18
J 12, 16, 19

Go On ▶

25. What number completes the number sentence?

$$4 \times \blacksquare = 20 + 8$$

A 5
B 6
C 7
D 8

26. What is the missing factor?

$$1 \times \blacksquare = 5$$

F 4
G 5
H 6
J 7

27. What multiplication sentence matches the array?

A 2 + 7 = 9
B 2 × 3 = 6
C 7 + 7 = 14
D 2 × 7 = 14

28.
```
   7
 × 7
 ───
```
F 14
G 28
H 49
J 56

29. What is the missing factor?

$$\blacksquare \times 10 = 70$$

A 6
B 7
C 9
D 60

30. What is the product of 0 and 6?

F 0
G 3
H 6
J 9

31. There are 8 hamburger buns in each package. How many buns are in 6 packages?

A 14
B 48
C 56
D 64

32. What symbol makes this true?

$$5 + 15 \bullet 2 \times 10$$

F <   G >   H =

33. What number sentence matches the problem?

$$6 + 6 + 6 + 6 = 24$$

A 4 × 6 = 24
B 6 × 3 = 18
C 12 + 10 = 24
D 30 − 6 = 24

Stop

Write the correct answer.

1. The product of 4 and another factor is 12. What is the other factor?

   _____

2.
   $$\begin{array}{r} 6 \\ \times\ 3 \\ \hline \end{array}$$

3. Which is true? Circle it.

   $6 \times 7 > 5 \times 9$

   $3 \times 8 = 6 \times 4$

4. Write a rule for this table.

Boxes	1	2	3	4
Invitations	8	16	24	32

   _____

   _____

5. Six students each sold 8 items for a playground fund-raiser. How many items did they sell in all?

   _____

For 6, use the pictograph.

NUMBER OF VOLUNTEERS	
School Clean-Up	🧍 🧍 🧍
Hospital Visit	🧍 🧍
Park Clean-Up	🧍 🧍 🧍 🧍 🧍
Food Pantry	🧍 🧍 🧍 🧍

Key: Each 🧍 = 4 people.

6. How many more people volunteered at the food pantry than visited the hospital?

   _____ more people

7. Write whether the problem has **too much**, **too little**, or **the right amount** of information.

   Jason lives 8 miles from school. Anna lives 5 miles from school. How far is the school from the library?

   _____

8. Mrs. Martinez has 2 daughters. She buys 2 packages of hair bows for each daughter. Each package has 5 bows. Circle the expression that shows how many hair bows there are in all.

   $2 + (2 \times 5)$

   $2 \times (2 \times 5)$

   Go On

9. Write the rule and the next three numbers in this pattern.

_____

8, 13, 18, 23, _____, _____, _____

10. Write the missing factor.

$9 \times 3 = 3 \times$ _____

11. What is the product of 4 and 9?

_____

12. Compare. Write $<$, $>$, or $=$ in the ◯.

6×5 ◯ 4×7

13. $7 \times (1 \times 3) =$ _____

14. Compare. Write $<$, $>$, or $=$ in the ◯.

3×1 ◯ 9×0

15. There are 6 jars of paint in each box. Jarred has 2 boxes. How many jars of paint does he have?

_____ jars

16. Circle the property you would use to find the product of 9×0.

Identity Property

Zero Property

Associative Property

Distributive Property

17. Doug is thinking of a number pattern. The first four numbers are 2, 8, 14, and 20. Write a rule for the pattern.

_____

Go On

Name _____

18. 5
    $\times\ 2$

19. $3 \times 10 =$ _____

20. Diane has 4 boxes of fruit drinks. Each box contains 2 cherry, 2 grape, and 2 orange drinks. How many drinks does she have in all?

_____ fruit drinks

21. A large poster costs $4. A small poster costs $2. How much would it cost to buy 3 large posters and 5 small posters?

_____

22. Write the missing factor.

_____ $\times\ 6 = 36$

23. Write whether the problem has **too much**, **too little**, or **the right amount** of information.

Johnny runs 2 miles every day for 5 days. It takes him 20 minutes to run a mile. How many miles does he run in 5 days?

_____

24. Write a rule for the table. Then complete the table.

Shirts	1	2	3	4	5	6
Buttons	9	18	27			

_____

_____

25. Complete.

$7 \times$ _____ $= 20 + 15$

26. $9 \times$ _____ $= 9$

Go On

Form B • Free Response　　　　　　　**Assessment Guide　AG 75**

27. Complete.

000000
000000
000000

_____ rows of _____ = _____

_____ × _____ = _____

28.   7
       × 8

29. Write the missing factor.

4 × _____ = 36

30. What is the product of 0 and 4?

_____

31. There are 4 students at each table. Each student needs 6 sheets of paper. How many sheets of paper are needed for the students at each table?

_____ sheets

32. Compare. Write $<$, $>$, or $=$ in the ◯.

5×6 ◯ 3×10

33. Circle the number sentence that matches the problem.

$5 + 5 + 5 = 15$

$5 \times 5 = 25$

$3 \times 5 = 15$

Stop

Choose the correct answer.

1. Kara has 10 pennies. She wants to share them equally with a friend. How many pennies will each get?

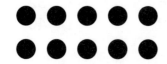

A 2 C 5
B 4 D 10

2. Four friends want to share 16 pieces of pizza equally. How many pieces will each get?

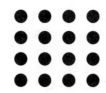

F 2 H 6
G 4 J 8

3. Ellie has 20 counters. She puts them into 4 equal groups. How many counters are in each group?

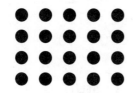

A 3 C 5
B 4 D 6

4. Which division sentence is shown by the number line?

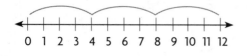

F $0 \div 4 = 0$ H $12 \div 6 = 2$
G $8 \div 8 = 1$ J $12 \div 4 = 3$

5. Which division sentence is shown by the repeated subtraction?

$$\begin{array}{cccc} 24 & 18 & 12 & 6 \\ -6 & -6 & -6 & -6 \\ \hline 18 & 12 & 6 & 0 \end{array}$$

A $20 \div 4 = 5$ C $24 \div 3 = 8$
B $24 \div 6 = 4$ D $24 \div 8 = 3$

6. Which division sentence is shown by the repeated subtraction?

$$\begin{array}{ccc} 27 & 18 & 9 \\ -9 & -9 & -9 \\ \hline 18 & 9 & 0 \end{array}$$

F $27 \div 9 = 3$ H $18 \div 6 = 3$
G $9 \div 3 = 3$ J $0 \div 9 = 0$

7. What symbol makes this number sentence true?

$$10 \bullet 2 = 16 \div 2$$

A + B − C × D ÷

8. What symbol makes this number sentence true?

$$30 \div 6 = 4 \bullet 1$$

F + G − H × J ÷

9. Which division sentence is represented by an array of 3 rows of 7?

A $21 \div 3 = 7$
B $21 \div 1 = 21$
C $35 \div 5 = 7$
D $28 \div 7 = 4$

Go On

10. Which division sentence is represented by 6 rows of 4?

F $24 \div 6 = 4$ **H** $24 \div 3 = 8$
G $24 \div 8 = 3$ **J** $12 \div 4 = 3$

11. Which multiplication sentence is represented by 6 rows of 8?

A $6 \times 8 = 48$ **C** $6 \times 6 = 36$
B $4 \times 8 = 32$ **D** $8 \times 8 = 64$

12. Which number completes the number sentence?

$$3 \times 3 = \blacksquare \div 3$$

F 1 **H** 9
G 3 **J** 27

13. Which number does the variable stand for?

$$18 \div 6 = p$$

A 12 **C** 4
B 6 **D** 3

14. Which number sentence does NOT belong in the fact family for 2, 4, and 8?

F $2 \times 4 = 8$ **H** $8 - 4 = 4$
G $8 \div 4 = 2$ **J** $4 \times 2 = 8$

15. $16 \div 8 = \blacksquare$

A 2 **C** 6
B 4 **D** 8

16. Which number completes the number sentence?

$$4 \times \blacksquare = 20 \div 5$$

F 5 **H** 1
G 4 **J** 0

17. Four friends share a box of candy. Each friend gets 8 pieces of candy. How many pieces of candy were in the box?

A 16 **C** 32
B 18 **D** 40

18. Amy has 60 pictures. Her album has 9 pages. Each page holds 6 pictures. Which number sentence shows how to find the number of pictures her album holds?

F $60 - 9 = 51$ **H** $6 \times 9 = 54$
G $60 \div 6 = 10$ **J** $9 + 6 = 15$

19. Al wants to share 20 cookies equally among 10 friends. Which number sentence shows how to find the number of cookies each friend will get?

A $30 \div 3 = 10$
B $20 \div 10 = 2$
C $20 - 2 = 18$
D $20 - 10 = 10$

20. Pat has 12 stuffed animals to put on 3 shelves. She wants to put an equal number of animals on each shelf. Which number sentence shows how to find the number of animals that will go on each shelf?

F $3 + 4 = 7$
G $12 - 3 = 9$
H $12 + 3 = 15$
J $12 \div 3 = 4$

Stop

Name _____

Write the correct answer.

1. Dawn has 8 cookies. She wants to share them equally with a friend. How many cookies will each person get?

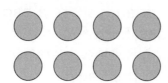

_____ cookies

2. Five friends want to share 10 pieces of pizza equally. How many pieces will each friend get?

_____ pieces

3. Doug has 15 counters. He puts them into 5 equal groups. How many counters are in each group?

_____ counters

4. Write the division sentence shown by the number line.

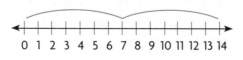

_____ ÷ _____ = _____

5. Write the division sentence shown by the repeated subtraction.

$$\begin{array}{ccc} 15 & 10 & 5 \\ -\ 5 & -\ 5 & -\ 5 \\ \hline 10 & 5 & 0 \end{array}$$

_____

6. Write the division sentence shown by the repeated subtraction.

$$\begin{array}{cccc} 16 & 12 & 8 & 4 \\ -\ 4 & -\ 4 & -\ 4 & -\ 4 \\ \hline 12 & 8 & 4 & 0 \end{array}$$

_____

7. Write +, −, ×, or ÷ to make the number sentence true.

$$5 \bigcirc 2 = 21 \div 3$$

8. Write the symbol that makes this number sentence true.

$$2 \times 4 = 32 \bigcirc 4$$

9. Complete the division sentence that is represented by 4 rows of 7.

_____ ÷ 4 = _____

Go On

Form B • Free Response

10. Complete the division sentence that is represented by 8 rows of 7.

_____ ÷ 8 = _____

11. Complete the multiplication sentence that is represented by 6 rows of 9.

_____ × 9 = _____

12. Write the number that makes this number sentence true.

$4 \times 1 = $ _____ ÷ 4

13. Write the number that the variable stands for.

$8 \div 4 = p$

$p = $ _____

14. Write the number sentence that is missing from the fact family for 2, 5, and 10.

$2 \times 5 = 10$

$5 \times 2 = 10$

$10 \div 2 = 5$

_____ ÷ _____ = _____

15. $25 \div 5 = $ _____

16. Write the number that makes this number sentence true.

$3 \times $ _____ $= 18 \div 3$

17. Three friends share a bag of oranges. Each friend gets 2 oranges. How many oranges were in the bag?

_____ oranges

18. Mr. Armstrong has 90 markers. He has 9 containers. Each container holds 8 markers. Write a number sentence that shows how many markers will fit in his containers.

_____

19. Joy has 28 pencils. She and 3 friends share them equally. Write a number sentence to show the number of pencils each person gets.

_____ ÷ _____ = _____

20. Matt has 15 model cars. He puts an equal number on each of 3 shelves. Write a number sentence that shows how many cars are on each shelf.

_____

Stop

Choose the correct answer.

1. What number completes both number sentences?

$$5 \times \blacksquare = 30 \qquad 30 \div 5 = \blacksquare$$

A 7   C 5
B 6   D 4

2. $2\overline{)14}$

F 16   H 7
G 12   J 6

3. $2\overline{)18}$

A 8   C 14
B 9   D 16

4. Amber has 40 stickers. She divides the stickers equally among her 5 friends. How many stickers does each friend get?

F 10   H 6
G 8   J 5

5. Eric has 25 pennies. He spends 5 of them to buy a pencil and divides the rest equally among his 4 sisters. How many pennies does each sister get?

A 20   C 5
B 16   D 1

6. Two numbers have a product of 16 and a quotient of 1. What are the numbers?

F 8 and 2   H 4 and 4
G 6 and 3   J 3 and 3

7. Which number completes the number sentence?

$$27 \div \blacksquare = 18 \div 2$$

A 3   C 8
B 6   D 9

8. $24 \div 3 = \blacksquare$

F 27   H 8
G 21   J 7

9. Which multiplication fact can be used to find $32 \div 4$?

A $2 \times 16 = 32$
B $4 \times 8 = 32$
C $4 \times 9 = 36$
D $4 \times 10 = 40$

10. $0 \div 4 = \blacksquare$

F 0   H 2
G 1   J 4

11. What symbol makes this number sentence true?

$$0 \div 9 \bullet 8 \div 8$$

A $<$ B $>$ C $=$

Go On ▶

12. $8 \div 1 = \blacksquare$

   F 0   **H** 8

   G 1   **J** 9

13. Tyler has 3 bags of carrots. There are 10 carrots in each bag. Which expression shows the number of carrots Tyler has in all?

   A $10 + 3$ **C** $10 + 10 + 3$

   B $10 - 3$ **D** 10×3

14. Dennis had 28 packages of raisins. He gave 4 packages to each of his friends. Which expression shows the number of friends that received raisins?

   F $28 \div 4$ **H** $28 + 28$

   G $28 - 4$ **J** $4 + 4$

15. A pet store has 8 puppies. Each puppy gets 2 treats each day. Which expression shows the number of treats that are needed each day?

   A $8 + 2$ **C** $8 \div 2$

   B 8×2 **D** $2 + 2 + 2$

16. Sean saw 3 ducks flying overhead and 6 ducks swimming in the pond. Which expression shows the number of ducks he saw in all?

   F 6×3

   G $6 \div 3$

   H $6 - 3$

   J $6 + 3$

17. Miss Jana received 20 flowers from her students. Each student brought 2 flowers. Which number sentence shows how to find the number of students who brought flowers?

   A $20 \div 2 = 10$

   B $20 - 2 = 18$

   C $20 + 2 = 22$

   D $20 + 20 = 40$

18. Each box contains 6 candy bars. Which number sentence shows how to find the number of bars in 3 boxes?

   F $6 \div 3 = 2$

   G $6 - 3 = 3$

   H $3 + 6 = 9$

   J $3 \times 6 = 18$

19. Mrs. Walls received 5 pieces of mail on Monday and 10 on Tuesday. Which number sentence shows how to find the number of pieces she received in all?

   A $10 \div 5 = 2$

   B $10 - 5 = 5$

   C $10 + 5 = 15$

   D $10 \times 5 = 50$

20. Jon has 18 games. Barry has 6 games. Which number sentence shows how to find how many more games Jon has than Barry?

   F $6 + 6 + 6 = 18$

   G $18 \div 6 = 3$

   H $6 + 18 = 24$

   J $18 - 6 = 12$

Stop

Write the correct answer.

1. Write the missing factor and quotient.

$5 \times$ _____ $= 35$ $35 \div 5 =$ _____

2. $2\overline{)16}$

_____

3. $2\overline{)12}$

_____

4. Deanna has 35 cookies. She puts the same number of cookies in each of 5 plastic bags. How many cookies are in each bag?

_____ cookies

5. Sue has 22 pencils. She takes 2 pencils to school and divides the rest equally among 4 boxes. How many pencils are in each box?

_____ pencils

6. The product of 2 numbers is 9. The quotient of the numbers is 1. What are the numbers?

_____ and _____

7. Write the number that makes this division sentence true.

$24 \div$ _____ $= 40 \div 5$

8. $27 \div 3 =$ _____

9. Write the multiplication fact that can be used to find $28 \div 4$.

_____ $\times$ _____ $=$ _____

10. Write a multiplication fact that can be used to find $0 \div 6$.

_____ $\times$ _____ $=$ _____

11. Compare. Write $<$, $>$, or $=$ in the $\bigcirc$.

$5 \div 5 \bigcirc 7 \div 7$

12. $9 \div 1 =$ _____

Go On ➡

Form B • Free Response

13. In each package of pizza snacks there are 8 mini pizzas. Write an expression that shows the number of mini pizzas there are in 4 packages.

_____ ◯ _____

14. Donna has 28 apples. She divides them equally among 7 friends. Write an expression to show how many apples each friend gets.

_____ ◯ _____

15. Five students are working on an art project. Each student needs 7 markers. Circle the expression that shows how many markers are needed in all.

5 + 7   5 × 7

7 − 5   7 ÷ 5

16. Jeff counted 5 red trucks and 10 white trucks in the parking lot. Write an expression to show how many trucks he counted in all.

_____ ◯ _____

17. Kevin found 9 seashells on Saturday and 10 seashells on Sunday. Write a number sentence to find the number of seashells he found in all.

_____ ◯ _____ = _____

18. There are 24 students going to lunch. Four students sit at each table. Write a number sentence to find how many tables they need.

_____ ◯ _____ = _____

19. Mr. Gant bought 5 boxes of pencils. There are 10 pencils in each box. Circle the number sentence that can be used to find how many pencils Mr. Gant has in all.

10 + 5 = 15   5 × 10 = 50

10 ÷ 5 = 2   10 − 5 = 2

20. Jake has 12 model cars. Ben has 8 model cars. Write a number sentence to find how many more model cars Jake has than Ben.

_____ ◯ _____ = _____

Stop

Form B • Free Response

Choose the correct answer.

1. $40 \div 8 = \blacksquare$

   A 4   **C** 6
   B 5   **D** 7

2. $6\overline{)54}$

   F 7   **H** 9
   G 8   **J** 10

3. $\blacksquare = 14 \div 7$

   A 98   **C** 7
   B 21   **D** 2

4. What number completes the number sentence?

$$32 \div \blacksquare = 9 - 5$$

   F 4   **H** 8
   G 6   **J** 9

5. Morgan worked 16 hours in 3 days. He worked 4 hours 1 day and the same number of hours on each of the other 2 days. How many hours did he work on each of the other days?

   A 2   **C** 6
   B 3   **D** 7

6. $9\overline{)36}$

   F 2   **H** 4
   G 3   **J** 5

7. $81 \div 9 = \blacksquare$

   A 7   **C** 9
   B 8   **D** 10

8. $10\overline{)50}$

   F 4   **H** 6
   G 5   **J** 7

9. Compare. What symbol makes this number sentence true?

$$9 \bullet 9 = 5 - 4$$

   A $+$ **C** $\times$
   B $-$ **D** $\div$

10. Paul bought 60 pencils. There were 10 pencils in each box. How many boxes did he buy?

   F 70   **H** 16
   G 50   **J** 6

Go On ➡

11. Compare. What symbol makes this true?

$$2 \times 3 \bullet 72 \div 9$$

  A   <   **B**   >   **C**   =

12. Find the missing factor and quotient.

$$7 \times \blacksquare = 21 \qquad 21 \div 7 = \blacksquare$$

  F   3   **H**   14
  G   7   **J**   28

13. Divide 0 by 10.

  A   0   **C**   7
  B   1   **D**   8

14. Each watermelon costs $2. How much will 10 watermelons cost?

  F $5   **H** $15
  G $10   **J** $20

15. Greta bought 8 yards of ribbon. She gave the clerk $40 and got $8 in change. How much did one yard of ribbon cost?

  A $3   **C** $13
  B $4   **D** $24

16. Each ticket costs $5. How much will 6 tickets cost?

  F $42   **H** $18
  G $30   **J** $11

17. Eight notebooks cost $24. How much does 1 notebook cost?

  A $3   **C** $8
  B $4   **D** $16

18. Mrs. Wilson spends $15 for 5 sandwiches. How much does each sandwich cost?

  F $3   **H** $6
  G $5   **J** $7

19. Bob threw 6 of the fish he caught back in the water. He divided the rest equally among 4 people. Each person got 4 fish. How many fish did Bob catch?

  A   12   **C**   22
  B   13   **D**   27

20. Angie was thinking of a number. She added 5 to the number. She divided that sum by 2 and got 10. What was her number?

  F   0   **H**   15
  G   10   **J**   25

Stop

Write the correct answer.

1. $32 \div 8 =$ _____

2. $6\overline{)24}$

_____

3. _____ $= 28 \div 7$

4. Write the number that makes this number sentence true.

$48 \div$ _____ $= 2 + 4$

5. Rich collected 24 leaves. He used 12 leaves to decorate his photo album. He divided the rest equally among 2 boxes. How many leaves were in each box?

_____ leaves

6. $9\overline{)54}$

_____

7. $72 \div 9 =$ _____

8. $10\overline{)70}$

_____

9. Compare. Write $+$, $-$, $\times$, or $\div$ to make the number sentence true.

$81 \bigcirc 9 = 16 - 7$

10. Lauren has 50 stickers. Ten stickers fit on each page of a notebook. How many pages can she fill?

_____ pages

Go On

Name _____

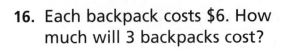
11. Compare. Write <, >, or = to make this true.

$$45 \div 5 \bigcirc 3 \times 4$$

12. Write the missing factor and quotient.

$7 \times$ ___ $= 28$ $28 \div 7 =$ ___

13. Divide 0 by 8.

_____

14. Each box of cereal costs $3. How much will 6 boxes cost?

_____

15. Lisa bought 5 hamburgers. She paid with a $20 bill. She got $5 in change. How much did each hamburger cost?

_____

16. Each backpack costs $6. How much will 3 backpacks cost?

_____

17. Four boxes of popcorn cost $8. How much does 1 box cost?

_____

18. Five puzzles cost $20. How much does 1 puzzle cost?

_____

19. Todd cooked 3 batches of chicken strips. He ate 2 strips. Then there were 16 strips left. How many chicken strips were in each batch?

_____ strips

20. Barb was thinking of a number. She added 4 to her number. She divided her answer by 3 and got 5. What was her number?

_____

Stop

Choose the correct answer.

1. What division sentence is represented by an array of 8 rows of 6?

A $48 \div 1 = 48$
B $24 \div 8 = 3$
C $48 \div 8 = 6$
D $24 \div 6 = 4$

2. What division sentence is shown by the number line?

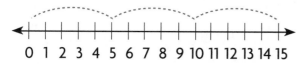

0 1 2 3 4 5 6 7 8 9 10 11 12 13 14 15

F $15 \div 5 = 3$
G $10 \div 2 = 5$
H $15 \div 1 = 15$
J $10 \div 1 = 10$

3. Which division sentence is represented by an array of 3 rows of 6?

A $18 \div 3 = 6$
B $18 \div 18 = 1$
C $18 \div 1 = 18$
D $0 \div 18 = 0$

4. Which number completes the division sentence?

$12 \div \blacksquare = 4$

F 8   **H** 4
G 6   **J** 3

5. What is the number that the variable stands for?

$12 \div 3 = r$

A 3
B 4
C 9
D 15

6. What multiplication fact can be used to find $20 \div 4$?

F $4 \times 7 = 28$
G $20 \times 1 = 20$
H $4 \times 5 = 20$
J $2 \times 10 = 20$

7. Find the missing factor and quotient.

$5 \times \blacksquare = 35$ $35 \div 5 = \blacksquare$

A 4
B 5
C 6
D 7

8. Eric has 21 crackers. He wants to give 3 crackers to each of his friends. Which number sentence shows how many friends will get crackers?

F $21 \div 3 = 7$
G $3 \times 9 = 27$
H $21 - 3 = 18$
J $21 + 3 = 24$

Go On

9. Kevin has 40 airplanes in his collection. A case holds 8 airplanes. What number sentence shows how many cases Kevin needs for his collection?

   A $40 - 8 = 32$
   B $40 + 8 = 48$
   C $8 + 8 = 16$
   D $40 \div 8 = 5$

10. Mary has 25 tulip bulbs. She divides them equally among 5 friends. How many tulip bulbs will each friend get?

    F 10
    G 7
    H 5
    J 4

11. $2\overline{)14}$

    A 6
    B 7
    C 8
    D 9

12. There are 30 blocks in a set. There are 5 blocks of each color. How many colors are in the set of blocks?

    F 5
    G 6
    H 7
    J 25

13. $27 \div 3 = \blacksquare$

    A 6
    B 7
    C 8
    D 9

14. What number completes the number sentence?

    $3 \times 3 = \blacksquare \div 3$

    F 30
    G 27
    H 18
    J 9

15. $0 \div 6 = \blacksquare$

    A 0
    B 1
    C 6
    D 16

16. $5 \div 1 = \blacksquare$

    F 0
    G 1
    H 4
    J 5

Go On

17. Gwen has 24 balloons. She divides them equally among 4 friends. What expression shows how many balloons each friend gets?

A $24 - 4$ C $24 + 4$
B $24 \div 4$ D $4 + 4$

18. Which symbol makes the number sentence true?

$6 \bullet 2 = 16 \div 2$

F $+$ H $\times$
G $-$ J $\div$

19. There are 8 bagels in each bag. Pam has 4 bags. What expression shows how many bagels Pam has in all?

A $4 + 8$ C $8 \div 4$
B 4×8 D $8 + 8$

20. Steve has 14 toy cars. He puts the same number of cars on each of 2 shelves. What number sentence can be used to find how many cars he puts on each shelf?

F $14 \div 2 = 7$
G $14 - 2 = 12$
H $14 + 2 = 16$
J $14 \times 2 = 28$

21. $\blacksquare = 49 \div 7$

A 6
B 7
C 8
D 9

22. Eight friends want to share 24 books equally. How many books will each friend get?

F 16
G 8
H 6
J 3

23. $6\overline{)42}$

A 8
B 7
C 6
D 5

24. $10\overline{)80}$

F 8
G 10
H 70
J 80

25. $9\overline{)45}$

A 4
B 5
C 6
D 7

Go On

26. What number completes the number sentence?

    $24 \div \blacksquare = 32 \div 4$

    F 3
    G 4
    H 6
    J 8

27. $9\overline{)72}$

    A 6
    B 7
    C 8
    D 9

28. James buys 5 roast beef sandwiches for $10. How much does each sandwich cost?

    F $2
    G $5
    H $10
    J $15

29. Two bags of apples cost $6. How much does one bag cost?

    A $2
    B $3
    C $4
    D $5

30. Each bag of popcorn costs $2. How much would 7 bags of popcorn cost?

    F $12
    G $14
    H $21
    J $35

31. Rich buys 6 bags of marbles. He gives the clerk $20 and gets $8 back. How much does one bag of marbles cost?

    A $2
    B $6
    C $8
    D $12

32. Marta baked 4 batches of cupcakes. She made 3 extra cupcakes with some left over batter. If Marta made 39 cupcakes in all, how many cupcakes were in each batch?

    F 4
    G 8
    H 9
    J 12

33. Ashley spent $30 at a bookstore. She bought a calendar for $14 and 4 books that each cost the same amount. How much did each book cost?

    A $2   C $4
    B $3   D $5

Stop

Form A • Multiple Choice

Write the correct answer.

1. What division sentence is represented by an array of 7 rows of 6?

_____

2. What division sentence is shown by the number line?

_____

3. Write a division sentence that is represented by an array of 4 rows of 5.

_____

4. What number completes the division sentence?

$36 \div$ _____ $= 6$

5. Find the number that the variable stands for.

$24 \div 6 = r$

$r =$ _____

6. Write a multiplication fact that can be used to find the quotient $35 \div 7$.

_____

7. Write the missing factor and quotient.

$7 \times$ ■ $= 56$ $56 \div 7 =$ ■

_____

8. Ross has 21 keys. He wants to give 3 keys to each of his friends. Write a number sentence to show how to find the number of friends who will get keys.

_____

Go On

Name _____

9. Valerie has 15 dance outfits. A bag holds 5 outfits. Write a number sentence to show how many bags Valerie will need to carry all of her dance outfits.

_____

10. Eddie has 36 feathers. He divides them equally among 6 friends. How many feathers does each friend get?

_____ feathers

11. 2)‾10‾

12. There are 45 cans of paint in Howard's Supply Store. There are 9 colors of paint and the same number of cans of each color. How many cans of each color are in the store?

_____ cans

13. $24 \div 3 =$ _____

14. $2 \times 2 =$ _____ $\div 2$

15. $0 \div 7 =$ _____

16. $6 \div 1 =$ _____

17. Gail has 18 cans of soda for her party. She divides them equally among 9 family members. Write an expression that shows how many cans each family member will get.

_____

Go On

Form B • Free Response

Name _____

18. What symbol makes the number sentence true?

$$10 \bigcirc 4 = 30 \div 5$$

19. There are 8 rolls in each package. Pam has 4 packages. Write an expression to show how many rolls Pam has in all.

_____

20. Ben has 12 masks in his collection. He wants to display them on his wall in 2 equal rows. Write a number sentence to show how many masks there will be in each row.

_____

21. _____ $= 81 \div 9$

22. Four friends want to share 28 pieces of candy equally. How many pieces of candy will each friend get?

_____ pieces of candy

23. $5\overline{)40}$

24. $10\overline{)60}$

25. $9\overline{)63}$

Form B • Free Response

26. What number completes the number sentence?

$$45 \div \underline{\hspace{2cm}} = 2 + 7$$

27. $9\overline{)54}$

28. Frances buys 2 watermelons for $8. How much does each watermelon cost?

_____

29. Four notebooks cost $12. How much does one notebook cost?

_____

30. Each bottle of water costs $2. How much would 8 bottles cost?

_____

31. Felix buys 6 books. Each book costs the same amount. He gives the clerk $20 and gets $2 back. How much does one book cost?

_____

32. Joshua made popcorn for the school carnival. He filled 26 bags and packed them into 3 boxes. He had 2 extra bags of popcorn. How many bags of popcorn were in each box?

_____ bags of popcorn

33. Sarah spent $50 at a clothing store. She bought a skirt for $23 and 3 shirts that each cost the same amount. How much did each shirt cost?

_____

Stop

Choose the correct answer.

For 1–3, use the tally table.

FAVORITE FOOD	
Name	Tally
Hamburger	IIII
Taco	卌
Chicken	III
Grilled Cheese	卌 I

1. How many students answered this survey?

   A 18   C 20
   B 19   D 21

2. How many more students chose taco than chose chicken?

   F 1   H 3
   G 2   J 5

3. How many students in all chose hamburger and grilled cheese?

   A 10   C 8
   B 9   D 7

For 4–7, use the frequency table.

FAVORITE CAR COLOR	
Color	Number
White	30
Blue	18
Black	23
Red	17

4. How many people were surveyed?

   F 78   H 98
   G 88   J 100

5. How many more people chose white than red?

   A 23   C 12
   B 13   D 7

6. Which group of colors is in order from **greatest** to **least** votes?

   F white, black, red, blue
   G white, red, blue, black
   H white, blue, red, black
   J white, black, blue, red

7. How many fewer people chose blue than chose black?

   A 12   C 5
   B 6   D 2

For 8–10, use the following information.

Jordan is doing an experiment with a cube numbered 1 through 6. He will roll the cube 30 times and record the number in a tally table.

8. How many tallies should there be on Jordan's table?

   F 6   H 30
   G 24   J 36

9. What will Jordan be able to find out from his table?

   A the number rolled most often
   B the difference between the numbers
   C the color rolled most often
   D the sum of the numbers from 1 through 6

Go On

10. Which number should Jordan NOT list on his tally table?

F 2   H 6
G 5   J 7

For 11–12, use the two spinners.

Sally is doing an experiment. She will use the two spinners 25 times and record the sum of the two numbers.

11. How many tallies should there be on Sally's table?

A 5   B 10   C 20   D 25

12. What sums should Sally list on her tally table?

F 1, 2, 3, 4   H 3, 4, 5, 6
G 2, 3, 4, 6   J 2, 4, 6, 9

For 13–16, use the line plot.

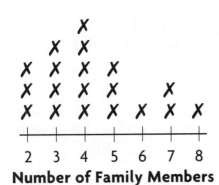

Number of Family Members

13. What is the mode for this set of data?

A 7   C 3
B 4   D 2

14. What is the range for this set of data?

F 4   H 6
G 5   J 7

15. How many families have 3 or fewer members?

A 3   C 10
B 7   D 14

16. What is the **greatest** number of family members in this set of data?

F 5   H 7
G 6   J 8

For 17–18, find the median.

17. 8, 12, 5, 9, 11

A 8   C 11
B 9   D 12

18. 5, 9, 2, 1, 7, 6, 8

F 2   H 5
G 4   J 6

For 19–20, find the mean.

19. 8, 1, 9

A 1   C 6
B 3   D 18

20. 1, 9, 3, 7, 5

F 1   H 9
G 5   J 25

Stop

Write the correct answer.

For 1–3, use the tally table.

FAVORITE STUFFED ANIMAL	
Animal	**Tally**
Rabbit	卌 I
Bear	卌 卌 II
Dog	卌 IIII
Cat	卌

1. How many students voted for their favorite stuffed animal?

_____ students

2. How many more students chose the dog than the cat?

_____ more students

3. How many students in all chose the rabbit and the bear?

_____ students

For 4–7, use the frequency table.

FAVORITE BOOK BAG COLOR	
Color	**Number**
Red	8
Purple	20
Blue	12
Black	13

4. How many people were surveyed?

_____ people

5. How many **more** people voted for purple than for red?

_____ more people

6. Write the colors in order from the **greatest** to the **least** votes.

_____

7. How many **fewer** people voted for red than for black?

_____ people

For 8–10, use the following information.

You are doing a spinner experiment. The spinner is divided into 6 equal parts numbered 1–6. You will use the spinner 25 times to see which number the pointer lands on most often. You will record the results in a tally table.

8. How many tallies will be on your tally table?

_____ tallies

9. What are you asked to find in this experiment?

_____

10. The numbers you might spin in your experiment should be on your tally table. What are these numbers?

____, ____, ____, ____, ____, ____

For 11–12, use the spinners.

Kelly is doing an experiment. She uses the two spinners 20 times and records the sums of the two numbers.

11. How many tallies should Kelly have in her table?

_____ tallies

12. What sums can Kelly get?

____, ____, ____, ____, ____, ____

For 13–16, use the line plot.

13. What is the mode for this set of data?

_____

14. What is the range for this set of data?

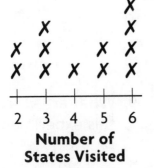

Number of States Visited

_____

15. How many students have visited 4 or fewer states?

_____ students

16. How many students have visited exactly 5 states?

_____ students

For 17–18, find the median.

17. 15, 3, 7, 4, 11

_____

18. 3, 1, 5, 7, 9, 2, 8

_____

For 19–20, find the mean.

19. 5, 9, 7

_____

20. 2, 8, 4, 6, 10

_____

Stop

Choose the correct answer.

For 1–4, use this data.

Some students made pictographs using this data.

FAVORITE SOUP	
Soup	Number of Votes
Chicken	30
Vegetable	15
Chili	10

1. Al used a key of 5. How many symbols should he draw to show the votes for chicken soup?

   A 3   C 5
   B 4   D 6

2. Joel used a key of 2. How many symbols should he draw to show the votes for chili?

   F 5   H 3
   G 4   J 2

3. What key did Haley use if she drew 3 symbols to show the votes for chicken soup?

   A 3   C 10
   B 5   D 30

4. What key did Ethan use if he drew $1\frac{1}{2}$ symbols to show the votes for vegetable soup?

   F 10   H 5
   G 6   J 4

For 5–7, use the graph.

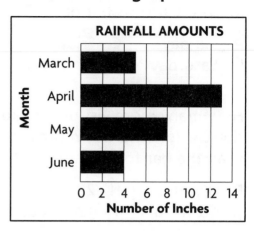

5. How many inches of rain fell in May?

   A 4   B 6   C 8   D 10

6. Which month had the most rain?

   F March   H May
   G April   J June

7. How many more inches of rain fell in May than in June?

   A 2   B 4   C 5   D 8

For 8–11, use the table below.

MUSEUM VISITORS	
Day	Number
Thursday	30
Friday	48
Saturday	76
Sunday	82

8. What would be the **best** scale for a bar graph of this data?

   F by 1s   H by 3s
   G by 2s   J by 10s

Go On ➡

9. Which day would have the longest bar on a bar graph?

  A Sunday   C Friday
  B Saturday   D Thursday

10. How many more visitors would the bar for Saturday represent than the bar for Friday?

  F 0 visitors   H 28 visitors
  G 18 visitors   J 124 visitors

11. How many people in all visited the museum on Saturday and Sunday?

  A 78   C 168
  B 158   D 206

For 12–15, use the grid.

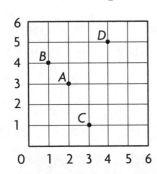

12. What is the ordered pair for point *D*?

  F (4,5)   H (3,1)
  G (5,4)   J (4,2)

13. What is the ordered pair for point *C*?

  A (2,3)   C (3,1)
  B (1,3)   D (4,2)

14. What point is named by the ordered pair (1,4)?

  F *A*   H *C*
  G *B*   J *D*

15. Start at 0. Which directions tell how to get to point *A* on the grid?

  A move 2 right and 3 up
  B move 2 up and 3 right
  C move 4 right and 2 up
  D move 3 right and 1 up

For 16–18, use the line graph.

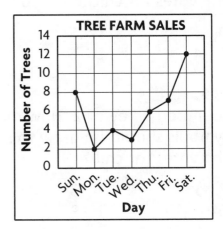

16. On what day were the most trees sold?

  F Sunday   H Friday
  G Thursday   J Saturday

17. How many trees were sold on Wednesday?

  A 2   C 4
  B 3   D 5

18. How many more trees were sold on Saturday than on Monday?

  F 5   G 6   H 9   J 10

  Stop

Name _____

Write the correct answer.

For 1–4, use the data below.

Some students made pictographs using the data in this table.

FAVORITE SMALL PET	
Pet	Number of Votes
Gerbil	16
Hamster	24
Tropical Fish	12
Bird	9

1. Pam used a key of 4. How many symbols should she draw to show the votes for hamster?

   _____ symbols

2. What key did Mark use if he drew $1\frac{1}{2}$ symbols to show the votes for bird?

   Key: Each symbol = _____ votes.

3. Charles used a key of 2. How many symbols should he draw to show the votes for tropical fish?

   _____ symbols

4. What key did Kendra use if she drew 4 symbols to show the votes for gerbil?

   Key: Each symbol = _____ votes.

For 5–7, use the bar graph.

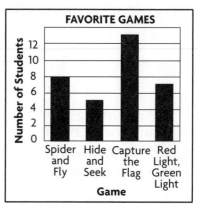

5. How many students voted for Spider and Fly?

   _____ students

6. What game received the **greatest** number of votes?

   _____

7. How many more students voted for Spider and Fly than for Hide and Seek?

   _____ more students

For 8–11, use the table below.

RAINY DAYS	
Month	Number
March	8
April	14
May	10
June	7

8. Circle the best scale for a bar graph of this data.

   by 2s   by 5s

   by 3s   by 10s

9. Which month would have the longest bar on a bar graph?

_____

10. How many more rainy days would the bar for May represent than the bar for June?

_____ more days

11. How many days in all did it rain from April to June?

_____ days

For 12–15, use the grid.

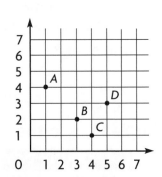

12. Write the ordered pair for point B.

(_____, _____)

13. Write the letter of the point named by the ordered pair (4,1).

_____

14. Write the ordered pair for point D.

(_____, _____)

15. Explain how to find point A on the grid.

_____

_____

For 16–18, use the line graph.

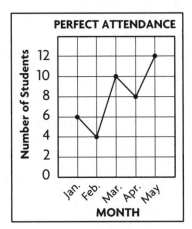

16. How many students had perfect attendance in January?

_____ students

17. How many more students had perfect attendance in May than in February?

_____ more students

18. In which months did more than 8 students have perfect attendance?

_____

Stop

Form B • Free Response

Choose the correct answer.

1. Measure the paper clip to the nearest inch.

   A 1 in.   **C** 2 in.

   B $1\frac{1}{2}$ in.   **D** $2\frac{1}{2}$ in.

2. Measure the ribbon to the nearest half inch.

   F 2 in.   **H** 3 in.

   G $2\frac{1}{2}$ in.   **J** $3\frac{1}{2}$ in.

3. A picture measures $4\frac{1}{2}$ inches. The end of the picture is between which two inch marks?

   A 3 and 4
   B 4 and 5
   C 5 and 6
   D 6 and 7

4. Choose the best unit of measure for the length of a shoe.

   F inch   **H** yard
   G feet   **J** mile

5. Choose the best unit of measure for the distance from your school to a school in another city.

   A inch   **C** yard
   B foot   **D** mile

6. A banana is about 6 __?__ long.

   F inches   **H** yards
   G feet   **J** miles

7. Choose the best unit of measure.

   A bedroom is about 12 __?__ long.

   A inches   **C** yards
   B feet   **D** miles

8. Choose the better estimate.

   F 2 cups   **G** 2 gallons

9. Which unit would be used to measure the amount of water it takes to fill a swimming pool?

   A pint   **C** cup
   B quart   **D** gallon

10. Compare the amounts.

    2 cups ● 2 quarts

    F <   **G** >   **H** =

Go On ▶

Form A • Multiple Choice

11. Choose the best unit of measure for the weight of a cherry.

A cup   C ounce
B foot   D pound

12. Choose the better estimate.

F 50 ounces   G 50 pounds

13. Which object weighs about 5 pounds?

A apple
B box of cereal
C watermelon
D slice of bread

14. ■ cups = 3 pints

cups	2	4	6	8
pints	1	2	3	4

F 1   H 6
G 4   J 10

For 15–16, use the table.

quarts	4	8	12	16	20
gallons	1	2	3	4	5

15. Jaime made 5 gallons of tea. How many quarts is this?

A 4   C 12
B 8   D 20

16. Mrs. Owens bought 3 gallons of milk. How many quarts is this?

F 6   H 10
G 7   J 12

17. Mr. Wagstar's garden is 3 yards long. How many feet long is it?

A 3 feet   C 6 feet
B 5 feet   D 9 feet

18. Bryce plants 8 trees. He needs to give each tree about 2 pints of water every day. Should he estimate or measure the water?

F estimate   G measure

19. Antonia needs a piece of ribbon to tie flowers together. Can she estimate the length or does she need to measure the ribbon?

A measure   B estimate

20. Katie's bread recipe calls for 2 cups of flour. Should she estimate or measure the flour?

F estimate   G measure

Stop

Form A • Multiple Choice

Name _____

Write the correct answer.

1. Measure the pencil to the nearest inch.

_____ inches

2. Measure the string to the nearest half inch.

_____ inches

3. A bookmark is $8\frac{1}{2}$ inches long. The end of the bookmark is between which two inch marks?

_____ and _____

4. Circle the better unit to use to measure the length of your bed.

inch   mile

5. Circle the better unit to use to measure the distance a bus could go in an hour.

feet   mile

6. Circle the better estimate. The door to your classroom is about 8 __?__ high.

inches   feet

7. Choose the best unit of measure. Write **inches, feet, yards,** or **miles**.

A car is about 8 _____ long.

8. Circle the better estimate for how much the sink can hold.

2 cups   2 gallons

9. Circle the better unit to use to measure the amount of water a bathtub can hold.

cup   gallon

10. Write <, >, or = to make the sentence true.

3 gallons ◯ 3 quarts

Go On

11. Circle the better unit to use to weigh your desk.

ounce   pound

12. Circle the better estimate.

2 ounces   2 pounds

13. Circle the object that weighs less than 10 pounds.

orange   kitchen table

14.

cups	2	4	6	8
pints	1	2	3	4

■ cups = 4 pints

_____ cups

For 15–16, use the table.

gallons	1	2	3	4
pints	8	16	24	32

15. Margo has 3 gallons of ice cream. How many pints is this?

_____ pints

16. A restaurant sold 16 pints of milk. How many gallons is this?

_____ gallons

17. A nightstand is 2 feet long. How many inches long is it?

_____ inches

18. Julia is making water globes for the winter fair. She needs about 1 tablespoon of glitter for each globe. Can she estimate or does she need to measure the glitter?

estimate   measure

19. Max wants to make a wooden picture frame. He needs exactly 2 feet of wood. Should he estimate or measure the wood?

estimate   measure

20. Louis is making juice from a powdered mix. The package says to use 2 quarts of water per package. Should Louis estimate or measure the water?

estimate   measure

■ Stop

Choose the correct answer.

1. Measure the pencil to the nearest centimeter.

A 2 cm   C 4 cm
B 3 cm   D 5 cm

2. Measure the string to the nearest centimeter.

F 2 cm   H 4 cm
G 3 cm   J 5 cm

3. Which unit would be used to measure the distance from one city to another city?

A cm   C m
B dm   D km

4. Which unit would be best to measure the length of a playground?

F cm   H m
G dm   J km

For 5–8, use the tables.

Table 1	m	1	2	3	4
	cm	100	200	300	400

Table 2	km	1	2	3	4
	m	1,000	2,000	3,000	4,000

Table 3	cm	10	20	30	40
	dm	1	2	3	4

Table 4	dm	10	20	30	40
	m	1	2	3	4

5. Which table helps to find how many centimeters there are in 2 meters?

A Table 1   C Table 3
B Table 2   D Table 4

6. Kahli walked three kilometers. How many meters did she walk?

F 3   H 1,000
G 300   J 3,000

7. Andre needs a new shoelace that is 40 centimeters long. How many decimeters long is the shoelace?

A 1   C 3
B 2   D 4

8. How many decimeters are in one meter?

F 1   H 100
G 10   J 1,000

9. Which unit would be used to measure the amount of apple juice in a cup?

A km   C mL
B m   D L

Go On

10. Which is the best estimate for the amount of water a bathtub can hold?

F   45 m   H   45 L
G   45 km   J   45 mL

11. Which best describes capacity?

A   the length of a container
B   the amount a container holds
C   the distance a container moves
D   the temperature of a container

12. Which container holds about 5 liters?

F   a water pitcher
G   a cup
H   a medicine dropper
J   a sink

13. Which object has the **greatest** mass?

A   a grape
B   an apple
C   a banana
D   a watermelon

14. Which unit would be used to measure the mass of a bicycle?

F   kg   H   g
G   L   J   mL

15. Compare the amounts.

1 g ● 1 kg

A   <   B   >   C   =

16. Which tool would you use to measure the mass of an orange?

F   a paper clip
G   a ruler
H   a liter
J   a simple balance

17. What temperature does the thermometer show?

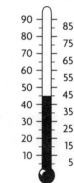

A   40°F
B   45°F
C   50°F
D   55°F

18. What temperature does the thermometer show?

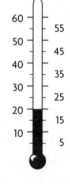

F   15°C
G   20°C
H   25°C
J   30°C

19. What might the temperature be outside if people are swimming at the beach?

A   0°C   C   20°C
B   10°C   D   30°C

20. What might the temperature be if people need to wear winter coats, hats, and gloves?

F   20°F   H   80°F
G   75°F   J   85°F

Stop

Name _____

Write the correct answer.

1. Measure the pencil to the nearest centimeter.

_____ cm

2. Measure the string to the nearest centimeter.

_____ cm

3. Which unit would be used to measure the distance a train travels in 2 hours? Write **m** or **km**.

_____

4. Which unit would be used to measure the length of a car? Write **m** or **km**.

_____

For 5–8, use the tables.

Table 1

m	1	2	3	4
cm	100	200	300	400

Table 2

km	1	2	3	4
m	1,000	2,000	3,000	4,000

5. Which table helps to find how many meters are in 300 centimeters?

Table _____

6. Maria Elena needs a string for her kite that is 2 kilometers long. How many meters long is her kite string?

_____ m

7. Jerome tossed a bean bag 4 meters. Write how many centimeters Jerome tossed the bean bag.

_____ cm

8. How many kilometers are in 3,000 meters?

_____ km

9. Which unit would be used to measure the amount of water in a small glass? Write **mL** or **L**.

_____

10. Circle the better estimate for the amount of water it would take to fill a kitchen sink.

10 mL   10 L

Go On ▶

11. Circle the correct answer.

____?____ is the amount a container can hold.

Mass   Capacity   Weight

12. Circle the item that holds about 2 liters.

bucket   cup

13. Circle the object with the **greater** mass.

book   desk

14. Which unit would be used to measure the mass of a desk? Write **g** or **kg**.

_____

15. Compare. Write <, >, or = in the ◯.

2 kg ◯ 2 g

16. Circle the unit you would use to measure the mass of a banana.

L   g   mL   cm

17. Write the temperature shown on the thermometer.

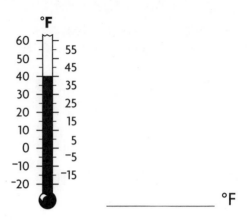

_____ °F

18. Write the temperature shown on the thermometer.

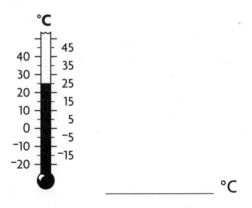

_____ °C

19. What would the temperature be outside if people are shoveling snow? Write 0°C or 20°C.

_____

20. What would the temperature be if people are swimming outside in a swimming pool? Write 90°F or 19°F.

_____

Stop

Choose the correct answer.

For 1–2, use the tally table.

FAVORITE FIELD TRIP	
Trip	Tally
Science Museum	IIII
Animal Park	卌 III
Nature Walk	卌 卌 I
Sculpture Garden	卌

1. How many students answered the survey?

   A 4　　　　C 28
   B 11　　　D 30

2. How many **more** students chose the nature walk than chose the science museum?

   F 4　　　　H 11
   G 7　　　　J 15

For 3–4, use the frequency table.

COLOR OF STUDENTS' CLOTHES			
	Blue	White	Black
Pants	10	1	6
Shorts	4	2	3
Skirts	2	0	1

3. How many students wore shorts?

   A 2　　　　C 4
   B 3　　　　D 9

4. How many students answered this survey?

   F 16　　　H 29
   G 19　　　J 30

For 5–6, use the following information.

Tony is experimenting with a cube numbered 1, 2, 3, 3, 3, 4. He will roll the cube 25 times and record the numbers in a tally table.

5. How many tallies should there be on Tony's table?

   A 3　　　　C 20
   B 6　　　　D 25

6. What are the possible outcomes for Tony's number cube?

   F 3　　　　　H 2, 3, 4
   G 1, 2, 3　　J 1, 2, 3, 4

For 7–8, use the line plot.

Magazines Sold by Students

7. How many students sold 1 or 2 magazines?

   A 2　　　　C 7
   B 5　　　　D 10

8. What is the range for this set of data?

   F 1　　　　H 3
   G 2　　　　J 4

Go On ►

9. What is the median for this set of numbers?

9, 13, 5, 4, 7

A 13   C 7
B 9   D 4

10. What is the mean for this set of data?

3, 10, 6, 7, 4

F 1   H 7
G 6   J 30

For 11–12, use the data in this table.

FAVORITE PIE	
Name	Number
Apple	8
Banana	6
Cherry	3
Chocolate	11

11. Keri makes a pictograph using this data. She uses a key of 2. How many symbols should she draw to show the votes for banana pie?

A 1   C 3
B 2   D 6

12. What key would Keri use if she drew 2 symbols to show the votes for apple pie?

F key of 2   H key of 6
G key of 4   J key of 8

For 13–14, use the bar graph.

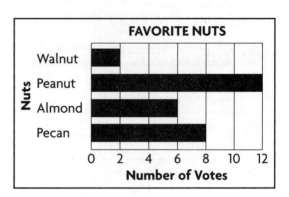

13. What type of graph is this?

A horizontal bar graph
B vertical bar graph

14. How many more students chose pecan than chose walnut?

F 2   H 8
G 6   J 10

For 15–16, use the grid.

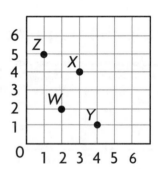

15. What is the ordered pair for point *Y*?

A (2,2)   C (3,4)
B (1,4)   D (4,1)

16. What point is named by the ordered pair (3,4)?

F *W*   H *Y*
G *X*   J *Z*

Go On

For 17–18, use the line graph.

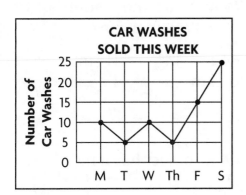

17. On what day were the most car washes sold?

    A Monday   C Friday
    B Wednesday   D Saturday

18. How many more car washes were sold on Saturday than on Tuesday?

    F 3   H 20
    G 5   J 25

19. Measure the string to the nearest inch.

    A 1 in.   C 2 in.

    B $1\frac{1}{2}$ in.   D $2\frac{1}{2}$ in.

20. Choose the best customary unit to measure the distance from your house to the library.

    F inch   H yard
    G foot   J mile

21. Compare the amounts.

    1 gallon ● 1 cup

    A <   B >   C =

22. Choose the best customary unit to weigh a strawberry.

    F ounce
    G foot
    H cup
    J pound

23. There are 4 quarts in a gallon. How many quarts are in 2 gallons?

    A 12 quarts
    B 8 quarts
    C 4 quarts
    D 2 quarts

24. There are 2 cups in a pint. How many cups are in 4 pints?

    F 2 cups
    G 4 cups
    H 6 cups
    J 8 cups

25. Jason has 4 plants. He gives each plant about 1 cup of water every week. Should he estimate or measure the water?

    A estimate
    B measure

Go On

Form A • Multiple Choice

26. Measure the paper clip to the nearest centimeter.

   F 2 cm
   G 3 cm
   H 5 cm
   J 6 cm

27. Measure the eraser to the nearest centimeter.

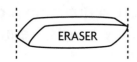

   A 1 cm
   B 2 cm
   C 3 cm
   D 4 cm

28. Paul needs 400 centimeters of string for a project. How many meters of string does he need?

   F 1 m   H 3 m
   G 2 m   J 4 m

29. Mike will walk 2,000 meters. How many kilometers will he walk?

   A 1 km
   B 2 km
   C 4 km
   D 20 km

30. What metric unit would be used to measure the amount of hot chocolate in a cup?

   F mL   H m
   G km   J L

31. What object has a mass greater than that of a toothbrush?

   A book
   B sheet of paper
   C feather
   D paper clip

32. What temperature does the thermometer show?

   F 40°F
   G 35°F
   H 34°F
   J 30°F

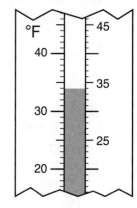

33. What temperature does the thermometer show?

   A 10°C
   B 11°C
   C 12°C
   D 13°C

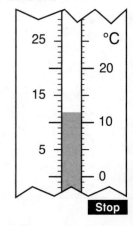

Stop

Write the correct answer.

For 1–2, use the tally table.

FAVORITE SUBJECT	
Subject	**Tally**
Reading	卌 I
Science	卌 卌 IIII
Art	IIII
Music	卌 卌

1. How many students answered the survey?

   _____

2. How many more students chose music than chose art?

   _____

For 3–4, use the frequency table.

HAIR COLOR			
	Brown	**Red**	**Black**
Boys	5	0	4
Girls	6	1	3

3. How many students have brown hair?

   _____

4. How many students answered the survey?

   _____

For 5–6, use this information.

Denise puts 3 yellow marbles, 4 blue marbles, 6 white marbles, and 1 black marble into a bag. She draws one marble from the bag, records the color on a tally table, and replaces the marble.

5. If she does this 8 times, how many marks will be on her tally table?

   _____

6. What are the possible outcomes in her experiment?

   _____

For 7–8, use the line plot.

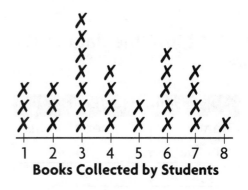

Books Collected by Students

7. How many students collected 6 or 7 books?

   _____

8. What is the range for this set of data?

   _____

Go On

9. What is the median for this set of numbers?

3, 7, 10, 4, 5

_____

10. What is the mean for this set of numbers?

2, 7, 5, 4, 2

_____

For 11–12, use the data in this table.

FAVORITE PIZZA	
Name	Number of Votes
Cheese	16
Pepperoni	9
Veggie	4
Meat	6

11. Ian makes a pictograph using this data. He uses a key of 2. How many symbols should he draw to show the votes for cheese pizza?

_____

12. What key would Minh use if she drew three symbols for pepperoni pizza?

_____

For 13–14, use the bar graph.

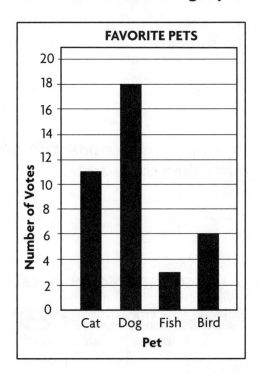

13. Is this a **vertical** or **horizontal** bar graph?

_____

14. How many more students chose cats than chose birds?

_____

Go On ▶

For 15–16, use the grid.

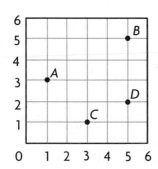

15. What is the ordered pair for point *D*?

_____

16. What point is found at the ordered pair (1,3)?

_____

For 17–18, use the line graph.

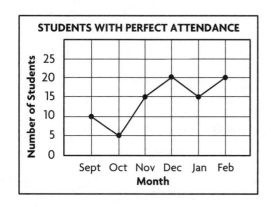

17. In which month did the fewest students have perfect attendance?

_____

18. How many more students had perfect attendance in February than in September?

_____

19. Measure the length of the string to the nearest inch.

_____

20. What is the best customary unit to measure the distance from your house to the grocery store?

_____

21. Compare the amounts. Write <, >, or = in the ◯.

1 cup ◯ 1 quart

22. What is the best customary unit to weigh a cherry?

_____

23. There are 4 quarts in a gallon. How many quarts are in 3 gallons?

_____ quarts

Go On

24. There are 2 cups in a pint. How many cups are in 3 pints?

_____ cups

25. Julia is mixing dye to color T-shirts. The instructions for dark blue dye say to mix one box of dye with 1 cup of water. Should she estimate or measure the water?

_____

26. Measure the paper clip to the nearest centimeter.

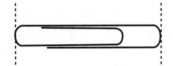

about _____ centimeters

27. Measure the crayon to the nearest centimeter.

about _____ centimeters

28. Chris needs 300 centimeters of wire for his science project. How many meters of wire does he need?

_____ meters

29. Susan is going to run 5,000 meters. How many kilometers will she run?

_____ kilometers

30. What is the best metric unit to measure the amount of water needed to fill a bathtub?

_____

31. List these objects in order from the **least** to the **greatest** mass: paper clip, book, ruler.

_____

32. What temperature does the thermometer show?

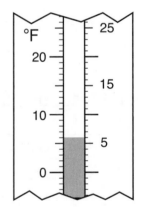

_____

33. What temperature does the thermometer show?

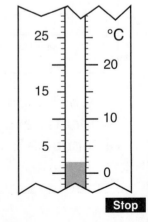

_____

Stop

Choose the correct answer.

1. What is straight, continues in both directions, and does not end?

   A point **C** line segment
   B line   **D** ray

2. What figure is formed by two rays with the same endpoint?

   F square **H** triangle
   G angle   **J** circle

3. I am part of a line. I have one endpoint. I am straight and continue in one direction. What am I?

   A line **C** line segment
   B ray   **D** angle

4. Emile's teacher drew this figure on the board. Which best describes the figure?

   F angle **H** parallel lines
   G line   **J** line segment

5. The answer to a question asked by a teacher is, "Two lines that never cross." What could be the question?

   A What are parallel lines?
   B What is a line?
   C What is an angle?
   D What are intersecting lines?

6. What figure is shown?

   F intersecting lines
   G a ray
   H an angle
   J parallel lines

7. Which best describes the figure shown below?

   A point
   B line
   C parallel lines
   D intersecting lines

For 8–9, use the figures below.

8. Which figure is a quadrilateral?

   F figure A **H** figure C
   G figure B **J** figure D

9. Which figure is NOT a polygon?

   A figure A **C** figure C
   B figure B **D** figure D

Go On ▶

For 10–13, use these triangles.

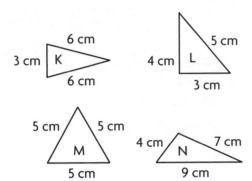

10. Which triangle has a right angle?

F triangle K   **H** triangle L
G triangle M   **J** triangle N

11. Which triangle has an obtuse angle?

A triangle K   **C** triangle L
B triangle M   **D** triangle N

12. What kind of triangle is figure K?

F equilateral **H** right
G scalene   **J** isosceles

13. Which figure is an equilateral triangle?

A figure K   **C** figure M
B figure L   **D** figure N

For 14–16, use these figures.

14. Which figure has 4 equal sides and NO right angles?

F figure L   **H** figure N
G figure M   **J** figure P

15. Which figure has 4 equal sides and 4 right angles?

A figure L   **C** figure N
B figure M   **D** figure P

16. Which figure has NO pairs of parallel sides and NO right angles?

F figure L   **H** figure N
G figure M   **J** figure P

For 17–18, use the following information.

Peter used the labels **multiples of 2** and **multiples of 3** for the sets in his Venn diagram.

17. Which number could be in the area where the sets overlap?

A 3   **C** 12
B 9   **D** 15

18. Which number would NOT be in the area where the sets overlap?

F 6   **H** 12
G 9   **J** 18

Stop

Write the correct answer.

1. What is the part of a line that has two endpoints called?

_____

2. An angle that forms a square corner is called a

_____ angle.

3. Circle the correct answer.

An angle is formed by two __?__ with the same endpoint.

    rays   circles

4.

Amanda drew this figure on the chalkboard. Write a name that describes the figure.

_____

5. What kind of lines never cross?

_____ lines

6. Circle the name of the figure shown in the drawing.

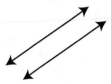

    parallel lines   intersecting lines

7.

Describe the lines in the drawing.

_____

For 8–9, use the figures.

8. Which figure is NOT a polygon?

_____

9. Which figure is a hexagon?

_____

For 10–13, use these triangles.

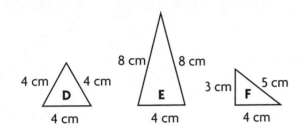

10. Which triangle is a right triangle?

_____

11. Which triangle has three equal angles?

_____

12. What kind of triangle is triangle D? Write **scalene** or **equilateral**.

_____

13. Which triangle is isosceles?

_____

For 14–16, use these figures.

14. Which figure does NOT have 4 equal sides?

_____

15. Which figure has 4 equal sides and 4 right angles?

_____

16. Which figure has 2 pairs of parallel sides, 4 equal sides, and NO right angles?

_____

For 17–18, use the following information.

Sandy used the labels **multiples of 3** and **multiples of 4** for the sets in her Venn diagram.

17. Circle the number that could be in the area where the sets overlap.

   6   9   12   16

18. Circle the number that could NOT be in the area where the sets overlap.

   12   15   24   36

Stop

Choose the correct answer.

1. Choose the two figures that are congruent.

A

B

C

D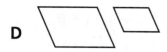

2. What figure is congruent to this figure?

F ◯   H ⬡

G ▭   J ⬠

3. Two figures are congruent if they have the same __?__.

   A position on a page
   B number of sides
   C number of angles
   D size and shape

4. What figure shows a line of symmetry?

F   H

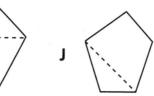

G   J

5. How many lines of symmetry does this figure have?

   A 0   C 2
   B 1   D 3

6. How many lines of symmetry does this figure have?

   F 0   H 2
   G 1   J 3

7. Which pair of figures appear to be similiar?

A   C

B   D

Name _____

8. Which two figures appear to be similar?

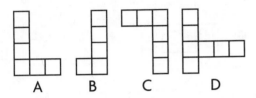

A B C   D

F A and B **H** C and D
G A and C **J** B and D

9. Which statement is true about similar figures?

A Similar figures must be in the same position.

B Similar figures must be congruent.

C Similar figures must have the same size.

D Similar figures must have the same shape.

For 10–12, tell what motion was used to move the plane figure.

10.

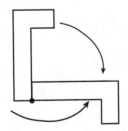

F slide
G flip
H turn

11.

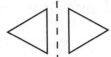

A slide
B flip
C turn

12.

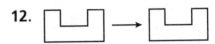

F slide
G flip
H turn

Use for questions 13–14.

Willis made this model of a triangle using pattern blocks. He used 4 pattern block triangles and put them into 2 rows.

13. How many pattern block triangles would Willis use to make a model of a triangle with 3 rows?

A 4   **C** 7
B 5   **D** 9

14. How many pattern block triangles would Willis use to make a model of a triangle with 5 rows?

F 45   **H** 16
G 25   **J** 5

Stop

Write the correct answer.

1. Circle the two figures that are congruent.

2. Circle the figure that is congruent to the one shown inside the box.

3. If two figures have the same size and shape, they are __?__.

_____

4. What letter has a line of symmetry? Write F, E, or P.

F E P

_____

5. How many lines of symmetry does this figure have?

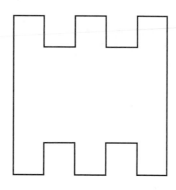

_____

6. How many lines of symmetry does this figure have?

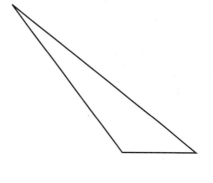

_____

7. Circle the pair of figures that appear to be similiar.

8. Which two figures appear to be similar?

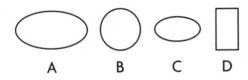

A   B   C   D

Figures _____ and _____

9. Circle the statement that is NOT true about similar figures.

Similar figures do not have to be in the same position.

Similar figures are sometimes congruent.

Similar figures must have the same size.

Similar figures must have the same shape.

For 10–12, tell what kind of motion was used to move each plane figure. Write turn, flip, or slide.

10.

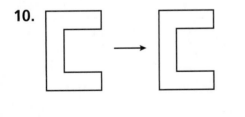

_____

11.

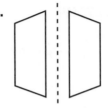

_____

12.

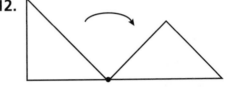

_____

Use for questions 13–14.

Sheli wanted to use triangle pattern blocks to model different plane figures.

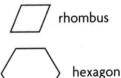
triangle

rhombus

hexagon

13. How many triangles would Sheli need to make a rhombus?

_____ triangles

14. How many triangles would Sheli need to make a hexagon?

_____ triangles

■ **Stop**

Choose the correct answer.

1. What solid figure has a shape like a box of cereal?

   A rectangular prism
   B cylinder
   C sphere
   D cone

2. How many edges does a rectangular prism have?

   F 6   H 12
   G 8   J 14

3. I am a solid figure. I look like a bowling ball. What figure am I?

   A a cube
   B a sphere
   C a cylinder
   D a cone

4. Which best describes the faces of a cube?

   F pentagons
   G circles
   H triangles
   J squares

5. What solid figure has 5 faces, 8 edges, and 5 vertices?

   A cube
   B square pyramid
   C sphere
   D rectangular prism

6. What solid figures are used to make the object?

   F cone, cylinder
   G cone, sphere
   H cone, square pyramid
   J cylinder, sphere

7. What solid figures are used to make the object?

   A cone, cube
   B square pyramid, cone
   C sphere, cube
   D cube, square pyramid

8. What solid figures are used to make the object?

   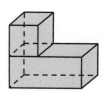

   F cube, cylinder
   G cube, rectangular prism
   H cube, sphere
   J cone, cube

Go On ➡

9. Which figure will NOT tessellate?

A ◯   C △

B ▢   D ⬡

10. Which figure will tessellate?

F ◇   H ◯

G (arrow shape)   J (blob shape)

11. Which figure will NOT tessellate?

A △   C ⬭

B ▭   D ⬡

12. Which figure will NOT tessellate?

F ⬡   H △

G ▢   J ⬠

13. How many line segments are needed to draw an octagon?

A 8   C 6
B 7   D 5

14. Which figure can be drawn with 4 line segments?

F hexagon   H pyramid
G rectangle   J cylinder

15. How many angles does a pentagon have?

A 8   C 5
B 7   D 2

16. How many vertices does a parallelogram have?

F 8   H 5
G 6   J 4

Use this figure for 17 and 18.

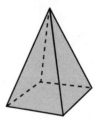

17. Which figure is the bottom view of a square pyramid?

A square   C circle
B triangle   D rectangle

18. Which figure is the side view of a square pyramid?

F square   H triangle
G circle   J rectangle

Stop

Form A • Multiple Choice

Write the correct answer.

1. Jody bought a can of peaches. What solid figure has a shape like a can?

   _____

2. How many faces does a cube have?

   _____

3. What solid figure looks like a cereal box?

   _____

4. Circle the word that best describes the faces of a cube.

   squares   circles

5.

   Name the two solid figures used to make this object.

   _____

6.

   Name the solid figures used to make the object.

   _____

7.

   Name the two solid figures used to make the object.

   _____

8. Name two figures that have 6 faces, 12 edges, and 8 vertices.

   _____

9. Tell if this is a tessellation. Write **yes** or **no**.

Form B • Free Response

10. Circle the figure that will tessellate.

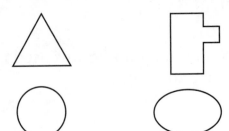

11. Circle the figure that will NOT tessellate.

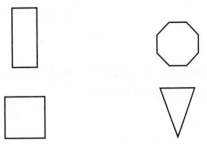

12. Circle the figure that will NOT tessellate.

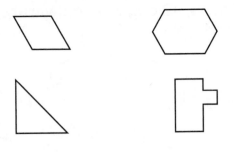

13. How many line segments are needed to draw a hexagon?

_____ line segments

14. Circle the figure can be drawn with 4 line segments.

octagon

rhombus

hexagon

pentagon

15. How many angles does an octagon have?

_____ angles

16. How many vertices does a rhombus have?

_____ vertices

17. Name the figure that is the bottom view of a cylinder.

_____

18. Name the figure that is the bottom view of a cube.

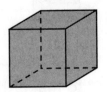

_____

Stop

Choose the correct answer.

For 1–4, find the perimeter of each figure.

1.

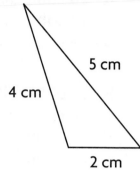

5 cm

4 cm

2 cm

A 16 cm   C 13 cm
B 15 cm   D 11 cm

2.

F 10 units   H 30 units
G 20 units   J 32 units

3.

A 8 units   C 12 units
B 10 units   D 14 units

4.

F 6 units   H 12 units
G 10 units   J 16 units

5. What is the perimeter of a rectangle that is 4 inches long and 3 inches wide?

A 7 in.   C 21 in.
B 14 in.   D 28 in.

6. What is the perimeter of a square whose sides are each 6 inches long?

F 12 in.   H 24 in.
G 18 in.   J 30 in.

For 7–10, find the area of each figure.

7.

A 9 square units
B 10 square units
C 11 square units
D 14 square units

8.

F 22 square units
G 18 square units
H 16 square units
J 14 square units

9.

5 ft

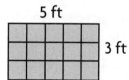

3 ft

A 16 square feet
B 15 square feet
C 13 square feet
D 8 square feet

10.

F 12 square units
G 10 square units
H 8 square units
J 6 square units

Go On

11. Sara wants to make a picture and put ribbon around the edge of it. Which picture would have the **greatest** area?

   A 3 in. wide, 6 in. long
   B 4 in. wide, 5 in. long
   C 2 in. wide, 7 in. long
   D 1 in. wide, 8 in. long

12. Sarah has 20 feet of wood to make a border around her garden. If she wants the **greatest** possible area, how long and how wide should each side of her border be?

   F 2 feet wide, 8 feet long
   G 4 feet wide, 6 feet long
   H 3 feet wide, 7 feet long
   J 5 feet wide, 5 feet long

13. Masaaki has 16 feet of streamers. He wants to decorate a square area. How long and how wide should each side be?

   A 4 feet   C 6 feet
   B 5 feet   D 8 feet

14. Paul has 30 feet of fencing to make a dog pen. Which pen would have the **least** area?

   F 5 ft wide, 10 ft long
   G 6 ft wide, 9 ft long
   H 7 ft wide, 8 ft long
   J 12 ft wide, 3 ft long

For 15–19, find the volume of each figure.

15.

   A 8 cubic units
   B 10 cubic units
   C 12 cubic units
   D 13 cubic units

16.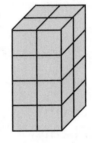

   F 8 cubic units
   G 10 cubic units
   H 16 cubic units
   J 20 cubic units

17.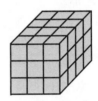

   A 10 cubic units
   B 13 cubic units
   C 36 cubic units
   D 54 cubic units

18.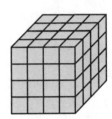

   F 16 cubic units
   G 24 cubic units
   H 32 cubic units
   J 64 cubic units

19.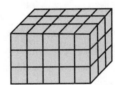

   A 15 cubic units
   B 24 cubic units
   C 30 cubic units
   D 45 cubic units

20. Tom made a figure that was 4 cubes long, 3 cubes wide, and 1 cube high. How many cubes did he use?

   F 8   H 14
   G 12   J 16

   ▮ Stop

Name _____

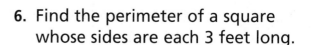
Write the correct answer.

For 1–4, find the perimeter of each figure.

1.

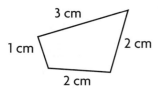

_____ cm

2.

_____ units

3.

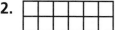

_____ units

4.

_____ units

5. Find the perimeter of a rectangle that is 5 inches long and 4 inches wide.

_____ inches

6. Find the perimeter of a square whose sides are each 3 feet long.

_____ feet

For 7–10, find the area of each figure.

7.

_____ square units

8.

_____ square units

9.

_____ square units

10.

_____ square units

Go On

Form B • Free Response   **Assessment Guide   AG135**

11. Maggie has 24 feet of fencing. Circle the choice that would fence in the least area.

    4 feet wide, 8 feet long

    6 feet wide, 6 feet long

12. Angela has 12 feet of fencing to build a play area for her gerbil. If she wants the **greatest** possible area, how long and how wide should each side of the play area be?

_____ feet wide,

_____ feet long

13. Justin is building a sandbox for his little sister. He has 24 feet of wood to build a square sandbox. How long should each side be?

_____ feet

14. Mark has 20 feet of fencing to put around a chicken pen. Circle the measurements of the pen that would have the **greater** area.

    4 feet wide, 6 feet long

    5 feet wide, 5 feet long

For 15–19, find the volume of the figure.

15.

_____ cubic units

16.

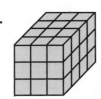

_____ cubic units

17.

_____ cubic units

18.

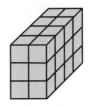

_____ cubic units

19.

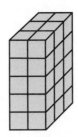

_____ cubic units

20. Diane has a box that is 3 cubes long, 2 cubes wide, and 1 cube high. How many cubes are in the box?

_____ cubes

Stop

Choose the correct answer.

1. Which is a name for this figure?

   A line
   B angle
   C line segment
   D ray

2. Which names this angle?

   F right angle
   G acute angle
   H obtuse angle

3. Which names this figure?

   A ray
   B right angle
   C parallel lines
   D intersecting lines

4. Which names this figure?

   F intersecting lines
   G line segment
   H parallel lines
   J point

5. Which figure is a polygon?

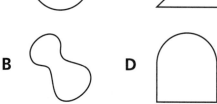

6. Which figure is a quadrilateral?

7. Which names the angle in the triangle?

   A right angle
   B obtuse angle
   C acute angle

Go On ▶

For 8–9, use these figures.

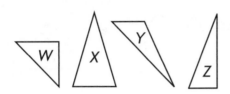

8. Choose the name for figure Y.

   F equilateral triangle
   G scalene triangle
   H right triangle
   J isosceles triangle

9. Which figure has 2 equal sides and 1 right angle?

   A figure W
   B figure X
   C figure Y
   D figure Z

For 10–11, use these figures.

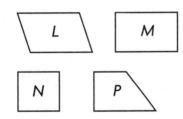

10. Choose the name for figure M.

   F triangle   H rectangle
   G rhombus   J square

11. Which figure has only 2 right angles and 1 pair of parallel sides?

   A figure L   C figure N
   B figure M   D figure P

For 12, use the Venn diagram.

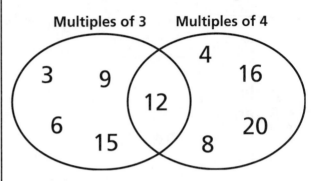

12. Which number is both a multiple of 3 and a multiple of 4?

   F 3   H 12
   G 4   J 16

13. Choose the two figures that are congruent.

14. Which figure is congruent to the one shown?

   F

   G

   H

   J

Go On ▶

15. Which shows a line of symmetry?

 A   C

B 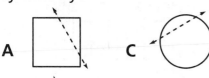 D

16. Which two figures appear to be similar?

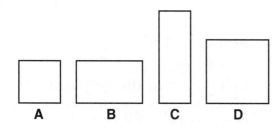

A   B   C   D

F A and B   **H** C and D
G A and D   **J** B and C

17. What kind of motion was used to move the figure?

A flip   **C** slide
B turn

18. What kind of motion was used to move the figure?

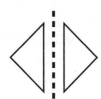

F flip   **H** slide
G turn

For 19–20, use pattern blocks to solve.

19. How many green triangles are needed to make a figure that is congruent to a yellow hexagon?

A 3   **C** 6
B 4   **D** 8

20. How many blue rhombuses are needed to make a figure that is congruent to a yellow hexagon?

F 2   **H** 4
G 3   **J** 5

21. Which names this figure?

A cone
B sphere
C cylinder
D rectangular prism

22. Which solid figure has the faces shown?

F cube
G rectangular prism
H sphere
J square pyramid

23. Which solid figures make this object?

A cube and cylinder
B cube and rectangle
C cube and sphere
D cube and cone

Go On ▶

24. Which solid figures make this object?

   F cone and sphere
   G cylinder and cone
   H cone and square pyramid
   J cylinder and sphere

25. Which shows figures combined to form a tessellation?

   A 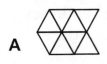   C

   B    D

26. How many line segments are needed to draw a pentagon?

   F 8   H 6
   G 7   J 5

27. What figure is the side view of a square pyramid?

   A square   C triangle
   B rectangle   D circle

28. What is the perimeter of the triangle?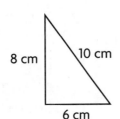

   8 cm   10 cm
   6 cm

   F 80 cm
   G 60 cm
   H 48 cm
   J 24 cm

29. What is the perimeter of a rectangle that is 5 inches long and 3 inches wide?

   A 16 in.   C 8 in.
   B 10 in.   D 6 in.

30. What is the area of the figure?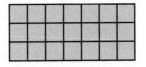

   F 20 square units
   G 21 square units
   H 24 square units
   J 30 square units

31. Phil has 24 feet of fencing to make a garden. Which rectangle will give him the **greatest** area?

   A 2 ft wide, 10 ft long
   B 3 ft wide, 9 ft long
   C 4 ft wide, 8 ft long
   D 5 ft wide, 7 ft long

32. What is the volume of the solid figure?

   F 24 cubic units
   G 8 cubic units
   H 6 cubic units
   J 4 cubic units

33. What is the volume of the solid figure?

   A 18 cubic units
   B 12 cubic units
   C 9 cubic units
   D 6 cubic units

   Stop

Write the correct answer.

1. What is the name of this figure?

_____

2. Name the angle.

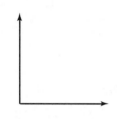

_____

3. What is another name for these intersecting lines?

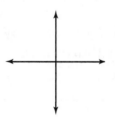

_____

4. Circle the name of the figure shown.

parallel lines

intersecting lines

5. Name the figure that is NOT a polygon.

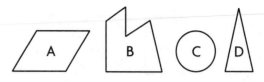

_____

6. How many sides does a quadrilateral have?

_____

7. Name the angle in the triangle.

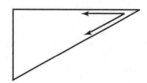

_____

8. Name the triangle by its sides.

_____

9. What triangle has 3 equal sides?

_____

Go On ▶

For 10–11, use these plane figures.

10. Write the name for figure *R*.

_____

11. Which figure has 5 sides and 5 angles?

_____

For 12, use the Venn diagram.

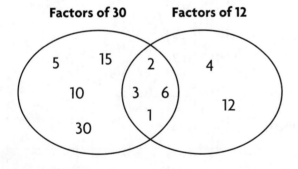

12. Name a number that is both a factor of 12 and a factor of 30.

_____

13. Circle the two figures that are congruent.

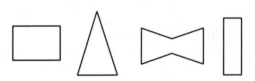

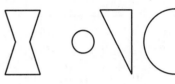

14. Draw a figure that is congruent to the one shown.

15. How many lines of symmetry does a square have?

_____

16. Which two figures appear to be similar?

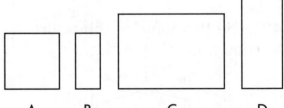

17. What kind of motion was used to move the figure?

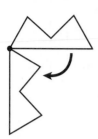

_____

18. What kind of motion was used to move the figure?

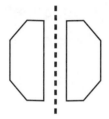

_____

Use for questions 19–20.

Aaron wanted to use pattern blocks to model different plane figures.

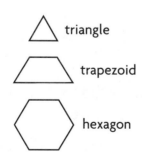
triangle

trapezoid

hexagon

19. How many triangles are needed to make a figure that is congruent to a trapezoid?

_____

20. How many trapezoids are needed to make a figure that is congruent to a hexagon?

_____

21. What solid figure names the shape of the Earth?

_____

22. Name the solid figure that has the faces shown.

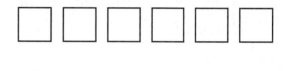

_____

23. Name the solid figures used to make this object.

_____

24. Name the solid figures used to make this object.

_____

Go On

25. Which figure tessellates?

_____

26. How many line segments are needed to draw an octagon?

_____

27. What figure is the bottom view of a cylinder?

_____

28. What is the perimeter of the triangle?

5 in.   4 in.

3 in.

_____ in.

29. What is the perimeter of a rectangle that is 4 inches long and 3 inches wide?

_____ inches

30. What is the area of the figure?

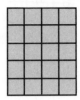

_____ square units

31. Lynda wants to fence in a flower garden with 22 feet of fencing. Circle the rectangle that will give her the greatest area.

   5 feet long, 6 feet wide

   7 feet long, 4 feet wide

32. What is the volume of the solid figure?

_____ cubic units

33. What is the volume of the solid figure?

_____ cubic units

Stop

Form B • Free Response

Choose the correct answer.

1. What is the pattern unit?

- A circle, circle, square
- B circle, square, circle
- C square, circle, square
- D circle, square, square

2. Which shape is next?

 ?

- F triangle   H square
- G rectangle   J pentagon

3. What is the pattern unit?

- A triangle, square
- B square, triangle
- C triangle, triangle
- D square, square

4. Which two shapes are next?

 ?   ?

- F triangle, circle
- G square, circle
- H circle, triangle
- J triangle, square

5. What is the pattern rule?

- A add two squares
- B subtract two squares
- C add four squares
- D multiply by two squares

6. What is the pattern rule?

△△△
△△△ △△△
△△△ △△△ △△△

- F Multiply the triangles by 3.
- G Add 2 triangles.
- H Multiply the triangles by 2.
- J Add a row of 3 triangles.

7. What is the pattern rule?

☐   ☐☐☐   ☐☐☐☐☐

- A add 4 tiles   C add 2 tiles
- B add 3 tiles   D add 1 tile

8. What is the pattern rule?

- F Add 1 column of dots
- G Subtract 1 column of dots
- H Add 4 dots to each row
- J Subtract 4 dots from each row

9. What is the rule for the number pattern?

25, 29, 33, 37, 41, 45

- A add 2   C add 4
- B add 3   D add 5

10. Find the missing numbers.

831, 811, 791, ■, 751, ■

- F 781, 731   H 781, 741
- G 771, 741   J 771, 731

Go On

11. What is the rule for the number pattern?

36, 42, 48, 54, 60, 66, 72

A divide by 6
B multiply by 6
C add 6
D subtract 6

12. Find the missing numbers.

204, 200, 196, ■, 188, 184, ■

F 194, 182   H 192, 180
G 190, 180   J 192, 182

13. Which pattern uses 3 shapes and is repeated two times?

A ○ △ ○ △ ○ △

B ○ □ △ ○ □ △

C △ □ ○ □ ○ △

D ○ ○ □ □ △ △

14. Which pattern shows a number multiplied by 2 to find the next number?

F 2, 4, 8, 16, 32
G 32, 16, 8, 4, 2
H 2, 4, 6, 8, 10
J 1, 1, 2, 4, 6, 10

15. What pattern uses 2 shapes and is repeated three times?

A □ □ □ △ △ △

B △ △ □ □ △ △

C □ △ □ △ □ △

D △ □ □ □ □ △

16. Which pattern shows the previous 2 numbers being added to find the next number?

F 3, 6, 12, 24, 48, 96
G 10, 6, 4, 2, 1, 1
H 1, 3, 5, 7, 9, 11
J 1, 1, 2, 3, 5, 8, 13

17. There are 5 boxes numbered 14, 22, 30, 38, and ■. What is the missing number?

A 42   C 48
B 46   D 56

18. A garden has a pattern unit of two red flowers, one yellow flower, one pink flower, and one orange flower. What color is the tenth flower?

F red   H orange
G pink   J yellow

19. A tower uses a cube, cylinder, and rectangular prism pattern. Which shape would be eighth ?

A cylinder
B cube
C rectangular prism

20. Find the next number in the pattern to solve.

28, 21, 14, ■

F 0   H 35
G 7   J 42

Stop

Form A • Multiple Choice

1. Draw the pattern unit.

□ △ □ □ △ □

_____

2. Which shape is next?

□ □ △ ○ □ △ ○ _?_

_____

3. Name the shapes in the pattern unit.

▭ ○ ▭ ○ ▭ ○

_____ and _____

4. Draw the two shapes that are next in the pattern.

○ △ ○ □ ○ △ ○ □

_____

5. What is the rule for the pattern?

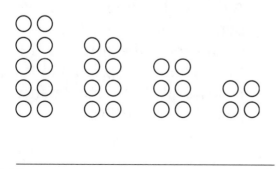

_____

For 6–8, circle the rule for the pattern.

6.

Multiply by 2.

Add 2 dots.

7.

□
□□□
□□□□□
□□□□□□□

Add 2 tiles.

Add 3 tiles.

8. △△
△△△
△△△△
△△△△△

Add 1 triangle.

Subtract 2 triangles.

9. What is the rule for the number pattern?

111, 113, 115, 117, 119, 121

_____

10. Write the missing numbers.

381, 376, 371, _____, 361, _____

Go On ▶

11. What is the rule for the number pattern?

70, 64, 58, 52, 46

_____

12. Write the missing numbers.

3, 6, 12, _____, 48, _____

13. Which pattern uses 4 shapes and is repeated two times? Circle it.

14. Write a pattern that shows a number divided by 2 to find the next number.

_____

15. Which pattern uses 3 shapes and is repeated two times? Circle it.

16. Write a pattern that shows subtracting 3 and then adding 1.

_____

17. Write the missing number.

102, 106, _____, 114, 118

18. There are paper kites in a classroom window. The kites are in a pattern of blue, green, orange, red, and yellow. What color is the eleventh kite in the window?

_____

19. Kevin drew a picture using a pattern of circle, triangle, and square. What is the eighth shape in the picture?

_____

20. A dance class lined up for a performance. There were 6 dancers in the first row, 12 in the second row, and 24 in the fourth row. How many dancers were in the third row?

_____

Stop

Choose the correct answer.

For 1–2, use this information.

A box has 3 red, 6 blue, 1 white, and 10 green cubes in it.

1. Which color is **most likely** to be pulled out of the box?

   A red   **C** white
   B blue   **D** green

2. What is the chance of pulling a red cube out of the box?

   F 3 out of 20   **H** 3 out of 4
   G 3 out of 10   **J** 1 out of 4

For 3–5, use this spinner.

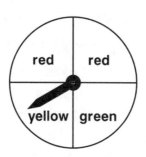

3. What are the outcomes for this spinner?

   A red, yellow, green
   B red, white, yellow
   C red, yellow, blue
   D red, blue, green

4. What is the chance that you will spin red?

   F 1 out of 3   **H** 2 out of 4
   G 1 out of 4   **J** 2 out of 3

5. Which outcomes are **equally likely**?

   A red, yellow
   B red, green
   C yellow, green
   D green, blue

For 6–7, use this tally table.

The tally table shows the results of an experiment using a bag of colored counters.

OUTCOMES	
Color	Tallies
Red	IIII
Yellow	HHT IIII
Blue	I
Green	IIII

6. Name the color that is **most likely** to be pulled next.

   F red   **H** blue
   G yellow   **J** green

7. Name the color that is **most unlikely** to be pulled next.

   A red   **C** blue
   B yellow   **D** green

For 8–9, use this line plot.

8. Predict the number that is **most likely** to be pulled out of the bag next.

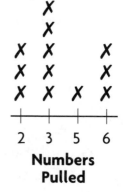

   F 2   **G** 3   **H** 5   **J** 6

9. Predict the number that is **most unlikely** to be pulled out of the bag next.

   A 2   **B** 3   **C** 5   **D** 6

Go On

For 10–11, use the bar graph.

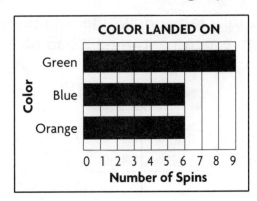

10. Which color did the spinner land on **most often**?

    F green   **G** blue   **H** orange

11. Which colors had **equally likely** outcomes?

    A green and blue
    B blue and orange
    C orange and green

12. What is NOT a combination shown by this tree diagram?

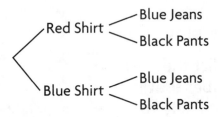

    F red shirt, blue jeans
    G red shirt, blue shirt
    H blue shirt, blue jeans
    J blue shirt, black pants

13. Henry has 2 shirts and 2 pairs of pants to choose from. How many possible combinations can he create?

    A 8   **B** 4   **C** 3   **D** 2

14. There are 4 flowers and 2 vases. How many different combinations can be created using 1 flower and 1 vase?

    F 4   **G** 6   **H** 8   **J** 16

Use this information to make a list to solve 15–16.

Luke, Garrett, Jessica, and Stephanie are arranged in a line.

15. How many different ways can they be arranged?

    A 24   **B** 20   **C** 12   **D** 8

16. What is NOT a way they can be arranged in line?

    F Luke, Stephanie, Garrett, Jessica
    G Stephanie, Garrett, Luke, Jessica
    H Garrett, Jessica, Luke, Garrett
    J Jessica, Luke, Garrett, Stephanie

Use this information to make a list to solve 17–18.

Ben is making a three-digit number using the digits 7, 4, and 2.

17. How many different ways can Ben arrange his numbers?

    A 13   **B** 12   **C** 6   **D** 2

18. Which is NOT a way Ben can arrange his numbers?

    F 742 **G** 427 **H** 274 **J** 272

    `Stop`

Write the correct answer.

For 1–3, use this information.

A box has 4 red, 1 blue, 3 white, and 7 green cubes in it.

1. Name the color you are **most likely** to pull out of the box.

_____

2. What is the chance of pulling a white cube out of the box?

_____ out of _____

For 3–5, use this spinner.

B = Blue
R = Red
Y = Yellow

3. How many outcomes are there for this spinner?

_____

4. What is the chance that you will spin yellow?

_____ out of _____

5. Which outcomes are **equally likely**?

_____

For 6–7, use this tally table.

The tally table shows the number of pulls from a bag of marbles.

OUTCOMES	
Color	Tallies
White	ⵊⵊⵊ ǁ
Red	ⵊⵊⵊ ⵊⵊⵊ ǁ
Green	ǀ

6. Name the color that is **most likely** to be pulled.

_____

7. Name the color that is **most unlikely** to be pulled.

_____

For 8–9, use this line plot.

```
X
X
X        X
X        X  X  X
X        X  X  X
X  X  X  X  X
+--+--+--+--+--+
1  2  3  4  5
   Numbers
   Pulled
```

8. Predict the number that is **most likely** to be pulled out of the bag next.

_____

9. Predict the number that is **most unlikely** to be pulled out of the bag next.

_____

Go On

For 10–11, use the bar graph.

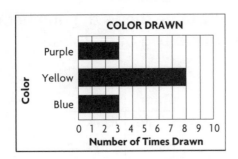

COLOR DRAWN

Color

Purple
Yellow
Blue

0 1 2 3 4 5 6 7 8 9 10
Number of Times Drawn

10. Which color was drawn from the bag **most often**?

_____

11. Which colors had **equally likely** outcomes?

_____

12. Circle the combination NOT shown by this tree diagram.

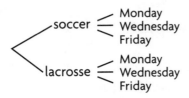

soccer — Monday / Wednesday / Friday
lacrosse — Monday / Wednesday / Friday

soccer, Monday

soccer, lacrosse

lacrosse, Friday

lacrosse, Wednesday

13. Keisha has 3 shirts and 2 pairs of pants to choose from. How many possible combinations can she create?

_____

14. There are 4 car styles and 3 color choices. How many different combinations of style and color are there?

_____

Use this information to make a list to solve 15–16.

Judson, Sergio, and Nigella are arranged in a line.

15. How many different ways can they be arranged?

_____

16. Circle a way they can NOT be arranged in line.

Judson, Nigella, Sergio

Nigella, Sergio, Judson

Sergio, Judson, Sergio

Judson, Sergio, Nigella

Use this information for questions 17–18.

Ken is making a four-digit number using the numbers 7, 5, 3, and 2.

17. How many different ways can Ken arrange his numbers?

_____

18. Circle the way Ken can NOT arrange his numbers.

7 5 3 2   5 2 3 7

7 3 2 5   2 3 3 5

Stop

Choose the correct answer.

1. Name the pattern unit.

△ △ ⌂ △ △ ⌂

A triangle, triangle, pentagon
B triangle, pentagon, triangle
C pentagon, triangle, pentagon
D triangle, pentagon, pentagon

2. What is the next shape in the pattern?

□ △ ▭ ▭ □ △ ▭

F △

G ▭

H □

J ⬠

3. What is the rule for the pattern?

○   ○○   ○○○
○   ○○   ○○○
○   ○○   ○○○

A Add 1 circle to each row.
B Add 2 circles to each row.
C Add 3 circles to each row.
D Add 4 circles to each row.

4. What is the rule for the pattern?

○○
○○   ○○
○○   ○○   ○○

F Add a row of 3 dots.
G Subtract 2 dots from each row.
H Subtract a row of 2 dots.
J Add a row of 2 dots.

5. What is the rule for the pattern?

13, 17, 21, 25, 29, 33

A Add 2.
B Add 3.
C Add 4.
D Add 5.

6. Which numbers are missing from the pattern?

707, 717, 727, ■, 747, 757, ■

F 737, 747
G 737, 757
H 737, 777
J 737, 767

Go On ▶

7. What is the rule for the pattern?

   64, 60, 56, 52, 48, 44, 40

   A Add 4.
   B Subtract 4.
   C Add 5.
   D Subtract 5.

8. Which pattern shows 7 added to each number?

   F 1, 8, 15, 22, 29, 36
   G 56, 49, 42, 35, 28, 21
   H 0, 7, 13, 18, 22, 25
   J 14, 20, 26, 32, 38, 44

9. Which pattern uses a pattern unit with 2 shapes that are repeated three times?

   A ○ ○ ▭ ○ ○

   B ▭ ▭ ▭ ○

   C ○ ▭ ○ ▭ ○ ▭

   D ▭ ○ ○ ▭ ○ ▭

10. In the front row of the class, there are 3 students. In the second row, there are 6 students. In the third row, there are 9 students. If the pattern continues, how many students are in the fifth row?

    F 12
    G 15
    H 18
    J 21

11. Benji wrote the following pattern.

    115, 118, 121, 124, ■, 130, ■

    What numbers are missing in Benji's pattern?

    A 127, 136
    B 128, 133
    C 127, 133
    D 128, 136

12. Trey is experimenting with a cube numbered 1, 2, 2, 3, 3, 3. Which describes his chance of rolling the number 1?

    F impossible
    G unlikely
    H likely
    J certain

Go On ▶

For 13–15, use the spinner.

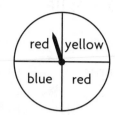

13. What possible outcomes should be included on a tally table?

    A red, yellow, brown
    B red, yellow, blue
    C red, green, yellow
    D red, purple, green

14. Which outcomes are equally likely?

    F red and yellow
    G red and blue
    H red and green
    J yellow and blue

15. What is the chance of spinning red?

    A 1 out of 3
    B 2 out of 4
    C 2 out of 3
    D 1 out of 4

For 16–18, use these spinners.

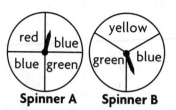

Spinner A   Spinner B

16. Melanie used these spinners for an experiment. Which statement about these spinners is true?

    F Spinner A has 5 possible outcomes.
    G The chance of spinning yellow on Spinner B is 1 out of 3.
    H It is impossible to spin blue on Spinner B.
    J The chance of spinning green on Spinner A is 1 out of 3.

17. For Spinner A, which outcomes are equally likely?

    A red, blue, green
    B red, blue
    C red, green
    D blue, green, brown

18. Which describes the chance of spinning yellow on Spinner A?

    F impossible
    G unlikely
    H likely
    J certain

Go On

For 19–20, use the line plot. It shows the results of spinning a spinner.

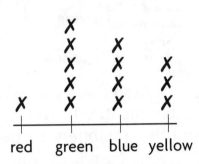

Number of Spins of Each Color

19. Predict which color you are most likely to spin.

   A red
   B green
   C blue
   D yellow

20. Predict which color you are unlikely to spin.

   F red
   G green
   H blue
   J yellow

21. Casey has 3 pairs of pants and 2 shirts. How many combinations of pants and shirts can she make using 1 pair of pants and 1 shirt?

   A 4
   B 6
   C 8
   D 16

22. Which combination is NOT shown by this tree diagram?

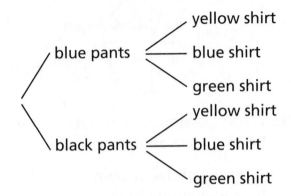

   F blue shirt, blue pants
   G blue shirt, yellow shirt
   H green shirt, blue pants
   J yellow shirt, black pants

For 23–24, use the information below.

Staci is making a 3-digit number using the digits 4, 2, and 9.

23. How many ways can Staci arrange the numbers?

   A 13
   B 12
   C 6
   D 2

24. Which does NOT show how Staci can arrange the numbers?

   F 429
   G 924
   H 249
   J 949

Stop

Write the correct answer.

1. Name the pattern unit.

_____

2. What is the next shape in the pattern?

 ?

_____

3. What is the rule for the pattern?

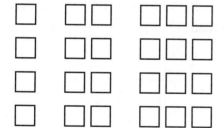

_____

4. What is the rule for the pattern?

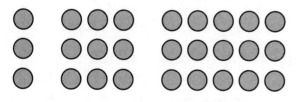

_____

5. What is the rule for the pattern?

1, 4, 7, 10, 13, 16

_____

6. Which numbers are missing from the pattern?

602, 607, 612, 617, ■, 627, ■

_____

7. What is the rule for the pattern?

41, 32, 23, 14, 5

_____

8. Make a pattern using a 2-digit number that shows 2 added to each number. Write the first four numbers in the pattern.

_____

Go On ▶

Form B • Free Response

Assessment Guide   AG157

9. Make a pattern whose pattern unit uses 3 shapes and is repeated two times.

_____

10. A bookshelf has 2 pictures on the first shelf, 5 pictures on the second shelf, and 8 pictures on the third shelf. If this pattern continues, how many pictures will be on the fifth shelf?

_____ pictures

11. Zack wrote the following pattern.

135, 131, 127, 123, ■, 115, ■

What numbers are missing in Zack's pattern?

_____

12. Denise puts 3 yellow marbles, 4 blue marbles, 6 white marbles, and 1 black marble into a bag. What word describes her chance of drawing the black marble from the bag?

_____

For 13–15, use the following information.

Sheli has a cube numbered 1, 2, 2, 2, 3, 4.

13. What possible outcomes should she include on her tally table?

_____

14. Which outcomes are equally likely?

_____

15. What is the chance that she will roll a 2?

_____

For 16–18, use this information about the bags of marbles used in an experiment.

Bag A—2 red, 2 white, 3 green

Bag B—1 yellow, 5 red, 3 blue

16. Is the following statement true or false? The chance of pulling a yellow marble from Bag B is 1 out of 10.

_____

Go On ▶

17. For Bag A, which two outcomes are **equally likely**?

_____

18. From which bag is it **impossible** to pull a green marble?

_____

For 19–20, use the line plot. It shows the results of pulling numbers from a bag.

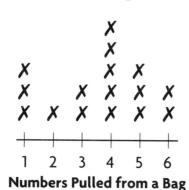

Numbers Pulled from a Bag

19. Predict which number is **unlikely** to be pulled from the bag.

_____

20. Predict which number is **most likely** to be pulled from the bag.

_____

21. June has 3 pairs of socks and 2 pairs of shoes. How many combinations of socks and shoes can she make, using 1 pair of socks and 1 pair of shoes in each?

_____

22. Use the tree diagram to tell how many combinations of pizza are possible.

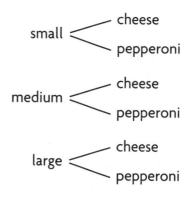

_____

For 23–24, use the information below.

Gina is making a code using the letters A, G, K, and M.

23. How many ways can Gina arrange the letters?

_____

24. Which does NOT show how Gina can arrange the letters? Circle it.

AGKM   AGAK

KMAG   GKMA

Stop

Name _____

Choose the correct answer.

1. Which fraction describes the shaded part of the figure?

A $\frac{1}{2}$ **C** $\frac{2}{3}$

B $\frac{1}{3}$ **D** $\frac{3}{3}$

2. What fraction names the point for the letter *x* on the number line?

$$\frac{0}{4} \quad \frac{1}{4} \quad x \quad \frac{3}{4} \quad \frac{4}{4}$$

0   1

F $\frac{1}{4}$ **H** $\frac{3}{4}$

G $\frac{2}{4}$ **J** $\frac{1}{5}$

For 3–5, choose the fraction that names the shaded part of the group.

3.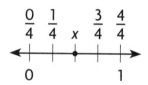

A $\frac{2}{5}$ **B** $\frac{1}{6}$ **C** $\frac{2}{6}$ **D** $\frac{3}{6}$

4. ▨▨▢▢▢

F $\frac{3}{5}$ **G** $\frac{1}{2}$ **H** $\frac{2}{5}$ **J** $\frac{1}{5}$

5. ●●○ / ●●○ / ●●○

A $\frac{3}{6}$ **C** $\frac{6}{9}$

B $\frac{3}{9}$ **D** $\frac{6}{6}$

6. Barb has 12 stickers. Of those stickers, $\frac{9}{12}$ are stars. The rest are hearts. How many heart stickers does she have?

F 3   **H** 12

G 9   **J** 21

For 7–8, find the missing numerator.

7.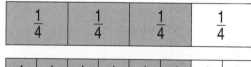

$$\frac{1}{2} = \frac{\blacksquare}{10}$$

A 1   **C** 5

B 2   **D** 10

8.

$$\frac{\blacksquare}{4} = \frac{6}{8}$$

F 1   **H** 4

G 3   **J** 6

Go On ➡

Form A • Multiple Choice

9. What group of fractions is in order from **least** to **greatest**?

$\frac{1}{2}$	$\frac{1}{2}$

$\frac{1}{3}$	$\frac{1}{3}$	$\frac{1}{3}$

$\frac{1}{4}$	$\frac{1}{4}$	$\frac{1}{4}$	$\frac{1}{4}$

A $\frac{1}{2}, \frac{2}{3}, \frac{1}{4}$ **C** $\frac{1}{4}, \frac{2}{3}, \frac{1}{2}$

B $\frac{1}{4}, \frac{1}{2}, \frac{2}{3}$ **D** $\frac{2}{3}, \frac{1}{2}, \frac{1}{4}$

10. Compare the fractions.

$\frac{1}{4}$	$\frac{1}{4}$	$\frac{1}{4}$	$\frac{1}{4}$

$\frac{1}{5}$	$\frac{1}{5}$	$\frac{1}{5}$	$\frac{1}{5}$	$\frac{1}{5}$

$$\frac{2}{4} \bullet \frac{3}{5}$$

F $<$ **G** $>$ **H** $=$

For 11–14, you may want to draw fraction bars to compare.

11. Which is true?

A $\frac{1}{2} < \frac{1}{3}$ **C** $\frac{1}{2} > \frac{2}{3}$

B $\frac{1}{4} > \frac{1}{3}$ **D** $\frac{1}{2} > \frac{1}{4}$

12. Which of these fractions is **greatest**?

F $\frac{1}{2}$ **H** $\frac{3}{4}$

G $\frac{2}{3}$ **J** $\frac{1}{5}$

13. Alan spent $\frac{1}{6}$ of his allowance on a pencil, $\frac{1}{10}$ on gum, $\frac{1}{3}$ on food, and $\frac{1}{5}$ on a book. On which item did he spend the **greatest** part of his allowance?

A pencil   **C** book
B gum   **D** food

14. Karry lives $\frac{4}{5}$ mile from school, Lynn lives $\frac{2}{3}$ mile from school, and Joe lives $\frac{1}{2}$ mile from school. Who lives the **greatest** distance from school?

F Karry   **H** Mark
G Joe   **J** Lynn

15. Choose the mixed number that names the shaded parts of the group.

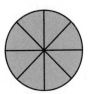

A $1\frac{1}{8}$ **C** $1\frac{2}{6}$

B $1\frac{2}{8}$ **D** $1\frac{6}{8}$

16. Sam is making a model to show $2\frac{2}{3}$. How many thirds will he need for his model?

F 10 thirds   **H** 6 thirds
G 8 thirds   **J** 4 thirds

`Stop`

Name _____

Write the correct answer.

1. Write the fraction that names the shaded part of the figure.

_____

2. What fraction names the point for the letter *x* on the number line?

$$\frac{0}{3} \quad \frac{1}{3} \quad X \quad \frac{3}{3}$$

0   1

_____

For 3–5, write the fraction that names the shaded part of the group.

3.

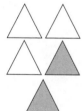

_____

4.

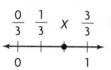

_____

5.

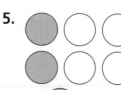

_____

6. Maggie has 10 stuffed animals. Of the animals, $\frac{4}{10}$ are bears. The rest are dogs. How many stuffed dogs does she have?

_____

For 7–8, find the missing numerator.

7.

$\frac{1}{4}$		$\frac{1}{4}$		$\frac{1}{4}$		$\frac{1}{4}$	
$\frac{1}{8}$	$\frac{1}{8}$	$\frac{1}{8}$	$\frac{1}{8}$	$\frac{1}{8}$	$\frac{1}{8}$	$\frac{1}{8}$	$\frac{1}{8}$

$$\frac{1}{4} = \frac{\blacksquare}{8}$$

_____

8.

$\frac{1}{3}$		$\frac{1}{3}$		$\frac{1}{3}$	
$\frac{1}{6}$	$\frac{1}{6}$	$\frac{1}{6}$	$\frac{1}{6}$	$\frac{1}{6}$	$\frac{1}{6}$

$$\frac{2}{3} = \frac{\blacksquare}{6}$$

_____

Go On

Form B • Free Response

9. Write $\frac{1}{2}$, $\frac{3}{4}$, and $\frac{3}{5}$ in order from **least** to **greatest**.

_____ , _____ , _____

10. Compare. Write $<$, $>$, or $=$ in the ○.

$\frac{4}{5}$ ○ $\frac{3}{4}$

For 11–14, draw fraction bars to help answer the question.

11. Circle the statement that is true.

$\frac{1}{5} > \frac{1}{3}$ $\frac{1}{2} < \frac{8}{10}$

12. Circle the **greatest** fraction.

$\frac{1}{2}$ $\frac{3}{4}$ $\frac{2}{5}$

13. Nathan spent $\frac{1}{6}$ of his allowance on food, $\frac{1}{2}$ on the movies, and $\frac{1}{3}$ on school supplies. On which item did he spend the **greatest** part of his allowance?

_____

14. Susan walks $\frac{5}{6}$ of a mile on Monday, $\frac{1}{3}$ of a mile on Wednesday, and $\frac{1}{2}$ of a mile on Friday. On which day does she walk the **greatest** distance?

_____

15. Write the mixed number that names the shaded parts of the group.

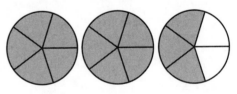

_____

16. Celine is making a model to show $3\frac{7}{8}$. How many eighths will she need for her model?

_____

`Stop`

Choose the correct answer.

For 1–5, use fraction bars to find the sum.

1. $\frac{2}{5} + \frac{1}{5} = $ ■

   A $\frac{2}{10}$ C $\frac{2}{5}$

   B $\frac{3}{10}$ D $\frac{3}{5}$

2. $\frac{6}{8} + \frac{1}{8} = $ ■

   F $\frac{5}{16}$ H $\frac{5}{8}$

   G $\frac{7}{16}$ J $\frac{7}{8}$

3. $\frac{1}{6} + \frac{2}{6} = $ ■

   A $\frac{3}{6}$ C $\frac{3}{12}$

   B $\frac{4}{6}$ D $\frac{4}{12}$

4. Lamont has 3 dog stickers, 4 cat stickers, and 1 car sticker. What fraction of the stickers are animals?

   F $\frac{1}{8}$ H $\frac{4}{8}$

   G $\frac{3}{8}$ J $\frac{7}{8}$

5. Emily did $\frac{1}{4}$ of her homework before supper and $\frac{2}{4}$ after supper. What part of her homework did she do in all?

   A $\frac{3}{4}$ C $\frac{3}{8}$

   B $\frac{2}{4}$ D $\frac{1}{4}$

For 6–8, find the sum in simplest form. Use fraction bars if you wish.

6. $\frac{1}{4} + \frac{2}{4} = $ ■

   F $\frac{3}{8}$ H $\frac{2}{4}$

   G $\frac{1}{4}$ J $\frac{3}{4}$

7. $\frac{3}{8} + \frac{2}{8} = $ ■

   A $\frac{1}{16}$ C $\frac{5}{16}$

   B $\frac{1}{8}$ D $\frac{5}{8}$

8. $\frac{3}{10} + \frac{3}{10} = $ ■

   F $\frac{3}{20}$ H $\frac{9}{20}$

   G $\frac{3}{10}$ J $\frac{3}{5}$

For 9–12, use fraction bars to find the difference.

9. $\frac{6}{8} - \frac{3}{8} = $ ■

   A $\frac{3}{1}$ C $\frac{3}{8}$

   B $\frac{9}{16}$ D $\frac{3}{16}$

10. $\frac{5}{6} - \frac{1}{6} = $ ■

   F $\frac{4}{12}$ H $\frac{6}{6}$

   G $\frac{4}{6}$ J $\frac{4}{4}$

Go On ▶

Form A • Multiple Choice

11. Pablo has $\frac{3}{4}$ of a pizza to share. Amy and Tim eat $\frac{2}{4}$ of the pizza. How much of the pizza is left?

   A $\frac{1}{8}$ C $\frac{5}{8}$

   B $\frac{1}{4}$ D $\frac{2}{4}$

12. George shared a bag of raisins with Ellen. George ate $\frac{3}{5}$ of the bag and Ellen ate $\frac{1}{5}$. How much of the bag of raisins is left?

   F $\frac{4}{5}$ H $\frac{1}{5}$

   G $\frac{4}{10}$ J $\frac{1}{10}$

For 13–16, find the difference in simplest form. Use fraction bars if you wish.

13. $\frac{5}{10} - \frac{1}{10} = \blacksquare$

   A $\frac{6}{20}$ C $\frac{2}{5}$

   B $\frac{1}{2}$ D $\frac{6}{10}$

14. $\frac{2}{6} - \frac{1}{6} = \blacksquare$

   F $\frac{1}{12}$ H $\frac{3}{12}$

   G $\frac{1}{6}$ J $\frac{1}{3}$

15. $\frac{8}{10} - \frac{5}{10} = \blacksquare$

   A $\frac{3}{20}$ C $\frac{13}{20}$

   B $\frac{3}{10}$ D $\frac{8}{10}$

16. $\frac{5}{12} - \frac{1}{12} = \blacksquare$

   F $\frac{1}{2}$ H $\frac{6}{24}$

   G $\frac{1}{3}$ J $\frac{4}{24}$

17. Ryan finished $\frac{3}{4}$ of his homework at school. How much does he need to finish at home?

   A $\frac{4}{4}$ C $\frac{1}{4}$

   B $\frac{1}{3}$ D $\frac{1}{7}$

18. April's mother ate $\frac{1}{5}$ of a watermelon. April and some friends ate $\frac{3}{5}$ of the melon. How much of the melon is left?

   F $\frac{1}{10}$ H $\frac{2}{5}$

   G $\frac{1}{5}$ J $\frac{7}{10}$

19. Ashley read $\frac{1}{6}$ of a new book on Monday and $\frac{1}{6}$ on Tuesday. How much of the book does she have left to read?

   A $\frac{2}{3}$ C $\frac{1}{6}$

   B $\frac{1}{3}$ D $\frac{0}{6}$

20. Becky painted $\frac{1}{8}$ of her room. How much of the room does she still have to paint?

   F $\frac{7}{8}$ H $\frac{1}{7}$

   G $\frac{3}{8}$ J $\frac{1}{8}$

Stop

Write the correct answer.

For 1–5, use fraction bars to find the sum.

1. $\frac{4}{8} + \frac{3}{8} = \blacksquare$

_____

2. $\frac{2}{10} + \frac{5}{10} = \blacksquare$

_____

3. $\frac{3}{8} + \frac{1}{8} = \blacksquare$

_____

4. Damon has a bag filled with 3 apples, 2 oranges, and 4 books. What fraction of the bag is filled with fruit?

_____ of the bag

5. Amy cleaned $\frac{1}{5}$ of her room in the morning and $\frac{2}{5}$ in the afternoon. How much of her room did she clean in all?

_____ of her room

For 6–8, find the sum. Write the answer in simplest form. Use fraction bars if you wish.

6. $\frac{1}{3} + \frac{1}{3}$

_____

7. $\frac{5}{8} + \frac{2}{8}$

_____

8. $\frac{2}{6} + \frac{1}{6}$

_____

For 9–12, use fraction bars to find the difference.

9. $\frac{5}{6} - \frac{4}{6} = \blacksquare$

_____

10. $\frac{3}{8} - \frac{1}{8} = \blacksquare$

_____

11. Mary Jo has $\frac{2}{3}$ of an apple pie to share. She gives $\frac{1}{3}$ of the pie to Jamie. How much of the pie is left?

_____ of the pie

12. Erin shared a bag of popcorn with Patrick. Erin ate $\frac{3}{8}$ of the bag of popcorn and Patrick ate $\frac{2}{8}$. How much of the bag of popcorn is left?

_____ of the bag

17. Todd cleaned $\frac{2}{5}$ of the basement before lunch. How much of the basement is left to clean after lunch?

_____ of the basement

For 13–16, find the difference. Write the answer in simplest form. Use fraction bars if you wish.

13. $\frac{5}{6} - \frac{3}{6}$

_____

18. Patty did $\frac{1}{6}$ of her homework at school. She came home and did $\frac{4}{6}$ of her homework before supper. How much of her homework is left to do?

_____ of her homework

14. $\frac{7}{8} - \frac{2}{8}$

_____

19. Andrew did $\frac{2}{5}$ of an art project on Tuesday and $\frac{1}{5}$ on Thursday. How much of the art project does he have left to do?

_____ of the project

15. $\frac{7}{10} - \frac{4}{10}$

_____

20. Peggy read $\frac{1}{4}$ of a book. How much of the book is left for her to read?

16. $\frac{3}{4} - \frac{1}{4}$

_____

_____ of the book

Stop

Form B • Free Response

Choose the correct answer.

1. What is the decimal for the shaded part?

   A   6

   B   0.6

   C   0.4

   D $\frac{6}{100}$

2. What is the decimal for the shaded part?

   F   10
   G   9
   H   0.9
   J   0.09

3. How is $\frac{5}{10}$ written as a decimal?

   A   510   C   0.5
   B   5   D   0.05

4. How is $\frac{3}{10}$ written as a decimal?

   F   0.13   H   0.03
   G   0.31   J   0.3

5. How is 0.9 written as a fraction?

   A $\frac{1}{9}$ C $\frac{9}{90}$
   B $\frac{9}{10}$ D $\frac{9}{100}$

6. Which of these names the same amount as $\frac{7}{100}$?

   F   710   H   0.7
   G   7   J   0.07

7. How is $\frac{29}{100}$ written as a decimal?

   A   29   C   2.09
   B   2.9   D   0.29

8. How is 0.15 written as a fraction?

   F $\frac{15}{10}$ H $\frac{15}{100}$
   G $\frac{10}{15}$ J $\frac{1}{5}$

9. How is 0.37 written as a fraction?

   A $\frac{3}{100}$ C $\frac{3}{7}$
   B $\frac{37}{100}$ D $\frac{37}{10}$

10. How is 4.76 written in expanded form?

   F   47 + 0.6
   G   4 + 0.7 + 0.06
   H   400 + 70 + 6
   J   476 + 100

11. What is the missing number?

   5.82 = 5 ones ■ tenths 2 hundredths

   A   2   C   8
   B   5   D   10

12. How is 2.09 written in word form?

   F   2 ones and nine hundredths
   G   2 ones and nine tenths
   H   2 tenths and nine hundredths
   J   2 tenths and nine ones

Go On

Form A • Multiple Choice

13. How is four ones and four hundredths written in standard form?

    A 404   **C** 0.4

    B 4.4   **D** 4.04

14. Compare these decimals.

    0.04 ● 0.05

    F <   **G** >   **H** =

For 15–18, identify problems with too little information. Solve problems with too much or the right amount of information.

15. Mrs. Barnard made cookies for her family. She gave 3 cookies to each member of her family. How many cookies did she bake?

    A too little information

    B 6

    C 9

    D 12

16. Harry bought 8 pencils, 10 markers, and 2 packages of paper at the store. He used 2 pencils at school. What fraction of the pencils were used?

    F too little information

    G $\frac{1}{4}$

    H $\frac{1}{2}$

    J $\frac{1}{8}$

17. At track practice, Kevin ran 2.9 miles, Louis ran 3.1 miles, and Jorge ran farther than both Kevin and Louis. How much farther did Jorge run than Kevin?

    A too little information

    B 0.2 miles

    C 1.2 miles

    D 6.0 miles

18. Janet spent $14 for dinner. She gave her waitress $20. How much change did Janet receive back?

    F too little information

    G $34

    H $6

    J $4

Use the number line for 19 and 20.

0 0.1 0.2 0.3 0.4 0.5 0.6 0.7 0.8 0.9 1.0

19. Which group of decimals is in order from **greatest** to **least**?

    A 0.2, 0.9, 0.5

    B 0.9, 0.2, 0.5

    C 0.2, 0.5, 0.9

    D 0.9, 0.5, 0.2

20. Pat bought 0.9 pound of cherries, 0.4 pound of grapes, and 0.6 pound of bananas. Which kind of fruit did she buy the most of?

    F cherries   **H** bananas

    G grapes   **J** oranges

Stop

Write the correct answer.

1. Write the decimal for the shaded part.

_____

2. Write the decimal for the shaded part.

_____

3. Write $\frac{7}{10}$ as a decimal.

_____

4. Write $\frac{2}{10}$ as a decimal.

_____

5. Write 0.9 as a fraction.

_____

6. Write $\frac{1}{100}$ as a decimal.

_____

7. Write $\frac{18}{100}$ as a decimal.

_____

8. Write 0.19 as a fraction.

_____

9. Write 0.68 as a fraction.

_____

10. Write 6.24 in expanded form.

_____

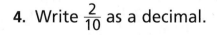

11. Write the missing number.

3.75 = 3 ones _____ tenths
         5 hundredths

12. Write 9.32 in word form.

_____

13. Write eight ones and eighty-eight hundredths in standard form.

_____

14. Compare. Write <, >, or = in the ◯.

0.06 ◯ 0.5

For 15–18, identify problems with too little information. Solve problems with too much or the right amount of information.

15. Cody left for soccer practice at 4:30. When he arrived home he spent 45 minutes on homework. What time did he finish his homework?

_____

16. There are 18 players on the basketball team and 20 players on the soccer team. Half of the soccer team also plays basketball. How many soccer players also play basketball?

_____

17. Eve worked for 4.5 hours Saturday and 5 hours on Sunday every weekend. How many hours did she work during January?

_____

18. It cost Mr. Wendell $34 to have his dog groomed. If he gave the groomer $50, how much change did he receive?

_____

Use the number line for 19 and 20.

19. Write the decimals 0.3, 0.6, and 0.1 in order from **greatest** to **least**.

_____ , _____ , _____

20. Jake bought 0.5 pound of oranges and 0.8 pound of apples. Which kind of fruit did he buy more of?

_____

Stop

Choose the correct answer.

1. What fraction of a dollar is shown?

A $\frac{1}{4}$ **C** $\frac{1}{2}$

B $\frac{3}{4}$ **D** $\frac{1}{5}$

2. What fraction of a dollar is shown?

F $\frac{1}{8}$ **H** $\frac{1}{2}$

G $\frac{1}{4}$ **J** $\frac{3}{4}$

3. What fraction of a dollar is shown?

A $\frac{1}{5}$ **C** $\frac{1}{2}$

B $\frac{1}{4}$ **D** $\frac{3}{4}$

4. What fraction of a dollar is shown?

F $\frac{1}{10}$ **H** $\frac{1}{4}$

G $\frac{1}{5}$ **J** $\frac{1}{2}$

5. What amount of money is $\frac{17}{100}$ of a dollar?

A $0.17   **C** $1.70
B $1.07   **D** $17.00

6. Marita has $\frac{1}{10}$ of a dollar. How much money is this?

F $0.01   **H** $0.25
G $0.10   **J** $0.50

7. Find the missing numbers.

$0.38 = ■ dimes ■ pennies

A 3, 8   **C** 8, 3
B 38, 0   **D** 30, 8

8. What amount of money is $\frac{4}{100}$ of a dollar?

F $40   **H** $0.40
G $4   **J** $0.04

9. What amount of money is $\frac{89}{100}$ of a dollar?

A $89   **C** $8.09
B $8.90   **D** $0.89

10. $0.36
        + $0.25
        —————
                   F $0.61
                   G $0.51
                   H $0.41
                   J $0.11

Go On ▶

11. $2.57
       + $1.39

    A $3.96
    B $3.89
    C $3.86
    D $3.22

12. $0.82
       − $0.39

    F $0.57
    G $0.47
    H $0.43
    J $0.11

13. 2.90
       − 1.26

    A 1.76
    B 1.74
    C 1.64
    D 1.54

14. A package of crackers costs $0.29 and a can of soup costs $0.59. How much would it cost to buy one of each?

    F $0.88   H $0.71
    G $0.78   J $0.30

15. Mr. Dyer's yard is 0.25 acre and Mr. Bartley's is 0.33 acre. How much land do they have in all?

    A 0.95 acre
    B 0.58 acre
    C 0.23 acre
    D 0.08 acre

16. Justin has $0.55 and Ben has $0.39. How much more money does Justin have than Ben?

    F $0.94   H $0.24
    G $0.81   J $0.16

17. Sue has $5 to spend at the book fair. She buys one book and two pencils. Books are $1.99 each and pencils are $0.65 each. How much money does Sue have left?

    A $1.75   C $1.65
    B $1.71   D $1.61

18. Rachel buys a loaf of bread for $0.79 and 2 pounds of potatoes. One pound of potatoes costs $0.25. How much change should she get back from $5?

    F $1.29   H $3.81
    G $3.71   J $4.29

19.

| Box of Cake Mix | $0.79 |
| Can of Pie Filling | $0.69 |

Leonard buys 2 boxes of cake mix and 1 can of pie filling. How much change should he get back from $5?

    A $3.93   C $3.28
    B $3.38   D $2.73

20. One bagel costs $0.43 and one roll costs $0.36. Ron buys 3 bagels and 2 rolls. How much change should he get back from $3?

    F $2.21   H $0.79
    G $0.99   J $0.06

Stop

Write the correct answer.

1. What fraction of a dollar is shown?

_____ of a dollar

2. What fraction of a dollar is shown?

_____ of a dollar

3. What fraction of a dollar is shown?

_____ of a dollar

4. What fraction of a dollar is shown?

_____ of a dollar

5. What amount of money is 32 hundredths of a dollar?

_____

6. Todd has $\frac{3}{4}$ of a dollar. How much money is this?

_____

7. Write the missing numbers.

$0.27 = ____ dimes ____ pennies

8. What amount of money is $\frac{6}{100}$ of a dollar?

_____

9. What amount of money is $\frac{54}{100}$ of a dollar?

_____

Go On ▶

10. $0.47
    $+ \$0.34$

11. $3.36
    $+ \$2.15$

12. $0.74
    $- \$0.56$

13.   4.70
    $- 2.18$

14. A can of peas costs $0.39 and a can of corn costs $0.49. How much would it cost to buy one of each?

_____

15. The Owens' backyard is 0.35 acre and the Fords' backyard is 0.59 acre. How many acres is that in all?

_____ acre

16. Greg has $0.81 and Dennis has $0.45. How much more money does Greg have than Dennis?

_____

17. Mark has $5 to spend at the hobby shop. He buys a model car and 3 paint brushes. A model car is $2.59 and each paint brush costs $0.45. How much money will Mark have left?

_____

18. Cassie buys 2 apples for $0.35 each and a pint of milk for $0.89. How much change should she get back from $5?

_____

19.

| BANANAS $0.39 PER POUND |
| PINEAPPLES $0.79 EACH |

Charlie buys 2 pounds of bananas and 1 pineapple. How much change should he get back from $5?

_____

20. A pint of orange juice costs $0.79 and a muffin costs $0.35. Janice buys 2 pints of orange juice and 2 muffins. How much change should she get back from $3?

_____

Stop

Name _____

Choose the correct answer.

1. What fraction names the point of the letter *x* on the number line?

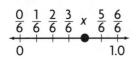

$$\frac{0}{6}\ \frac{1}{6}\ \frac{2}{6}\ \frac{3}{6}\ x\ \frac{5}{6}\ \frac{6}{6}$$
0   1.0

A $\frac{4}{6}$ **B** $\frac{3}{6}$ **C** $\frac{1}{2}$ **D** $\frac{1}{4}$

2. What fraction names the shaded part of the group?

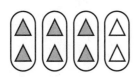

F $\frac{1}{4}$ **G** $\frac{3}{4}$ **H** $\frac{2}{8}$ **J** $\frac{8}{8}$

3. Use the fraction bars. Find an equivalent fraction.

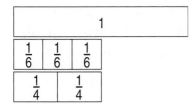

$$\frac{3}{6} = \frac{\blacksquare}{4}$$

A 4   **B** 3   **C** 2   **D** 1

4.   0.59
      + 0.33

F $0.86   **H** $0.92
G $0.82   **J** $1.26

5. Use the fraction bars. Find an equivalent fraction.

1

$\frac{1}{5}$	$\frac{1}{5}$

$\frac{1}{10}$	$\frac{1}{10}$	$\frac{1}{10}$	$\frac{1}{10}$

$$\frac{2}{5} = \frac{\blacksquare}{10}$$

A 10   **B** 4   **C** 2   **D** 1

6. Compare the fractions. Choose <, >, or =.

$\frac{1}{6}$	$\frac{1}{6}$

$\frac{1}{3}$	$\frac{1}{3}$

$$\frac{2}{6} \bullet \frac{2}{3}$$

F <   **G** >   **H** =

7. Use the fraction bars to compare. Order $\frac{1}{3}$, $\frac{2}{5}$, and $\frac{1}{6}$ from **least** to **greatest**.

$\frac{1}{5}$	$\frac{1}{5}$

$\frac{1}{3}$

$\frac{1}{6}$

A $\frac{1}{3}, \frac{2}{5}, \frac{1}{6}$ **C** $\frac{1}{3}, \frac{1}{6}, \frac{2}{5}$

B $\frac{1}{6}, \frac{1}{3}, \frac{2}{5}$ **D** $\frac{1}{6}, \frac{2}{5}, \frac{1}{3}$

8.   0.92
      − 0.56

F 0.36   **H** 0.46
G 0.38   **J** 0.55

Go On

Form A • Multiple Choice

Name _____

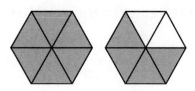

9. Use the model below to solve the problem. Jason ate $\frac{1}{2}$ of his sandwich. Jeff ate $\frac{3}{4}$ of his sandwich. Justin ate $\frac{2}{5}$ of his sandwich. Who ate the **greatest** part of his sandwich?

$\frac{1}{5}$	$\frac{1}{5}$	
$\frac{1}{2}$		
$\frac{1}{4}$	$\frac{1}{4}$	$\frac{1}{4}$

A Jeff
B Jason
C Justin

10. Tasha has $5.00 to spend. She buys 2 muffins at $0.29 each and a carton of juice for $0.89. How much money will she have left?

F $4.63 **H** $3.82
G $4.53 **J** $3.53

11. Ron walked $\frac{2}{3}$ of a mile. Casey walked $\frac{3}{5}$ of a mile. Josie walked $\frac{3}{4}$ of a mile. Who walked the farthest?

$\frac{1}{5}$	$\frac{1}{5}$	$\frac{1}{5}$
$\frac{1}{3}$	$\frac{1}{3}$	
$\frac{1}{4}$	$\frac{1}{4}$	$\frac{1}{4}$

A Josie
B Casey
C Ron

12. What fraction names the shaded parts?

F $1\frac{1}{6}$ **H** $1\frac{4}{6}$
G $1\frac{3}{6}$ **J** $1\frac{5}{6}$

13. Use the fraction bars. Find the sum.

| $\frac{1}{8}$ | $\frac{1}{8}$ | $\frac{1}{8}$ | $\frac{1}{8}$ | $\frac{1}{8}$ | $\frac{1}{8}$ |

$\frac{5}{8} + \frac{1}{8} = \blacksquare$

A $\frac{1}{2}$ **B** $\frac{5}{8}$ **C** $\frac{6}{8}$ **D** $\frac{5}{16}$

14. Danielle and Jimmy shared a granola bar. Danielle ate $\frac{2}{6}$ of the bar, and Jimmy ate $\frac{3}{6}$ of the bar. What fraction of the granola bar did they eat?

F $\frac{1}{2}$ **G** $\frac{1}{6}$ **H** $\frac{1}{4}$ **J** $\frac{5}{6}$

15. What is the sum in simplest form?

| $\frac{1}{6}$ | $\frac{1}{6}$ | $\frac{1}{6}$ | $\frac{1}{6}$ |
| $\frac{1}{3}$ | | $\frac{1}{3}$ | |

$\frac{2}{6} + \frac{2}{6} = \blacksquare$

A $\frac{1}{6}$ **B** $\frac{2}{6}$ **C** $\frac{1}{3}$ **D** $\frac{2}{3}$

Go On

16. Kevin rode his bike $\frac{2}{8}$ of a mile. Alan rode $\frac{4}{8}$ of a mile. How far did they ride their bikes altogether?

F $\frac{2}{16}$ of a mile H $\frac{6}{16}$ of a mile

G $\frac{3}{4}$ of a mile J $\frac{1}{2}$ of a mile

17. Find the difference.

$\frac{6}{8} - \frac{3}{8} = \blacksquare$

$\frac{1}{8}$	$\frac{1}{8}$	$\frac{1}{8}$	$\frac{1}{8}$	$\frac{1}{8}$	$\frac{1}{8}$

A $\frac{5}{8}$ B $\frac{4}{8}$ C $\frac{3}{8}$ D $\frac{2}{8}$

18. Jenny cut a loaf of bread into 8 equal slices. She ate 3 slices. What fraction shows how much of the loaf was left?

F $\frac{2}{3}$ G $\frac{3}{8}$ H $\frac{5}{8}$ J 5

19. What is the difference in simplest form?

$\frac{5}{6} - \frac{1}{6} = \blacksquare$

A $\frac{1}{6}$ B $\frac{2}{3}$ C $\frac{1}{3}$ D $\frac{1}{2}$

20. Jake ran $\frac{7}{10}$ of a mile. Denise ran $\frac{2}{10}$ of a mile. How much farther did Jake run than Denise?

F $\frac{9}{10}$ of a mile

G $\frac{9}{20}$ of a mile

H $\frac{1}{10}$ of a mile

J $\frac{1}{2}$ of a mile

21. Karen mowed $\frac{1}{7}$ of the grass in the morning and then $\frac{3}{7}$ of it in the afternoon. Her brother mowed the rest. How do you find the fraction of the grass that her brother mowed?

A Add $\frac{1}{7} + \frac{3}{7}$.

B Subtract $\frac{3}{7} - \frac{1}{7}$, and then subtract from $\frac{7}{7}$.

C Add $\frac{1}{7} + \frac{1}{7}$.

D Add $\frac{1}{7} + \frac{3}{7}$, and then subtract from $\frac{7}{7}$.

22. What is the decimal for the fraction $\frac{3}{10}$?

F 0.1 G 0.2 H 0.3 J 3.0

23. What is the decimal for the shaded part?

A 7.0   C 0.7
B 0.9   D 0.3

24. What is $\frac{8}{10}$ written as a decimal?

F 810   H 0.8
G 0.08   J 1.8

Go On

25. What is 0.47 written as a fraction?

A $\frac{47}{100}$ C 47.00

B $\frac{47}{10}$ D $\frac{4}{7}$

26. What is 4.36 written in expanded form?

F $4.0 + 0.3 + 0.06$
G $4.0 + 0.60 + 0.03$
H $400 + 30 + 6$
J $4 + 30 + 100$

27. Which shows 0.8, 0.3, and 0.5 in order from **greatest** to **least**?

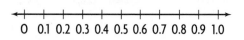

0 0.1 0.2 0.3 0.4 0.5 0.6 0.7 0.8 0.9 1.0

A 0.8, 0.3, 0.5
B 0.8, 0.5, 0.3
C 0.5, 0.3, 0.8
D 0.3, 0.5, 0.8

For 28–29, identify problems with too little information. Solve the problems with too much or the right amount of information.

28. Dylan ran after school. He ran 4 days each week. How far did Dylan run in 1 week?

F too little information
G 4 miles
H 10 miles
J 14 miles

29. Kendra bought 3 notebooks, 2 packs of pencils, and 1 package of markers. Each notebook cost $1.39. How much did Kendra spend on notebooks?

A too little information
B $4.17
C $4.71
D $6.95

30. What fraction of a dollar is shown?

F $\frac{1}{10}$ of a dollar

G $\frac{1}{5}$ of a dollar

H $\frac{1}{4}$ of a dollar

J $\frac{1}{2}$ of a dollar

31. What amount of money is $\frac{3}{4}$ of a dollar?

A $750   C $0.75
B $75   D $0.57

32. Find the missing numbers.

$0.42 =$ ■ dimes ■ pennies

F 2, 4   H 4, 200
G 4, 2   J 2, 40

33. Larry has $5.00. He buys 2 pounds of apples at $0.39 a pound and a head of lettuce for $0.99. How much money is left?

A $4.33   C $3.62
B $4.23   D $3.23

■ Stop

Name _____

Write the correct answer.

1. Name the fraction shown by the point on the number line.

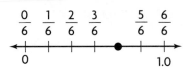

_____

2. Write the fraction that names the shaded part of the group.

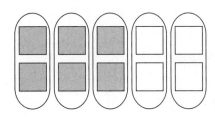

_____

3. Use the fraction bars. Find an equivalent fraction.

1

$\frac{1}{8}$	$\frac{1}{8}$

$\frac{1}{4}$

$$\frac{2}{8} = \frac{\blacksquare}{4}$$

_____

4. Add. $5.75
      + $3.50

_____

5. Use the fraction bars. Find an equivalent fraction.

1

$\frac{1}{8}$	$\frac{1}{8}$	$\frac{1}{8}$	$\frac{1}{8}$	$\frac{1}{8}$	$\frac{1}{8}$

$\frac{1}{4}$	$\frac{1}{4}$	$\frac{1}{4}$

$$\frac{6}{8} = \frac{\blacksquare}{4}$$

_____

6. Compare the fractions. Write <, >, or = in the ◯.

$\frac{1}{5}$	$\frac{1}{5}$	$\frac{1}{5}$	$\frac{1}{5}$

$\frac{1}{4}$	$\frac{1}{4}$

$$\frac{4}{5} \bigcirc \frac{2}{4}$$

7. Use the fraction bars to compare. Order $\frac{1}{2}$, $\frac{2}{5}$, and $\frac{1}{3}$ from **least** to **greatest**.

$\frac{1}{2}$

$\frac{1}{5}$	$\frac{1}{5}$

$\frac{1}{3}$

_____ , _____ , _____

8. Subtract.   0.87
      − 0.56

_____

Form B • Free Response   **Assessment Guide   AG181**

9. Use the model below to solve the problem.

Kendra has $\frac{1}{5}$ of her room clean. Matt has $\frac{2}{3}$ of his room clean. Jermaine has $\frac{1}{4}$ of his room clean. Who cleaned the **greatest** part of his or her room?

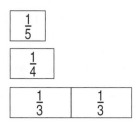

_____

10. Yuki has $5.00. He buys 2 pencils for $0.39 each, a calculator for $2.99, and a notebook for $1.09. How much money does he have left?

_____

11. Use the model below to solve the problem.

Tasha drank $\frac{1}{4}$ of her milk. Jacob drank $\frac{2}{5}$ of his milk. Robert drank $\frac{2}{3}$ of his milk. Who drank the **least** amount of milk?

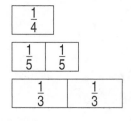

_____

12. Write the mixed number that names the shaded parts.

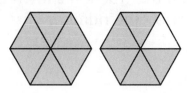

_____

13. Use the fraction bar. Find the sum.

| $\frac{1}{10}$ | $\frac{1}{10}$ | $\frac{1}{10}$ | $\frac{1}{10}$ | $\frac{1}{10}$ | $\frac{1}{10}$ | $\frac{1}{10}$ |

$\frac{4}{10} + \frac{3}{10} =$ _____

14. Rita washed $\frac{2}{8}$ of the dishes, and Jose washed $\frac{3}{8}$ of the dishes. What fraction of the dishes were washed?

_____

15. Find the sum. Write it in simplest form.

| $\frac{1}{8}$ | $\frac{1}{8}$ | $\frac{1}{8}$ | $\frac{1}{8}$ |
| $\frac{1}{2}$ | | | |

$\frac{2}{8} + \frac{2}{8} =$ _____

Go On

16. Ellen walked $\frac{4}{10}$ of a mile. Anna walked $\frac{2}{10}$ of a mile. How far did they walk altogether? Write your answer in simplest form.

$\frac{4}{10} + \frac{2}{10} =$ _____ of a mile

17. Find the difference.

$\frac{1}{5}$	$\frac{1}{5}$	$\frac{1}{5}$

$\frac{3}{5} - \frac{2}{5} =$ _____

18. Wyatt ate 3 pieces of a pizza that was cut into 10 equal slices. What fraction of the pizza was left?

_____

19. Find the sum. Write it in simplest form.

$\frac{1}{8} + \frac{3}{8} = \blacksquare$

_____

20. Denny swept $\frac{5}{8}$ of the driveway. Barbara swept $\frac{2}{8}$ of the driveway. How much more of the driveway did Denny sweep than Barbara?

_____

21. Darrell read $\frac{1}{5}$ of a book to the class before lunch and $\frac{2}{5}$ of the book after lunch. Carrie finished reading the book. How do you find the fraction of the book Carrie read?

_____

_____

22. Write $\frac{8}{10}$ as a decimal.

_____

23. Write the decimal name for the shaded part.

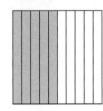

_____

24. Write $\frac{3}{10}$ as a decimal.

_____

Go On ▶

25. Write 0.33 as a fraction.

_____

26. Write 1.28 in expanded form.

_____

27. Order 0.9, 0.3, and 0.7 from **greatest** to **least**.

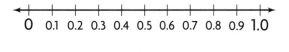

_____ , _____ , _____

For 28–29, tell whether the problem has too little information. Solve the problems with too much or the right amount of information.

28. Casey has 2 cats, 3 dogs, and several gerbils. What fraction of her pets are cats?

_____

29. Jose started his homework at 4:30. He took a fifteen-minute break that lasted until 5:15. He finished his homework one hour later. What time did Jose finish his homework?

_____

30. Write the fraction of a dollar shown below.

_____ of a dollar

31. What amount of money is $\frac{1}{4}$ of a dollar?

_____

32. Write the missing numbers.

$0.52 = $ ■ quarters ■ pennies

_____

33. Latanya has $5.00. She buys a bracelet for $1.99 and 2 hair clips for $0.69 each. How much money is left?

_____

Stop

Choose the correct answer.

1. Complete the number pattern.

   $7 \times 3 = 21$
   $7 \times 30 = 210$
   $7 \times \blacksquare = 2{,}100$

   A 100   **C** 300
   B 200   **D** 400

2. $7 \times 50 = \blacksquare$

   F 35   **H** 500
   G 350   **J** 750

3. $9 \times 10 = \blacksquare$

   A 19   **C** 91
   B 90   **D** 190

4. $8 \times 400 = \blacksquare$

   F 320   **H** 3,200
   G 480   **J** 4,800

5. $3 \times 70 = \blacksquare$

   A 93   **C** 210
   B 170   **D** 370

6. Use the base-ten blocks to find the product.

   $2 \times 13 = \blacksquare$

   F 62   **H** 26
   G 46   **J** 13

7. Jon made an array of 3 rows of 15 tiles. Which multiplication sentence does his array show?

   A $3 \times 15 = 45$
   B $10 \times 5 = 50$
   C $15 \times 10 = 150$
   D $15 \times 15 = 225$

8. Use the base-ten blocks to find the product.

   $3 \times 25 = \blacksquare$

   F 75   **H** 50
   G 65   **J** 25

9. Phil makes an array with 2 rows of 14 tiles. How many tiles are in his array?

   A 14   **C** 42
   B 28   **D** 56

10. Use the base-ten blocks to find the product.

    $3 \times 14 = \blacksquare$

    F 42   **H** 54
    G 44   **J** 56

Go On ▶

11. Balloons cost 75¢ each. Which number sentence shows how to find the cost of 3 balloons?

   A 75¢ + 3 = ■
   B 75¢ − 3 = ■
   C 3 × 75¢ = ■
   D 75¢ ÷ 3 = ■

12. Carolyn read 30 minutes on Monday and 50 minutes on Wednesday. Which could you use to find the number of minutes she read in all?

   F addition   H multiplication
   G subtraction   J division

13. Jerry has 45 model cars and Tom has 9. Which number sentence shows how to find how many more cars Jerry has than Tom?

   A 45 + 9 = ■
   B 45 − 9 = ■
   C 9 × 45 = ■
   D 45 ÷ 5 = ■

14. Jill paid $33 for 3 rosebushes. Which number sentence could you use to find the cost of one rosebush?

   F $33 + 3 = ■
   G $33 ÷ 3 = ■
   H $33 × 3 = ■
   J $33 − 3 = ■

For 15–20, choose a method and solve.

15. 142
   × 6

   A 856
   B 852
   C 582
   D 148

16. 129
   × 3

   F 497
   G 487
   H 387
   J 307

17.   64
   × 5

   A 80
   B 160
   C 240
   D 320

18. 102
   × 4

   F 308
   G 388
   H 408
   J 418

19. Photos of local historic sites sell for $2 each. How much would 42 pictures cost?

   A $84   B $64   C $44   D $21

20. An elementary school yearbook costs $5. How much would 30 yearbooks cost?

   F $15   G $45   H $120   J $150

Stop

Write the correct answer.

1. Complete the number pattern.

$8 \times 4 = 32$

$8 \times 40 = 320$

$8 \times$ _____ $= 3,200$

2. $8 \times 20 =$ _____

3. $8 \times 10 =$ _____

4. $7 \times 800 =$ _____

5. $6 \times 700 =$ _____

6. Use the array to find the product.

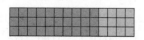

$3 \times 14 =$ _____

7. Kristi made an array of 2 rows of 17 tiles. Write a multiplication sentence to show her array. You may draw a picture to help.

_____

8. Use the base-ten blocks to find the product.

$2 \times 26 =$ _____

9. Tim makes an array with 5 rows of 16 tiles. How many tiles are in his array? You may draw a picture to help.

_____ tiles

10. Use the base-ten blocks to find the product.

$4 \times 23 =$ _____

Go On ▶

11. Wild animal stamps cost $0.33 each. Write a number sentence that shows how to find the cost of buying 6 stamps.

_____

12. Sheila jogged 40 minutes on Monday and 30 minutes on Tuesday. Write whether you would **add**, **subtract**, **multiply**, or **divide** to find the number of minutes she jogged in all.

_____

13. Pete has 36 books and Rich has 19 books. Write a number sentence that shows how many more books Pete has than Rich.

_____

14. Brandon has 24 stickers. He wants to put an equal number on each of 4 pages in a notebook. Write a number sentence that shows the number of stickers on each page.

_____

For 15–20, choose a method and solve.

15.   253
$\times$ 5

16.   103
$\times$ 6

17.   27
$\times$ 5

18.   114
$\times$ 3

19. Mike sold ticket packs for games at the school fair for $3 each. He sold 22 ticket packs. How much money did he make?

_____

20. The community center sells tickets to the talent show for $4 per ticket. They sold 45 tickets for the show. How much money did the community center make?

_____

Stop

Choose the correct answer.

1. $11 \div 3 = \blacksquare$

A 3 r2
B 4 r1
C 6 r3
D 8 r1

2. $6\overline{)23}$

F 6
G 5 r2
H 4 r1
J 3 r5

3. $8\overline{)53}$

A 6 r3
B 6 r5
C 8 r6
D 8 r7

4. $6\overline{)25}$

F 5 r1
G 4 r1
H 3 r2
J 2 r4

5. $18 \div 5 = \blacksquare$

A 4
B 3 r4
C 3 r3
D 2 r4

6. $4\overline{)50}$

F 10
G 11 r2
H 12
J 12 r2

7. $7\overline{)83}$

A 12
B 11 r6
C 11 r3
D 10 r3

8. A florist has 49 flowers. She ties 3 flowers together in each bunch. How many flowers are left over?

F 1   H 15
G 2   J 16

9. There are 90 students on a stage. The teacher puts 5 students in each row. How many rows of students will there be?

A 16   C 19
B 18   D 20

10. A librarian has 92 books to put into boxes. Each box holds 6 books. How many books will be left over after 15 boxes are filled?

F 0   H 4
G 2   J 6

Go On ▶

11. Each shelf can hold 9 cans. There are 58 cans. How many shelves will be full?

A 3   C 5
B 4   D 6

12. Peggy has 65 yards of lace. She needs 6 yards to make each tablecloth. How many tablecloths can she make?

F 13   H 10
G 11   J 8

13. Mark has 87 marshmallows for a party. He puts 7 in each cup. How many cups can he fill?

A 9   C 12
B 10   D 14

14. Five people can sit on each bench. How many benches are needed for 93 people?

F 20   H 16
G 19   J 15

15. $5\overline{)335}$

A 61
B 67
C 70
D 71

16. $432 \div 9 = \blacksquare$

F 41
G 47
H 48
J 53

17. $8\overline{)280}$

A 35
B 38
C 40
D 42

18. $736 \div 8 = \blacksquare$

F 87
G 92
H 112
J 117

19. A nursery has 324 plants to divide equally into boxes. Each box holds 4 plants. How many boxes will they need?

A 80   C 100
B 81   D 124

20. There are 636 people attending a play. They are seated in 6 sections. If there are an equal number of people in each section, how many people are in each section?

F 106   H 136
G 116   J 160

Stop

Write the correct answer.

1. $18 \div 5 =$ _____

2. $3\overline{)11}$

_____

3. $2\overline{)17}$

_____

4. $7\overline{)29}$

_____

5. $17 \div 3 =$ _____

6. $3\overline{)68}$

_____

7. $4\overline{)65}$

_____

8. Nick has 53 tulip bulbs. He plants 3 bulbs in each flower box. How many tulip bulbs are left over?

_____ tulip bulbs

9. There are 88 students eating lunch at tables in the cafeteria. There are 4 students seated at each table. How many tables are there?

_____ tables

10. Ellen has 81 strawberries to put in bowls. Each bowl holds 6 strawberries. How many strawberries are left over after 13 bowls are filled?

_____ strawberries left

Go On

11. Each box holds 5 sandwiches. How many boxes are needed if there are 75 sandwiches?

_____ boxes

12. Lisa has 68 inches of ribbon. She needs 5 inches of ribbon to make each bow. How many bows can she make?

_____ bows

13. Kate has 49 apples for fruit baskets. She puts 3 apples in each basket. How many baskets can she fill?

_____ baskets

14. A ride at an amusement park holds 6 people in each car. How many cars are needed to hold 82 people?

_____ cars

15. $4\overline{)172}$

_____

16. $234 \div 9 =$ _____

17. $9\overline{)279}$

_____

18. $156 \div 2 =$ _____

19. A bakery has 126 rolls to divide equally into bags. Each bag holds 6 rolls. How many bags will be needed?

_____ bags

20. There are 424 snacks to put in 4 boxes. Each box will have an equal number of snacks. How many snacks will be in each box?

_____ snacks

Stop

Choose the correct answer.

1. $2 \times 80 = $ ■

   A 82
   B 100
   C 160
   D 280

2. $5 \times 500 = $ ■

   F 2,500
   G 505
   H 250
   J 25

3. $9 \times 60 = $ ■

   A 630
   B 540
   C 450
   D 170

4. Use the array to find the product.

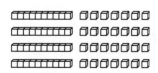

   $4 \times 17 = $ ■

   F 88
   G 68
   H 58
   J 47

5. Use the array to find the product.

$3 \times 15 = $ ■

   A 30
   B 35
   C 45
   D 85

6. $5 \times 73 = $ ■

   F 78
   G 315
   H 355
   J 365

Choose whether you would add, subtract, multiply, or divide.

7. Mike read for 40 minutes on Monday and 50 minutes on Tuesday. How many minutes did he read in all?

   A add
   B subtract
   C multiply
   D divide

Go On ▶

8. Kai bought 8 apples for 24¢ each. Which number sentence shows how to find the cost of the 8 apples?

   F $24¢ - 8¢ = $ ■
   G $24¢ ÷ 8 = $ ■
   H $8¢ + 24¢ = $ ■
   J $8 \times 24¢ = $ ■

Choose whether you would add, subtract, multiply, or divide.

9. A train car has 90 seats. What is the total number of seats on a 7 car train?

   A add
   B subtract
   C multiply
   D divide

For 10–12, choose a method. Find the product.

10.   14
   $\times 8$

       F 122
       G 112
       H 92
       J 22

11. $3 \times 45 = $ ■

   A 150   **C** 120
   B 135   **D** 15

12. $7 \times 83 = $ ■

   F 77
   G 90
   H 581
   J 5,621

13. Use the counters to find the quotient and remainder.

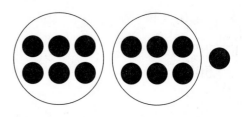

   $13 ÷ 2 = $ ■

   A 6 r1
   B 12 r1
   C 3 r1
   D 2 r1

For 14–15, find the quotient and remainder. Use counters or draw a picture to help.

14. $22 ÷ 5 = $ ■

   F 4
   G 4 r2
   H 5
   J 5 r2

15. $19 ÷ 4 = $ ■

   A 4
   B 4 r1
   C 4 r2
   D 4 r3

Go On ▶

For items 16–18, use the model to find the quotient and remainder.

16. 37 ÷ 3 = ■

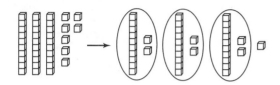

   F 3 r1
   G 3 r3
   H 12 r1
   J 36 r1

17. 43 ÷ 3 = ■

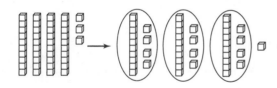

   A 13 r2
   B 14
   C 14 r1
   D 14 r2

18. 35 ÷ 4 = ■

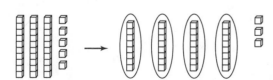

   F 7 r3
   G 8 r1
   H 8 r3
   J 9 r3

19. Linda has 66 balloons. How many groups of 5 balloons each can she make?

   A 11
   B 12
   C 13
   D 14

20. Joey has 542 trading cards in his collection. He can put 9 cards on each page of his album. How many pages will his collection use?

   F 600
   G 61
   H 9
   J 6

21. Each taxicab holds 4 people. How many taxicabs are needed to take 78 people to a ball game?

   A 18
   B 19
   C 20
   D 21

Go On

22. 5)460

    F 80
    G 90
    H 91
    J 92

For 25–28, ESTIMATE the quotient.

25. 6)491

    A 70
    B 80
    C 90
    D 100

26. 9)823

    F 70
    G 80
    H 90
    J 100

23. 8)944

    A 116
    B 117
    C 118
    D 119

27. $492 \div 5 = $ ■

    A 70
    B 80
    C 90
    D 100

28. $327 \div 4 = $ ■

24. 4)356

    F 89
    G 88
    H 81
    J 79

    F 80
    G 70
    H 60
    J 50

Stop

Write the correct answer.

For 1–3, use mental math and basic facts to find the product.

1. $4 \times 70 =$ ▪

_____

2. $3 \times 800 =$ ▪

_____

3. $4 \times 90 =$ ▪

_____

4. Use the array to find the product.

$3 \times 16 =$ _____

5. Use the array to find the product.

$4 \times 12 =$ _____

6. $4 \times 87 =$ _____

Choose whether you would add, subtract, multiply, or divide.

7. Carmen read for 25 minutes on Tuesday and 45 minutes on Thursday. How many minutes did she read in all?

_____

8. Jason bought 6 pencils for $0.30 each. Write a number sentence that shows the cost of the 6 pencils.

_____

Go On ▶

Choose whether you would add, subtract, multiply, or divide.

9. There were 53 people on a bus. At the first stop, 37 people got off the bus. What is the number of people left on the bus?

_____

For 10–12, choose a method. Find the product.

10.   24
    $\times\ 3$

11. $4 \times 36 = $ ■

_____

12. $6 \times 29 = $ ■

_____

13. Use the counters to find the quotient and remainder.

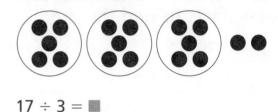

$17 \div 3 = $ ■

_____

For 14–15, find the quotient and remainder. Use counters or draw a picture to help.

14. $19 \div 3 = $ ■

_____

15. $22 \div 4 = $ ■

_____

For 16–18, use the model to find the quotient and remainder.

16. Find the quotient and the remainder.

$25 \div 4 = $ ■

_____

Go On ▶

17.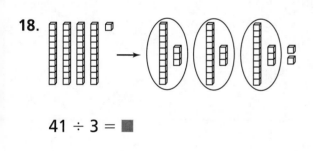

$32 \div 3 = \blacksquare$

_____

18.

$41 \div 3 = \blacksquare$

_____

19. Chris has 74 marbles. He puts them into groups of 8. How many groups of marbles can he make?

_____ groups

20. Jason has 245 shells in his collection. He can put 8 shells in each display box. How many display boxes does he need to hold his collection?

_____ boxes

21. Each van holds 8 people. How many vans are needed to take 102 people to a park?

_____ vans

22. $6\overline{)432}$

23. $7\overline{)847}$

24. $6\overline{)426}$

Go On

For 25–28, ESTIMATE the quotient.

25. $7\overline{)647}$

_____

26. $8\overline{)812}$

_____

27. $631 \div 9 = ■$

_____

28. $137 \div 6 = ■$

_____

Name _____

Choose the correct answer.

1. What is the value of the 5 in 5,307?

   A 5,000   **C** 50
   B 500   **D** 5

2. Compare the numbers.

7,412 ● 7,413

   F <   **G** >   **H** =

3. Which operation symbol makes the number sentence true?

130 ● 15 = 115

   A ÷   **B** ×   **C** −   **D** +

4.
```
  704
−  88
```
   F 516
   G 612
   H 606
   J 616

5. What amount is shown?

   A $2.61   **C** $2.31
   B $2.56   **D** $2.16

6.
```
  $4.65
−$2.90
```
   F $7.65
   G $2.75
   H $1.95
   J $1.75

For 7, use the schedule.

MORNING
CLASS SCHEDULE

Activity	Time
Reading	8:15 A.M. – 9:00 A.M.
Math	9:00 A.M. – 10:00 A.M.
Recess	10:00 A.M. – 10:20 A.M.
Art	10:20 A.M. – 11:00 A.M.
Spelling	11:00 A.M. – 11:35 A.M.

7. Which activity is the longest?

   A reading   **C** spelling
   B math   **D** art

8. There are 8 oranges in each bag. Kyle buys 2 bags. How many oranges does he buy in all?

   F 6   **H** 14
   G 10   **J** 16

9.
```
  9
× 3
```
   A 36
   B 27
   C 18
   D 12

Go On ➡

Form A • Multiple Choice

10. Compare. Choose $<$, $>$, or $=$ for the ●.

0×8 ● 1×6

F $<$ **G** $>$ **H** $=$

11. Luke buys 8 packages of balloons. Each package has 4 balloons in it. How many balloons does he buy in all?

A 40   **C** 24
B 32   **D** 12

12. ■ $= 10 \times 8$

F 18   **H** 80
G 70   **J** 108

For 13, use the pictograph.

NEW LIBRARY BOOKS	
Fiction	📖 📖 📖
Science	📖 📖
History	📖 📖
Art	📖 📖 📖

Key: Each 📖 = 4 books.

13. How many more new art books than science books are in the library?

A 1   **C** 4
B 2   **D** 8

14. What is the rule for the table?

Chairs	1	2	3	4	5
Legs	4	8	12	16	20

F Multiply chairs by 4.
G Divide chairs by 4.
H Add 1 to chairs.
J Add 2 to legs.

15. An adult's ticket costs $8. A child's ticket costs $4. How much would tickets cost for 3 adults and 7 children?

A $22   **C** $52
B $24   **D** $53

16. Which number makes the number sentences true?

$7 \times$ ■ $= 28$ $28 \div 7 =$ ■

F 2   **H** 4
G 3   **J** 5

17. $42 \div 7 =$ ■

A 8   **C** 6
B 7   **D** 5

18. What is the rule for the pattern?

345, 360, 375, 390, 405, 420

F Add 10.
G Add 15.
H Add 25.
J Subtract 15.

Go On ▶

For 19–20, use the bar graph.

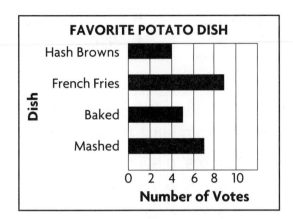

FAVORITE POTATO DISH

19. Which potato dish got the **greatest** number of votes?

   A   hash browns
   B   french fries
   C   baked
   D   mashed

20. How many more votes were for mashed than for baked potatoes?

   F   2   G   3   H   7   J   12

21. Which unit would you use to measure the length of your math book?

   A   mile   C   foot
   B   yard   D   inch

22. Which word describes a triangle that has 3 equal sides?

   F   acute
   G   obtuse
   H   isosceles
   J   equilateral

23. Which quadrilateral has only 1 pair of parallel sides?

   A   C

   B   D

24. Which figure has 6 faces?

   F   rectangular prism
   G   sphere
   H   cylinder
   J   cone

25. Judy has 16 feet of fencing to build a play area for her puppy. If she wants the **greatest** possible area, how long and wide should the sides of the play area be?

   A   4 feet long, 4 feet wide
   B   5 feet long, 3 feet wide
   C   8 feet long, 8 feet wide
   D   16 feet long, 16 feet wide

26. What is the volume of the figure?

   F   8 cubic units
   G   16 cubic units
   H   24 cubic units
   J   32 cubic units

Go On ▶

27. Which color are you **most likely** to spin?

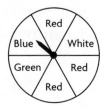

A red   C green
B blue   D white

28. Lucy is arranging her vases on a shelf. She has a blue vase, a yellow vase, a red vase, and a purple vase. How many ways can she arrange her vases?

F 4   G 12   H 16   J 24

29. Compare. Choose <, >, or =.

$\frac{1}{6}$	$\frac{1}{6}$	$\frac{1}{6}$

$\frac{1}{4}$	$\frac{1}{4}$	$\frac{1}{4}$

$\frac{3}{6}$ ● $\frac{3}{4}$

A <   B >   C =

30. What is the sum in simplest form?

$\frac{3}{10} + \frac{2}{10} = $ ■

F $\frac{1}{2}$ G $\frac{2}{5}$ H $\frac{5}{20}$ J $\frac{1}{20}$

31. What is the difference in simplest form?

$\frac{7}{8} - \frac{5}{8} = $ ■

A $\frac{2}{16}$ B $\frac{1}{2}$ C $\frac{1}{4}$ D $\frac{1}{8}$

32. What is $\frac{9}{10}$ written as a decimal?

F 0.09   H 9.1
G 0.9   J 910

33. Which shows the decimals in order from **least** to **greatest**?

A 0.4, 0.8, 0.6
B 0.8, 0.6, 0.4
C 0.4, 0.6, 0.8
D 0.6, 0.4, 0.8

34.   0.17
    + 2.81
    ‾‾‾‾‾

F 4.51   H 2.98
G 3.15   J 2.64

35. Lauren exercises for 35 minutes each day. How many minutes does she exercise in 7 days?

A 42 minutes
B 56 minutes
C 215 minutes
D 245 minutes

36. A group of 68 students is going to a museum. Each van can hold 8 students. How many vans do the students need?

F 7 vans
G 8 vans
H 9 vans
J 10 vans

Stop

Write the correct answer.

1. Write the value of the 9 in 8,903.

_____

2. Compare the numbers. Write <, >, or = in the ◯.

3,920 ◯ 3,290

3. Write + or − to complete the number sentence.

220 ◯ 25 = 245

4.   405
    − 67

5. Write the amount.

_____

6. $8.30
    − $3.85

_____

For 7, use the schedule.

| AFTERNOON CLASS SCHEDULE ||
Activity	Time
Lunch	12:10 P.M. – 12:45 P.M.
Science	12:45 P.M. – 1:30 P.M.
Reading	1:30 P.M. – 2:30 P.M.
Music	2:30 P.M. – 3:10 A.M.

7. Which activity lasts 45 minutes?

_____

Go On

8. Mrs. George gave Kelly and her brother 4 crackers each. How many crackers did Kelly and her brother get in all?

_____ crackers

9.   7
   × 3

   _____

10. Compare. Write <, >, or = in the ◯.

   7 × 1 ◯ 1 × 7

11. There are 6 juice drinks in each box. How many juice drinks are there in 4 boxes?

   _____ juice drinks

12. _____ = 8 × 8

For 13, use the pictograph.

FAVORITE SPORT	
Baseball	🧍 🧍 🧍 🧍
Swimming	🧍 🧍
Hockey	🧍
Football	🧍 🧍 🧍

Key: Each 🧍 = 4 votes.

13. How many more students voted for baseball than football?

   _____ more students

14. Write a rule for the table?

Cars	1	2	3	4	5
Tires	4	8	12	16	20

   _____

15. A pizza costs $9. Sandwiches cost $5. How much would it cost to buy 2 pizzas and 5 sandwiches?

   _____

16. Find the missing factor and quotient.

   $4 \times$ _____ $= 36$

   $36 \div 4 =$ _____

17. $35 \div 7 =$ _____

18. What is the rule for the pattern?

   410, 395, 380, 365, 350, 335

   _____

Go On

For 19–20, use the bar graph.

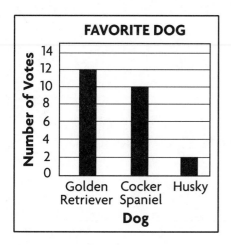

19. Which dog got the **greatest** number of votes?

_____

20. How many more votes were for Cocker Spaniel than for Husky?

_____ more votes

21. Choose the unit you would use to measure the height of your classroom. Write **inch, foot, yard,** or **mile.**

_____

22. What is the name of a triangle with exactly 2 equal sides?

_____

23. Which quadrilateral has 2 pairs of parallel sides and 4 sides of equal length?

_____

24. Circle the name of the solid figure that has exactly 5 faces.

   cube   square pyramid

   sphere   cylinder

25. Julie has 20 feet of fencing to build a play area for her rabbits. If she wants the **greatest** possible area, how long and wide should the sides of the play area be?

_____ feet long,

_____ feet wide

26. Find the volume of the figure.

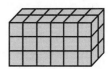

_____ cubic units

▶ Go On

27. Which color are you **most likely** to spin?

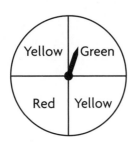

_____

28. Mike is arranging books on a shelf. He has a math book, a science book, a reading book, and a social studies book. How many ways can Mike arrange his books?

_____

29. Compare. Write $<$, $>$, or $=$ in the ◯.

| $\frac{1}{8}$ | $\frac{1}{8}$ | $\frac{1}{8}$ |

| $\frac{1}{4}$ | $\frac{1}{4}$ |

$\frac{3}{8}$ ◯ $\frac{2}{4}$

30. Find the sum in simplest form.

$\frac{2}{10} + \frac{2}{10} =$ _____

31. Find the difference in simplest form.

$\frac{5}{6} - \frac{2}{6} =$ _____

32. Write $\frac{2}{10}$ as a decimal.

_____

33. Write the decimals in order from **least** to **greatest**.

0.7, 0.3, 0.5

_____

34.   0.22
   $+ 1.37$

_____

35. Erik jogs for 45 minutes each day. How many minutes does he jog in 5 days?

_____

36. A group of 62 students is going to the zoo. Each van can hold 9 students. How many vans do the students need?

_____

Stop

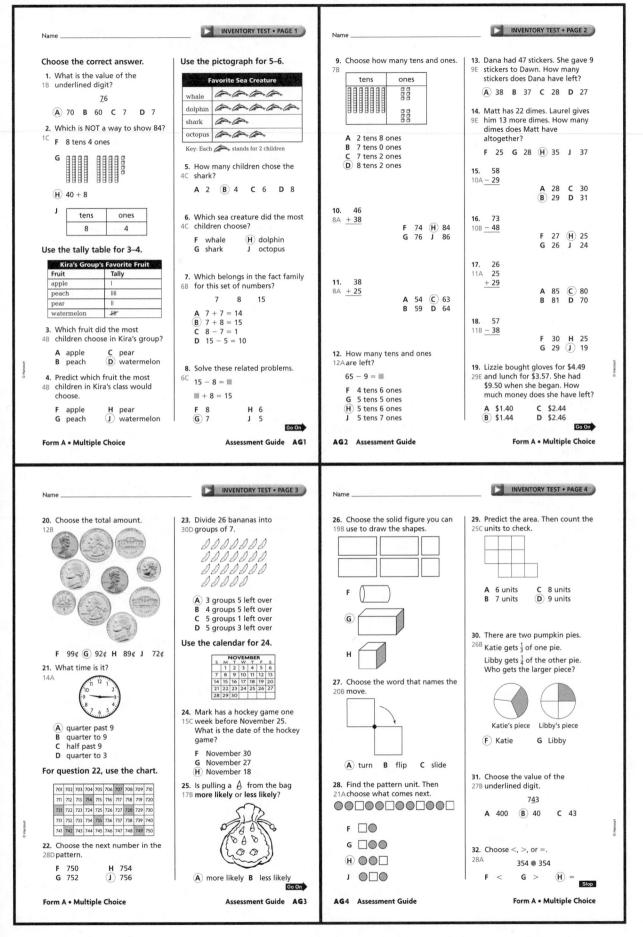

INVENTORY TEST • PAGE 1

Name _____

Choose the correct answer.

1. What is the value of the
1B underlined digit?

7̲6

(A) 70 B 60 C 7 D 7

2. Which is NOT a way to show 84?
1C F 8 tens 4 ones

G

(H) 40 + 8

J

tens	ones
8	4

Use the tally table for 3–4.

Kira's Group's Favorite Fruit	
Fruit	**Tally**
apple	I
peach	IIII
pear	II
watermelon	JHH

3. Which fruit did the most
4B children choose in Kira's group?

A apple C pear
B peach (D) watermelon

4. Predict which fruit the most
4B children in Kira's class would
choose.

F apple H pear
G peach (J) watermelon

Form A • Multiple Choice

Use the pictograph for 5–6.

Favorite Sea Creature	
whale	🐬🐬🐬
dolphin	🐬🐬🐬🐬
shark	🐬🐬
octopus	🐬

Key: Each 🐬 stands for 2 children

5. How many children chose the
4C shark?

A 2 (B) 4 C 6 D 8

6. Which sea creature did the most
4C children choose?

F whale (H) dolphin
G shark J octopus

7. Which belongs in the fact family
6B for this set of numbers?

7   8   15

A 7 + 7 = 14
(B) 7 + 8 = 15
C 8 − 7 = 1
D 15 − 5 = 10

8. Solve these related problems.
6C
15 − 8 = ■

■ + 8 = 15

F 8 H 6
(G) 7 J 5

Go On

Assessment Guide AG1

INVENTORY TEST • PAGE 2

Name _____

9. Choose how many tens and ones.
7B

tens	ones

A 2 tens 8 ones
B 7 tens 0 ones
C 7 tens 2 ones
(D) 8 tens 2 ones

10.   46
8A + 38

F 74 (H) 84
G 76 J 86

11.   38
8A + 25

A 54 (C) 63
B 59 D 64

12. How many tens and ones
12A are left?

65 − 9 = ■

F 4 tens 6 ones
G 5 tens 5 ones
(H) 5 tens 6 ones
J 5 tens 7 ones

13. Dana had 47 stickers. She gave 9
9E stickers to Dawn. How many
stickers does Dana have left?

(A) 38 B 37 C 28 D 27

14. Matt has 22 dimes. Laurel gives
9E him 13 more dimes. How many
dimes does Matt have
altogether?

F 25 G 28 (H) 35 J 37

15.   58
10A − 29

A 28 C 30
(B) 29 D 31

16.   73
10B − 48

F 27 (H) 25
G 26 J 24

17.   26
11A   25
    + 29

A 85 (C) 80
B 81 D 70

18.   57
11B − 38

F 30 H 25
G 29 (J) 19

19. Lizzie bought gloves for $4.49
29E and lunch for $3.57. She had
$9.50 when she began. How
much money does she have left?

A $1.40 C $2.44
(B) $1.44 D $2.46

Go On

AG2 Assessment Guide

Form A • Multiple Choice

INVENTORY TEST • PAGE 3

Name _____

20. Choose the total amount.
12B

F 99¢ (G) 92¢ H 89¢ J 72¢

21. What time is it?
14A

A quarter past 9
B quarter to 9
C half past 9
D quarter to 3

For question 22, use the chart.

701	702	703	704	705	706	707	708	709	710
711	712	713	714	715	716	717	718	719	720
721	722	723	724	725	726	727	728	729	730
731	732	733	734	735	736	737	738	739	740
741	742	743	744	745	746	747	748	749	750

22. Choose the next number in the
28D pattern.

F 750 H 754
G 752 (J) 756

Form A • Multiple Choice

23. Divide 26 bananas into
30D groups of 7.

(A) 3 groups 5 left over
B 4 groups 5 left over
C 5 groups 1 left over
D 5 groups 3 left over

Use the calendar for 24.

NOVEMBER						
S	M	T	W	T	F	S
				1	2	3
4	5	6	7	8	9	10
11	12	13	14	15	16	17
18	19	20	21	22	23	24
25	26	27	28	29	30	

24. Mark has a hockey game one
15C week before November 25.
What is the date of the hockey
game?

F November 30
G November 27
(H) November 18

25. Is pulling a 💧 from the bag
17B more likely or less likely?

(A) more likely B less likely

Go On

Assessment Guide AG3

INVENTORY TEST • PAGE 4

Name _____

26. Choose the solid figure you can
19B use to draw the shapes.

F
(G)
H

27. Choose the word that names the
20B move.

(A) turn B flip C slide

28. Find the pattern unit. Then
21A choose what comes next.

F
G
(H)
J

29. Predict the area. Then count the
25C units to check.

A 6 units C 8 units
B 7 units (D) 9 units

30. There are two pumpkin pies.
26B Katie gets $\frac{1}{3}$ of one pie.

Libby gets $\frac{1}{4}$ of the other pie.
Who gets the larger piece?

Katie's piece   Libby's piece

(F) Katie G Libby

31. Choose the value of the
27B underlined digit.

7̲43

A 400 (B) 40 C 43

32. Choose <, >, or =.
28A
354 ● 354

F < G > (H) =

Stop

AG4 Assessment Guide

Form A • Multiple Choice

INVENTORY TEST • PAGE 1

Name _____

Write the correct answer.

1. What is the value of the
1B underlined digit?

9<u>3</u>

_____ 90

2. Which is NOT a way to show the
1C number 47? Circle it.

⬭ 7 tens 4 ones ⬮

tens	ones
4	7

tens	ones
(rods)	(cubes)

40 + 7

Use the tally table for 3–4.

Owen's Group's Favorite Pet	
Pet	Tally
cat	II
dog	III
hamster	IIII I
fish	IIII

3. Which pet did the most students
4B choose in Owen's group?

_____ hamster

4. Predict which pet the most
4B students in Owen's class would
choose.

_____ hamster

Use the pictograph for 5–6.

Ways to Travel	
cars	🚗🚗🚗🚗🚗
buses	🚌🚌
trains	🚆🚆🚆
planes	✈✈✈✈✈

Key: Each 🚗🚌🚆✈
stands for 2 choices.

5. How many students chose
4C trains?

_____ 6

6. Which way to travel did the
4C **least** students choose?

_____ buses

7. Which belongs in the fact family
6B for this set of numbers? Circle it.

3   8   11

4 + 4 = 8   ⬭ 11 − 8 = 3 ⬮

11 + 8 = 19   8 − 3 = 5

Go On ▶

Form B • Free Response

Assessment Guide **AG5**

INVENTORY TEST • PAGE 2

Name _____

8. Solve these related problems.
6C 10 − 7 = _____ 3

_____ 3 + 7 = 10

9. Write how many tens and ones.
7B

tens	ones
(rods)	(cubes)

_____ 6 tens _____ 4 ones

10. 47
8A + 36
_____
83

11. 59
8A + 37
_____
96

12. How many tens and ones
12A are left?

85 − 7 = ▪

_____ 7 tens _____ 8 ones

13. Tori has 21 walnuts. She gives
9E 6 walnuts to Alma. How many
walnuts does Tori have left?

_____ 15 walnuts

14. Sam has 55 baseball cards. Luke
9E gives him 17 more cards. How
many baseball cards does Sam
have altogether?

_____ 72 baseball cards

15. 87
10A − 58
_____
29

16. 48
10B − 39
_____
9

17. 21
11A 19
+ 48
_____
88

18. 84
11B − 26
_____
58

Go On ▶

AG6 **Assessment Guide**

Form B • Free Response

INVENTORY TEST • PAGE 3

Name _____

19. Lori spent $3.24 to buy a
29E birthday card. Then her mother
gave her $3.75. Lori had $7.50
when she began. How much
money does Lori have now?

_____ $8.01

20. Write the total amount.
12B

_____ 78¢

21. What time is it?
14A

1 : 45

Use the chart for question 22.

901	902	903	904	905	906	907	908	909	910
911	912	913	914	915	916	917	918	919	920
921	922	923	924	925	926	927	928	929	930
931	932	933	934	935	936	937	938	939	940
941	942	943	944	945	946	947	948	949	950

22. Write the next number in the
28D pattern.

_____ 954

23. Divide 23 apples into groups
30D of 8.

_____ 2 groups _____ 7 left over

Use the calendar for 24.

FEBRUARY						
S	M	T	W	T	F	S
						1
2	3	4	5	6	7	8
9	10	11	12	13	14	15
16	17	18	19	20	21	22
23	24	25	26	27	28	

24. Miranda's birthday is two weeks
15C after Valentine's Day. Valentine's
Day is February 14. When is
Miranda's birthday?

_____ February 28

Go On ▶

Form B • Free Response

Assessment Guide **AG7**

INVENTORY TEST • PAGE 4

Name _____

25. Is pulling a △ from the bag
17B **more likely** or **less likely**?

more likely   ⬭ less likely ⬮

26. Circle the solid figure you can
19B use to draw the shapes.

27. Write the word that names the
20B move.

_____ flip

28. Circle the pattern unit. Then
21A draw what comes next.

29. Write the area of the figure.
25C

_____ 14 units

30. There are 2 sheets of art paper.
26B Jesse gets $\frac{1}{2}$ of one sheet.
Alan gets $\frac{1}{5}$ of the other sheet.
Who gets the larger piece?

Jesse's piece   Alan's piece

_____ Jesse

31. Write the value of the
27B underlined digit.

<u>7</u>15

_____ 700

32. Write <, >, or = in the ◯.
28A

694 ⬭ > ⬮ 469

Stop ■

AG8 **Assessment Guide**

Form B • Free Response

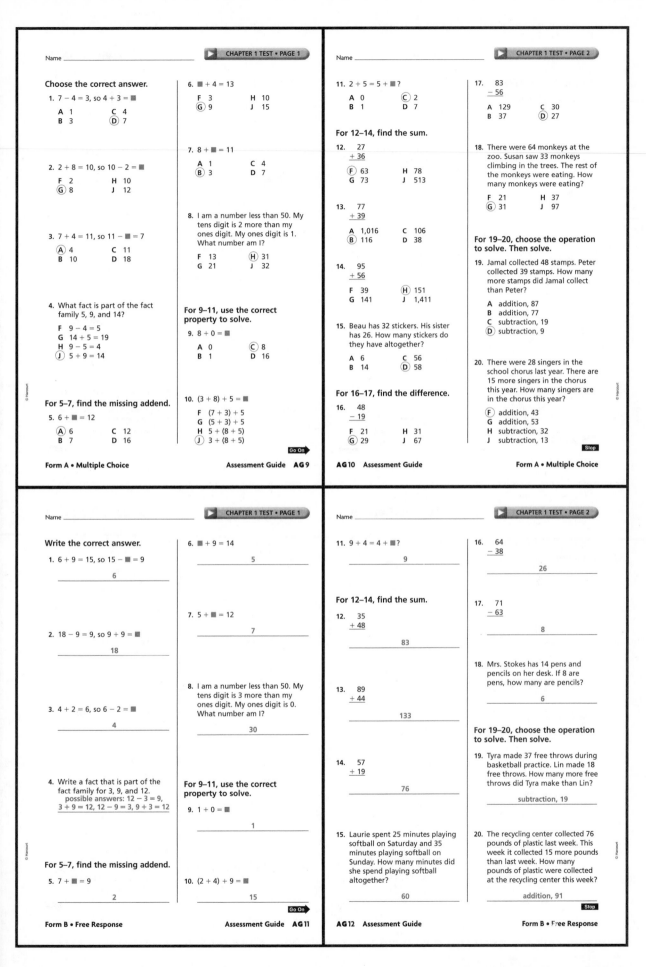

Choose the correct answer.

1. 7 − 4 = 3, so 4 + 3 = ■
- **A** 1
- **B** 3
- **C** 4
- **(D)** 7

2. 2 + 8 = 10, so 10 − 2 = ■
- **F** 2
- **(G)** 8
- **H** 10
- **J** 12

3. 7 + 4 = 11, so 11 − ■ = 7
- **(A)** 4
- **B** 10
- **C** 11
- **D** 18

4. What fact is part of the fact family 5, 9, and 14?
- **F** 9 − 4 = 5
- **G** 14 + 5 = 19
- **H** 9 − 5 = 4
- **(J)** 5 + 9 = 14

For 5–7, find the missing addend.

5. 6 + ■ = 12
- **(A)** 6
- **B** 7
- **C** 12
- **D** 16

6. ■ + 4 = 13
- **F** 3
- **(G)** 9
- **H** 10
- **J** 15

7. 8 + ■ = 11
- **A** 1
- **(B)** 3
- **C** 4
- **D** 7

8. I am a number less than 50. My tens digit is 2 more than my ones digit. My ones digit is 1. What number am I?
- **F** 13
- **G** 21
- **(H)** 31
- **J** 32

For 9–11, use the correct property to solve.

9. 8 + 0 = ■
- **A** 0
- **B** 1
- **(C)** 8
- **D** 16

10. (3 + 8) + 5 = ■
- **F** (7 + 3) + 5
- **G** (5 + 3) + 5
- **H** 5 + (8 + 5)
- **(J)** 3 + (8 + 5)

Go On ➡

Form A • Multiple Choice   **Assessment Guide AG 9**

---

11. 2 + 5 = 5 + ■ ?
- **A** 0
- **B** 1
- **(C)** 2
- **D** 7

For 12–14, find the sum.

12. 27
      + 36
- **(F)** 63
- **G** 73
- **H** 78
- **J** 513

13. 77
      + 39
- **A** 1,016
- **(B)** 116
- **C** 106
- **D** 38

14. 95
      + 56
- **F** 39
- **G** 141
- **(H)** 151
- **J** 1,411

15. Beau has 32 stickers. His sister has 26. How many stickers do they have altogether?
- **A** 6
- **B** 14
- **C** 56
- **(D)** 58

For 16–17, find the difference.

16. 48
      − 19
- **F** 21
- **(G)** 29
- **H** 31
- **J** 67

17. 83
      − 56
- **A** 129
- **B** 37
- **C** 30
- **(D)** 27

18. There were 64 monkeys at the zoo. Susan saw 33 monkeys climbing in the trees. The rest of the monkeys were eating. How many monkeys were eating?
- **F** 21
- **(G)** 31
- **H** 37
- **J** 97

For 19–20, choose the operation to solve. Then solve.

19. Jamal collected 48 stamps. Peter collected 39 stamps. How many more stamps did Jamal collect than Peter?
- **A** addition, 87
- **B** addition, 77
- **C** subtraction, 19
- **(D)** subtraction, 9

20. There were 28 singers in the school chorus last year. There are 15 more singers in the chorus this year. How many singers are in the chorus this year?
- **(F)** addition, 43
- **G** addition, 53
- **H** subtraction, 32
- **J** subtraction, 13

Stop ⬛

AG 10 Assessment Guide   **Form A • Multiple Choice**

Write the correct answer.

1. 6 + 9 = 15, so 15 − ■ = 9

_____6_____

2. 18 − 9 = 9, so 9 + 9 = ■

_____18_____

3. 4 + 2 = 6, so 6 − 2 = ■

_____4_____

4. Write a fact that is part of the fact family for 3, 9, and 12.
possible answers: 12 − 3 = 9, 3 + 9 = 12, 12 − 9 = 3, 9 + 3 = 12

For 5–7, find the missing addend.

5. 7 + ■ = 9

_____2_____

6. ■ + 9 = 14

_____5_____

7. 5 + ■ = 12

_____7_____

8. I am a number less than 50. My tens digit is 3 more than my ones digit. My ones digit is 0. What number am I?

_____30_____

For 9–11, use the correct property to solve.

9. 1 + 0 = ■

_____1_____

10. (2 + 4) + 9 = ■

_____15_____

Go On ➡

Form B • Free Response   **Assessment Guide AG 11**

---

11. 9 + 4 = 4 + ■ ?

_____9_____

For 12–14, find the sum.

12. 35
      + 48

_____83_____

13. 89
      + 44

_____133_____

14. 57
      + 19

_____76_____

15. Laurie spent 25 minutes playing softball on Saturday and 35 minutes playing softball on Sunday. How many minutes did she spend playing softball altogether?

_____60_____

16. 64
      − 38

_____26_____

17. 71
      − 63

_____8_____

18. Mrs. Stokes has 14 pens and pencils on her desk. If 8 are pens, how many are pencils?

_____6_____

For 19–20, choose the operation to solve. Then solve.

19. Tyra made 37 free throws during basketball practice. Lin made 18 free throws. How many more free throws did Tyra make than Lin?

_____subtraction, 19_____

20. The recycling center collected 76 pounds of plastic last week. This week it collected 15 more pounds than last week. How many pounds of plastic were collected at the recycling center this week?

_____addition, 91_____

Stop ⬛

AG 12 Assessment Guide   **Form B • Free Response**

Choose the correct answer.

1. What number is **odd**?

A 18   C 66
B 47   D 94

2. What is the value of the 5 in 4,572?

F 5   H 500
G 50   J 5,000

3. What is 345 written in expanded form?

A 300 + 40 + 5
B 30 + 45
C 34 + 5
D 3 + 4 + 5

4. What number is **even**?

F 133   H 358
G 247   J 581

5. What is the value of the 8 in 683,472?

A 800
B 8,000
C 80,000
D 800,000

6. Predict the next number in the pattern.

33, 37, 41, 45, _____

F 47   H 51
G 49   J 59

7. What is 700 + 50 + 8 written in standard form?

A 7,508   C 758
B 7,058   D 20

8. Jesse modeled 133 with base-ten blocks. He used 1 hundred and 2 tens. How many ones did he use?

F 33   H 13
G 23   J 3

9. What is 8,734 written in expanded form?

A 87 + 34
B 800 + 734
C 800 + 70 + 34
D 8,000 + 700 + 30 + 4

10. Which number is **odd**?

F 244   H 658
G 401   J 972

[Go On]

Form A • Multiple Choice

---

11. What is 18,329 written in expanded form?

A 10,000 + 8,000 + 300 + 20 + 9
B 18,000 + 3,000 + 29
C 1,800 + 300 + 20 + 9
D 1 + 8 + 3 + 2 + 9

12. What is four thousand, six hundred five written in standard form?

F 4,065   H 4,650
G 4,605   J 46,005

13. What is eight hundred seventy-two written in standard form?

A 80,072   C 8,072
B 8,702   D 872

14. What number completes the number sentence?

8,000 + 400 + ■ + 5 = 8,425

F 2,000   H 20
G 25   J 2

15. Jenny skip-counts by threes. She says, "3, 6, 9, 12." What numbers should Jenny say next?

A 15, 18, 21   C 16, 18, 21
B 16, 17, 18   D 20, 25, 30

16. The code to a safe is a number pattern that skip-counts by hundreds. The first number is 432. The second number is 532. The third number is 632. What is the fourth number of the code?

F 732   H 832
G 782   J 1,632

17. What is two hundred fifty-five thousand, four hundred eight written in standard form?

A 255,408   C 255,048
B 255,084   D 25,548

18. What is the greatest 4-digit number that can be written using 3,8,5, and 6?

F 8,653   H 8,563
G 8,635   J 8,536

19. What is the greatest 3-digit number that can be written using 5, 7, and 2?

A 257   C 725
B 572   D 752

20. Brittany made a model using base-ten blocks. She used 4 hundreds, 17 tens, and 6 ones. What number did she model?

F 476   H 516
G 486   J 576

[Stop]

Form A • Multiple Choice

Write the correct answer.

1. Is 33 **even** or **odd**?

_____ odd _____

2. Write the value of the 3 in the number 2,385.

_____ 300 _____

3. Write 471 in expanded form.

_____ 400 + 70 + 1 _____

4. Is 326 **even** or **odd**?

_____ even _____

5. Write the value of the 5 in 752,034.

_____ 50,000 _____

6. Predict the next number in the pattern.

46, 49, 52, 55,

_____ 58 _____

7. Write this number in standard form.

300 + 20 + 8

_____ 328 _____

8. Luke modeled 354 with base-ten blocks. He used 2 hundreds and 4 ones. How many tens did he use?

_____ 15 _____

9. Write 9,256 in expanded form.

_____ 9,000 + 200 + 50 + 6 _____

10. Circle the **even** number.

(392)
491
763
807

[Go On]

Form B • Free Response

---

11. Write 14,752 in expanded form.

_____ 10,000 + 4,000 + 700 + 50 + 2 _____

12. Write five thousand, eight hundred two in standard form.

_____ 5,802 _____

13. Write two hundred sixty-four in standard form.

_____ 264 _____

14. Write the number that completes the number sentence.

5,000 + 300 + _70_ + 2 = 5,372

15. Peggy skip-counted by twos. She said, "4, 6, 8, 10." Write the next three numbers.

_12_ , _14_ , _16_

16. Rachel made a number pattern that skip-counts by tens. The first number is 791. The second number is 801. The third number is 811. What is the fourth number of her pattern?

_____ 821 _____

17. Write four hundred thirty-seven thousand, six hundred four in standard form.

_____ 437,604 _____

18. Write the **greatest** 4-digit number possible using 2, 5, 9, and 4.

_____ 9,542 _____

19. Write the **greatest** 3-digit number possible using 0, 6, and 2.

_____ 620 _____

20. Toby made a model using base-ten blocks. He used 2 hundreds, 7 tens, and 23 ones. What number did he model?

_____ 293 _____

[Stop]

Form B • Free Response

Name _____

Choose the correct answer.

1. What is 585 rounded to the nearest hundred?

   (A) 600   C 580
   B 590   D 500

2. Choose a benchmark of 10, 100, 500, or 1,000 to ESTIMATE the number of players on a hockey team.

   F 1,000   H 100
   G 500   (J) 10

3. Which group of numbers is in order from **least** to **greatest**?

   A 5,592; 5,583; 4,785
   B 5,583; 5,592; 4,785
   C 4,785; 5,592; 5,583
   (D) 4,785; 5,583; 5,592

4. Which number is **greater than** 7,560?

   F 7,559   H 7,000
   G 7,060   (J) 7,801

5. What is 14,781 rounded to the nearest thousand?

   (A) 15,000   C 14,000
   B 14,700   D 10,000

6. Choose a benchmark of 10, 50, 100, or 1,000 to ESTIMATE the number of peanuts in a large bag.

   F 10   (H) 100
   G 50   J 1,000

7. Which group of numbers is in order from **least** to **greatest**?

   A 737,869; 733,457; 825,789
   B 737,869; 825,789; 733,457
   C 825,789; 733,457; 737,869
   (D) 733,457; 737,869; 825,789

8. Which group of numbers is in order from **greatest** to **least**?

   F 38,621; 38,479; 38,512
   (G) 38,621; 38,512; 38,479
   H 38,512; 38,479; 38,621
   J 38,479; 38,512; 38,621

9. What is 7,356 rounded to the nearest thousand?

   A 8,000   C 7,300
   B 7,400   (D) 7,000

10. What is the **greatest** place-value position in which the digits of 8,451 and 8,579 are different?

    F ones   (H) hundreds
    G tens   J thousands

11. What is 355 rounded to the nearest ten?

    A 300   (C) 360
    B 350   D 400

12. The height of Grand Teton is 13,766 ft. What is this number rounded to the nearest thousand?

    (F) 14,000   H 13,600
    G 13,700   J 10,000

   Go On

Form A • Multiple Choice

Name _____

13. What is 7,642 rounded to the nearest hundred?

    A 8,000   C 7,640
    B 7,700   (D) 7,600

14. Which is a true statement?

    (F) 4,895 > 4,871
    G 4,356 < 3,789
    H 389 > 398
    J 861 < 816

For 15–17, use the bar graph.

U.S. NATIONAL PARKS

Badlands 244,000
Big Cypress 729,000
Craters of the Moon 714,000
Dismal Swamp 107,000
Shenandoah 199,000

Size in Acres

15. Which two national parks are **smaller** than Badlands?

    A Big Cypress and Shenandoah
    B Dismal Swamp and Big Cypress
    C Craters of the Moon and Shenandoah
    (D) Shenandoah and Dismal Swamp

16. Which two parks have areas **greater than** 300,000 acres?

    F Big Cypress and Badlands
    G Dismal Swamp and Big Cypress
    (H) Big Cypress and Craters of the Moon
    J Badlands and Dismal Swamp

17. Which lists these parks in order from **least** to **greatest**?

    (A) Dismal Swamp, Shenandoah, Badlands
    B Big Cypress, Craters of the Moon, Badlands
    C Shenandoah, Dismal Swamp, Badlands
    D Badlands, Shenandoah, Dismal Swamp

18. Which number is **less than** 383,064?

    F 383,064   H 384,000
    G 383,100   (J) 383,060

For 19–20, use the table.

BASEBALL GAME ATTENDANCE	
Day	Number of People
Friday	8,749
Saturday	9,322
Sunday	4,886

19. To the nearest hundred, how many people attended the baseball game on Friday?

    A 9,000   (C) 8,700
    B 8,750   D 8,000

20. To the nearest thousand, how many people attended the games on Saturday and Sunday altogether?

    F 10,000   (H) 14,000
    G 13,000   J 15,000

   Stop

Form A • Multiple Choice

Name _____

Write the correct answer.

1. **Round 639 to the nearest hundred.**

   ___600___

2. Circle a benchmark to ESTIMATE the number of players on a baseball team.

   (10)   100   500

3. Write the numbers 4,481; 3,539; and 4,492 in order from **least** to **greatest**.

   3,539 ; 4,481 ; 4,492

4. Circle the number **greater than** 6,380.

   6,372   (6,384)   6,299

5. **Round 23,603 to the nearest thousand.**

   ___24,000___

6. Circle a benchmark to ESTIMATE the number of pages in a photo album.

   5   (50)   500

7. Write the numbers 647,729; 747,538; and 647,810 in order from **least** to **greatest**.

   647,729 ; 647,810 ; 747,538

8. Write the numbers 24,039; 23,507; and 24,258 in order from **greatest** to **least**.

   24,258 ; 24,039 ; 23,507

9. Round 8,206 to the nearest thousand.

   ___8,000___

10. Circle the name of the **greatest** place-value position in which 5,398 and 5,379 are different.

    Ones   (Tens)
    Hundreds   Thousands

11. **Round 659 to the nearest ten.**

    ___660___

12. There were 12,499 people at a football game. **Round this number to the nearest thousand.**

    ___12,000___

   Go On

Form B • Free Response

Name _____

13. **Round 5,362 to the nearest hundred.**

    ___5,400___

14. Compare the numbers. Write <, >, or = in the ◯.

    2,533 (<) 2,542

For 15–17, use the bar graph.

SEA ANIMAL WEIGHTS

Beluga Whale 3,307
Killer Whale 9,982
Manatee 1,394
Bottlenose Dolphin 595
Walrus 2,756

Weight in Pounds

15. Circle the three sea animals that weigh **less than** the beluga whale.

    killer whale, manatee, walrus

    bottlenose dolphin, walrus, killer whale

    walrus, killer whale, bottlenose dolphin

    (manatee, bottlenose dolphin, walrus)

16. Which sea animal is **heavier than** a manatee, but **lighter than** a beluga whale?

    ___walrus___

17. Which sea animal from this chart weighs the most?

    ___killer whale___

18. Circle the number **less than** 894,057.

    894,108   (894,049)   904,039

For 19–20, use the table.

NEWSPAPER RECYCLING	
Day	Pounds of Paper
Monday	1,650
Wednesday	1,049
Friday	1,670

19. To the **nearest hundred**, how many pounds of paper were collected on Monday?

    ___1,700___ pounds

20. To the **nearest thousand**, how many pounds of paper were collected on Monday and Wednesday altogether?

    ___3,000___ pounds

   Stop

Form B • Free Response

Choose the correct answer.

1. Which group of numbers is in order from **greatest** to **least**?

   A 243,918; 242,927; 243,876
   B 242,927; 243,876; 243,918
   C 243,876; 242,927; 243,918
   D 243,918; 243,876; 242,927 ⊙

2. What is the value of the 4 in 248,216?

   F 400
   G 4,000
   H 40,000 ⊙
   J 400,000

3. At 3:00 there were 67 skaters in the park. By 7:00 there were 92 skaters. Which number sentence would help you find how many more skaters were in the park at 7:00 than at 3:00?

   A 92 − 67 = ■ ⊙
   B 92 + 67 = ■
   C 92 − 24 = ■
   D 67 + 92 = ■

4. Predict the next number in the pattern.

   438, 441, 444, 447, ■

   F 449
   G 450 ⊙
   H 451
   J 453

5. Use the benchmark to estimate the number of flowers in the garden.

   20 flowers   ___?___ flowers

   A 10
   B 25
   C 100 ⊙
   D 500

6. Which subtraction fact is in the same fact family as 8 + 6 = 14?

   F 14 − 9 = 5
   G 8 − 6 = 2
   H 14 − 8 = 6 ⊙
   J 8 − 5 = 3

7. 3,000 + 700 + 3 = ■

   A 3,730
   B 3,703 ⊙
   C 3,073
   D 3,037

8. 9 + ■ = 14

   F 5 ⊙
   G 7
   H 9
   J 23

   Go On ▶

9. 73 + 67 = ■

   A 6
   B 34
   C 140 ⊙
   D 150

10. What is the value of the 2 in 867,281?

   F 2
   G 200 ⊙
   H 2,000
   J 20,000

11. Use the benchmark to estimate the number of marbles in Jar B.

   A   B

   5 marbles   ? marbles

   A about 5
   B about 10
   C about 20
   D about 100

12. 54 − 37 = ■

   F 13
   G 17 ⊙
   H 23
   J 91

13. Which number is **even**?

   A 45
   B 33
   C 72 ⊙
   D 81

For 14–15, use the bar graph.

Annual Adoptions

Dogs 358
Cats 527
Lizards 109
Horses 42

Number Adopted

14. Which animal was adopted **more than** lizards, but **less than** cats?

   F horses
   G cats
   H dogs ⊙
   J lizards

15. Which two animals were adopted most often?

   A cats and dogs ⊙
   B cats and horses
   C lizards and horses
   D horses and cats

16. What is 8,524 **rounded to the nearest thousand**?

   F 7,000
   G 8,000
   H 8,500
   J 9,000 ⊙

17. What is the **greatest** place-value position in which the digits of 5,456 and 5,179 are different?

   A ones
   B tens
   C hundreds
   D thousands

   Go On ▶

18. Which property of addition is shown by 1 + 0 = ■ ?

   F Zero Property of Addition ⊙
   G Order Property of Addition
   H Grouping Property of Addition

19. Which addition fact is in the same fact family as 18 − 9 = 9?

   A 18 + 9 = 27
   B 6 + 6 = 12
   C 9 + 9 = 18 ⊙
   D 10 + 8 = 18

20. What is three hundred thirty-two thousand, twelve written in standard form?

   F 32,012   H 303,212
   G 302,021   J 332,012 ⊙

21. 700 + 90 + 1 = ■

   A 7,910
   B 7,901
   C 7,091
   D 791 ⊙

22. Which number is **greater than** 457,950 but **less than** 458,950?

   F 457,850   H 458,962
   G 458,430 ⊙   J 459,750

23. There are 73 students in the school band. 56 students play a wind instrument. How many students do NOT play a wind instrument?

   A 17 ⊙
   B 23
   C 29
   D 129

24. What is 735 written in expanded form?

   F 700 + 35
   G 700 + 30 + 5 ⊙
   H 70 + 35
   J 7 + 3 + 5

25. Billy had 7 video games. His brother gave Billy some games. Billy now has 15 video games. How many video games did Billy's brother give him?

   A 7
   B 8 ⊙
   C 21
   D 22

   Go On ▶

26. What is 3,692 **rounded to the nearest thousand**?

   F 1,000
   G 3,000
   H 3,700
   J 4,000 ⊙

27. Which number completes this number sentence?

   ■ + 2 = 2

   A 4
   B 2
   C 1
   D 0 ⊙

28. I am a 3-digit number. The sum of my digits is 4. I have the same number of hundreds and ones. My middle digit is NOT a zero. Which number am I?

   F 112
   G 121 ⊙
   H 211
   J 400

29. How many hundreds are in 5,000?

   A 5
   B 15
   C 50 ⊙
   D 500

30. What types of numbers are 12, 46, 74, and 98?

   F odd
   G even ⊙
   H both odd and even
   J neither odd or even

31. What is 572 **rounded to the nearest hundred**?

   A 500
   B 570
   C 580
   D 600 ⊙

32. There are 43 third grade students and 48 fourth grade students at Tanglewood Elementary. How many third and fourth grade students are there altogether?

   F 5
   G 81
   H 85
   J 91 ⊙

33. What is 883 rounded to the nearest ten?

   A 900
   B 880 ⊙
   C 830
   D 800

   Stop

Name _____

Write the correct answer.

1. Circle the numbers that are in order from **greatest** to **least**.

   (873,938; 873,398; 872,498)

   872,498; 873,398; 873,938

   873,398; 872,498; 873,938

   873,398; 873,938; 872,498

2. Write the value of the 8 in 383,451.

   _____ 80,000 _____

3. There are 87 fish in a small tank and 94 fish in a larger tank. Write a number sentence that shows how to find how many more fish were in the larger tank.

   _____ 94 − 87 = 7 _____

4. Write the next number in the pattern.

   870, 860, 850, 840, ■

   830

5. Use the benchmark to estimate the number of pictures on the bulletin board. Circle the number.

   5 pictures _____?_____ pictures

   5   (20)   100

6. Write a subtraction fact that is in the same fact family as 7 + 4 = 11.

   _____ 11 − 7 = 4, or 11 − 4 = 7 _____

7. Write 9,000 + 30 + 1 in standard form.

   _____ 9,031 _____

8. Write the missing number.

   7 + ■ = 16

   9

   Go On

Name _____

9. Add.

   76 + 36 = ■

   _____ 112 _____

10. Write the value of the 4 in 704,852.

    _____ 4,000 _____

11. Use the benchmark to estimate the number of CDs on the rack. Circle the number.

    4 CDs _____?_____ CDs

    8   (12)   20

12. Subtract.

    47 − 8 = ■

    _____ 39 _____

13. Write whether 48 is **odd** or **even**.

    _____ even _____

For 14–15, use the bar graph.

Hockey Game Attendance

14. Which day had more people attending than Friday?

    _____ Saturday _____

15. Which two days had the most people attending the hockey games?

    _____ Friday _____ and _____ Saturday _____

16. Round 5,239 to the nearest thousand.

    _____ 5,000 _____

    Go On

Name _____

17. Write the greatest place-value position in which the digits of 25,610 and 26,634 are different.

    _____ thousands _____ place

18. Circle the property of addition that is shown by the following:

    (1 + 9) + 3 = 1 + (9 + 3)

    (Grouping Property of Addition)

    Order Property of Addition

    Zero Property of Addition

19. Write the addition fact that is in the same fact family as 12 − 6 = 6.

    _____ 6 + 6 = 12 _____

20. Write four hundred twenty-two thousand, fifteen in standard form.

    _____ 422,015 _____

21. Write 2,000 + 700 + 50 in standard form.

    _____ 2,750 _____

22. Which number is **greater than** 744,838 but **less than** 745,838?

    745,938   754,938

    (744,938)   754,389

23. In the museum there are 96 paintings and 57 statues. How many more paintings than statues are there in the museum?

    _____ 39 _____

24. Write 682 in expanded form.

    _____ 600 + 80 + 2 _____

25. In the morning there were 8 cows in the field. Later in the day there were 14 cows in the field. How many more cows were in the field in the afternoon?

    _____ 6 _____

    Go On

Name _____

26. Round 34,720 to the nearest thousand.

    _____ 35,000 _____

27. Write the missing number.

    ■ + 7 = 7

    _____ 0 _____

28. I am a 2-digit number. The sum of my digits is 12. My tens digit is 4 more than my ones digit. What number am I?

    _____ 84 _____

29. How many 100s are in 4,000?

    _____ 40 _____

30. Are the numbers 15, 33, 57, and 89 **even** or **odd**?

    _____ odd _____

31. Round 480 to the nearest hundred.

    _____ 500 _____

32. Natalie counted 32 tomatoes and 29 cucumbers in her garden. How many tomatoes and cucumbers were there in all?

    _____ 61 _____

33. Round 752 to the nearest ten.

    _____ 750 _____

    Stop

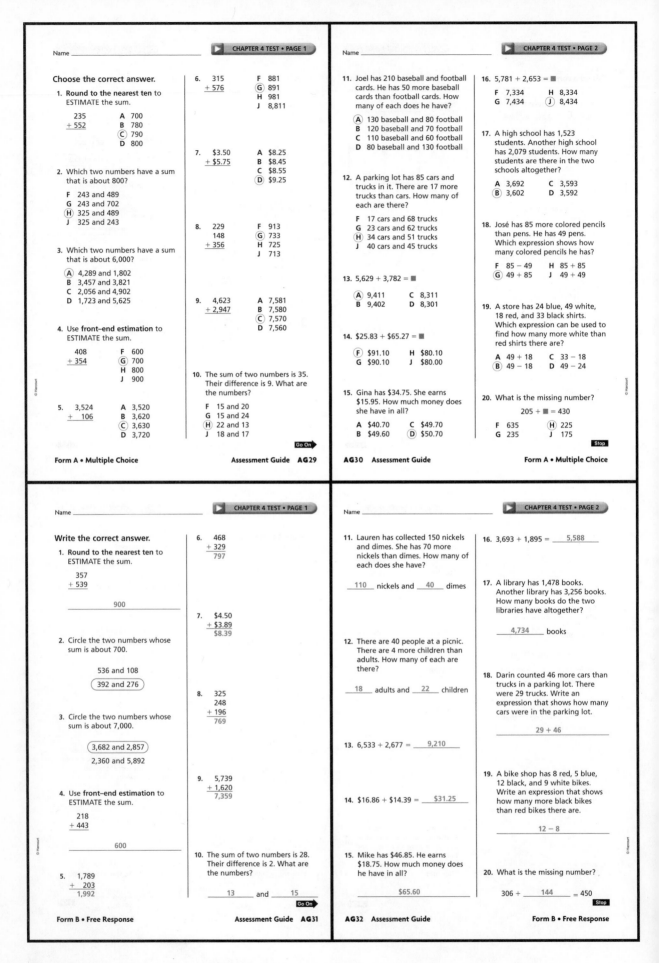

Name _____

Choose the correct answer.

1. **Round to the nearest ten** to ESTIMATE the sum.

   235
   + 552

   A 700
   B 780
   (C) 790
   D 800

2. Which two numbers have a sum that is about 800?

   F 243 and 489
   G 243 and 702
   (H) 325 and 489
   J 325 and 243

3. Which two numbers have a sum that is about 6,000?

   (A) 4,289 and 1,802
   B 3,457 and 3,821
   C 2,056 and 4,902
   D 1,723 and 5,625

4. Use **front–end estimation** to ESTIMATE the sum.

   408
   + 354

   F 600
   (G) 700
   H 800
   J 900

5. 3,524
   + 106

   A 3,520
   B 3,620
   (C) 3,630
   D 3,720

6. 315
   + 576

   F 881
   (G) 891
   H 981
   J 8,811

7. $3.50
   + $5.75

   A $8.25
   B $8.45
   C $8.55
   (D) $9.25

8. 229
   148
   + 356

   F 913
   (G) 733
   H 725
   J 713

9. 4,623
   + 2,947

   A 7,581
   B 7,580
   (C) 7,570
   D 7,560

10. The sum of two numbers is 35. Their difference is 9. What are the numbers?

    F 15 and 20
    G 15 and 24
    (H) 22 and 13
    J 18 and 17

Go On

Form A • Multiple Choice   Assessment Guide   **AG29**

Name _____

11. Joel has 210 baseball and football cards. He has 50 more baseball cards than football cards. How many of each does he have?

    (A) 130 baseball and 80 football
    B 120 baseball and 70 football
    C 110 baseball and 60 football
    D 80 baseball and 130 football

12. A parking lot has 85 cars and trucks in it. There are 17 more trucks than cars. How many of each are there?

    F 17 cars and 68 trucks
    G 23 cars and 62 trucks
    (H) 34 cars and 51 trucks
    J 40 cars and 45 trucks

13. 5,629 + 3,782 = ■

    (A) 9,411   C 8,311
    B 9,402   D 8,301

14. $25.83 + $65.27 = ■

    (F) $91.10   H $80.10
    G $90.10   J $80.00

15. Gina has $34.75. She earns $15.95. How much money does she have in all?

    A $40.70   C $49.70
    B $49.60   (D) $50.70

16. 5,781 + 2,653 = ■

    F 7,334   H 8,334
    G 7,434   (J) 8,434

17. A high school has 1,523 students. Another high school has 2,079 students. How many students are there in the two schools altogether?

    A 3,692   C 3,593
    (B) 3,602   D 3,592

18. José has 85 more colored pencils than pens. He has 49 pens. Which expression shows how many colored pencils he has?

    F 85 − 49   H 85 + 85
    (G) 49 + 85   J 49 + 49

19. A store has 24 blue, 49 white, 18 red, and 33 black shirts. Which expression can be used to find how many more white than red shirts there are?

    A 49 + 18   C 33 − 18
    (B) 49 − 18   D 49 − 24

20. What is the missing number?

    205 + ■ = 430

    F 635   (H) 225
    G 235   J 175

Stop

AG30   Assessment Guide   **Form A • Multiple Choice**

Name _____

Write the correct answer.

1. **Round to the nearest ten** to ESTIMATE the sum.

   357
   + 539

   _____900_____

2. Circle the two numbers whose sum is about 700.

   536 and 108

   (392 and 276)

3. Circle the two numbers whose sum is about 7,000.

   (3,682 and 2,857)

   2,360 and 5,892

4. Use **front–end estimation** to ESTIMATE the sum.

   218
   + 443

   _____600_____

5. 1,789
   + 203
   1,992

6. 468
   + 329
   797

7. $4.50
   + $3.89
   $8.39

8. 325
   248
   + 196
   769

9. 5,739
   + 1,620
   7,359

10. The sum of two numbers is 28. Their difference is 2. What are the numbers?

    ___13___ and ___15___

Go On

Form B • Free Response   Assessment Guide   **AG31**

Name _____

11. Lauren has collected 150 nickels and dimes. She has 70 more nickels than dimes. How many of each does she have?

    ___110___ nickels and ___40___ dimes

12. There are 40 people at a picnic. There are 4 more children than adults. How many of each are there?

    ___18___ adults and ___22___ children

13. 6,533 + 2,677 = ___9,210___

14. $16.86 + $14.39 = ___$31.25___

15. Mike has $46.85. He earns $18.75. How much money does he have in all?

    ___$65.60___

16. 3,693 + 1,895 = ___5,588___

17. A library has 1,478 books. Another library has 3,256 books. How many books do the two libraries have altogether?

    ___4,734___ books

18. Darin counted 46 more cars than trucks in a parking lot. There were 29 trucks. Write an expression that shows how many cars were in the parking lot.

    ___29 + 46___

19. A bike shop has 8 red, 5 blue, 12 black, and 9 white bikes. Write an expression that shows how many more black bikes than red bikes there are.

    ___12 − 8___

20. What is the missing number?

    306 + ___144___ = 450

Stop

AG32   Assessment Guide   **Form B • Free Response**

Choose the correct answer.

1. Which two numbers have a difference that is about 300?

   A 871 and 495
   B 839 and 272
   C 710 and 482
   (D) 792 and 546

2. **Round to the nearest hundred** to ESTIMATE the difference.

   5,679
   − 4,458

   F 200   (H) 1,200
   G 1,100   J 1,300

3. Laura watched 618 minutes of TV in May and 389 minutes in June. About how many more minutes of TV did she watch in May than in June?

   A 600   (C) 200
   B 400   D 100

4. Use **front-end estimation** to ESTIMATE the difference.

   4,727 − 1,283

   F 6,000   H 4,000
   G 5,000   (J) 3,000

5. **Round to the nearest ten** to ESTIMATE the sum.

   329
   + 544

   A 800   (C) 870
   B 850   D 880

6. **Round to the nearest dollar** to ESTIMATE the difference.

   $7.28
   − $4.80

   (F) $2.00   H $3.00
   G $2.50   J $12.00

7.   562
    − 288

   (A) 274   C 386
   B 326   D 850

8. 606 − 311 = ■

   F 315   (H) 295
   G 305   J 285

9. $8.74
    − $2.75

   (A) $5.99   C $6.09
   B $6.01   D $6.79

10.   900
     − 126

   F 764   H 864
   (G) 774   J 884

Go On ▶

Form A • Multiple Choice   **Assessment Guide AG33**

---

11. Joe has 24 CDs, 208 stickers, and 134 trading cards. How many more stickers than trading cards does he have?

   A 342   C 110
   B 184   (D) 74

12.   6,000
     − 3,859

   F 2,140
   (G) 2,141
   H 3,251
   J 3,859

13. 5,246 − 789 = ■
   (A) 4,457
   B 4,547
   C 5,447
   D 5,543

14.   5,668
     − 792

   (F) 4,876
   G 4,966
   H 5,876
   J 5,976

15. Mr. Gomez traveled 5,389 miles last year. Mr. Burton traveled 7,912 miles. How many more miles did Mr. Burton travel than Mr. Gomez?

   A 2,517   C 2,673
   (B) 2,523   D 2,677

16. Kayla lives 2,379 miles away from her grandparents. Marcus lives 1,480 miles away from his grandparents. How much farther from her grandparents does Kayla live than Marcus?

   F 1,299 miles (H) 899 miles
   G 1,119 miles J 859 miles

17. A restaurant will serve pancakes to 25 adults and 13 children. Each person will eat 2 pancakes. About how many pancakes should the cook make?

   A 50   (C) 80
   B 60   D 100

18. A store sells pens for $1.29 and paper for $1.49. Margo has $5.00. How much money will she have left if she buys paper?

   (F) $3.51   H $4.81
   G $4.61   J $6.49

For 19–20, use this information.
Tasha's dad spent $35.06 at the grocery store. Tasha's mom spent $47.50 at the hardware store.

19. Which expression can you use to show how much money Tasha's mom and dad spent in all?

   A $35.06 + $35.06
   (B) $35.06 + $47.50
   C $47.50 − $35.06
   D $47.50 + $47.50

20. How much money did Tasha's mom and dad spend in all?

   F $12.44   (H) $82.56
   G $70.12   J $95.00

Stop

AG34 Assessment Guide   **Form A • Multiple Choice**

Write the correct answer.

1. Circle the two numbers whose difference is about 200.

   571 and 308
   (425 and 216)

2. **Round to the nearest hundred** to ESTIMATE the difference.

   4,221
   − 3,449
   _____800_____

3. Martin collected 129 pounds of paper for recycling in March and 288 pounds in April. About how many more pounds did he collect in April than in March?
   Check student's estimate.

   about ___200___ pounds

4. Use **front-end estimation** to ESTIMATE the difference.

   3,829 − 1,346

   _____2,000_____

5. **Round to the nearest ten** to ESTIMATE the difference.

   373
   − 89
   _____280_____

6. **Round to the nearest dollar** to ESTIMATE the difference.

   $8.32
   − $3.97
   _____$4.00_____

7.   621
    − 454
    _____167_____

8. 508 − 133 = _____375_____

9. $7.63
    − $3.64
    _____$3.99_____

10.   800
     − 334
     _____466_____

Go On ▶

Form B • Free Response   **Assessment Guide AG35**

---

11. A nursery has 202 evergreens, 56 vines, and 129 roses. How many more evergreens than roses does the nursery have?

   _____73_____ evergreens

12.   5,000
     − 2,412
     _____2,588_____

13. 4,325 − 537 = _____3,788_____

14.   6,486
     − 663
     _____5,823_____

15. Jay flew 2,573 miles in an airplane to visit his cousins. Jody flew 1,175 miles to visit her cousins. How many more miles did Jay fly than Jody?

   _____1,398_____ miles

16. Find the difference between 5,285 and 3,492.

   _____1,793_____

17. A third-grade class is planning a family picnic for 22 students and 37 adults. Each person will drink 2 sodas at the picnic. About how many sodas will they need?
   Check student's estimate.
   about _____120_____ sodas

18. A deli sells roast beef sandwiches for $2.79 and ham sandwiches for $2.99.

   Linda has $5.00. How much money will she have left if she buys a ham sandwich?

   _____$2.01_____

For 19–20, use this information.
Kai's sister spent $19.08 at the sporting goods store. Kai's brother spent $52.66 at the art supplies store.

19. Write an expression you can use to show how much money Kai's brother and sister spent in all.

   _____$19.08 + $52.66 or $52.66 + $19.08_____

20. How much money did Kai's brother and sister spend in all?

   _____$71.74_____

Stop

AG36 Assessment Guide   **Form B • Free Response**

Name _____

Choose the correct answer.

1. Which is an equivalent set for $0.89?
   - A 8 dimes, 2 nickels
   - B 7 dimes, 5 nickels
   - (C) 3 quarters, 1 dime, 4 pennies
   - D 3 quarters, 1 nickel, 4 pennies

2. Which is the **greatest** amount of money?
   - F 3 quarters, 6 dimes, 4 nickels
   - G 3 quarters, 7 dimes, 4 nickels
   - (H) 4 quarters, 7 dimes
   - J 5 quarters, 2 dimes, 8 pennies

3. A soda costs $0.86. Darren pays with a $1 bill. Which set of coins should he get in change?
   - A 2 dimes
   - B 1 dime, 1 nickel
   - C 1 dime, 1 nickel, 4 pennies
   - (D) 1 dime, 4 pennies

4. Make a table to find how many ways you can make $0.30.
   - F 4
   - G 5
   - H 6
   - (J) more than 6

5. $5.37 + $4.72 = ■
   - (A) $10.09
   - B $9.45
   - C $9.09
   - D $9.00

6. Which is an equivalent set for $1.32?
   - F one $1 bill, 1 quarter
   - (G) one $1 bill, 3 dimes, 2 pennies
   - H one $1 bill, 6 nickels
   - J one $1 bill, 2 dimes

7. Andre spent $2.36. He gave the clerk a $5 bill. How much change should he get?
   - (A) $2.64
   - B $2.74
   - C $3.36
   - D $3.74

8. Which is the **greatest** amount of money?
   - F two $1 bills, 10 nickels
   - G two $1 bills, 5 dimes, 4 nickels
   - H two $1 bills, 6 dimes
   - (J) two $1 bills, 3 quarters

9. $8.34 − $5.65 = ■
   - (A) $2.69
   - B $2.71
   - C $2.79
   - D $3.31

10. Kamar has 2 quarters, 4 dimes, and 3 nickels. How many ways can he pay for a can of juice that costs $0.55?
    - F 2
    - G 3
    - (H) 4
    - J 5

Go On

Form A • Multiple Choice

Name _____

11. Which is an **equivalent** set for $3.55?
    - A three $1 bills, 5 dimes
    - B three $1 bills, 5 nickels
    - (C) three $1 bills, 2 quarters, 1 nickel
    - D three $1 bills, 2 quarters

12. Joan has $2.68 and Bob has $4.97. How much money do they have in all?
    - F $2.29
    - G $6.55
    - H $7.55
    - (J) $7.65

13. Pat has 3 quarters and 5 dimes. Marc has 2 quarters and 7 dimes. Sue has 5 quarters. Tim has 3 quarters and 5 nickels. Which two people have the same amount of money?
    - A Pat and Marc
    - (B) Pat and Sue
    - C Marc and Sue
    - D Tim and Marc

14. Make a table to find how many ways you can make $0.18.
    - F 10
    - (G) 6
    - H 2
    - J 1

15. A box of soap costs $4.65. Jean pays with a $5 bill. Which set of coins should she get in change?
    - A 1 quarter, 3 nickels
    - B 1 quarter, 5 pennies
    - (C) 1 quarter, 1 dime
    - D 1 quarter, 2 dimes

16. What amount of money is equivalent to four $1 bills, 1 quarter, and 4 pennies?
    - F $4.39
    - G $4.34
    - (H) $4.29
    - J $4.24

17. Kim spends $6.79. Amy spends $9.33. How much more money does Amy spend than Kim?
    - A $2.46
    - (B) $2.54
    - C $3.54
    - D $3.56

18. Kay bought a sandwich for $2.45. She paid for it with three $1 bills. Which set of coins should she get in change?
    - (F) 2 quarters, 1 nickel
    - G 4 dimes, 1 nickel
    - H 2 quarters, 4 nickels
    - J 2 quarters, 1 dime

19. Tao has 5 quarters, 2 dimes, 3 nickels, and 8 pennies. How many different sets of coins could he use to make $1.22?
    - A 10
    - B 8
    - (C) 4
    - D 1

20. Lynne has one $1 bill, 2 quarters, and 3 dimes. Leo has 5 quarters and 8 nickels. Meg has 6 quarters and 4 dimes. Jan has 2 quarters and 9 dimes. Who has the **greatest** amount of money?
    - F Lynne
    - (G) Meg
    - H Leo
    - J Jan

Stop

Form A • Multiple Choice

Name _____

Write the correct answer.

1. Circle the set of coins that is **equivalent** to $0.68.

   2 quarters, 1 nickel, 2 pennies

   OR

   (2 quarters, 1 dime, 1 nickel, 3 pennies)

2. Circle the amount that is **greater**.

   (3 quarters, 1 dime)

   OR

   2 quarters, 2 dimes, 2 nickels

3. A notebook costs $0.78. You pay with a $1 bill. What coins should you get in change?

   __2__ dimes __2__ pennies

4. Make a table to find how many ways you can make $0.12.

   __4__ ways
   (1 dime, 2 pennies; 2 nickels, 2 pennies; 1 nickel, 7 pennies; 12 pennies)

5. $4.58 + $5.61 = __$10.19__

6. Circle the set of bills and coins that is equivalent to $1.26.

   (One $1 bill, 1 quarter, 1 penny)

   OR

   One $1 bill, 1 dime, 6 pennies

7. Kendra bought a book for $3.26. She paid with a $5 bill. How much change should she get?

   __$1.74__

8. Circle the amount that is **greater**.

   (Two $1 bills, 2 quarters, 3 nickels)

   OR

   Two $1 bills, 1 quarter, 3 dimes

9. $9.27 − $6.48 = __$2.79__

10. Donna has 3 quarters, 2 dimes, and 6 pennies. She buys an orange drink for $0.65. How many quarters, dimes, and pennies could she use to make $0.65?

    __2__ quarters __1__ dime
    __5__ pennies

Go On

Form B • Free Response

Name _____

11. Circle the set that is **equivalent** to $2.45.

    Two $1 bills, 1 quarter, 2 nickels

    OR

    (Two $1 bills, 4 dimes, 1 nickel)

12. Kate has $3.29 and Joey has $4.09. How much money do they have in all?

    __$7.38__

13. Rodney has 2 quarters and 6 dimes. Don has 4 quarters and 5 nickels. Pat has 5 quarters. Which two people have the same amount of money?

    __Don__ and __Pat__

14. Make a table to find how many ways you can make $0.15.

    __6__ ways

15. Kathy buys a box of fabric softener for $4.20. She pays with a $5 bill. What coins should she get in change?

    __3__ quarters __1__ nickels

16. Make a set of $1 bills, quarters, and pennies that is **equivalent** to $3.53.

    __3__ $1 bills __2__ quarters
    __3__ pennies

17. Jason saves $7.28. Carla saves $9.12. How much more money does Carla save than Jason?

    __$1.84__

18. Calvin buys a notebook for $3.29. He pays with four $1 bills. How many of each coin should he get in change?

    __2__ quarters __2__ dimes
    __1__ pennies

19. Ryan has 6 quarters, 3 dimes, 2 nickels and 4 pennies. How many different sets of coins could he use to make $1.50?

    __2__ sets

20. Joann has two $1 bills and 3 dimes. Peter has 6 quarters and 2 dimes. Who has the **greater** amount of money?

    __Joann__

Stop

Form B • Free Response

Choose the correct answer.

1. What time does the clock show?

    A 2:14
    (B) 3:14
    C 3:46
    D 4:14

2. School starts at 8:00 A.M. After 3 hours and 35 minutes it is time for lunch. What time is lunch?

    F 10:25 A.M. H 11:05 A.M.
    G 10:35 A.M. (J) 11:35 A.M.

3. What time does the clock show?

    A 7:23
    B 5:36
    (C) 4:36
    D 4:33

4. Find the elapsed time from 8:15 P.M. to 8:45 P.M.

    F 15 minutes (H) 30 minutes
    G 20 minutes J 45 minutes

5. Which of these activities would you **most likely** do at 3:00 A.M.?

    (A) sleep   C play outside
    B go shopping D eat lunch

6. The clock shows when school starts. At what time does school start?

    F 7:25 A.M.
    G 7:30 A.M.
    (H) 7:35 A.M.
    J 8:25 A.M.

For 7–8, use this clock.

7. What time does the clock show?

    A 11:07   C 10:07
    B 10:53   (D) 9:53

8. What is another way to read the time?

    (F) 7 minutes before 10
    G 7 minutes after 10
    H 53 minutes before 11
    J 30 minutes before 10

9. A movie began at 8:05 P.M. and ended at 10:00 P.M. How long was the movie?

    A 2 hours
    (B) 1 hour 55 minutes
    C 1 hour 50 minutes
    D 1 hour 40 minutes

10. Ken started piano practice at 4:45 P.M. He practiced for 1 hour 30 minutes. At what time did he stop practicing?

    (F) 6:15 P.M. H 5:45 P.M.
    G 6:00 P.M. J 5:00 P.M.

For 11–13, use this calendar.

APRIL						
Sun	Mon	Tue	Wed	Thu	Fri	Sat
	1	2	3	4	5	6
7	8	9	10	11	12	13
14	15	16	17	18	19	20
21	22	23	24	25	26	27
28	29	30				

11. The sun was shining every day from April 3 to April 24. How many weeks of sun were there?

    A 1   B 2   (C) 3   D 4

    Go On ▶

Form A • Multiple Choice

---

12. Practice is Monday through Friday and begins on April 1. It ends on April 26. How many days of practice are there?

    F 28 (G) 20 H 12 J 11

13. Spring softball practice begins on April 5 and lasts for 2 weeks and 3 days. When does practice end?

    A April 19 C April 23
    (B) April 22 D April 24

For 14–16, use this schedule.

APPOINTMENT SCHEDULE	
Person	Time
May	8:00 A.M.–9:00 A.M.
Peg	9:00 A.M.–9:45 A.M.
Jon	9:45 A.M.–10:45 A.M.
Sue	9:45 A.M.–11:10 A.M.

14. Which person's appointment is 45 minutes long?

    F May   H Jon
    (G) Peg   J Sue

15. Which person's appointment ends at 9:00 A.M.?

    (A) May   C Jon
    B Peg   D Sue

16. Who has the longest appointment?

    F May   H Jon
    G Peg   (J) Sue

For 17–20, use the table. You may want to draw a time line to help.

YEAR OF STATEHOOD	
State	Year
Florida	1845
Idaho	1890
Indiana	1816
Oklahoma	1907
Virginia	1788
Hawaii	1959

17. Which became a state before Indiana?

    A Idaho   C Oklahoma
    B Florida   (D) Virginia

18. Which became a state between Idaho and Hawaii?

    F Indiana (H) Oklahoma
    G Florida   J Virginia

19. Wisconsin became a state in 1848. Between which two states should Wisconsin appear on a time line?

    (A) Florida and Idaho
    B Indiana and Florida
    C Virginia and Florida
    D Idaho and Oklahoma

20. New Mexico became a state in 1912. Which became a state five years before New Mexico?

    F Hawaii   H Indiana
    G Idaho   (J) Oklahoma

    Stop ■

Form A • Multiple Choice

Write the correct answer.

1. What time does the clock show?

    ___2___ : ___26___

2. A soccer game begins at 6:00 P.M. After 2 hours and 10 minutes the game ends. What time does the game end? Circle A.M. or P.M.

    ___8___ : ___10___   A.M. / (P.M.)

3. What time does the clock show?

    ___6___ : ___08___

4. Find the elapsed time from 3:30 P.M. to 3:45 P.M.

    ___15___ minutes

5. Circle the activity that would **most likely** happen at 9:00 A.M.

    go to bed for the night
    (start school day)

6. The clock shows the time the amusement park closes. What time does the amusement park close? Circle A.M. or P.M.

    ___9___ : ___30___   A.M. / (P.M.)

For 7–8, use this clock.

7. What time does the clock show?

    ___8___ : ___48___

8. Circle another way to read the time.

    12 minutes after 8
    (12 minutes before 9)

9. A play began at 7:30 P.M. and ended at 8:50 P.M. How long was the play?

    ___1___ hour(s) ___20___ minute(s)

10. Mac went outside to play with his friends at 3:30 P.M. He played for 1 hour and 45 minutes and went inside. What time did he go inside? Circle A.M. or P.M.

    ___5___ : ___15___   A.M. / (P.M.)

    Go On ▶

Form B • Free Response

For 11–13, use this calendar.

11. Practice for the winter play is Monday through Friday and begins on January 14. It ends on January 29. How many days of practice are there?

JANUARY						
S	M	T	W	T	F	S
		1	2	3	4	5
6	7	8	9	10	11	12
13	14	15	16	17	18	19
20	21	22	23	24	25	26
27	28	29	30	31		

    ___12___ days

12. It rained every day from January 3 to January 17. How many weeks did it rain?

    ___2___ weeks

13. Fred's father goes out of town for 1 week and 4 days on January 7. When will he return?

    ___January 18___

For 14–16, use this schedule.

FIELD TRIP SCHEDULE	
Activity	Time
Drive to zoo	9:45 A.M.–10:15 A.M.
Unload busses	10:15 A.M.–10:30 A.M.
See animals	10:30 A.M.–Noon
Lunch	Noon–1:00 P.M.
Watch movie	1:00 P.M.–1:45 P.M.

14. Which activity is 45 minutes?

    ___watch movie___

15. Which activity ends at 10:15?

    ___drive to zoo___

16. Which activity is the longest?

    ___see animals___

For 17–20, use the table. You may want to draw a time line to help.

YEAR ELECTED	
President	Year
Lincoln	1860
Kennedy	1960
Carter	1976
Jackson	1828
Taft	1908
Reagan	1980

17. Who was a President of the United States before Lincoln?

    ___Jackson___

18. Who was a President between Kennedy and Reagan?

    ___Carter___

19. James Garfield was elected President in 1880. Between which two presidents should Garfield appear on a time line?

    ___Lincoln___ and ___Taft___

20. John Quincy Adams was elected President in 1824. Who was elected four years later?

    ___Jackson___

    Stop ■

Form B • Free Response

Choose the correct answer.

1. A sandwich costs $4.19. Walt pays with a $5 bill. Which set of coins should he get in change?

(A) 3 quarters, 1 nickel, 1 penny
B 3 quarters, 1 nickel
C 3 quarters, 1 penny
D 2 quarters, 4 dimes

For 2–3, use the chart. You may want to draw a time line to help.

YEAR OF BIRTH	
Family Member	**Year**
Felix	1987
Mom	1962
Crystal	1996
Uncle Clayton	1971
Dad	1964

Crystal wrote down the years that some of her family members were born.

2. Who was born 23 years before Felix?

F Mom   H Uncle Clayton
G Crystal   (J) Dad

3. Aunt Dafina was born in 1973. Between which two family members should Aunt Dafina appear on a time line?

A Mom and Dad
(B) Uncle Clayton and Felix
C Mom and Uncle Clayton
D Felix and Crystal

4. 3,000
   − 1,488

F 2,612
G 2,512
H 2,488
(J) 1,512

5. Make a table to find how many different equivalent sets can be made with a value of $0.20.

A 1   C 3
B 2   (D) more than 4

6. Karen has 1 quarter and 3 dimes. Dan has 5 dimes. Who has **more** money?

(F) Karen   G Dan

7. The sum of two numbers is 29. Their difference is 3. What are the numbers?

A 14 and 15
(B) 13 and 16
C 12 and 17
D 12 and 15

8. $34.51
   + $12.69

F $46.10
G $47.10
(H) $47.20
J $57.20

Go On ▶

9. Which is an equivalent set of coins for $0.63?

A 2 quarters, 1 nickel, 3 pennies
(B) 2 quarters, 1 dime, 3 pennies
C 5 dimes, 3 pennies
D 4 dimes, 3 nickels, 3 pennies

10. Nicole buys a sandwich for $3.79. She pays with a $5 bill. How much change should she get?

F $2.21   (H) $1.21
G $1.79   J $1.09

For 11–12, use this calendar.

OCTOBER						
S	M	T	W	T	F	S
			1	2	3	4
5	6	7	8	9	10	11
12	13	14	15	16	17	18
19	20	21	22	23	24	25
26	27	28	29	30	31	

11. An art show starts on October 7 and ends on October 25. How many days long is the art show?

A 14 days   (C) 19 days
B 15 days   D 25 days

12. Peggy will move to a new house in 2 weeks. Today is October 2. When will she move?

F October 14
(G) October 16
H October 18
J October 19

13. 847
   − 568

(A) 279
B 315
C 321
D 339

14. Maria has 23 more dolls than stuffed animals. She has 18 stuffed animals. Which expression shows how many dolls she has?

(F) 18 + 23
G 18 + 18
H 23 − 18
J 23 + 23

15. Mark spent $2.75 on Monday and $4.80 on Tuesday. How much did Mark spend in all?

A $2.05
B $5.16
C $6.55
(D) $7.55

16. 618 + 199 = ■

F 861
(G) 817
H 771
J 717

Go On ▶

17. Jake buys an apple for $0.35. He pays with a $1 bill. What change should he get?

A 1 quarter, 3 dimes
B 1 quarter, 3 dimes, 1 nickel
C 2 quarters, 1 nickel
(D) 2 quarters, 1 dime, 1 nickel

18. Sue has $5.19 and Megan has $8.58. How much more money does Megan have than Sue?

F $3.49   (H) $3.39
G $3.41   J $2.39

19. Which number sentence is true?

A 752 − 147 = 615
(B) 208 + 32 + 9 = 249
C 501 − 88 = 589
D 630 + 219 = 839

20. The clock shows the time reading class begins. What time does reading class begin?

F 3:50 A.M.   (H) 10:15 A.M.
G 3:50 P.M.   J 10:15 P.M.

For 21–22, use this schedule.

MUSIC LESSONS	
Instrument	**Time**
Piano	2:00 P.M.–2:40 P.M.
Flute	2:45 P.M.–3:25 P.M.
Tuba	3:25 P.M.–4:00 P.M.
Clarinet	4:00 P.M.–5:00 P.M.

21. Which lesson is one hour long?

A piano   C tuba
B flute   (D) clarinet

22. Which lessons last the same amount of time?

(F) piano and flute
G piano and tuba
H flute and tuba
J tuba and clarinet

23. $9.21
   − $5.77

(A) $3.44
B $4.54
C $4.56
D $4.98

24. $3.78 + $6.49 = ■

(F) $10.27
G $9.27
H $9.17
J $9.07

Go On ▶

25. Use **front-end estimation** to ESTIMATE the difference.

927 − 688

(A) 300   C 100
B 200   D 60

26. 822 − 374 = ■

F 448
G 458
H 549
J 552

27. Which is the **least** amount of money?

(A) 6 dimes, 1 nickel
B 3 quarters, 1 dime
C 3 quarters, 1 nickel, 1 penny
D 2 quarters, 3 dimes

28. **Round to the nearest hundred** to ESTIMATE the sum.

  294
+ 632

F 700
G 800
(H) 900
J 1000

29. What is the elapsed time from 6:45 A.M. to 7:30 A.M.?

A 15 minutes
B 30 minutes
(C) 45 minutes
D 50 minutes

30. $7.15 − $4.29 = ■

(F) $2.86
G $3.14
H $3.86
J $3.96

For 31–32, use this clock.

31. What time does the clock show?

A 8:42   (C) 7:42
B 8:32   D 7:35

32. What is another way to read the time?

F 42 minutes before 8
(G) 18 minutes before 8
H 18 minutes after 8
J 15 minutes before 9

33. Which is an equivalent set for $2.26?

A two $1 bills, 2 dimes, 1 nickel
B one $1 bill, 2 dimes, 1 nickel, 1 penny
C 4 quarters, 2 dimes, 6 pennies
(D) two $1 bills, 2 dimes, 6 pennies

Stop ■

Name _____

Write the correct answer.

1. Phil buys a pair of sunglasses for $3.69. He pays with a $5 bill. How much change should he get?

   _____ $1.31 _____

For 2–3, use the chart. You may want to draw a time line to help.

YEAR OF BIRTH	
Family Member	**Year**
Uncle Mihir	1948
Jeevan	1997
Mom	1963
Sushila	1991
Dad	1961

Jeevan wrote down the years that some of his family members were born.

2. Who was born 36 years before Jeevan?

   _____ Dad _____

3. Aunt Vajra was born in 1952. Between which two family members should Aunt Vajra appear on a time line?

   Uncle Mihir and _____ Dad _____

4. 6,000
   − 3,561
   ‾‾‾‾‾‾‾
    2,439

5. Make a table to show how many different equivalent sets can be made with a value of $0.17.

   _____ 6 _____ sets

6. Jill has 3 quarters and 2 dimes. Jamie has 2 quarters, 2 dimes, and 3 nickels. Who has **less** money?

   _____ Jamie _____

7. The sum of two numbers is 26. Their difference is 4. What are the numbers?

   _____ 11 _____ and _____ 15 _____

8. $56.24
   + $14.87
   ‾‾‾‾‾‾‾
    $71.11

Go On

Form B • Free Response
Assessment Guide **AG49**

Name _____

9. Circle the set of coins with a value of $0.80.

   2 quarters, 2 dimes

   OR

   (3 quarters, 1 nickel)

10. Maggie buys a brush for $4.18. She pays with a $5 bill. How much change should she get?

    _____ $0.82 _____

For 11–13, use this calendar.

APRIL						
S	M	T	W	T	F	S
					1	2
3	4	5	6	7	8	9
10	11	12	13	14	15	16
17	18	19	20	21	22	23
24	25	26	27	28	29	30

11. Softball practice ends 4 weeks after April 2. On what date does softball practice end?

    _____ April 30 _____

12. Today is April 3. The science test is in 1 week and 2 days. Write the date of the science test.

    _____ April 12 _____

13. 621
    − 256
    ‾‾‾‾‾
     365

14. Paul has 15 more action figures than he has cars. He has 8 cars. Write an expression to show how many action figures he has.

    _____ 15 + 8 _____

15. A coloring book costs $2.89. A box of colored pencils costs $1.79. How much do the items cost in all?

    _____ $4.68 _____

16. 589
    + 236
    ‾‾‾‾‾
     825

17. A large can of tomato juice costs $0.79. Joey pays with a $1 bill. Circle the change he should get.

    (2 dimes, 1 penny)

    OR

    3 dimes, 1 penny

Go On

AG50 Assessment Guide
Form B • Free Response

Name _____

18. Judy has $7.25. Katie has $8.45. How much more money does Katie have than Judy?

    _____ $1.20 _____

19. Circle the number sentence that is true.

    782 − 359 = 427

    (307 + 45 + 8 = 360)

20. Write the time shown on the clock.

    _____ 11:15 _____

For 21–22, use this schedule.

LIBRARY STORY TIME	
Group	**Time (A.M.)**
Ages 3–4	9:00–9:20
Ages 5–6	9:20–9:50
Ages 7–8	9:50–10:20
Ages 9–10	10:20–11:00

21. Which group's story time lasts 40 minutes?

    Ages _____ 9–10 _____

22. Which two groups' story times last for the same amount of time?

    Ages _____ 5–6 _____

    and

    Ages _____ 7–8 _____

23. $7.31
    − $3.46
    ‾‾‾‾‾‾
     $3.85

24. $4.52 + $5.86 = _____ $10.38 _____

25. Use **front-end estimation** to ESTIMATE the difference.

    783 − 512 = _____ 200 _____

26. 936 − 457 = _____ 479 _____

Go On

Form B • Free Response
Assessment Guide **AG51**

Name _____

27. Circle the **least** amount of money.

    (2 quarters, 2 dimes, 1 nickel)

    OR

    3 quarters, 1 dime

28. **Round to the nearest hundred** to ESTIMATE the sum.

     287
    + 516
    ‾‾‾‾‾

    _____ 800 _____

29. Write the elapsed time from 5:45 P.M. to 6:15 P.M.

    _____ 30 _____ minutes

30. $5.21 − $2.32 = _____ $2.89 _____

For 31–32, use this clock.

31. Write the time.

    _____ 3:55 _____

32. Circle another way to read the time.

    5 minutes after 4

    OR

    (5 minutes before 4)

33. Circle the equivalent set for $3.35.

    Three $1 bills, 1 quarter, 1 nickel

    OR

    (Three $1 bills, 3 dimes, 1 nickel)

Stop

AG52 Assessment Guide
Form B • Free Response

Assessment Guide AG 221

Choose the correct answer.

1. Which number sentence matches the problem?

$7 + 7 + 7 = 21$

A $20 + 1 = 21$
(B) $3 \times 7 = 21$
C $7 \times 7 = 49$
D $14 + 14 = 28$

2. What are the factors in the number sentence $5 \times 8 = 40$?

F 5 and 40   H 8 and 40
(G) 5 and 8   J 4 and 0

3. Which multiplication sentence matches the array?

A $2 + 8 = 10$
(B) $2 \times 8 = 16$
C $8 + 8 = 16$
D $2 \times 2 = 4$

4. $3 \times 9 = $ ■

F 12   (H) 27
G 18   J 39

5. Tom and Kelli walked to the store in 15 minutes. At the store they bought 2 candy bars. How much did they spend in all?

A $30
B $17
C 30 minutes
(D) Too little information

6.

4 groups of 5 equals ■

F 9   (H) 20
G 14   J 45

7. Soccer practice lasts for 2 hours, 3 nights a week. Izumi also spends 4 hours playing basketball. How many hours does he practice soccer in a week?

A 5
(B) 6
C 10
D Too little information

8.   9
   $\times 2$

F 29
(G) 18
H 16
J 11

9. What is the missing factor?

$7 \times 3 = $ ■ $\times 7$

A 6   C 4
B 5   (D) 3

10.

$5 \times 2 = $ ■

F 7   H 20
(G) 10   J 25

Go On

Form A • Multiple Choice

11. Lisa bought 2 packages of pencils. There are 6 pencils in each package. How many pencils did Lisa buy?

A 4   (C) 12
B 8   D 26

12. There are 5 snack bars in each package. Each package costs $2.00. How many bars are in 4 packages?

F 9
G 11
(H) 20
J 22

13. There are 6 apples in a box. If Ben buys 3 boxes, how many apples will he buy?

(A) 18   C 6
B 9   D 3

14. Doug bought 3 packages of socks. There are 4 pairs of socks in each package. How many pairs of socks did he buy?

F 3   H 7
G 4   (J) 12

15. ■ rows of ■ = ■

(A) 3 rows of 9 = 27
B 3 rows of 9 = 39
C 2 rows of 8 = 28
D 2 rows of 9 = 29

16. Marta has 5 pairs of shoes. How many shoes does she have?

F 5   (H) 10
G 7   J 25

17. It takes 2 eggs to make each cake. A box of cake mix costs $0.79. Teri needs to make 4 cakes. How many eggs will she need?

A 2
B 6
(C) 8
D Too little information

18. Which number sentence is another way to find $3 \times 5 = 15$?

(F) $5 + 5 + 5 = 15$
G $7 + 8 = 15$
H $3 \times 3 = 9$
J $5 \times 5 = 15$

19. Margo spends 3 hours each day, 7 days a week practicing ice-skating. How many hours does she spend ice-skating in one week?

A 7   C 14
B 10   (D) 21

20. $6 \times 5 = $ ■

F 14   (H) 30
G 24   J 68

Stop

Form A • Multiple Choice

Write the correct answer.

1. Write a multiplication sentence that matches the problem.

$3 + 3 + 3 + 3 + 3 = 15$

_5_ × _3_ = _15_

2. What are the factors in the number sentence $4 \times 2 = 8$?

_4_ and _2_

3. Complete the multiplication sentence that matches the array.

$2 \times$ _6_ = _12_

4. $3 \times 6 = $ _18_

5. Write whether the problem has **too much, too little,** or **the right amount** of information. Solve if you can.

Richard has 2 books of stamps. He bought 10 new stamps. How much did the stamps cost?

too little

6.

2 groups of 5 equals _10_

7. Write whether the problem has **too much, too little,** or **the right amount** of information. Solve if you can.

Mary performed in a 2-hour play 4 nights last week. She spent 7 hours ice-skating. How many hours did she perform in the play last week?

too much; 8 hours

8.   8
   $\times 2$
   16

9. What is the missing factor?

$8 \times 3 = $ _3_ $\times 8$

10.

$4 \times 5 = $ _20_

Go On

Form B • Free Response

11. Ron bought 2 boxes of muffins. There are 9 muffins in each box. How many muffins did he buy?

_18_ muffins

12. There are 5 green peppers in each bag. A bag costs $2.00. How many peppers are in 3 bags?

_15_ peppers

13. Glasses come in cartons of 8. If Joe buys 3 cartons, how many glasses will he buy?

_24_ glasses

14. There are 3 flowers in each pot. You buy 2 pots. How many flowers will you have?

_6_ flowers

15.

5 rows of _6_ = _30_

16. Greta has 5 packages of balloons. Each package has 8 balloons in it. How many balloons does Greta have?

_40_ balloons

17. Write whether the problem has **too much, too little,** or **the right amount** of information. Solve if you can.

There are 4 bags of crackers inside each box. Joe buys 2 boxes. How many bags of crackers does he have?

the right amount; 8 bags

18. Circle the number sentence that is another way to find $2 \times 7 = 14$.

($7 + 7 = 14$) $4 + 10 = 14$

19. Larry has 3 boxes with 3 toy cars in each box. How many cars does he have?

_9_ cars

20.

$4 \times 3 = $ _12_

Stop

Form B • Free Response

Name _____

Choose the correct answer.

1. 1
    × 4

    A 1   (C) 4
    B 3   D   5

2. 8 × 1 = ■

    F 0   (H) 8
    G 1   J   9

3. What is the missing factor?

    5 × ■ = 25

    A 2   C   4
    B 3   (D) 5

4. 6 × 1 = ■

    F 7   H   5
    (G) 6   J   0

5. What are the next 3 numbers in the pattern?

    5, 7, 9, 11, ____, ____, ____

    A 12, 14, 16
    (B) 13, 15, 17
    C 14, 17, 20
    D 15, 19, 23

6. What is the product of 4 and 7?

    F 3   (H) 28
    G 11   J   47

7. Amy made 4 cups of hot chocolate. She put 4 small marshmallows in each cup. How many marshmallows did she use?

    A 20   C   12
    (B) 16   D   8

8. Jill is thinking of a number pattern. The first four numbers in her pattern are 5, 10, 15, and 20. What is a rule for her pattern?

    F   multiply by 2
    (G) add 5
    H   subtract 4
    J   add 10

9. A classroom has 6 rows with 4 desks in each row. How many desks are in the room?

    (A) 24   C   12
    B   20   D   10

10. What is the product of 0 and 8?

    (F) 0   H   8
    G   4   J   12

Go On

Form A • Multiple Choice   **Assessment Guide   AG57**

Name _____

11. When 8 is multiplied by a number, the answer is 24. What is the number?

    A 2   C   4
    (B) 3   D   5

12. Each package of pens contains 3 blue and 5 black pens. How many pens are in 4 packages?

    F 12   H   23
    G 17   (J) 32

13. Abby is thinking of a number pattern. Her pattern starts with 8, 14, 20, 26, and 32. Which number doesn't fit the pattern if it continues?

    A 56   C   50
    (B) 52   D   44

14. 9 × ■ = 0

    (F) 0   H   9
    G   1   J   90

15. Eric has 4 nickels. Each nickel is worth 5 cents. How much money does Eric have?

    A 4¢   C   9¢
    B 5¢   (D) 20¢

16. The product of 2 and another factor is 18. Which number sentence could be used to find the missing factor?

    F   2 + ■ = 18
    (G) 2 × ■ = 18
    H   18 − ■ = 2
    J   ■ − 2 = 18

17. There are 4 apartments in each building. How many apartments are there in 9 buildings?

    A 5   C   18
    B 13   (D) 36

18. Phil's mom buys 5 boxes of cereal. Each box should have 1 prize in it. Phil found 0 prizes in each box. How many prizes did he get?

    F 6   H   4
    G 5   (J) 0

19. Josh's number pattern starts with 38, 36, 37, 35, 36, 34, and 35. What are the next 3 numbers in the number pattern?

    A 36, 35, 37
    (B) 33, 34, 32
    C 34, 36, 35
    D 31, 32, 29

20. A number multiplied by 4 equals 12. What is the number?

    F 2   H   8
    (G) 3   J   16

Stop

AG58   Assessment Guide   **Form A • Multiple Choice**

Name _____

Write the correct answer.

1. 6
    × 4
    ——
    24

2. 6 × 1 = ___6___

3. Write the missing factor.

    4 × ___4___ = 16

4. 8 × 1 = ___8___

5. Write the next 3 numbers in the pattern.

    6, 9, 12, 15, _18_, _21_, _24_

6. Write the product of 4 and 5.

    ___20___

7. Andrea is planting tulips. She plants 4 bulbs in each hole. She dug 7 holes. How many bulbs does she need?

    ___28___ bulbs

8. Karen is thinking of a number pattern. The first four numbers in her pattern are 20, 17, 14, and 11. What is a rule for her pattern?

    ___subtract 3___

9. Jim arranges his model planes in 4 rows with 3 planes in each row. How many model planes does he have?

    ___12___ planes

10. What is the product of 0 and 3?

    ___0___

11. When 5 is multiplied by another factor, the answer is 10. What is the other factor?

    ___2___

Go On

Form B • Free Response   **Assessment Guide   AG59**

Name _____

12. John bought 4 bags of bagels. Each bag contains 8 bagels. How many bagels did he buy in all?

    ___32___ bagels

13. Alex is thinking of a number pattern. His pattern is 5, 9, 13, 17, and 21. Circle the number that doesn't fit in the pattern if it continues.

    (26)   33   37

14. 8 × ___0___ = 0

15. Bruce has 4 boxes. He puts 1 car in each box. How many cars does he have in all?

    ___4___ cars

16. The product of 3 and another factor is 15. Circle the number sentence that could be used to find the missing factor.

    3 + ■ = 15
    (3 × ■ = 15)

17. There are 9 cookies on each tray. How many cookies are there on 4 trays?

    ___36___ cookies

18. A store gave free bags to its customers. Some of the bags had a prize inside. Chris opened 6 bags. Each bag had 0 prizes inside. How many prizes did Chris find?

    ___0___ prizes

19. Paul's number pattern is 34, 32, 29, 27, 24 and 22. What are the next three numbers in the pattern?

    _19_, _17_, _14_

20. A number multiplied by 5 equals 25. What is the number?

    ___5___

Stop

AG60   Assessment Guide   **Form B • Free Response**

Assessment Guide   AG 223

Choose the correct answer.

1. $2 \times 7 = \blacksquare$
   A 5   (C) 14
   B 9   D 27

2. Which of the following is true?
   F $7 \times 3 > 4 \times 6$
   G $7 \times 5 < 6 \times 5$
   H $8 \times 4 = 7 \times 6$
   (J) $3 \times 8 = 4 \times 6$

3. What is the missing factor?
   $5 \times \blacksquare = 30$
   (A) 6   C 4
   B 5   D 3

4. Which symbol makes the following true?
   $7 \times 7 \bullet 6 \times 8$
   F $<$ (G) $>$ H $=$

5. Keith's father works 6 days each week. How many days does his father work in 7 weeks?
   A 13   (C) 42
   B 21   D 67

6. 9
   $\times 6$
                F 48
                (G) 54
                H 56
                J 63

7. Steve bought 7 boxes of cupcakes. There were 4 cupcakes in each box. Twelve cupcakes had white icing and the rest had chocolate icing. How many had chocolate icing?
   A 13   C 20
   (B) 16   D 28

8. What is the product of 8 and 9?
   F 1   (H) 72
   G 17   J 89

9. What number completes the number sentence?
   $3 \times \blacksquare = 20 + 1$
   A 10   C 8
   B 9   (D) 7

10. The product of two factors is 54. One of the factors is 6. What is the other factor?
    F 6   H 8
    G 7   (J) 9

Go On

---

11. Emily has 2 jobs. At one job she works 6 hours each day, 3 days a week. At her other job she works 8 hours each day, 2 days a week. How many hours does she work in one week?
    A 36   C 30
    (B) 34   D 28

12. Each bicycle has 2 wheels. What expression shows how many wheels there are on 6 bicycles?
    F $2 + 6$
    G $6 - 2$
    (H) 6×2
    J 6×6

13. There are 4 small pizzas in each box. Mrs. Owens buys 8 boxes. How many pizzas will she have?
    A 4   C 24
    B 12   (D) 32

14. Danny has 48 plants to arrange in his garden. He wants 6 rows with the same number of plants in each row. How many plants should be in each row?
    F 9   H 7
    (G) 8   J 6

15. Each roll of ribbon has 9 yards on it. Megan needs 63 yards. How many rolls should she buy in order to have enough?
    (A) 7   C 5
    B 6   D 4

16. Each week, Nate goes to school 5 days and spends 2 days at home. How many days does he spend at school in 7 weeks?
    F 14   (H) 35
    G 17   J 49

17. Cheryl was playing a math game. The answer was 40. Which of these could have been the problem?
    A $8 \times 6 = \blacksquare$ C $7 \times 6 = \blacksquare$
    (B) $8 \times 5 = \blacksquare$ D $7 \times 5 = \blacksquare$

For 18–20, use the pictograph.

FAVORITE PLACES TO VISIT	
City Park	🚗
Lake	🚗 🚗 🚗
Mountains	🚗 🚗
Amusement Park	🚗 🚗 🚗 🚗 🚗
Zoo	🚗 🚗 🚗 🚗 🚗
Nature Trail	🚗 🚗

Key: Each 🚗 = 4 votes.

18. How many more votes did the lake receive than the nature trail?
    F 1   (H) 4
    G 2   J 10

19. How many people altogether voted for the amusement park and the zoo?
    A 32   C 36
    (B) 34   D 40

20. Which three numbers represented on the pictograph are multiples of 4?
    F 4, 8, 10   H 8, 14, 16
    G 8, 10, 16   (J) 8, 12, 20

Stop

Write the correct answer.

1. $3 \times 7 = \underline{\quad 21 \quad}$

2. Compare. Write $<$, $>$, or $=$ in the $\bigcirc$.
   $3 \times 6 \;(>)\; 2 \times 7$

3. What is the missing factor?
   $6 \times \underline{\quad 4 \quad} = 24$

4. Compare. Write $<$, $>$, or $=$ in the $\bigcirc$.
   $7 \times 6 \;(<)\; 6 \times 8$

5. Carl has 6 pages of stickers. Each page holds 6 stickers. How many stickers does he have?
   $\underline{\quad 36 \quad}$ stickers

6. 5
   $\times 6$
   $\overline{\;30\;}$

7. Kim bought 7 packages of pens. There were 5 pens in each package. Twenty pens were red and the rest were blue. How many blue pens were there?
   $\underline{\quad 15 \quad}$ blue pens

8. What is the product of 8 and 5?
   $\underline{\quad 40 \quad}$

9. Complete.
   $7 \times \underline{\quad 1 \quad} = 2 + 5$

10. The product of two factors is 12. One of the factors is 6. What is the other factor?
    $\underline{\quad 2 \quad}$

11. Alex bought 6 containers of flowers. There were 4 flowers in each container. He also bought 8 containers that had 2 flowers in each container. How many flowers did he buy in all?
    $\underline{\quad 40 \quad}$ flowers

Go On

---

12. There are 3 apples in each box. Circle the expression that shows how many apples there are in 6 boxes.
    3×2 (6×3)

13. Kyle buys 8 packages of hamburger patties. Each package contains 4 patties. How many hamburger patties does he buy?
    $\underline{\quad 32 \quad}$ hamburger patties

14. Danielle has 24 CDs to arrange. She wants 8 CDs on each shelf. How many shelves will she need?
    $\underline{\quad 3 \quad}$ shelves

15. Each roll of wrapping paper is 7 feet long. How many feet of wrapping paper are there on 4 of these rolls?
    $\underline{\quad 28 \quad}$ feet

16. There are 7 days in a week. How many days are there in 8 weeks?
    $\underline{\quad 56 \quad}$ days

17. Molly was playing a math game. The answer was 64. Circle the problem with that answer.
    (8×8) 8×9

For 18–20, use the pictograph.

AMUSEMENT PARK RIDES SEATING CAPACITY	
Roller Coaster	🧍🧍🧍🧍🧍🧍
Spider	🧍🧍🧍
Raging River	🧍🧍🧍
Water Plunge	🧍🧍
Merry-Go-Round	🧍🧍🧍🧍🧍
Flying Carpet	🧍

Key: Each 🧍 = 4 seats.

18. How many more people can ride the Spider compared to the Flying Carpet?
    $\underline{\quad 10 \quad}$

19. Janet's class has 22 students. Which rides have enough seats for everyone in her class?
    $\underline{\quad Merry\text{-}Go\text{-}Round \quad}$
    $\underline{\quad and\ Roller\ Coaster \quad}$

20. Zach is waiting in line to ride the Raging River ride. There are 34 people in front of him. How many times will the seats fill up before he gets on the ride?
    $\underline{\quad 2 \quad}$

Stop

Name _____

Choose the correct answer.

1. What is the missing factor?

■ × 9 = 54

A 8　　　(C) 6
B 7　　　D 5

2. Find the product.

3 × (5 × 2) = ■

F 56　　　H 13
(G) 30　　J 10

3. What is the rule for the table?

Packages	1	2	3	4	5	6
Flowers	6	12	18	24	30	36

(A) Multiply the number of packages by 6.
B Add 5 to the number of packages.
C Subtract 5 from the number of flowers.
D Multiply the number of packages by 5.

4. What is the rule for the table?

Weeks	1	2	3	4	5	6
Days	7	14	21	28	35	42

F Multiply the number of days by 7.
G Add 6 to the number of weeks.
(H) Multiply the number of weeks by 7.
J Subtract 6 from the number of days.

For 5–6, find the missing number for each _____.

5. 2 × (4 × 3) = (_____ × 4) × 3

(A) 2　　　C 4
B 3　　　D 12

6. 7 × _____ = 8 × 7

F 1　　　(H) 8
G 4　　　J 56

For 7–8, tell what property you would use to find the product.

7. 1 × 8

A Associative Property
(B) Identity Property
C Distributive Property
D Commutative Property

8. 9 × 4

F Associative Property
G Identity Property
H Zero Property
(J) Distributive Property

For 9–10, use this table.

Packages	1	2	3	4	5	6
Cupcakes	2	4	6	■	■	■

9. Which numbers complete the table?

A 7, 8, 9　　　C 12, 14, 16
(B) 8, 10, 12　　D 9, 12, 15

10. Suppose you had 16 cupcakes. How many packages would you have?

F 7　　　H 9
(G) 8　　　J 10

Go On ►

Form A • Multiple Choice　　　　Assessment Guide　**AG 65**

Name _____

11. Ellen has $35. A pair of sunglasses sells for $7. A hair bow sells for $2. She buys 2 pairs of sunglasses and 4 hair bows. How much money does she have left?

A $3　　　C $8
B $7　　　(D) $13

12. The product of a number and 8 is 72. What is the number?

(F) 9　　　H 64
G 10　　　J 80

13. There are 4 cupcakes in each box. Each cupcake has 1 cherry on top. Crystal buys 5 boxes of cupcakes. How many cherries are there?

A 9　　　(C) 20
B 10　　　D 24

14. Adult tickets cost $3 each. Student tickets cost $2 each. How much will 5 adult tickets and 10 student tickets cost?

(F) $35　　　H $50
G $40　　　J $56

15. Which numbers complete the table?

Octopuses	3	4	5	6	7	8
Arms	24	32	40	■	■	■

A 44, 48, 52
B 45, 50, 55
C 46, 52, 58
(D) 48, 56, 64

16. Find the product.

(3 × 3) × 9 = ■

F 27　　　H 80
G 71　　　(J) 81

17. Which symbol makes the number sentence true?

18 + 15 ● 3 × 10

(A) >　　　B <　　　C =

18. Kate had 50 stickers. She gave 15 away on Monday and 24 on Tuesday. How many stickers does she have left?

(F) 11　　　H 59
G 21　　　J 81

19. A nickel has the same value as 5 pennies. John has 9 nickels. How many pennies would this be?

A 14　　　(C) 45
B 40　　　D 50

20. A restaurant sells roast beef sandwiches for $5 each. There are 2 sandwiches in a bag. Which expression shows how much it would cost to buy 4 bags?

(F) (2 × 5) × 4
G (4 + 2) × 5
H 4 + (2 × 5)
J 4 × (2 + 5)

Stop ■

AG 66　Assessment Guide　　　　　　　**Form A • Multiple Choice**

Name _____

Write the correct answer.

1. Write the missing factor.

_____4_____ × 9 = 36

2. Find the product.

4 × (3 × 1) = ___12___

3. Circle the rule for the table.

Flowers	2	3	4	5	6
Petals	10	15	20	25	30

(Multiply the flowers by 5.)
Add 8 to flowers.

4. Write a rule to find the number of pennies.

Dimes	1	2	3	4	5
Pennies	10	20	30	40	50

Multiply the number of dimes by 10.

5. Write the missing number.

4 × 6 = (4 × ___5___) + (4 × 1)

6. Write the missing number.

4 × (3 × 7) = (___4___ × 3) × 7

For 7–8, write the property you would use to find the product.

7. 7 × (5 × 3)

___Associative Property___

8. 8 × 6

___Distributive Property___

For 9–10, use this table.

Packages	2	3	4	5	6	7
Markers	8	12	16	■	■	■

9. Complete the table.

___20___, ___24___, ___28___

10. Suppose you have 32 markers. How many packages would you have?

___8___ packages

Go On ►

Form B • Free Response　　　　Assessment Guide　**AG 67**

Name _____

11. Kelly has $40. A pair of socks costs $2. A notebook costs $3. She buys 3 pairs of socks and 4 notebooks. How much money does she have left?

___$22___

12. The product of two factors is 45. One of the factors is 5. What is the other factor?

___9___

13. Evan gave each of his 2 friends 2 packages of sports cards. Each package contains 5 cards. How many cards did he give away?

___20___ cards

14. Large balls cost $5 each and small balls cost $2 each. How much would 4 large balls and 6 small balls cost?

___$32___

15. Complete the table.

Teams	1	2	3	4	5	6
Players	9	18	27	■	■	■

___36___, ___45___, ___54___

16. Find the product.

(4 × 2) × 8 = ___64___

17. Compare. Write <, >, or = in the ○.

13 + 17 (<) 4 × 10

18. Joel found 35 seashells. He gave his mother 10 and his grandmother 8. How many seashells does he have left?

___17___ seashells

19. A dime has the same value as 10 pennies. Bob has 9 dimes. How many pennies would this be?

___90___ pennies

20. Mrs. Gomez has 2 children. Each child needs 3 notebooks. The notebooks cost $2 each. Write an expression to show how much it will cost Mrs. Gomez to buy the notebooks.

___2___ × ___3___ × ___2___

Stop ■

AG 68　Assessment Guide　　　　　　　**Form B • Free Response**

Assessment Guide　AG 225

Choose the correct answer.

1. The product of 3 and another factor is 15. What is the other factor?

   A 18
   B 12
   Ⓒ 5
   D 4

2. 8
   × 3

   F 11
   G 16
   H 21
   Ⓙ 24

3. Which is true?

   Ⓐ 8 × 5 < 7 × 6
   B 8 × 3 = 7 × 4
   C 7 × 4 = 5 × 6
   D 6 × 4 > 8 × 4

4. What is a rule for this table?

Box	1	2	3	4	5
Glasses	4	8	12	16	20

   F Add 4 to the number of boxes.
   G Add 3 to the number of boxes.
   H Subtract 3 from the number of glasses.
   Ⓙ Multiply the number of boxes by 4.

5. Each school van seats 6 students. If there are 9 school vans, how many students can ride in the vans?

   A 3
   B 15
   Ⓒ 54
   D 58

For 6, use the pictograph.

WAYS TO TRAVEL	
Plane	☺ ☺ ☺ ☺ ☺
Car	☺ ☺ ☺
Train	☺ ☺ ☺ ☺
Boat	☺

Key: Each ☺ = 3 votes.

6. How many more people prefer to travel by train than by boat?

   F 12
   Ⓖ 9
   H 6
   J 3

7. Matt and Jackie have 3 dogs and 2 cats. They went shopping for pet food. How much would 2 bags of pet food cost?

   A $4
   B $5
   C $10
   Ⓓ Too little information

Go On

8. Three friends each wear 2 bracelets on each of their wrists. Which expression shows how to find how many bracelets they are wearing in all?

   F (2 + 3) + 2
   G (2 × 3) + 3
   Ⓗ (2 × 2) × 3
   J 3 × (2 + 1)

9. What are the next 3 numbers in the pattern?

   9, 12, 15, 18, ■, ■, ■

   A 19, 20, 21
   Ⓑ 21, 24, 27
   C 22, 26, 30
   D 23, 28, 33

10. What is the missing factor?

    3 × 4 = 4 × ■

    F 3
    G 4
    H 5
    J 6

11. What is the product of 4 and 5?

    A 1
    B 9
    Ⓒ 20
    D 45

12. What symbol makes this true?

    8 × 4 ● 7 × 5

    Ⓕ <   G >   H =

13. 8 × (4 × 1) = ■

    A 13
    Ⓑ 32
    C 40
    D 64

14. What symbol makes this true?

    5 × 0 ● 7 × 1

    Ⓕ <   G >   H =

15. There are 5 bananas in each bunch. Taylor buys 2 bunches. How many bananas does she buy?

    A 3
    B 7
    Ⓒ 10
    D 12

16. Which property would you use to find the product of 5 × 1?

    Ⓕ Identity Property
    G Zero Property
    H Distributive Property
    J Associative Property

Go On

17. Jeff is thinking of a number pattern. The first four numbers are 7, 11, 15, and 19. What is a rule for his pattern?

    Ⓐ Add 4.
    B Subtract 5.
    C Add 3.
    D Multiply by 2.

18. 4
    × 2

    F 2
    G 4
    H 6
    Ⓙ 8

19. ■ = 10 × 9

    A 19   Ⓒ 90
    B 60   D 109

20. Diane has 2 packages of socks. Each package contains 2 pairs of white socks, 1 pair of blue socks, and 1 pair of pink socks. How many pairs of socks does she have in all?

    F 10 pairs of socks
    Ⓖ 8 pairs of socks
    H 6 pairs of socks
    J 4 pairs of socks

21. An adult's dinner costs $7. A child's dinner costs $4. How much would it cost for 2 adults and 3 children to eat dinner?

    A $34   Ⓒ $26
    B $29   D $16

22. What is the missing factor?

    ■ × 6 = 30

    F 4   H 6
    Ⓖ 5   J 7

23. Mr. Bloom works 8 hours each day, 5 days a week. It takes him 1 hour to get to work. How many hours does he work each week?

    A 13 hours
    Ⓑ 40 hours
    C 45 hours
    D Too little information

24. Which numbers complete the table?

Tables	1	2	3	4	5	6
Legs	3	6	9	■	■	■

    F 10, 11, 12
    G 11, 14, 17
    Ⓗ 12, 15, 18
    J 12, 16, 19

Go On

25. What number completes the number sentence?

    4 × ■ = 20 + 8

    A 5
    B 6
    Ⓒ 7
    D 8

26. What is the missing factor?

    1 × ■ = 5

    F 4
    Ⓖ 5
    H 6
    J 7

27. What multiplication sentence matches the array?

    ■ ■ ■ ■ ■ ■ ■
    ■ ■ ■ ■ ■ ■ ■

    A 2 + 7 = 9
    B 2 × 3 = 6
    C 7 + 7 = 14
    Ⓓ 2 × 7 = 14

28. 7
    × 7

    F 14
    G 28
    Ⓗ 49
    J 56

29. What is the missing factor?

    ■ × 10 = 70

    A 6
    Ⓑ 7
    C 9
    D 60

30. What is the product of 0 and 6?

    Ⓕ 0
    G 3
    H 6
    J 9

31. There are 8 hamburger buns in each package. How many buns are in 6 packages?

    A 14
    Ⓑ 48
    C 56
    D 64

32. What symbol makes this true?

    5 + 15 ● 2 × 10

    F <   G >   Ⓗ =

33. What number sentence matches the problem?

    6 + 6 + 6 + 6 = 24

    Ⓐ 4 × 6 = 24
    B 6 × 3 = 18
    C 12 + 10 = 24
    D 30 − 6 = 24

Stop

Write the correct answer.

1. The product of 4 and another factor is 12. What is the other factor?

   _____ 3 _____

2.
   $$\begin{array}{r} 6 \\ \times\,3 \\ \hline 18 \end{array}$$

3. Which is true? Circle it.

   $6 \times 7 > 5 \times 9$

   $\boxed{3 \times 8 = 6 \times 4}$

4. Write a rule for this table.

Boxes	1	2	3	4
Invitations	8	16	24	32

   _____ Multiply the number of _____

   _____ boxes by 8. _____

5. Six students each sold 8 items for a playground fund-raiser. How many items did they sell in all?

   _____ 48 _____

For 6, use the pictograph.

NUMBER OF VOLUNTEERS	
School Clean-Up	🧍 🧍 🧍
Hospital Visit	🧍 🧍
Park Clean-Up	🧍 🧍 🧍 🧍 🧍
Food Pantry	🧍 🧍 🧍 🧍

Key: Each 🧍 = 4 people.

6. How many more people volunteered at the food pantry than visited the hospital?

   _____ 8 _____ more people

7. Write whether the problem has **too much, too little,** or **the right amount** of information.

   Jason lives 8 miles from school. Anna lives 5 miles from school. How far is the school from the library?

   _____ too little information _____

8. Mrs. Martinez has 2 daughters. She buys 2 packages of hair bows for each daughter. Each package has 5 bows. Circle the expression that shows how many hair bows there are in all.

   $2 + (2 \times 5)$

   $\boxed{2 \times (2 \times 5)}$

   `Go On`

---

9. Write the rule and the next three numbers in this pattern.

   _____ Add 5. _____

   8, 13, 18, 23, __28__ , __33__ , __38__

10. Write the missing factor.

    $9 \times 3 = 3 \times \underline{\quad 9 \quad}$

11. What is the product of 4 and 9?

    _____ 36 _____

12. Compare. Write <, >, or = in the ◯.

    $6 \times 5 \;\boxed{>}\; 4 \times 7$

13. $7 \times (1 \times 3) = \underline{\quad 21 \quad}$

14. Compare. Write <, >, or = in the ◯.

    $3 \times 1 \;\boxed{>}\; 9 \times 0$

15. There are 6 jars of paint in each box. Jarred has 2 boxes. How many jars of paint does he have?

    _____ 12 _____ jars

16. Circle the property you would use to find the product of 9×0.

    Identity Property

    $\boxed{\text{Zero Property}}$

    Associative Property

    Distributive Property

17. Doug is thinking of a number pattern. The first four numbers are 2, 8, 14, and 20. Write a rule for the pattern.

    _____ Add 6. _____

    `Go On`

18.
    $$\begin{array}{r} 5 \\ \times\,2 \\ \hline 10 \end{array}$$

19. $3 \times 10 = \underline{\quad 30 \quad}$

20. Diane has 4 boxes of fruit drinks. Each box contains 2 cherry, 2 grape, and 2 orange drinks. How many drinks does she have in all?

    _____ 24 _____ fruit drinks

21. A large poster costs $4. A small poster costs $2. How much would it cost to buy 3 large posters and 5 small posters?

    _____ $22 _____

22. Write the missing factor.

    $\underline{\quad 6 \quad} \times 6 = 36$

23. Write whether the problem has **too much, too little,** or **the right amount** of information.

    Johnny runs 2 miles every day for 5 days. It takes him 20 minutes to run a mile. How many miles does he run in 5 days?

    _____ too much information _____

24. Write a rule for the table. Then complete the table.

Shirts	1	2	3	4	5	6
Buttons	9	18	27	36	45	54

    _____ Multiply the number of _____

    _____ shirts by 9. _____

25. Complete.

    $7 \times \underline{\quad 5 \quad} = 20 + 15$

26. $9 \times \underline{\quad 1 \quad} = 9$

    `Go On`

---

27. Complete.

    🗆🗆🗆🗆🗆
    🗆🗆🗆🗆🗆
    🗆🗆🗆🗆🗆

    __3__ rows of __6__ = __18__

    __3__ × __6__ = __18__

28.
    $$\begin{array}{r} 7 \\ \times\,8 \\ \hline 56 \end{array}$$

29. Write the missing factor.

    $4 \times \underline{\quad 9 \quad} = 36$

30. What is the product of 0 and 4?

    _____ 0 _____

31. There are 4 students at each table. Each student needs 6 sheets of paper. How many sheets of paper are needed for the students at each table?

    _____ 24 _____ sheets

32. Compare. Write <, >, or = in the ◯.

    $5 \times 6 \;\boxed{=}\; 3 \times 10$

33. Circle the number sentence that matches the problem.

    $5 + 5 + 5 = 15$

    $5 \times 5 = 25$

    $\boxed{3 \times 5 = 15}$

    `Stop`

Choose the correct answer.

1. Kara has 10 pennies. She wants to share them equally with a friend. How many pennies will each get?

A 2
B 4
C 5
D 10

2. Four friends want to share 16 pieces of pizza equally. How many pieces will each get?

F 2
G 4
H 6
J 8

3. Ellie has 20 counters. She puts them into 4 equal groups. How many counters are in each group?

A 3
B 4
C 5
D 6

4. Which division sentence is shown by the number line?

F $0 \div 4 = 0$
G $8 \div 8 = 1$
H $12 \div 6 = 2$
J $12 \div 4 = 3$

5. Which division sentence is shown by the repeated subtraction?

$$\begin{array}{cccc} 24 & 18 & 12 & 6 \\ -6 & -6 & -6 & -6 \\ \hline 18 & 12 & 6 & 0 \end{array}$$

A $20 \div 4 = 5$ C $24 \div 3 = 8$
B $24 \div 6 = 4$ D $24 \div 8 = 3$

6. Which division sentence is shown by the repeated subtraction?

$$\begin{array}{ccc} 27 & 18 & 9 \\ -9 & -9 & -9 \\ \hline 18 & 9 & 0 \end{array}$$

F $27 \div 9 = 3$ H $18 \div 6 = 3$
G $9 \div 3 = 3$ J $0 \div 9 = 0$

7. What symbol makes this number sentence true?

$$10 \bullet 2 = 16 \div 2$$

A $+$ B $-$ C $\times$ D $\div$

8. What symbol makes this number sentence true?

$$30 \div 6 = 4 \bullet 1$$

F $+$ G $-$ H $\times$ J $\div$

9. Which division sentence is represented by an array of 3 rows of 7?

A $21 \div 3 = 7$
B $21 \div 1 = 21$
C $35 \div 5 = 7$
D $28 \div 7 = 4$

Go On

Form A • Multiple Choice   Assessment Guide **AG77**

---

10. Which division sentence is represented by 6 rows of 4?

F $24 \div 6 = 4$ H $24 \div 3 = 8$
G $24 \div 8 = 3$ J $12 \div 4 = 3$

11. Which multiplication sentence is represented by 6 rows of 8?

A $6 \times 8 = 48$ C $6 \times 6 = 36$
B $4 \times 8 = 32$ D $8 \times 8 = 64$

12. Which number completes the number sentence?

$$3 \times 3 = \blacksquare \div 3$$

F 1
G 3
H 9
J 27

13. Which number does the variable stand for?

$$18 \div 6 = p$$

A 12
B 6
C 4
D 3

14. Which number sentence does NOT belong in the fact family for 2, 4, and 8?

F $2 \times 4 = 8$ H $8 - 4 = 4$
G $8 \div 4 = 2$ J $4 \times 2 = 8$

15. $16 \div 8 = \blacksquare$

A 2
B 4
C 6
D 8

16. Which number completes the number sentence?

$$4 \times \blacksquare = 20 \div 5$$

F 5
G 4
H 1
J 0

17. Four friends share a box of candy. Each friend gets 8 pieces of candy. How many pieces of candy were in the box?

A 16
B 18
C 32
D 40

18. Amy has 60 pictures. Her album has 9 pages. Each page holds 6 pictures. Which number sentence shows how to find the number of pictures her album holds?

F $60 - 9 = 51$ H $6 \times 9 = 54$
G $60 \div 6 = 10$ J $9 + 6 = 15$

19. Al wants to share 20 cookies equally among 10 friends. Which number sentence shows how to find the number of cookies each friend will get?

A $30 \div 3 = 10$
B $20 \div 10 = 2$
C $20 - 2 = 18$
D $20 - 10 = 10$

20. Pat has 12 stuffed animals to put on 3 shelves. She wants to put an equal number of animals on each shelf. Which number sentence shows how to find the number of animals that will go on each shelf?

F $3 + 4 = 7$
G $12 - 3 = 9$
H $12 + 3 = 15$
J $12 \div 3 = 4$

Stop

AG78 Assessment Guide   **Form A • Multiple Choice**

Write the correct answer.

1. Dawn has 8 cookies. She wants to share them equally with a friend. How many cookies will each person get?

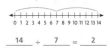

___4___ cookies

2. Five friends want to share 10 pieces of pizza equally. How many pieces will each friend get?

___2___ pieces

3. Doug has 15 counters. He puts them into 5 equal groups. How many counters are in each group?

___3___ counters

4. Write the division sentence shown by the number line.

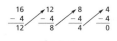

___14___ $\div$ ___7___ $=$ ___2___

5. Write the division sentence shown by the repeated subtraction.

$$\begin{array}{ccc} 15 & 10 & 5 \\ -5 & -5 & -5 \\ \hline 10 & 5 & 0 \end{array}$$

$$15 \div 5 = 3$$

6. Write the division sentence shown by the repeated subtraction.

$$\begin{array}{cccc} 16 & 12 & 8 & 4 \\ -4 & -4 & -4 & -4 \\ \hline 12 & 8 & 4 & 0 \end{array}$$

$$16 \div 4 = 4$$

7. Write $+$, $-$, $\times$, or $\div$ to make the number sentence true.

$$5 \; (+) \; 2 = 21 \div 3$$

8. Write the symbol that makes this number sentence true.

$$2 \times 4 = 32 \; (\div) \; 4$$

9. Complete the division sentence that is represented by 4 rows of 7.

___28___ $\div 4 =$ ___7___

Go On

Form B • Free Response   Assessment Guide **AG79**

---

10. Complete the division sentence that is represented by 8 rows of 7.

___56___ $\div 8 =$ ___7___

11. Complete the multiplication sentence that is represented by 6 rows of 9.

___6___ $\times 9 =$ ___54___

12. Write the number that makes this number sentence true.

$$4 \times 1 = \underline{\hspace{0.8cm} 16 \hspace{0.8cm}} \div 4$$

13. Write the number that the variable stands for.

$$8 \div 4 = p$$

$$p = \underline{\hspace{1cm} 2 \hspace{1cm}}$$

14. Write the number sentence that is missing from the fact family for 2, 5, and 10.

$$2 \times 5 = 10$$
$$5 \times 2 = 10$$
$$10 \div 2 = 5$$

___10___ $\div$ ___5___ $=$ ___2___

15. $25 \div 5 =$ ___5___

16. Write the number that makes this number sentence true.

$$3 \times \underline{\hspace{1cm} 2 \hspace{1cm}} = 18 \div 3$$

17. Three friends share a bag of oranges. Each friend gets 2 oranges. How many oranges were in the bag?

___6___ oranges

18. Mr. Armstrong has 90 markers. He has 9 containers. Each container holds 8 markers. Write a number sentence that shows how many markers will fit in his containers.

$$8 \times 9 = 72, \text{ or } 9 \times 8 = 72$$

19. Joy has 28 pencils. She and 3 friends share them equally. Write a number sentence to show the number of pencils each person gets.

___28___ $\div$ ___4___ $=$ ___7___

20. Matt has 15 model cars. He puts an equal number on each of 3 shelves. Write a number sentence that shows how many cars are on each shelf.

$$15 \div 3 = 5$$

Stop

AG80 Assessment Guide   **Form B • Free Response**

AG 228 Assessment Guide

Choose the correct answer.

1. What number completes both number sentences?

$5 \times \blacksquare = 30 \qquad 30 \div 5 = \blacksquare$

  A 7   C 5
  (B) 6   D 4

2. $2\overline{)14}$

  F 16   (H) 7
  G 12   J 6

3. $2\overline{)18}$

  A 8   C 14
  (B) 9   D 16

4. Amber has 40 stickers. She divides the stickers equally among her 5 friends. How many stickers does each friend get?

  F 10   H 6
  (G) 8   J 5

5. Eric has 25 pennies. He spends 5 of them to buy a pencil and divides the rest equally among his 4 sisters. How many pennies does each sister get?

  A 20   (C) 5
  B 16   D 1

6. Two numbers have a product of 16 and a quotient of 1. What are the numbers?

  F 8 and 2   (H) 4 and 4
  G 6 and 3   J 3 and 3

7. Which number completes the number sentence?

$27 \div \blacksquare = 18 \div 2$

  (A) 3   C 8
  B 6   D 9

8. $24 \div 3 = \blacksquare$

  F 27   (H) 8
  G 21   J 7

9. Which multiplication fact can be used to find $32 \div 4$?

  A $2 \times 16 = 32$
  (B) $4 \times 8 = 32$
  C $4 \times 9 = 36$
  D $4 \times 10 = 40$

10. $0 \div 4 = \blacksquare$

  (F) 0   H 2
  G 1   J 4

11. What symbol makes this number sentence true?

$0 \div 9 \bullet 8 \div 8$

  (A) <   B >   C =

---

12. $8 \div 1 = \blacksquare$

  F 0   (H) 8
  G 1   J 9

13. Tyler has 3 bags of carrots. There are 10 carrots in each bag. Which expression shows the number of carrots Tyler has in all?

  A $10 + 3$ C $10 + 10 + 3$
  B $10 - 3$ (D) 10×3

14. Dennis had 28 packages of raisins. He gave 4 packages to each of his friends. Which expression shows the number of friends that received raisins?

  (F) $28 \div 4$ H $28 + 28$
  G $28 - 4$ J $4 + 4$

15. A pet store has 8 puppies. Each puppy gets 2 treats each day. Which expression shows the number of treats that are needed each day?

  A $8 + 2$ C $8 \div 2$
  (B) 8×2 D $2 + 2 + 2$

16. Sean saw 3 ducks flying overhead and 6 ducks swimming in the pond. Which expression shows the number of ducks he saw in all?

  F 6×3
  G $6 \div 3$
  H $6 - 3$
  (J) $6 + 3$

17. Miss Jana received 20 flowers from her students. Each student brought 2 flowers. Which number sentence shows how to find the number of students who brought flowers?

  (A) $20 \div 2 = 10$
  B $20 - 2 = 18$
  C $20 + 2 = 22$
  D $20 + 20 = 40$

18. Each box contains 6 candy bars. Which number sentence shows how to find the number of bars in 3 boxes?

  F $6 \div 3 = 2$
  G $6 - 3 = 3$
  H $3 + 6 = 9$
  (J) $3 \times 6 = 18$

19. Mrs. Walls received 5 pieces of mail on Monday and 10 on Tuesday. Which number sentence shows how to find the number of pieces she received in all?

  A $10 \div 5 = 2$
  B $10 - 5 = 5$
  (C) $10 + 5 = 15$
  D $10 \times 5 = 50$

20. Jon has 18 games. Barry has 6 games. Which number sentence shows how to find how many more games Jon has than Barry?

  F $6 + 6 + 6 = 18$
  G $18 \div 6 = 3$
  H $6 + 18 = 24$
  (J) $18 - 6 = 12$

Stop

Write the correct answer.

1. Write the missing factor and quotient.

$5 \times \underline{7} = 35 \qquad 35 \div 5 = \underline{7}$

2. $2\overline{)16}$

      $\underline{8}$

3. $2\overline{)12}$

      $\underline{6}$

4. Deanna has 35 cookies. She puts the same number of cookies in each of 5 plastic bags. How many cookies are in each bag?

  $\underline{7}$ cookies

5. Sue has 22 pencils. She takes 2 pencils to school and divides the rest equally among 4 boxes. How many pencils are in each box?

  $\underline{5}$ pencils

6. The product of 2 numbers is 9. The quotient of the numbers is 1. What are the numbers?

  $\underline{3}$ and $\underline{3}$

7. Write the number that makes this division sentence true.

$24 \div \underline{3} = 40 \div 5$

8. $27 \div 3 = \underline{9}$

9. Write the multiplication fact that can be used to find $28 \div 4$.

$\underline{7} \times \underline{4} = \underline{28}$
or $4 \times 7 = 28$

10. Write a multiplication fact that can be used to find $0 \div 6$.

$\underline{0} \times \underline{6} = \underline{0}$
or $6 \times 0 = 0$

11. Compare. Write <, >, or = in the ◯.

$5 \div 5 \; \boxed{=} \; 7 \div 7$

12. $9 \div 1 = \underline{9}$

Go On

---

13. In each package of pizza snacks there are 8 mini pizzas. Write an expression that shows the number of mini pizzas there are in 4 packages.

$\underline{8} \;(\times)\; \underline{4}$
or 4×8

14. Donna has 28 apples. She divides them equally among 7 friends. Write an expression to show how many apples each friend gets.

$\underline{28} \;(\div)\; \underline{7}$

15. Five students are working on an art project. Each student needs 7 markers. Circle the expression that shows how many markers are needed in all.

  $5 + 7$ $\boxed{5 \times 7}$
  $7 - 5$ $7 \div 5$

16. Jeff counted 5 red trucks and 10 white trucks in the parking lot. Write an expression to show how many trucks he counted in all.

$\underline{10} \;(+)\; \underline{5}$
or $5 + 10$

17. Kevin found 9 seashells on Saturday and 10 seashells on Sunday. Write a number sentence to find the number of seashells he found in all.

$\underline{9} \;(+)\; \underline{10} = \underline{19}$
or $10 + 9 = 19$

18. There are 24 students going to lunch. Four students sit at each table. Write a number sentence to find how many tables they need.

$\underline{24} \;(\div)\; \underline{4} = \underline{6}$

19. Mr. Gant bought 5 boxes of pencils. There are 10 pencils in each box. Circle the number sentence that can be used to find how many pencils Mr. Gant has in all.

  $10 + 5 = 15$ $\boxed{5 \times 10 = 50}$
  $10 \div 5 = 2$ $10 - 5 = 2$

20. Jake has 12 model cars. Ben has 8 model cars. Write a number sentence to find how many more model cars Jake has than Ben.

$\underline{12} \;(-)\; \underline{8} = \underline{4}$

Stop

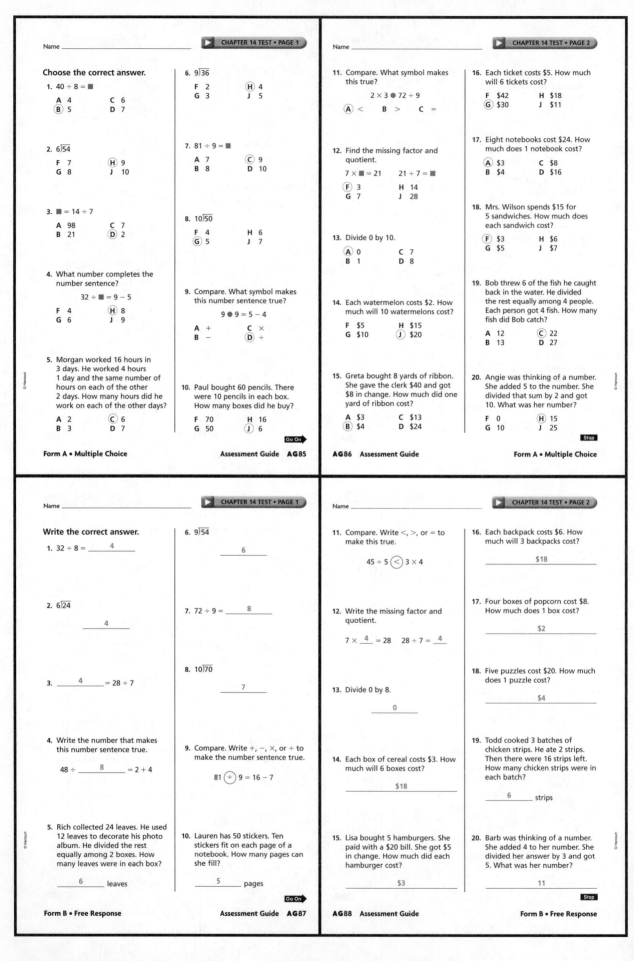

Choose the correct answer.

1. 40 ÷ 8 = ■

A 4 C 6
(B) 5 D 7

2. 6)54

F 7 (H) 9
G 8 J 10

3. ■ = 14 ÷ 7

A 98 C 7
B 21 (D) 2

4. What number completes the number sentence?

32 ÷ ■ = 9 − 5

F 4 (H) 8
G 6 J 9

5. Morgan worked 16 hours in 3 days. He worked 4 hours 1 day and the same number of hours on each of the other 2 days. How many hours did he work on each of the other days?

A 2 (C) 6
B 3 D 7

6. 9)36

F 2 (H) 4
G 3 J 5

7. 81 ÷ 9 = ■

A 7 (C) 9
B 8 D 10

8. 10)50

F 4 H 6
(G) 5 J 7

9. Compare. What symbol makes this number sentence true?

9 ● 9 = 5 − 4

A + C ×
B − (D) ÷

10. Paul bought 60 pencils. There were 10 pencils in each box. How many boxes did he buy?

F 70 H 16
G 50 (J) 6

> Go On

Form A • Multiple Choice   **Assessment Guide   AG85**

---

11. Compare. What symbol makes this true?

2 × 3 ● 72 ÷ 9

(A) <   B >   C =

12. Find the missing factor and quotient.

7 × ■ = 21   21 ÷ 7 = ■

(F) 3 H 14
G 7 J 28

13. Divide 0 by 10.

(A) 0 C 7
B 1 D 8

14. Each watermelon costs $2. How much will 10 watermelons cost?

F $5 H $15
G $10 (J) $20

15. Greta bought 8 yards of ribbon. She gave the clerk $40 and got $8 in change. How much did one yard of ribbon cost?

A $3 C $13
(B) $4 D $24

16. Each ticket costs $5. How much will 6 tickets cost?

F $42 H $18
(G) $30 J $11

17. Eight notebooks cost $24. How much does 1 notebook cost?

(A) $3 C $8
B $4 D $16

18. Mrs. Wilson spends $15 for 5 sandwiches. How much does each sandwich cost?

(F) $3 H $6
G $5 J $7

19. Bob threw 6 of the fish he caught back in the water. He divided the rest equally among 4 people. Each person got 4 fish. How many fish did Bob catch?

A 12 (C) 22
B 13 D 27

20. Angie was thinking of a number. She added 5 to the number. She divided that sum by 2 and got 10. What was her number?

F 0 (H) 15
G 10 J 25

> Stop

AG86   Assessment Guide   **Form A • Multiple Choice**

Write the correct answer.

1. 32 ÷ 8 = ___4___

2. 6)24
___4___

3. ___4___ = 28 ÷ 7

4. Write the number that makes this number sentence true.

48 ÷ ___8___ = 2 + 4

5. Rich collected 24 leaves. He used 12 leaves to decorate his photo album. He divided the rest equally among 2 boxes. How many leaves were in each box?

___6___ leaves

6. 9)54
___6___

7. 72 ÷ 9 = ___8___

8. 10)70
___7___

9. Compare. Write +, −, ×, or ÷ to make the number sentence true.

81 (÷) 9 = 16 − 7

10. Lauren has 50 stickers. Ten stickers fit on each page of a notebook. How many pages can she fill?

___5___ pages

> Go On

Form B • Free Response   **Assessment Guide   AG87**

---

11. Compare. Write <, >, or = to make this true.

45 ÷ 5 (<) 3 × 4

12. Write the missing factor and quotient.

7 × ___4___ = 28   28 ÷ 7 = ___4___

13. Divide 0 by 8.

___0___

14. Each box of cereal costs $3. How much will 6 boxes cost?

___$18___

15. Lisa bought 5 hamburgers. She paid with a $20 bill. She got $5 in change. How much did each hamburger cost?

___$3___

16. Each backpack costs $6. How much will 3 backpacks cost?

___$18___

17. Four boxes of popcorn cost $8. How much does 1 box cost?

___$2___

18. Five puzzles cost $20. How much does 1 puzzle cost?

___$4___

19. Todd cooked 3 batches of chicken strips. He ate 2 strips. Then there were 16 strips left. How many chicken strips were in each batch?

___6___ strips

20. Barb was thinking of a number. She added 4 to her number. She divided her answer by 3 and got 5. What was her number?

___11___

> Stop

AG88   Assessment Guide   **Form B • Free Response**

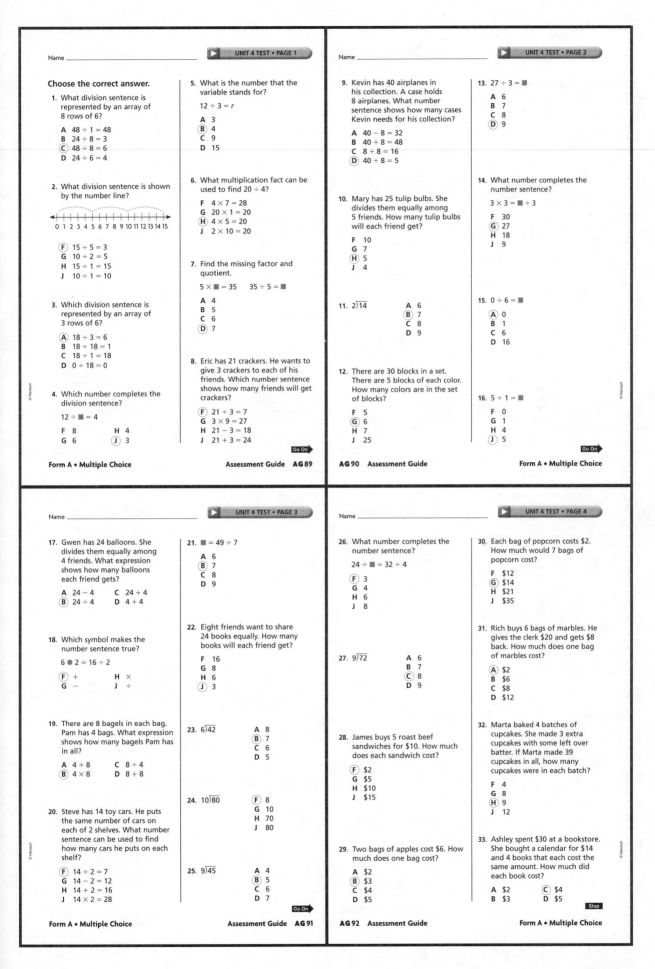

Name _____

Choose the correct answer.

1. What division sentence is represented by an array of 8 rows of 6?

   A 48 ÷ 1 = 48
   B 24 ÷ 8 = 3
   C 48 ÷ 8 = 6
   D 24 ÷ 6 = 4

2. What division sentence is shown by the number line?

   0 1 2 3 4 5 6 7 8 9 10 11 12 13 14 15

   F 15 ÷ 5 = 3
   G 10 ÷ 2 = 5
   H 15 ÷ 1 = 15
   J 10 ÷ 1 = 10

3. Which division sentence is represented by an array of 3 rows of 6?

   A 18 ÷ 3 = 6
   B 18 ÷ 18 = 1
   C 18 ÷ 1 = 18
   D 0 ÷ 18 = 0

4. Which number completes the division sentence?

   12 ÷ ■ = 4

   F 8   H 4
   G 6   J 3

5. What is the number that the variable stands for?

   12 ÷ 3 = r

   A 3
   B 4
   C 9
   D 15

6. What multiplication fact can be used to find 20 ÷ 4?

   F 4 × 7 = 28
   G 20 × 1 = 20
   H 4 × 5 = 20
   J 2 × 10 = 20

7. Find the missing factor and quotient.

   5 × ■ = 35   35 ÷ 5 = ■

   A 4
   B 5
   C 6
   D 7

8. Eric has 21 crackers. He wants to give 3 crackers to each of his friends. Which number sentence shows how many friends will get crackers?

   F 21 ÷ 3 = 7
   G 3 × 9 = 27
   H 21 − 3 = 18
   J 21 ÷ 3 = 24

   Go On

Name _____

9. Kevin has 40 airplanes in his collection. A case holds 8 airplanes. What number sentence shows how many cases Kevin needs for his collection?

   A 40 − 8 = 32
   B 40 + 8 = 48
   C 8 + 8 = 16
   D 40 ÷ 8 = 5

10. Mary has 25 tulip bulbs. She divides them equally among 5 friends. How many tulip bulbs will each friend get?

    F 10
    G 7
    H 5
    J 4

11. 2)14

    A 6
    B 7
    C 8
    D 9

12. There are 30 blocks in a set. There are 5 blocks of each color. How many colors are in the set of blocks?

    F 5
    G 6
    H 7
    J 25

13. 27 ÷ 3 = ■

    A 6
    B 7
    C 8
    D 9

14. What number completes the number sentence?

    3 × 3 = ■ ÷ 3

    F 30
    G 27
    H 18
    J 9

15. 0 ÷ 6 = ■

    A 0
    B 1
    C 6
    D 16

16. 5 ÷ 1 = ■

    F 0
    G 1
    H 4
    J 5

    Go On

Name _____

17. Gwen has 24 balloons. She divides them equally among 4 friends. What expression shows how many balloons each friend gets?

    A 24 − 4   C 24 + 4
    B 24 ÷ 4   D 4 + 4

18. Which symbol makes the number sentence true?

    6 ● 2 = 16 ÷ 2

    F +   H ×
    G −   J ÷

19. There are 8 bagels in each bag. Pam has 4 bags. What expression shows how many bagels Pam has in all?

    A 4 + 8   C 8 ÷ 4
    B 4 × 8   D 8 + 8

20. Steve has 14 toy cars. He puts the same number of cars on each of 2 shelves. What number sentence can be used to find how many cars he puts on each shelf?

    F 14 ÷ 2 = 7
    G 14 − 2 = 12
    H 14 + 2 = 16
    J 14 × 2 = 28

21. ■ = 49 ÷ 7

    A 6
    B 7
    C 8
    D 9

22. Eight friends want to share 24 books equally. How many books will each friend get?

    F 16
    G 8
    H 6
    J 3

23. 6)42

    A 8
    B 7
    C 6
    D 5

24. 10)80

    F 8
    G 10
    H 70
    J 80

25. 9)45

    A 4
    B 5
    C 6
    D 7

    Go On

Name _____

26. What number completes the number sentence?

    24 ÷ ■ = 32 ÷ 4

    F 3
    G 4
    H 6
    J 8

27. 9)72

    A 6
    B 7
    C 8
    D 9

28. James buys 5 roast beef sandwiches for $10. How much does each sandwich cost?

    F $2
    G $5
    H $10
    J $15

29. Two bags of apples cost $6. How much does one bag cost?

    A $2
    B $3
    C $4
    D $5

30. Each bag of popcorn costs $2. How much would 7 bags of popcorn cost?

    F $12
    G $14
    H $21
    J $35

31. Rich buys 6 bags of marbles. He gives the clerk $20 and gets $8 back. How much does one bag of marbles cost?

    A $2
    B $6
    C $8
    D $12

32. Marta baked 4 batches of cupcakes. She made 3 extra cupcakes with some left over batter. If Marta made 39 cupcakes in all, how many cupcakes were in each batch?

    F 4
    G 8
    H 9
    J 12

33. Ashley spent $30 at a bookstore. She bought a calendar for $14 and 4 books that each cost the same amount. How much did each book cost?

    A $2   C $4
    B $3   D $5

    Stop

Write the correct answer.

1. What division sentence is represented by an array of 7 rows of 6?

   _42 ÷ 7 = 6, or 42 ÷ 6 = 7_

2. What division sentence is shown by the number line?

   0 1 2 3 4 5 6 7 8 9 10 11 12

   _12 ÷ 6 = 2_

3. Write a division sentence that is represented by an array of 4 rows of 5.

   _20 ÷ 4 = 5, or 20 ÷ 5 = 4_

4. What number completes the division sentence?

   36 ÷ __6__ = 6

5. Find the number that the variable stands for.

   $24 ÷ 6 = r$

   $r =$ __4__

6. Write a multiplication fact that can be used to find the quotient 35 ÷ 7.

   _7 × 5 = 35, or 5 × 7 = 35_

7. Write the missing factor and quotient.

   7 × ■ = 56   56 ÷ 7 = ■

   _8_

8. Ross has 21 keys. He wants to give 3 keys to each of his friends. Write a number sentence to show how to find the number of friends who will get keys.

   _21 ÷ 3 = 7_

   Go On ▶

Form B • Free Response   Assessment Guide **AG 93**

---

9. Valerie has 15 dance outfits. A bag holds 5 outfits. Write a number sentence to show how many bags Valerie will need to carry all of her dance outfits.

   _15 ÷ 5 = 3_

10. Eddie has 36 feathers. He divides them equally among 6 friends. How many feathers does each friend get?

    __6__ feathers

11. $2\overline{)10}$ (quotient 5)

12. There are 45 cans of paint in Howard's Supply Store. There are 9 colors of paint and the same number of cans of each color. How many cans of each color are in the store?

    __5__ cans

13. 24 ÷ 3 = __8__

14. 2 × 2 = __8__ ÷ 2

15. 0 ÷ 7 = __0__

16. 6 ÷ 1 = __6__

17. Gail has 18 cans of soda for her party. She divides them equally among 9 family members. Write an expression that shows how many cans each family member will get.

    _18 ÷ 9_

    Go On ▶

AG 94 Assessment Guide   **Form B • Free Response**

---

18. What symbol makes the number sentence true?

    10 Ⓞ 4 = 30 ÷ 5   (symbol: −)

19. There are 8 rolls in each package. Pam has 4 packages. Write an expression to show how many rolls Pam has in all.

    _8 × 4 = 32, or 4 × 8 = 32_

20. Ben has 12 masks in his collection. He wants to display them on his wall in 2 equal rows. Write a number sentence to show how many masks there will be in each row.

    _12 ÷ 2 = 6_

21. __9__ = 81 ÷ 9

22. Four friends want to share 28 pieces of candy equally. How many pieces of candy will each friend get?

    __7__ pieces of candy

23. $5\overline{)40}$ (quotient 8)

24. $10\overline{)60}$ (quotient 6)

25. $9\overline{)63}$ (quotient 7)

    Go On ▶

Form B • Free Response   Assessment Guide **AG 95**

---

26. What number completes the number sentence?

    45 ÷ __5__ = 2 + 7

27. $9\overline{)54}$ (quotient 6)

28. Frances buys 2 watermelons for $8. How much does each watermelon cost?

    _$4_

29. Four notebooks cost $12. How much does one notebook cost?

    _$3_

30. Each bottle of water costs $2. How much would 8 bottles cost?

    _$16_

31. Felix buys 6 books. Each book costs the same amount. He gives the clerk $20 and gets $2 back. How much does one book cost?

    _$3_

32. Joshua made popcorn for the school carnival. He filled 26 bags and packed them into 3 boxes. He had 2 extra bags of popcorn. How many bags of popcorn were in each box?

    __8__ bags of popcorn

33. Sarah spent $50 at a clothing store. She bought a skirt for $23 and 3 shirts that each cost the same amount. How much did each shirt cost?

    _$9_

    Stop

AG 96 Assessment Guide   **Form B • Free Response**

AG 232   **Assessment Guide**

Choose the correct answer.

For 1–3, use the tally table.

FAVORITE FOOD	
Name	Tally
Hamburger	IIII
Taco	ЖII
Chicken	III
Grilled Cheese	ЖI

1. How many students answered this survey?
- (A) 18
- B 19
- C 20
- D 21

2. How many more students chose taco than chose chicken?
- F 1
- (G) 2
- H 3
- J 5

3. How many students in all chose hamburger and grilled cheese?
- (A) 10
- B 9
- C 8
- D 7

For 4–7, use the frequency table.

FAVORITE CAR COLOR	
Color	Number
White	30
Blue	18
Black	23
Red	17

4. How many people were surveyed?
- F 78
- (G) 88
- H 98
- J 100

5. How many more people chose white than red?
- A 23
- (B) 13
- C 12
- D 7

6. Which group of colors is in order from **greatest** to **least** votes?
- F white, black, red, blue
- G white, red, blue, black
- H white, blue, red, black
- (J) white, black, blue, red

7. How many fewer people chose blue than chose black?
- A 12
- B 6
- (C) 5
- D 2

For 8–10, use the following information.

Jordan is doing an experiment with a cube numbered 1 through 6. He will roll the cube 30 times and record the number in a tally table.

8. How many tallies should there be on Jordan's table?
- F 6
- G 24
- (H) 30
- J 36

9. What will Jordan be able to find out from his table?
- (A) the number rolled most often
- B the difference between the numbers
- C the color rolled most often
- D the sum of the numbers from 1 through 6

`Go On`

Form A • Multiple Choice

---

10. Which number should Jordan **NOT** list on his tally table?
- F 2
- G 5
- H 6
- (J) 7

For 11–12, use the two spinners.

Sally is doing an experiment. She will use the two spinners 25 times and record the sum of the two numbers.

11. How many tallies should there be on Sally's table?
- A 5
- B 10
- C 20
- (D) 25

12. What sums should Sally list on her tally table?
- F 1, 2, 3, 4
- G 2, 3, 4, 6
- (H) 3, 4, 5, 6
- J 2, 4, 6, 9

For 13–16, use the line plot.

Number of Family Members

13. What is the mode for this set of data?
- A 7
- (B) 4
- C 3
- D 2

14. What is the range for this set of data?
- F 4
- G 5
- (H) 6
- J 7

15. How many families have 3 or fewer members?
- A 3
- (B) 7
- C 10
- D 14

16. What is the **greatest** number of family members in this set of data?
- F 5
- G 6
- H 7
- (J) 8

For 17–18, find the median.

17. 8, 12, 5, 9, 11
- A 8
- (B) 9
- C 11
- D 12

18. 5, 9, 2, 1, 7, 6, 8
- F 2
- G 4
- H 5
- (J) 6

For 19–20, find the mean.

19. 8, 1, 9
- A 1
- B 3
- (C) 6
- D 18

20. 1, 9, 3, 7, 5
- F 1
- (G) 5
- H 9
- J 25

`Stop`

Form A • Multiple Choice

Write the correct answer.

For 1–3, use the tally table.

FAVORITE STUFFED ANIMAL	
Animal	Tally
Rabbit	ЖI
Bear	ЖЖII
Dog	ЖIIII
Cat	Ж

1. How many students voted for their favorite stuffed animal?

___32___ students

2. How many more students chose the dog than the cat?

___4___ more students

3. How many students in all chose the rabbit and the bear?

___18___ students

For 4–7, use the frequency table.

FAVORITE BOOK BAG COLOR	
Color	Number
Red	8
Purple	20
Blue	12
Black	13

4. How many people were surveyed?

___53___ people

5. How many **more** people voted for purple than for red?

___12___ more people

6. Write the colors in order from the **greatest** to the **least** votes.

__purple, black, blue, red__

7. How many **fewer** people voted for red than for black?

___5___ people

For 8–10, use the following information.

You are doing a spinner experiment. The spinner is divided into 6 equal parts numbered 1–6. You will use the spinner 25 times to see which number the pointer lands on most often. You will record the results in a tally table.

8. How many tallies will be on your tally table?

___25___ tallies

9. What are you asked to find in this experiment?
the number the pointer lands on most often

`Go On`

Form B • Free Response

---

10. The numbers you might spin in your experiment should be on your tally table. What are these numbers?

_1_, _2_, _3_, _4_, _5_, _6_

For 11–12, use the spinners.

Kelly is doing an experiment. She uses the two spinners 20 times and records the sums of the two numbers.

11. How many tallies should Kelly have in her table?

___20___ tallies

12. What sums can Kelly get?

_2_, _3_, _4_, _5_, _6_, _7_

For 13–16, use the line plot.

13. What is the mode for this set of data?

___6___

14. What is the range for this set of data?

___4___

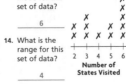
Number of States Visited

15. How many students have visited 4 or fewer states?

___6___ students

16. How many students have visited exactly 5 states?

___2___ students

For 17–18, find the median.

17. 15, 3, 7, 4, 11

___7___

18. 3, 1, 5, 7, 9, 2, 8

___5___

For 19–20, find the mean.

19. 5, 9, 7

___7___

20. 2, 8, 4, 6, 10

___6___

`Stop`

Form B • Free Response

Choose the correct answer.

For 1–4, use this data.

Some students made pictographs using this data.

FAVORITE SOUP	
Soup	Number of Votes
Chicken	30
Vegetable	15
Chili	10

1. Al used a key of 5. How many symbols should he draw to show the votes for chicken soup?

 A 3 C 5
 B 4 Ⓓ 6

2. Joel used a key of 2. How many symbols should he draw to show the votes for chili?

 Ⓕ 5 H 3
 G 4 J 2

3. What key did Haley use if she drew 3 symbols to show the votes for chicken soup?

 A 3 Ⓒ 10
 B 5 D 30

4. What key did Ethan use if he drew 1½ symbols to show the votes for vegetable soup?

 Ⓕ 10 H 5
 G 6 J 4

For 5–7, use the graph.

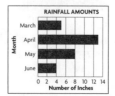

RAINFALL AMOUNTS

5. How many inches of rain fell in May?

 A 4 B 6 Ⓒ 8 D 10

6. Which month had the most rain?

 F March H May
 Ⓖ April J June

7. How many more inches of rain fell in May than in June?

 A 2 Ⓑ 4 C 5 D 8

For 8–11, use the table below.

MUSEUM VISITORS	
Day	Number
Thursday	30
Friday	48
Saturday	76
Sunday	82

8. What would be the **best** scale for a bar graph of this data?

 F by 1s H by 3s
 G by 2s Ⓙ by 10s

Form A • Multiple Choice

---

9. Which day would have the longest bar on a bar graph?

 Ⓐ Sunday C Friday
 B Saturday D Thursday

10. How many more visitors would the bar for Saturday represent than the bar for Friday?

 F 0 visitors Ⓗ 28 visitors
 G 18 visitors J 124 visitors

11. How many people in all visited the museum on Saturday and Sunday?

 A 78 C 168
 Ⓑ 158 D 206

For 12–15, use the grid.

12. What is the ordered pair for point *D*?

 Ⓕ (4,5) H (3,1)
 G (5,4) J (4,2)

13. What is the ordered pair for point *C*?

 A (2,3) Ⓒ (3,1)
 B (1,3) D (4,2)

14. What point is named by the ordered pair (1,4)?

 F A H C
 Ⓖ B J D

15. Start at 0. Which directions tell how to get to point *A* on the grid?

 Ⓐ move 2 right and 3 up
 B move 2 up and 3 right
 C move 4 right and 2 up
 D move 3 right and 1 up

For 16–18, use the line graph.

TREE FARM SALES

16. On what day were the most trees sold?

 F Sunday H Friday
 G Thursday Ⓙ Saturday

17. How many trees were sold on Wednesday?

 A 2 C 4
 Ⓑ 3 D 5

18. How many more trees were sold on Saturday than on Monday?

 F 5 G 6 H 9 Ⓙ 10

Form A • Multiple Choice

Write the correct answer.

For 1–4, use the data below.

Some students made pictographs using the data in this table.

FAVORITE SMALL PET	
Pet	Number of Votes
Gerbil	16
Hamster	24
Tropical Fish	12
Bird	9

1. Pam used a key of 4. How many symbols should she draw to show the votes for hamster?

 ___6___ symbols

2. What key did Mark use if he drew 1½ symbols to show the votes for bird?

 Key: Each symbol = ___6___ votes.

3. Charles used a key of 2. How many symbols should he draw to show the votes for tropical fish?

 ___6___ symbols

4. What key did Kendra use if she drew 4 symbols to show the votes for gerbil?

 Key: Each symbol = ___4___ votes.

For 5–7, use the bar graph.

FAVORITE GAMES

5. How many students voted for Spider and Fly?

 ___8___ students

6. What game received the **greatest** number of votes?

 ___Capture the Flag___

7. How many more students voted for Spider and Fly than for Hide and Seek?

 ___3___ more students

For 8–11, use the table below.

RAINY DAYS	
Month	Number
March	8
April	14
May	10
June	7

8. Circle the best scale for a bar graph of this data.

 (by 2s) by 5s
 by 3s by 10s

Form B • Free Response

---

9. Which month would have the longest bar on a bar graph?

 ___April___

10. How many more rainy days would the bar for May represent than the bar for June?

 ___3___ more days

11. How many days in all did it rain from April to June?

 ___31___ days

For 12–15, use the grid.

12. Write the ordered pair for point *B*.

 (___3___ , ___2___)

13. Write the letter of the point named by the ordered pair (4,1).

 ___C___

14. Write the ordered pair for point *D*.

 (___5___ , ___3___)

15. Explain how to find point *A* on the grid.

 ___Start at 0. Move 1 space to___
 ___the right and 4 spaces up.___

For 16–18, use the line graph.

PERFECT ATTENDANCE

16. How many students had perfect attendance in January?

 ___6___ students

17. How many more students had perfect attendance in May than in February?

 ___8___ more students

18. In which months did more than 8 students have perfect attendance?

 ___March and May___

Form B • Free Response

Choose the correct answer.

1. Measure the paper clip to the nearest inch.

   Ⓐ 1 in.   C 2 in.

   B 1½ in.   D 2½ in.

2. Measure the ribbon to the nearest half inch.

   F 2 in.   H 3 in.

   Ⓖ 2½ in.   J 3½ in.

3. A picture measures 4½ inches. The end of the picture is between which two inch marks?

   A 3 and 4
   Ⓑ 4 and 5
   C 5 and 6
   D 6 and 7

4. Choose the best unit of measure for the length of a shoe.

   Ⓕ inch   H yard
   G feet   J mile

5. Choose the best unit of measure for the distance from your school to a school in another city.

   A inch   C yard
   B foot   Ⓓ mile

6. A banana is about 6 _?_ long.

   Ⓕ inches   H yards
   G feet   J miles

7. Choose the best unit of measure. A bedroom is about 12 _?_ long.

   A inches   C yards
   Ⓑ feet   D miles

8. Choose the better estimate.

   Ⓕ 2 cups   G 2 gallons

9. Which unit would be used to measure the amount of water it takes to fill a swimming pool?

   A pint   C cup
   B quart   Ⓓ gallon

10. Compare the amounts.

    2 cups ● 2 quarts

    Ⓕ <   G >   H =

11. Choose the best unit of measure for the weight of a cherry.

    A cup   Ⓒ ounce
    B foot   D pound

12. Choose the better estimate.

    F 50 ounces   Ⓖ 50 pounds

13. Which object weighs about 5 pounds?

    A apple
    B box of cereal
    Ⓒ watermelon
    D slice of bread

14. ■ cups = 3 pints

cups	2	4	6	8
pints	1	2	3	4

    F 1   Ⓗ 6
    G 4   J 10

For 15–16, use the table.

quarts	4	8	12	16	20
gallons	1	2	3	4	5

15. Jaime made 5 gallons of tea. How many quarts is this?

    A 4   C 12
    B 8   Ⓓ 20

16. Mrs. Owens bought 3 gallons of milk. How many quarts is this?

    F 6   H 10
    G 7   Ⓙ 12

17. Mr. Wagstar's garden is 3 yards long. How many feet long is it?

    A 3 feet   C 6 feet
    B 5 feet   Ⓓ 9 feet

18. Bryce plants 8 trees. He needs to give each tree about 2 pints of water every day. Should he estimate or measure the water?

    Ⓕ estimate   G measure

19. Antonia needs a piece of ribbon to tie flowers together. Can she estimate the length or does she need to measure the ribbon?

    A measure   Ⓑ estimate

20. Katie's bread recipe calls for 2 cups of flour. Should she estimate or measure the flour?

    F estimate   Ⓖ measure

Write the correct answer.

1. Measure the pencil to the nearest inch.

   ___2___ inches

2. Measure the string to the nearest half inch.

   ___1½___ inches

3. A bookmark is 8½ inches long. The end of the bookmark is between which two inch marks?

   ___8___ and ___9___

4. Circle the better unit to use to measure the length of your bed.

   (inch)   mile

5. Circle the better unit to use to measure the distance a bus could go in an hour.

   feet   (mile)

6. Circle the better estimate. The door to your classroom is about 8 _?_ high.

   inches   (feet)

7. Choose the best unit of measure. Write **inches, feet, yards,** or **miles**.

   A car is about 8 ___feet___ long.

8. Circle the better estimate for how much the sink can hold.

   2 cups   (2 gallons)

9. Circle the better unit to use to measure the amount of water a bathtub can hold.

   cup   (gallon)

10. Write <, >, or = to make the sentence true.

    3 gallons (>) 3 quarts

11. Circle the better unit to use to weigh your desk.

    ounce   (pound)

12. Circle the better estimate.

    2 ounces   (2 pounds)

13. Circle the object that weighs less than 10 pounds.

    (orange)   kitchen table

14.
cups	2	4	6	8
pints	1	2	3	4

    ■ cups = 4 pints

    ___8___ cups

For 15–16, use the table.

gallons	1	2	3	4
pints	8	16	24	32

15. Margo has 3 gallons of ice cream. How many pints is this?

    ___24___ pints

16. A restaurant sold 16 pints of milk. How many gallons is this?

    ___2___ gallons

17. A nightstand is 2 feet long. How many inches long is it?

    ___24___ inches

18. Julia is making water globes for the winter fair. She needs about 1 tablespoon of glitter for each globe. Can she estimate or does she need to measure the glitter?

    (estimate)   measure

19. Max wants to make a wooden picture frame. He needs exactly 2 feet of wood. Should he estimate or measure the wood?

    estimate   (measure)

20. Louis is making juice from a powdered mix. The package says to use 2 quarts of water per package. Should Louis estimate or measure the water?

    estimate   (measure)

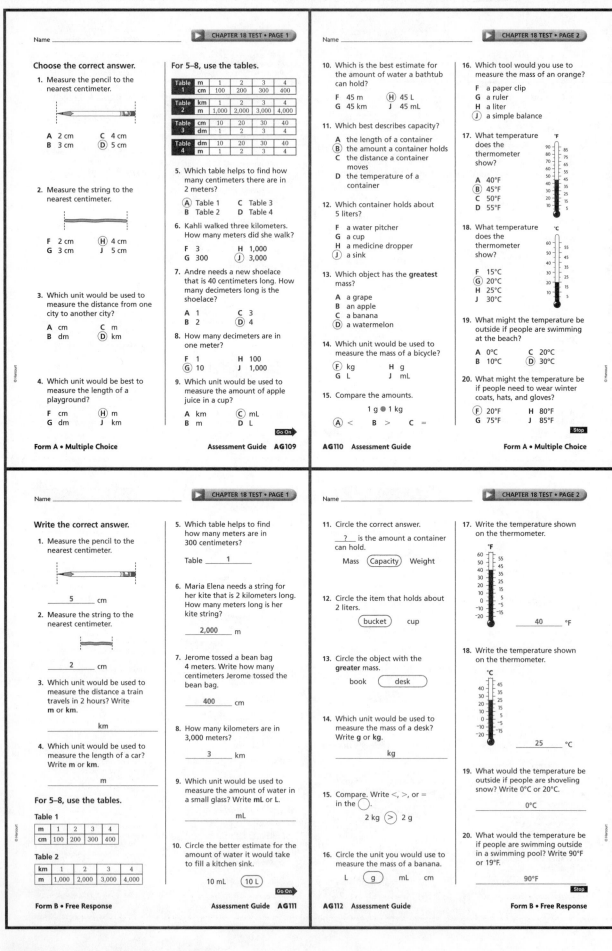

Choose the correct answer.

1. Measure the pencil to the nearest centimeter.

   A 2 cm   C 4 cm
   B 3 cm   (D) 5 cm

2. Measure the string to the nearest centimeter.

   F 2 cm   (H) 4 cm
   G 3 cm   J 5 cm

3. Which unit would be used to measure the distance from one city to another city?

   A cm   C m
   B dm   (D) km

4. Which unit would be best to measure the length of a playground?

   F cm   (H) m
   G dm   J km

For 5–8, use the tables.

Table 1	m	1	2	3	4
	cm	100	200	300	400

Table 2	km	1	2	3	4
	m	1,000	2,000	3,000	4,000

Table 3	cm	10	20	30	40
	dm	1	2	3	4

Table 4	dm	10	20	30	40
	m	1	2	3	4

5. Which table helps to find how many centimeters there are in 2 meters?

   (A) Table 1   C Table 3
   B Table 2   D Table 4

6. Kahli walked three kilometers. How many meters did she walk?

   F 3   H 1,000
   G 300   (J) 3,000

7. Andre needs a new shoelace that is 40 centimeters long. How many decimeters long is the shoelace?

   A 1   C 3
   B 2   (D) 4

8. How many decimeters are in one meter?

   F 1   H 100
   (G) 10   J 1,000

9. Which unit would be used to measure the amount of apple juice in a cup?

   A km   (C) mL
   B m   D L

10. Which is the best estimate for the amount of water a bathtub can hold?

    F 45 m   (H) 45 L
    G 45 km   J 45 mL

11. Which best describes capacity?

    A the length of a container
    (B) the amount a container holds
    C the distance a container moves
    D the temperature of a container

12. Which container holds about 5 liters?

    F a water pitcher
    G a cup
    H a medicine dropper
    (J) a sink

13. Which object has the **greatest** mass?

    A a grape
    B an apple
    C a banana
    (D) a watermelon

14. Which unit would be used to measure the mass of a bicycle?

    (F) kg   H g
    G L   J mL

15. Compare the amounts.

    1 g ● 1 kg

    (A) <   B >   C =

16. Which tool would you use to measure the mass of an orange?

    F a paper clip
    G a ruler
    H a liter
    (J) a simple balance

17. What temperature does the thermometer show?

    A 40°F
    (B) 45°F
    C 50°F
    D 55°F

18. What temperature does the thermometer show?

    F 15°C
    (G) 20°C
    H 25°C
    J 30°C

19. What might the temperature be outside if people are swimming at the beach?

    A 0°C   C 20°C
    B 10°C   (D) 30°C

20. What might the temperature be if people need to wear winter coats, hats, and gloves?

    (F) 20°F   H 80°F
    G 75°F   J 85°F

Write the correct answer.

1. Measure the pencil to the nearest centimeter.

   _____5_____ cm

2. Measure the string to the nearest centimeter.

   _____2_____ cm

3. Which unit would be used to measure the distance a train travels in 2 hours? Write **m** or **km**.

   _____ km

4. Which unit would be used to measure the length of a car? Write **m** or **km**.

   _____ m

For 5–8, use the tables.

Table 1

m	1	2	3	4
cm	100	200	300	400

Table 2

km	1	2	3	4
m	1,000	2,000	3,000	4,000

5. Which table helps to find how many meters are in 300 centimeters?

   Table _____1_____

6. Maria Elena needs a string for her kite that is 2 kilometers long. How many meters long is her kite string?

   _____2,000_____ m

7. Jerome tossed a bean bag 4 meters. Write how many centimeters Jerome tossed the bean bag.

   _____400_____ cm

8. How many kilometers are in 3,000 meters?

   _____3_____ km

9. Which unit would be used to measure the amount of water in a small glass? Write **mL** or **L**.

   _____ mL

10. Circle the better estimate for the amount of water it would take to fill a kitchen sink.

    10 mL   (10 L)

11. Circle the correct answer.

    ___?___ is the amount a container can hold.

    Mass   (Capacity)   Weight

12. Circle the item that holds about 2 liters.

    (bucket)   cup

13. Circle the object with the **greater** mass.

    book   (desk)

14. Which unit would be used to measure the mass of a desk? Write **g** or **kg**.

    _____ kg

15. Compare. Write <, >, or = in the ◯.

    2 kg (>) 2 g

16. Circle the unit you would use to measure the mass of a banana.

    L   (g)   mL   cm

17. Write the temperature shown on the thermometer.

    _____40_____ °F

18. Write the temperature shown on the thermometer.

    _____25_____ °C

19. What would the temperature be outside if people are shoveling snow? Write 0°C or 20°C.

    _____0°C_____

20. What would the temperature be if people are swimming outside in a swimming pool? Write 90°F or 19°F.

    _____90°F_____

Choose the correct answer.

For 1–2, use the tally table.

FAVORITE FIELD TRIP	
Trip	Tally
Science Museum	IIII
Animal Park	IIII III
Nature Walk	IIII IIII I
Sculpture Garden	IIII

1. How many students answered the survey?

   A 4
   Ⓒ 28
   B 11
   D 30

2. How many **more** students chose the nature walk than chose the science museum?

   F 4
   H 11
   Ⓖ 7
   J 15

For 3–4, use the frequency table.

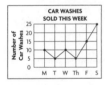

COLOR OF STUDENTS' CLOTHES			
	Blue	White	Black
Pants	10	1	6
Shorts	4	2	3
Skirts	2	0	1

3. How many students wore shorts?

   A 2
   C 4
   B 3
   Ⓓ 9

4. How many students answered this survey?

   F 16
   Ⓗ 29
   G 19
   J 30

For 5–6, use the following information.

Tony is experimenting with a cube numbered 1, 2, 3, 3, 3, 4. He will roll the cube 25 times and record the numbers in a tally table.

5. How many tallies should there be on Tony's table?

   A 3
   C 20
   B 6
   Ⓓ 25

6. What are the possible outcomes for Tony's number cube?

   F 3
   H 2, 3, 4
   G 1, 2, 3
   Ⓙ 1, 2, 3, 4

For 7–8, use the line plot.

Magazines Sold by Students

7. How many students sold 1 or 2 magazines?

   A 2
   Ⓒ 7
   B 5
   D 10

8. What is the range for this set of data?

   F 1
   Ⓗ 3
   G 2
   J 4

---

9. What is the median for this set of numbers?

   9, 13, 5, 4, 7

   A 13
   Ⓒ 7
   B 9
   D 4

10. What is the mean for this set of data?

   3, 10, 6, 7, 4

   F 1
   H 7
   Ⓖ 6
   J 30

For 11–12, use the data in this table.

FAVORITE PIE	
Name	Number
Apple	8
Banana	6
Cherry	3
Chocolate	11

11. Keri makes a pictograph using this data. She uses a key of 2. How many symbols should she draw to show the votes for banana pie?

   A 1
   Ⓒ 3
   B 2
   D 6

12. What key would Keri use if she drew 2 symbols to show the votes for apple pie?

   F key of 2
   H key of 6
   Ⓖ key of 4
   J key of 8

For 13–14, use the bar graph.

FAVORITE NUTS

13. What type of graph is this?

   Ⓐ horizontal bar graph
   B vertical bar graph

14. How many more students chose pecan than chose walnut?

   F 2
   H 8
   Ⓖ 6
   J 10

For 15–16, use the grid.

15. What is the ordered pair for point Y?

   A (2,2)
   C (3,4)
   B (1,4)
   Ⓓ (4,1)

16. What point is named by the ordered pair (3,4)?

   F W
   H Y
   Ⓖ X
   J Z

For 17–18, use the line graph.

CAR WASHES SOLD THIS WEEK

17. On what day were the most car washes sold?

   A Monday
   C Friday
   B Wednesday
   Ⓓ Saturday

18. How many more car washes were sold on Saturday than on Tuesday?

   F 3
   Ⓗ 20
   G 5
   J 25

19. Measure the string to the nearest inch.

   A 1 in.
   Ⓒ 2 in.
   B 1½ in.
   D 2½ in.

20. Choose the best customary unit to measure the distance from your house to the library.

   F inch
   H yard
   G foot
   Ⓙ mile

21. Compare the amounts.

   1 gallon ● 1 cup

   A <
   Ⓑ >
   C =

22. Choose the best customary unit to weigh a strawberry.

   Ⓕ ounce
   G foot
   H cup
   J pound

23. There are 4 quarts in a gallon. How many quarts are in 2 gallons?

   A 12 quarts
   Ⓑ 8 quarts
   C 4 quarts
   D 2 quarts

24. There are 2 cups in a pint. How many cups are in 4 pints?

   F 2 cups
   G 4 cups
   H 6 cups
   Ⓙ 8 cups

25. Jason has 4 plants. He gives each plant about 1 cup of water every week. Should he estimate or measure the water?

   Ⓐ estimate
   B measure

---

26. Measure the paper clip to the nearest centimeter.

   F 2 cm
   Ⓖ 3 cm
   H 5 cm
   J 6 cm

27. Measure the eraser to the nearest centimeter.

   ERASER

   A 1 cm
   B 2 cm
   Ⓒ 3 cm
   D 4 cm

28. Paul needs 400 centimeters of string for a project. How many meters of string does he need?

   F 1 m
   H 3 m
   G 2 m
   Ⓙ 4 m

29. Mike will walk 2,000 meters. How many kilometers will he walk?

   A 1 km
   Ⓑ 2 km
   C 4 km
   D 20 km

30. What metric unit would be used to measure the amount of hot chocolate in a cup?

   Ⓕ mL
   H m
   G km
   J L

31. What object has a mass greater than that of a toothbrush?

   Ⓐ book
   B sheet of paper
   C feather
   D paper clip

32. What temperature does the thermometer show?

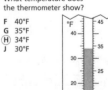

   F 40°F
   G 35°F
   Ⓗ 34°F
   J 30°F

33. What temperature does the thermometer show?

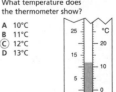

   A 10°C
   B 11°C
   Ⓒ 12°C
   D 13°C

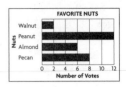

Write the correct answer.

For 1–2, use the tally table.

FAVORITE SUBJECT	
Subject	Tally
Reading	卌 I
Science	卌 卌 IIII
Art	IIII
Music	卌 卌

1. How many students answered the survey?

   _____ 34 _____

2. How many more students chose music than chose art?

   _____ 6 _____

For 3–4, use the frequency table.

HAIR COLOR			
	Brown	Red	Black
Boys	5	0	4
Girls	6	1	3

3. How many students have brown hair?

   _____ 11 _____

4. How many students answered the survey?

   _____ 19 _____

Form B • Free Response

For 5–6, use this information.

Denise puts 3 yellow marbles, 4 blue marbles, 6 white marbles, and 1 black marble into a bag. She draws one marble from the bag, records the color on a tally table, and replaces the marble.

5. If she does this 8 times, how many marks will be on her tally table?

   _____ 8 _____

6. What are the possible outcomes in her experiment?

   yellow, blue, white, black

For 7–8, use the line plot.

Books Collected by Students

7. How many students collected 6 or 7 books?

   _____ 9 _____

8. What is the range for this set of data?

   _____ 7 _____

Go On

Assessment Guide **AG117**

9. What is the median for this set of numbers?

   3, 7, 10, 4, 5

   _____ 5 _____

10. What is the mean for this set of numbers?

    2, 7, 5, 4, 2

    _____ 4 _____

For 11–12, use the data in this table.

FAVORITE PIZZA	
Name	Number of Votes
Cheese	16
Pepperoni	9
Veggie	4
Meat	6

11. Ian makes a pictograph using this data. He uses a key of 2. How many symbols should he draw to show the votes for cheese pizza?

    _____ 8 _____

12. What key would Minh use if she drew three symbols for pepperoni pizza?

    _____ key of 3 _____

For 13–14, use the bar graph.

FAVORITE PETS

13. Is this a **vertical** or **horizontal** bar graph?

    _____ vertical bar graph _____

14. How many more students chose cats than chose birds?

    _____ 5 _____

Go On

AG118 Assessment Guide

Form B • Free Response

For 15–16, use the grid.

15. What is the ordered pair for point *D*?

    _____ (5,2) _____

16. What point is found at the ordered pair (1,3)?

    _____ A _____

For 17–18, use the line graph.

STUDENTS WITH PERFECT ATTENDANCE

17. In which month did the fewest students have perfect attendance?

    _____ October _____

Form B • Free Response

18. How many more students had perfect attendance in February than in September?

    _____ 10 _____

19. Measure the length of the string to the nearest inch.

    _____ 2 in. _____

20. What is the best customary unit to measure the distance from your house to the grocery store?

    _____ mile _____

21. Compare the amounts. Write <, >, or = in the ◯.

    1 cup ⦵< 1 quart

22. What is the best customary unit to weigh a cherry?

    _____ oz or ounce _____

23. There are 4 quarts in a gallon. How many quarts are in 3 gallons?

    _____ 12 _____ quarts

Go On

Assessment Guide **AG119**

24. There are 2 cups in a pint. How many cups are in 3 pints?

    _____ 6 _____ cups

25. Julia is mixing dye to color T-shirts. The instructions for dark blue dye say to mix one box of dye with 1 cup of water. Should she estimate or measure the water?

    _____ measure _____

26. Measure the paper clip to the nearest centimeter.

    about _____ 4 _____ centimeters

27. Measure the crayon to the nearest centimeter.

    CRAYON

    about _____ 5 _____ centimeters

28. Chris needs 300 centimeters of wire for his science project. How many meters of wire does he need?

    _____ 3 _____ meters

AG120 Assessment Guide

29. Susan is going to run 5,000 meters. How many kilometers will she run?

    _____ 5 _____ kilometers

30. What is the best metric unit to measure the amount of water needed to fill a bathtub?

    _____ L _____

31. List these objects in order from the **least** to the **greatest** mass: paper clip, book, ruler.

    paper clip, ruler, book

32. What temperature does the thermometer show?

    _____ 6°F _____

33. What temperature does the thermometer show?

    _____ 2°C _____

Stop

Form B • Free Response

AG 238   Assessment Guide

Name _____

Choose the correct answer.

1. What is straight, continues in both directions, and does not end?

   A point   C line segment
   (B) line   D ray

2. What figure is formed by two rays with the same endpoint?

   F square   H triangle
   (G) angle   J circle

3. I am part of a line. I have one endpoint. I am straight and continue in one direction. What am I?

   A line   C line segment
   (B) ray   D angle

4. Emile's teacher drew this figure on the board. Which best describes the figure?

   F angle   H parallel lines
   G line   (J) line segment

5. The answer to a question asked by a teacher is, "Two lines that never cross." What could be the question?

   (A) What are parallel lines?
   B What is a line?
   C What is an angle?
   D What are intersecting lines?

6. What figure is shown?

   F intersecting lines
   G a ray
   H an angle
   (J) parallel lines

7. Which best describes the figure shown below?

   A point
   B line
   C parallel lines
   (D) intersecting lines

For 8–9, use the figures below.

8. Which figure is a quadrilateral?

   (F) figure A   H figure C
   G figure B   J figure D

9. Which figure is NOT a polygon?

   A figure A   C figure C
   (B) figure B   D figure D

Form A • Multiple Choice

Go On

Assessment Guide   **AG121**

Name _____

For 10–13, use these triangles.

10. Which triangle has a right angle?

    F triangle K   (H) triangle L
    G triangle M   J triangle N

11. Which triangle has an obtuse angle?

    A triangle K   C triangle L
    B triangle M   (D) triangle N

12. What kind of triangle is figure K?

    F equilateral   H right
    G scalene   (J) isosceles

13. Which figure is an equilateral triangle?

    A figure K   (C) figure M
    B figure L   D figure N

For 14–16, use these figures.

14. Which figure has 4 equal sides and NO right angles?

    F figure L   H figure N
    G figure M   (J) figure P

15. Which figure has 4 equal sides and 4 right angles?

    A figure L   C figure N
    (B) figure M   D figure P

16. Which figure has NO pairs of parallel sides and NO right angles?

    F figure L   (H) figure N
    G figure M   J figure P

For 17–18, use the following information.

Peter used the labels **multiples of 2** and **multiples of 3** for the sets in his Venn diagram.

17. Which number could be in the area where the sets overlap?

    A 3   (C) 12
    B 9   D 15

18. Which number would NOT be in the area where the sets overlap?

    F 6   H 12
    (G) 9   J 18

Stop

AG122   Assessment Guide

Form A • Multiple Choice

Name _____

Write the correct answer.

1. What is the part of a line that has two endpoints called?

   _____line segment_____

2. An angle that forms a square corner is called a

   _____right_____ angle.

3. Circle the correct answer.

   An angle is formed by two __?__ with the same endpoint.

   (rays)   circles

4.

   Amanda drew this figure on the chalkboard. Write a name that describes the figure.

   _____angle_____

5. What kind of lines never cross?

   _____parallel_____ lines

6. Circle the name of the figure shown in the drawing.

   (parallel lines)   intersecting lines

7.

   Describe the lines in the drawing.

   _____intersecting lines_____

For 8–9, use the figures.

8. Which figure is NOT a polygon?

   _____Figure C_____

9. Which figure is a hexagon?

   _____Figure A_____

Form B • Free Response

Go On

Assessment Guide   **AG123**

Name _____

For 10–13, use these triangles.

10. Which triangle is a right triangle?

    _____Triangle F_____

11. Which triangle has three equal angles?

    _____Triangle D_____

12. What kind of triangle is triangle D? Write **scalene** or **equilateral**.

    _____equilateral_____

13. Which triangle is isosceles?

    _____Triangle E_____

For 14–16, use these figures.

14. Which figure does NOT have 4 equal sides?

    _____Figure G_____

15. Which figure has 4 equal sides and 4 right angles?

    _____Figure H_____

16. Which figure has 2 pairs of parallel sides, 4 equal sides, and NO right angles?

    _____Figure J_____

For 17–18, use the following information.

Sandy used the labels **multiples of 3** and **multiples of 4** for the sets in her Venn diagram.

17. Circle the number that could be in the area where the sets overlap.

    6   9   (12)   16

18. Circle the number that could NOT be in the area where the sets overlap.

    12   (15)   24   36

Stop

AG124   Assessment Guide

Form B • Free Response

Assessment Guide   AG 239

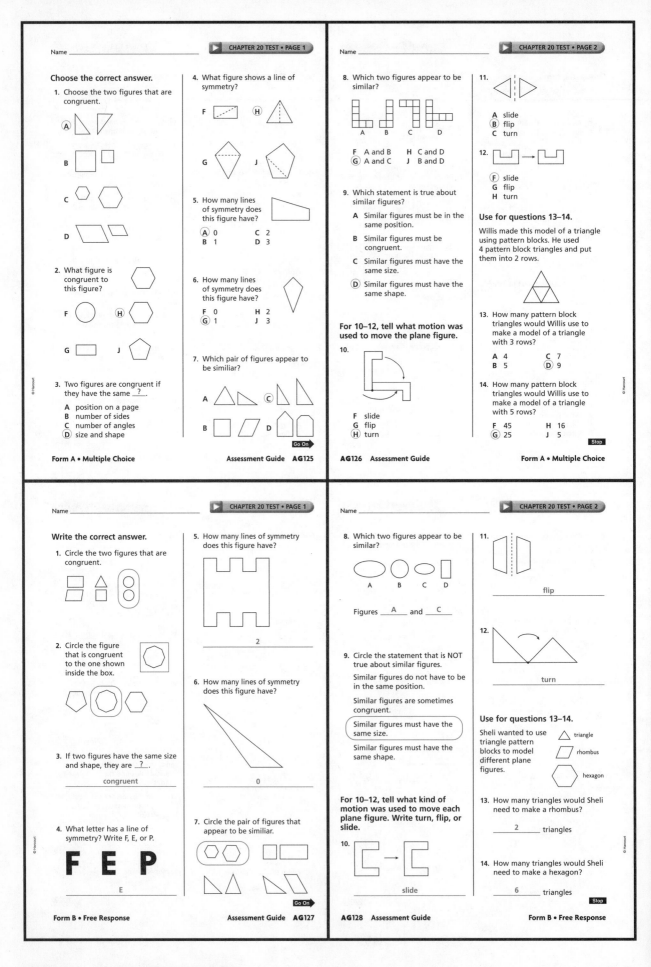

Name _____

Choose the correct answer.

1. Choose the two figures that are congruent.
   - (A)
   - B
   - C
   - D

2. What figure is congruent to this figure?
   - F
   - (H)
   - G
   - J

3. Two figures are congruent if they have the same __?__.
   - A position on a page
   - B number of sides
   - C number of angles
   - (D) size and shape

4. What figure shows a line of symmetry?
   - F
   - (H)
   - G
   - J

5. How many lines of symmetry does this figure have?
   - (A) 0
   - B 1
   - C 2
   - D 3

6. How many lines of symmetry does this figure have?
   - F 0
   - (G) 1
   - H 2
   - J 3

7. Which pair of figures appear to be similiar?
   - A
   - (C)
   - B
   - D

Name _____

8. Which two figures appear to be similar?
   - A   B   C   D
   - F A and B   H C and D
   - (G) A and C   J B and D

9. Which statement is true about similar figures?
   - A Similar figures must be in the same position.
   - B Similar figures must be congruent.
   - C Similar figures must have the same size.
   - (D) Similar figures must have the same shape.

For 10–12, tell what motion was used to move the plane figure.

10.
   - F slide
   - G flip
   - (H) turn

11.
   - A slide
   - (B) flip
   - C turn

12.
   - (F) slide
   - G flip
   - H turn

Use for questions 13–14.

Willis made this model of a triangle using pattern blocks. He used 4 pattern block triangles and put them into 2 rows.

13. How many pattern block triangles would Willis use to make a model of a triangle with 3 rows?
   - A 4
   - B 5
   - C 7
   - (D) 9

14. How many pattern block triangles would Willis use to make a model of a triangle with 5 rows?
   - F 45
   - (G) 25
   - H 16
   - J 5

Stop

Name _____

Write the correct answer.

1. Circle the two figures that are congruent.

2. Circle the figure that is congruent to the one shown inside the box.

3. If two figures have the same size and shape, they are __?__.
   congruent

4. What letter has a line of symmetry? Write F, E, or P.

   F E P
   E

5. How many lines of symmetry does this figure have?
   2

6. How many lines of symmetry does this figure have?
   0

7. Circle the pair of figures that appear to be similiar.

Go On

Name _____

8. Which two figures appear to be similar?
   - A   B   C   D
   Figures __A__ and __C__

9. Circle the statement that is NOT true about similar figures.
   - Similar figures do not have to be in the same position.
   - Similar figures are sometimes congruent.
   - (Similar figures must have the same size.)
   - Similar figures must have the same shape.

For 10–12, tell what kind of motion was used to move each plane figure. Write turn, flip, or slide.

10.
   slide

11.
   flip

12.
   turn

Use for questions 13–14.

Sheli wanted to use triangle pattern blocks to model different plane figures.
   - triangle
   - rhombus
   - hexagon

13. How many triangles would Sheli need to make a rhombus?
   __2__ triangles

14. How many triangles would Sheli need to make a hexagon?
   __6__ triangles

Stop

Name _____

Choose the correct answer.

1. What solid figure has a shape like a box of cereal?
   - (A) rectangular prism
   - B cylinder
   - C sphere
   - D cone

2. How many edges does a rectangular prism have?
   - F 6
   - G 8
   - (H) 12
   - J 14

3. I am a solid figure. I look like a bowling ball. What figure am I?
   - A a cube
   - (B) a sphere
   - C a cylinder
   - D a cone

4. Which best describes the faces of a cube?
   - F pentagons
   - G circles
   - H triangles
   - (J) squares

5. What solid figure has 5 faces, 8 edges, and 5 vertices?
   - A cube
   - (B) square pyramid
   - C sphere
   - D rectangular prism

6. What solid figures are used to make the object?
   - (F) cone, cylinder
   - G cone, sphere
   - H cone, square pyramid
   - J cylinder, sphere

7. What solid figures are used to make the object?
   - A cone, cube
   - B square pyramid, cone
   - C sphere, cube
   - (D) cube, square pyramid

8. What solid figures are used to make the object?
   - F cube, cylinder
   - (G) cube, rectangular prism
   - H cube, sphere
   - J cone, cube

Go On

Form A • Multiple Choice

Name _____

9. Which figure will NOT tessellate?
   - (A) ○
   - B □
   - C △
   - D ⬡

10. Which figure will tessellate?
    - (F) ◇
    - G ⬡⬡
    - H ○
    - J (shape)

11. Which figure will NOT tessellate?
    - A △
    - B ▭
    - (C) ○
    - D ⬡

12. Which figure will NOT tessellate?
    - F ⬡
    - G □
    - H △
    - (J) ⬠

13. How many line segments are needed to draw an octagon?
    - (A) 8
    - B 7
    - C 6
    - D 5

14. Which figure can be drawn with 4 line segments?
    - F hexagon
    - (G) rectangle
    - H pyramid
    - J cylinder

15. How many angles does a pentagon have?
    - A 8
    - B 7
    - (C) 5
    - D 2

16. How many vertices does a parallelogram have?
    - F 8
    - G 6
    - H 5
    - (J) 4

Use this figure for 17 and 18.

17. Which figure is the bottom view of a square pyramid?
    - (A) square
    - B triangle
    - C circle
    - D rectangle

18. Which figure is the side view of a square pyramid?
    - F square
    - G circle
    - (H) triangle
    - J rectangle

Stop

Form A • Multiple Choice

Name _____

Write the correct answer.

1. Jody bought a can of peaches. What solid figure has a shape like a can?

   _____cylinder_____

2. How many faces does a cube have?

   _____6_____

3. What solid figure looks like a cereal box?

   _____rectangular prism_____

4. Circle the word that best describes the faces of a cube.
   (squares)   circles

5.

   Name the two solid figures used to make this object.

   _____cube and square pyramid_____

6.

   Name the solid figures used to make the object.

   _____cube and cylinder_____

7.

   Name the two solid figures used to make the object.

   _____square pyramid and cylinder_____

8. Name two figures that have 6 faces, 12 edges, and 8 vertices.

   _____cube and rectangular prism_____

9. Tell if this is a tessellation. Write **yes** or **no**.

   _____yes_____

Go On

Form B • Free Response

Name _____

10. Circle the figure that will tessellate.

11. Circle the figure that will NOT tessellate.

12. Circle the figure that will NOT tessellate.

13. How many line segments are needed to draw a hexagon?

    _____6_____ line segments

14. Circle the figure can be drawn with 4 line segments.
    - octagon
    - (rhombus)
    - hexagon
    - pentagon

15. How many angles does an octagon have?

    _____8_____ angles

16. How many vertices does a rhombus have?

    _____4_____ vertices

17. Name the figure that is the bottom view of a cylinder.

    _____circle_____

18. Name the figure that is the bottom view of a cube.

    _____square_____

Stop

Form B • Free Response

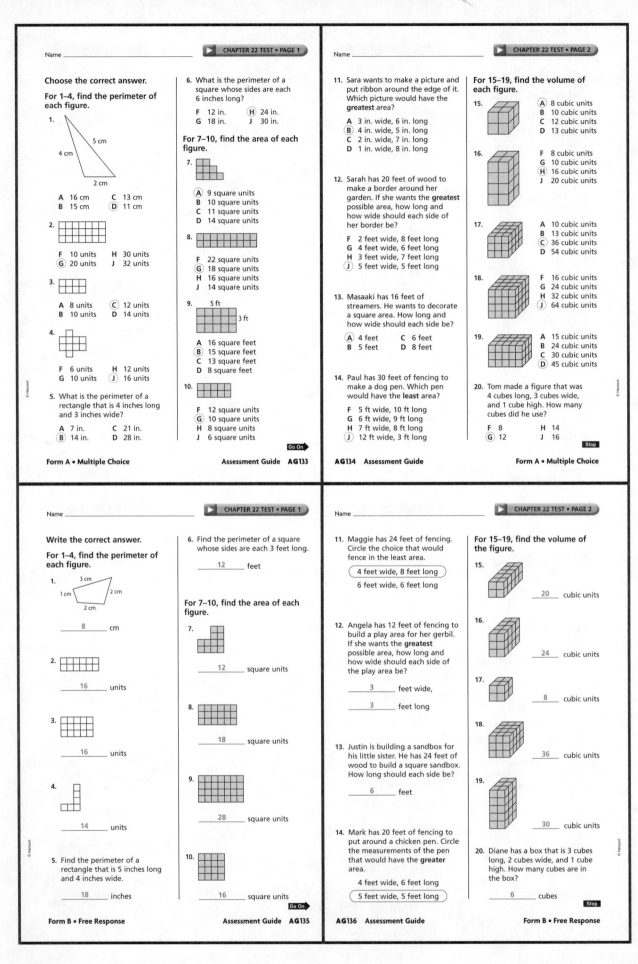

Name _____

Choose the correct answer.

For 1–4, find the perimeter of each figure.

1.

5 cm
4 cm
2 cm

A 16 cm   C 13 cm
B 15 cm   (D) 11 cm

2.

F 10 units   H 30 units
(G) 20 units   J 32 units

3.

A 8 units   (C) 12 units
B 10 units   D 14 units

4.

F 6 units   H 12 units
G 10 units   (J) 16 units

5. What is the perimeter of a rectangle that is 4 inches long and 3 inches wide?

A 7 in.   C 21 in.
(B) 14 in.   D 28 in.

6. What is the perimeter of a square whose sides are each 6 inches long?

F 12 in.   (H) 24 in.
G 18 in.   J 30 in.

For 7–10, find the area of each figure.

7.

(A) 9 square units
B 10 square units
C 11 square units
D 14 square units

8.

F 22 square units
(G) 18 square units
H 16 square units
J 14 square units

9.

5 ft
3 ft

A 16 square feet
(B) 15 square feet
C 13 square feet
D 8 square feet

10.

F 12 square units
(G) 10 square units
H 8 square units
J 6 square units

Go On

Form A • Multiple Choice   Assessment Guide **AG133**

Name _____

11. Sara wants to make a picture and put ribbon around the edge of it. Which picture would have the **greatest** area?

A 3 in. wide, 6 in. long
(B) 4 in. wide, 5 in. long
C 2 in. wide, 7 in. long
D 1 in. wide, 8 in. long

12. Sarah has 20 feet of wood to make a border around her garden. If she wants the **greatest** possible area, how long and how wide should each side of her border be?

F 2 feet wide, 8 feet long
G 4 feet wide, 6 feet long
H 3 feet wide, 7 feet long
(J) 5 feet wide, 5 feet long

13. Masaaki has 16 feet of streamers. He wants to decorate a square area. How long and how wide should each side be?

(A) 4 feet   C 6 feet
B 5 feet   D 8 feet

14. Paul has 30 feet of fencing to make a dog pen. Which pen would have the **least** area?

F 5 ft wide, 10 ft long
G 6 ft wide, 9 ft long
H 7 ft wide, 8 ft long
(J) 12 ft wide, 3 ft long

For 15–19, find the volume of each figure.

15.

(A) 8 cubic units
B 10 cubic units
C 12 cubic units
D 13 cubic units

16.

F 8 cubic units
G 10 cubic units
(H) 16 cubic units
J 20 cubic units

17.

A 10 cubic units
B 13 cubic units
(C) 36 cubic units
D 54 cubic units

18.

F 16 cubic units
G 24 cubic units
H 32 cubic units
(J) 64 cubic units

19.

A 15 cubic units
B 24 cubic units
C 30 cubic units
(D) 45 cubic units

20. Tom made a figure that was 4 cubes long, 3 cubes wide, and 1 cube high. How many cubes did he use?

F 8   H 14
(G) 12   J 16

Stop

AG134 Assessment Guide   Form A • Multiple Choice

Name _____

Write the correct answer.

For 1–4, find the perimeter of each figure.

1.

3 cm
1 cm
2 cm
2 cm

___8___ cm

2.

___16___ units

3.

___16___ units

4.

___14___ units

5. Find the perimeter of a rectangle that is 5 inches long and 4 inches wide.

___18___ inches

6. Find the perimeter of a square whose sides are each 3 feet long.

___12___ feet

For 7–10, find the area of each figure.

7.

___12___ square units

8.

___18___ square units

9.

___28___ square units

10.

___16___ square units

Go On

Form B • Free Response   Assessment Guide **AG135**

Name _____

11. Maggie has 24 feet of fencing. Circle the choice that would fence in the least area.

(4 feet wide, 8 feet long)
6 feet wide, 6 feet long

12. Angela has 12 feet of fencing to build a play area for her gerbil. If she wants the **greatest** possible area, how long and how wide should each side of the play area be?

___3___ feet wide,

___3___ feet long

13. Justin is building a sandbox for his little sister. He has 24 feet of wood to build a square sandbox. How long should each side be?

___6___ feet

14. Mark has 20 feet of fencing to put around a chicken pen. Circle the measurements of the pen that would have the **greater** area.

4 feet wide, 6 feet long
(5 feet wide, 5 feet long)

For 15–19, find the volume of the figure.

15.

___20___ cubic units

16.

___24___ cubic units

17.

___8___ cubic units

18.

___36___ cubic units

19.

___30___ cubic units

20. Diane has a box that is 3 cubes long, 2 cubes wide, and 1 cube high. How many cubes are in the box?

___6___ cubes

Stop

AG136 Assessment Guide   Form B • Free Response

AG 242   **Assessment Guide**

Name _____

Choose the correct answer.

1. Which is a name for this figure?

   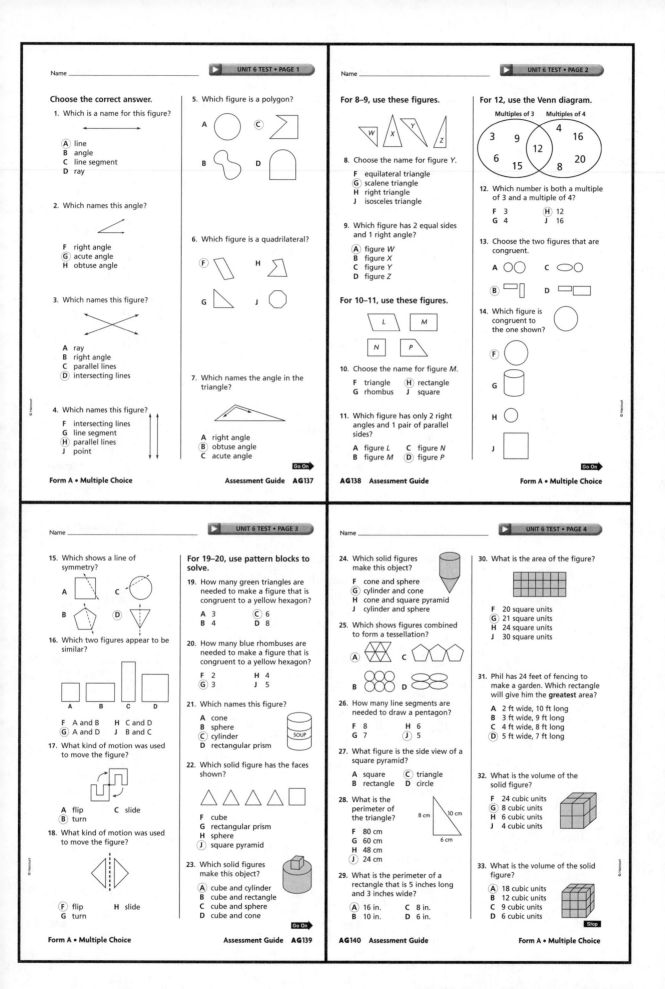

   (A) line
   B angle
   C line segment
   D ray

2. Which names this angle?

   F right angle
   (G) acute angle
   H obtuse angle

3. Which names this figure?

   A ray
   B right angle
   C parallel lines
   (D) intersecting lines

4. Which names this figure?
   F intersecting lines
   G line segment
   (H) parallel lines
   J point

5. Which figure is a polygon?

   A
   (C)
   B
   D

6. Which figure is a quadrilateral?

   (F)
   H
   G
   J

7. Which names the angle in the triangle?

   A right angle
   (B) obtuse angle
   C acute angle

   Go On ▶

Form A • Multiple Choice   **Assessment Guide   AG137**

Name _____

For 8–9, use these figures.

8. Choose the name for figure Y.
   F equilateral triangle
   (G) scalene triangle
   H right triangle
   J isosceles triangle

9. Which figure has 2 equal sides and 1 right angle?
   (A) figure W
   B figure X
   C figure Y
   D figure Z

For 10–11, use these figures.

10. Choose the name for figure M.
    F triangle   (H) rectangle
    G rhombus   J square

11. Which figure has only 2 right angles and 1 pair of parallel sides?
    A figure L   C figure N
    B figure M   (D) figure P

For 12, use the Venn diagram.

Multiples of 3   Multiples of 4

| 3 | 9 | 12 | 4 | 16 |
| 6 | 15 | | 8 | 20 |

12. Which number is both a multiple of 3 and a multiple of 4?
    F 3   (H) 12
    G 4   J 16

13. Choose the two figures that are congruent.

    A   C
    (B) D

14. Which figure is congruent to the one shown?

    (F)
    G
    H
    J

    Go On ▶

AG138   Assessment Guide   **Form A • Multiple Choice**

Name _____

15. Which shows a line of symmetry?

    A   C
    B   (D)

16. Which two figures appear to be similar?

    A   B   C   D

    F A and B   H C and D
    (G) A and D J B and C

17. What kind of motion was used to move the figure?

    A flip   C slide
    (B) turn

18. What kind of motion was used to move the figure?

    (F) flip   H slide
    G turn

For 19–20, use pattern blocks to solve.

19. How many green triangles are needed to make a figure that is congruent to a yellow hexagon?
    A 3   (C) 6
    B 4   D 8

20. How many blue rhombuses are needed to make a figure that is congruent to a yellow hexagon?
    F 2   H 4
    (G) 3   J 5

21. Which names this figure?
    A cone
    B sphere
    (C) cylinder
    D rectangular prism

22. Which solid figure has the faces shown?

    F cube
    G rectangular prism
    H sphere
    (J) square pyramid

23. Which solid figures make this object?
    (A) cube and cylinder
    B cube and rectangle
    C cube and sphere
    D cube and cone

    Go On ▶

Form A • Multiple Choice   **Assessment Guide   AG139**

Name _____

24. Which solid figures make this object?
    F cone and sphere
    (G) cylinder and cone
    H cone and square pyramid
    J cylinder and sphere

25. Which shows figures combined to form a tessellation?
    (A)   C
    B   D

26. How many line segments are needed to draw a pentagon?
    F 8   H 6
    G 7   (J) 5

27. What figure is the side view of a square pyramid?
    A square   (C) triangle
    B rectangle D circle

28. What is the perimeter of the triangle?
    F 80 cm
    G 60 cm
    H 48 cm
    (J) 24 cm

    8 cm   10 cm
       6 cm

29. What is the perimeter of a rectangle that is 5 inches long and 3 inches wide?
    (A) 16 in.   C 8 in.
    B 10 in.   D 6 in.

30. What is the area of the figure?

    F 20 square units
    (G) 21 square units
    H 24 square units
    J 30 square units

31. Phil has 24 feet of fencing to make a garden. Which rectangle will give him the **greatest** area?
    A 2 ft wide, 10 ft long
    B 3 ft wide, 9 ft long
    C 4 ft wide, 8 ft long
    (D) 5 ft wide, 7 ft long

32. What is the volume of the solid figure?
    F 24 cubic units
    (G) 8 cubic units
    H 6 cubic units
    J 4 cubic units

33. What is the volume of the solid figure?
    (A) 18 cubic units
    B 12 cubic units
    C 9 cubic units
    D 6 cubic units

    Stop ■

AG140   Assessment Guide   **Form A • Multiple Choice**

Assessment Guide   AG 243

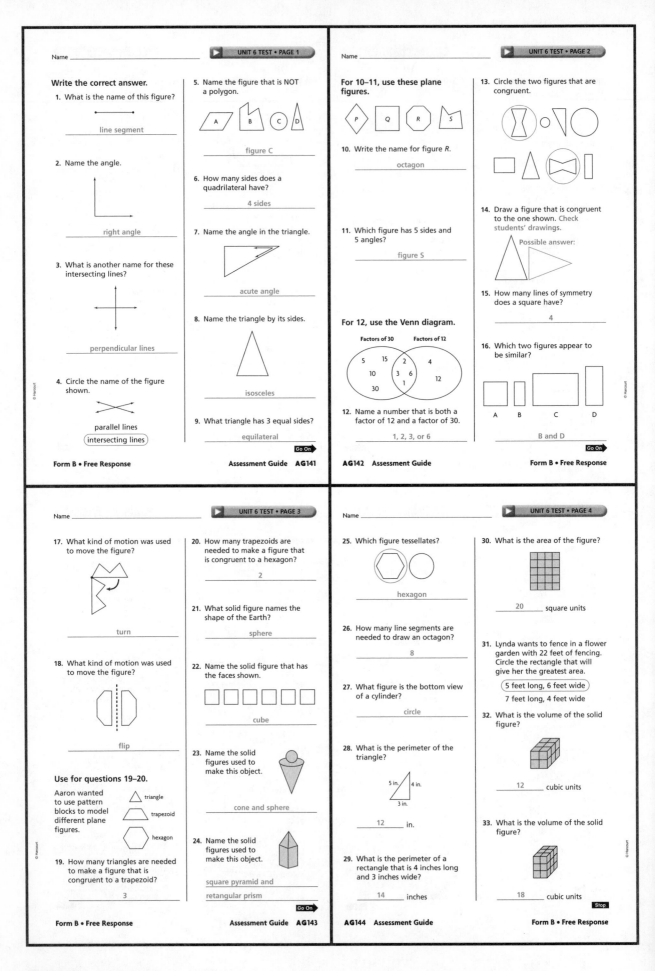

Write the correct answer.

1. What is the name of this figure?

   line segment

2. Name the angle.

   right angle

3. What is another name for these intersecting lines?

   perpendicular lines

4. Circle the name of the figure shown.

   parallel lines
   (intersecting lines)

5. Name the figure that is NOT a polygon.

   figure C

6. How many sides does a quadrilateral have?

   4 sides

7. Name the angle in the triangle.

   acute angle

8. Name the triangle by its sides.

   isosceles

9. What triangle has 3 equal sides?

   equilateral

   Go On

For 10–11, use these plane figures.

10. Write the name for figure R.

    octagon

11. Which figure has 5 sides and 5 angles?

    figure S

For 12, use the Venn diagram.

Factors of 30   Factors of 12

5 15   2   4
10   3 6
30   1   12

12. Name a number that is both a factor of 12 and a factor of 30.

    1, 2, 3, or 6

13. Circle the two figures that are congruent.

14. Draw a figure that is congruent to the one shown. Check students' drawings.

    Possible answer:

15. How many lines of symmetry does a square have?

    4

16. Which two figures appear to be similar?

    A   B   C   D

    B and D

    Go On

17. What kind of motion was used to move the figure?

    turn

18. What kind of motion was used to move the figure?

    flip

Use for questions 19–20.

Aaron wanted to use pattern blocks to model different plane figures.

   triangle
   trapezoid
   hexagon

19. How many triangles are needed to make a figure that is congruent to a trapezoid?

    3

20. How many trapezoids are needed to make a figure that is congruent to a hexagon?

    2

21. What solid figure names the shape of the Earth?

    sphere

22. Name the solid figure that has the faces shown.

    cube

23. Name the solid figures used to make this object.

    cone and sphere

24. Name the solid figures used to make this object.

    square pyramid and
    retangular prism

    Go On

25. Which figure tessellates?

    hexagon

26. How many line segments are needed to draw an octagon?

    8

27. What figure is the bottom view of a cylinder?

    circle

28. What is the perimeter of the triangle?

    5 in.   4 in.
       3 in.

    12   in.

29. What is the perimeter of a rectangle that is 4 inches long and 3 inches wide?

    14   inches

30. What is the area of the figure?

    20   square units

31. Lynda wants to fence in a flower garden with 22 feet of fencing. Circle the rectangle that will give her the greatest area.

    (5 feet long, 6 feet wide)
    7 feet long, 4 feet wide

32. What is the volume of the solid figure?

    12   cubic units

33. What is the volume of the solid figure?

    18   cubic units

    Stop

Name _____

Choose the correct answer.

1. What is the pattern unit?

   ○○□ ○○□ ○○□

   A circle, circle, square
   B circle, square, circle
   C square, circle, square
   D circle, square, square

2. Which shape is next?

   □ ⬠ △ □ ⬠ △ □ ?

   F triangle   **H** square
   G rectangle   **J** pentagon

3. What is the pattern unit?

   □ △ □ △ □ △

   A triangle, square
   B square, triangle
   C triangle, triangle
   D square, square

4. Which two shapes are next?

   □ ○ △ □ ○ △ ? ?

   F triangle, circle
   G square, circle
   H circle, triangle
   J triangle, square

5. What is the pattern rule?

   □□
   □□ □□
   □□ □□ □□

   A add two squares
   B subtract two squares
   C add four squares
   D multiply by two squares

6. What is the pattern rule?

   △△△
   △△△ △△△   △△△
   △△△ △△△   △△△

   F Multiply the triangles by 3.
   G Add 2 triangles.
   H Multiply the triangles by 2.
   J Add a row of 3 triangles.

7. What is the pattern rule?

   □   □□□   □□□□□

   A add 4 tiles   **C** add 2 tiles
   B add 3 tiles   **D** add 1 tile

8. What is the pattern rule?

   ● ●● ●●● ●●●●

   F Add 1 column of dots
   G Subtract 1 column of dots
   H Add 4 dots to each row
   J Subtract 4 dots from each row

9. What is the rule for the number pattern?

   25, 29, 33, 37, 41, 45

   A add 2   **C** add 4
   B add 3   **D** add 5

10. Find the missing numbers.

    831, 811, 791, ■, 751, ■

    F 781, 731   **H** 781, 741
    G 771, 741   **J** 771, 731

    Go On

Form A • Multiple Choice

Name _____

11. What is the rule for the number pattern?

    36, 42, 48, 54, 60, 66, 72

    A divide by 6
    B multiply by 6
    C add 6
    D subtract 6

12. Find the missing numbers.

    204, 200, 196, ■, 188, 184, ■

    F 194, 182   **H** 192, 180
    G 190, 180   **J** 192, 182

13. Which pattern uses 3 shapes and is repeated two times?

    A ○ △ ○ △ ○ △
    B ○ □ △ ○ □ △
    C △ □ ○ □ ○ △
    D ○ ○ □ □ △ △

14. Which pattern shows a number multiplied by 2 to find the next number?

    F 2, 4, 8, 16, 32
    G 32, 16, 8, 4, 2
    H 2, 4, 6, 8, 10
    J 1, 1, 2, 4, 6, 10

15. What pattern uses 2 shapes and is repeated three times?

    A □ □ □ △ △ △
    B △ △ □ △ △ △
    C □ △ □ △ □ △
    D △ □ □ □ □ △

16. Which pattern shows the previous 2 numbers being added to find the next number?

    F 3, 6, 12, 24, 48, 96
    G 10, 6, 4, 2, 1, 1
    H 1, 3, 5, 7, 9, 11
    J 1, 1, 2, 3, 5, 8, 13

17. There are 5 boxes numbered 14, 22, 30, 38, and ■. What is the missing number?

    A 42   **C** 48
    B 46   **D** 56

18. A garden has a pattern unit of two red flowers, one yellow flower, one pink flower, and one orange flower. What color is the tenth flower?

    F red   **H** orange
    G pink   **J** yellow

19. A tower uses a cube, cylinder, and rectangular prism pattern. Which shape would be eighth ?

    A cylinder
    B cube
    C rectangular prism

20. Find the next number in the pattern to solve.

    28, 21, 14, ■

    F 0   **H** 35
    G 7   **J** 42

    Stop

Form A • Multiple Choice

Name _____

1. Draw the pattern unit.

   □ △ □ △ □ △
   □ △ □

   _____

2. Which shape is next?

   □ △ ○ □ △ ○ ?

   □

3. Name the shapes in the pattern unit.

   □ ○ ▭ ○ □ ○

   rectangle and circle

4. Draw the two shapes that are next in the pattern.

   ○ △ ○ □ ○ △ ○ □

   ○ △

5. What is the rule for the pattern?

   ○○
   ○○ ○○
   ○○ ○○ ○○
   ○○ ○○ ○○ ○○

   Subtract two circles.

For 6–8, circle the rule for the pattern.

6.

   (dot pattern)

   Multiply by 2.
   Add 2 dots.

7.

   (tile pattern)

   Add 2 tiles.
   Add 3 tiles.

8.

   △△
   △△△
   △△△△
   △△△△△

   Add 1 triangle.
   Subtract 2 triangles.

9. What is the rule for the number pattern?

   111, 113, 115, 117, 119, 121

   add 2

10. Write the missing numbers.

    381, 376, 371, 366, 361, 356

    Go On

Form B • Free Response

Name _____

11. What is the rule for the number pattern?

    70, 64, 58, 52, 46

    subtract 6

12. Write the missing numbers.

    3, 6, 12, 24, 48, 96

13. Which pattern uses 4 shapes and is repeated two times? Circle it.

    ○ △ □ ○ △ □ □
    (○ △ ○ □ □ △ ○ □)
    □ ○ □ △ △ □ □
    □ □ ○ □ □ □ ○

14. Write a pattern that shows a number divided by 2 to find the next number.

    Possible answer: 32, 16, 8, 4, 2

15. Which pattern uses 3 shapes and is repeated two times? Circle it.

    □ △ □ △ □ △
    ○ △ □ △ ○ □
    (△ ○ □ △ ○ □)
    △ △ ○ ○ □ □

16. Write a pattern that shows subtracting 3 and then adding 1.

    Possible answer: 12, 9, 10, 7, 8, 5

17. Write the missing number.

    102, 106, 110, 114, 118

18. There are paper kites in a classroom window. The kites are in a pattern of blue, green, orange, red, and yellow. What color is the eleventh kite in the window?

    blue

19. Kevin drew a picture using a pattern of circle, triangle, and square. What is the eighth shape in the picture?

    triangle

20. A dance class lined up for a performance. There were 6 dancers in the first row, 12 in the second row, and 24 in the fourth row. How many dancers were in the third row?

    18

    Stop

Form B • Free Response

Choose the correct answer.

For 1–2, use this information.

A box has 3 red, 6 blue, 1 white, and 10 green cubes in it.

1. Which color is **most likely** to be pulled out of the box?

   A red   C white
   B blue   (D) green

2. What is the chance of pulling a red cube out of the box?

   (F) 3 out of 20 H 3 out of 4
   G 3 out of 10 J 1 out of 4

For 3–5, use this spinner.

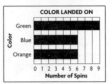

3. What are the outcomes for this spinner?

   (A) red, yellow, green
   B red, white, yellow
   C red, yellow, blue
   D red, blue, green

4. What is the chance that you will spin red?

   F 1 out of 3 (H) 2 out of 4
   G 1 out of 4 J 2 out of 3

5. Which outcomes are **equally likely**?

   A red, yellow
   B red, green
   (C) yellow, green
   D green, blue

For 6–7, use this tally table.

The tally table shows the results of an experiment using a bag of colored counters.

OUTCOMES	
Color	Tallies
Red	IIII
Yellow	IIII IIII
Blue	I
Green	IIII

6. Name the color that is **most likely** to be pulled next.

   F red   H blue
   (G) yellow J green

7. Name the color that is **most unlikely** to be pulled next.

   A red   (C) blue
   B yellow D green

For 8–9, use this line plot.

8. Predict the number that is **most likely** to be pulled out of the bag next.

```
            X
            X
   X    X   X
   X    X   X
   X  X X   X
   2  3 5   6
   Numbers
   Pulled
```

   F 2 (G) 3 H 5 J 6

9. Predict the number that is **most unlikely** to be pulled out of the bag next.

   A 2 B 3 (C) 5 D 6

Go On ▶

Form A • Multiple Choice   Assessment Guide **AG149**

For 10–11, use the bar graph.

COLOR LANDED ON

10. Which color did the spinner land on **most often**?

    (F) green G blue H orange

11. Which colors had **equally likely** outcomes?

    A green and blue
    (B) blue and orange
    C orange and green

12. What is NOT a combination shown by this tree diagram?

    F red shirt, blue jeans
    (G) red shirt, blue shirt
    H blue shirt, blue jeans
    J blue shirt, black pants

13. Henry has 2 shirts and 2 pairs of pants to choose from. How many possible combinations can he create?

    A 8 (B) 4 C 3 D 2

14. There are 4 flowers and 2 vases. How many different combinations can be created using 1 flower and 1 vase?

    F 4 G 6 (H) 8 J 16

Use this information to make a list to solve 15–16.

Luke, Garrett, Jessica, and Stephanie are arranged in a line.

15. How many different ways can they be arranged?

    (A) 24 B 20 C 12 D 8

16. What is NOT a way they can be arranged in line?

    F Luke, Stephanie, Garrett, Jessica
    G Stephanie, Garrett, Luke, Jessica
    (H) Garrett, Jessica, Luke, Garrett
    J Jessica, Luke, Garrett, Stephanie

Use this information to make a list to solve 17–18.

Ben is making a three-digit number using the digits 7, 4, and 2.

17. How many different ways can Ben arrange his numbers?

    A 13 B 12 (C) 6 D 2

18. Which is NOT a way Ben can arrange his numbers?

    F 742 G 427 H 274 (J) 272

Stop

AG150 Assessment Guide   Form A • Multiple Choice

Write the correct answer.

For 1–3, use this information.

A box has 4 red, 1 blue, 3 white, and 7 green cubes in it.

1. Name the color you are **most likely** to pull out of the box.

   _____green_____

2. What is the chance of pulling a white cube out of the box?

   __3__ out of __15__

For 3–5, use this spinner.

B = Blue
R = Red
Y = Yellow

3. How many outcomes are there for this spinner?

   _____3_____

4. What is the chance that you will spin yellow?

   __1__ out of __4__

5. Which outcomes are **equally likely**?

   _____red and yellow_____

For 6–7, use this tally table.

The tally table shows the number of pulls from a bag of marbles.

OUTCOMES	
Color	Tallies
White	IIII II
Red	IIII IIII II
Green	I

6. Name the color that is **most likely** to be pulled.

   _____red_____

7. Name the color that is **most unlikely** to be pulled.

   _____green_____

For 8–9, use this line plot.

8. Predict the number that is **most likely** to be pulled out of the bag next.

```
   X
   X
   X    X
   X  X X X
   X  X X X
   1  2 3 4 5
   Numbers
   Pulled
```

   _____1_____

9. Predict the number that is **most unlikely** to be pulled out of the bag next.

   _____2_____

Go On ▶

Form B • Free Response   Assessment Guide **AG151**

For 10–11, use the bar graph.

COLOR DRAWN

10. Which color was drawn from the bag **most often**?

    _____yellow_____

11. Which colors had **equally likely** outcomes?

    _____blue and purple_____

12. Circle the combination NOT shown by this tree diagram.

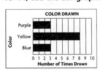

    soccer, Monday
    (soccer, lacrosse)
    lacrosse, Friday
    lacrosse, Wednesday

13. Keisha has 3 shirts and 2 pairs of pants to choose from. How many possible combinations can she create?

    _____6_____

14. There are 4 car styles and 3 color choices. How many different combinations of style and color are there?

    _____12_____

Use this information to make a list to solve 15–16.

Judson, Sergio, and Nigella are arranged in a line.

15. How many different ways can they be arranged?

    _____6_____

16. Circle a way they can NOT be arranged in line.

    Judson, Nigella, Sergio
    Nigella, Sergio, Judson
    (Sergio, Judson, Sergio)
    Judson, Sergio, Nigella

Use this information for questions 17–18.

Ken is making a four-digit number using the numbers 7, 5, 3, and 2.

17. How many different ways can Ken arrange his numbers?

    _____24_____

18. Circle the way Ken can NOT arrange his numbers.

    7 5 3 2   5 2 3 7
    7 3 2 5   (2 3 3 5)

Stop

AG152 Assessment Guide   Form B • Free Response

Choose the correct answer.

1. Name the pattern unit.

△ △ △ △ △ △

(A) triangle, triangle, pentagon
B triangle, pentagon, triangle
C pentagon, triangle, pentagon
D triangle, pentagon, pentagon

2. What is the next shape in the pattern?

☐ △ ☐ ☐ △ ☐

F △

G ☐

(H) ☐

J ⬠

3. What is the rule for the pattern?

○ ○○ ○○○
○ ○○ ○○○
○ ○○ ○○○

(A) Add 1 circle to each row.
B Add 2 circles to each row.
C Add 3 circles to each row.
D Add 4 circles to each row.

4. What is the rule for the pattern?

○○
○○ ○○
○○ ○○ ○○

F Add a row of 3 dots.
G Subtract 2 dots from each row.
H Subtract a row of 2 dots.
(J) Add a row of 2 dots.

5. What is the rule for the pattern?

13, 17, 21, 25, 29, 33

A Add 2.
B Add 3.
(C) Add 4.
D Add 5.

6. Which numbers are missing from the pattern?

707, 717, 727, ■, 747, 757, ■

F 737, 747
G 737, 757
H 737, 777
(J) 737, 767

▶ Go On

Form A • Multiple Choice   Assessment Guide **AG153**

---

7. What is the rule for the pattern?

64, 60, 56, 52, 48, 44, 40

A Add 4.
(B) Subtract 4.
C Add 5.
D Subtract 5.

8. Which pattern shows 7 added to each number?

(F) 1, 8, 15, 22, 29, 36
G 56, 49, 42, 35, 28, 21
H 0, 7, 13, 18, 22, 25
J 14, 20, 26, 32, 38, 44

9. Which pattern uses a pattern unit with 2 shapes that are repeated three times?

A ○ ○ ▭ ○ ○

B ▭ ▭ ▭ ○

(C) ○▭○▭○▭

D ▭ ○ ○ ▭ ○ ▭

10. In the front row of the class, there are 3 students. In the second row, there are 6 students. In the third row, there are 9 students. If the pattern continues, how many students are in the fifth row?

F 12
(G) 15
H 18
J 21

11. Benji wrote the following pattern.

115, 118, 121, 124, ■, 130, ■

What numbers are missing in Benji's pattern?

A 127, 136
B 128, 133
(C) 127, 133
D 128, 136

12. Trey is experimenting with a cube numbered 1, 2, 2, 3, 3, 3. Which describes his chance of rolling the number 1?

F impossible
(G) unlikely
H likely
J certain

▶ Go On

AG154 Assessment Guide   **Form A • Multiple Choice**

For 13–15, use the spinner.

red | yellow
blue | red

13. What possible outcomes should be included on a tally table?

A red, yellow, brown
(B) red, yellow, blue
C red, green, yellow
D red, purple, green

14. Which outcomes are equally likely?

F red and yellow
G red and blue
H red and green
(J) yellow and blue

15. What is the chance of spinning red?

A 1 out of 3
(B) 2 out of 4
C 2 out of 3
D 1 out of 4

For 16–18, use these spinners.

red | blue
blue | green
Spinner A

yellow
green | blue
Spinner B

16. Melanie used these spinners for an experiment. Which statement about these spinners is true?

F Spinner A has 5 possible outcomes.
(G) The chance of spinning yellow on Spinner B is 1 out of 3.
H It is impossible to spin blue on Spinner B.
J The chance of spinning green on Spinner A is 1 out of 3.

17. For Spinner A, which outcomes are equally likely?

A red, blue, green
B red, blue
(C) red, green
D blue, green, brown

18. Which describes the chance of spinning yellow on Spinner A?

(F) impossible
G unlikely
H likely
J certain

▶ Go On

Form A • Multiple Choice   Assessment Guide **AG155**

For 19–20, use the line plot. It shows the results of spinning a spinner.

```
        X
        X   X
        X   X   X
        X   X   X
    X   X   X   X
   red green blue yellow
```
Number of Spins of Each Color

19. Predict which color you are most likely to spin.

A red
(B) green
C blue
D yellow

20. Predict which color you are unlikely to spin.

(F) red
G green
H blue
J yellow

21. Casey has 3 pairs of pants and 2 shirts. How many combinations of pants and shirts can she make using 1 pair of pants and 1 shirt?

A 4
(B) 6
C 8
D 16

22. Which combination is NOT shown by this tree diagram?

blue pants — yellow shirt
            — blue shirt
            — green shirt
black pants — yellow shirt
            — blue shirt
            — green shirt

F blue shirt, blue pants
(G) blue shirt, yellow shirt
H green shirt, blue pants
J yellow shirt, black pants

For 23–24, use the information below.

Staci is making a 3-digit number using the digits 4, 2, and 9.

23. How many ways can Staci arrange the numbers?

A 13
B 12
(C) 6
D 2

24. Which does NOT show how Staci can arrange the numbers?

F 429
G 924
H 249
(J) 949

■ Stop

AG156 Assessment Guide   **Form A • Multiple Choice**

Assessment Guide AG247

Write the correct answer.

1. Name the pattern unit.

○ △ ○ ○ △ ○

circle, triangle, circle

2. What is the next shape in the pattern?

△ ○ □ △ ○ □ ?

△

3. What is the rule for the pattern?

□ □□ □□□
□ □□ □□□
□ □□ □□□
□ □□ □□□

Add 1 square to each row.

4. What is the rule for the pattern?

● ●●● ●●●●●
● ●●● ●●●●●
● ●●● ●●●●●

Add 2 dots to each row.

5. What is the rule for the pattern?

1, 4, 7, 10, 13, 16

Add 3.

6. Which numbers are missing from the pattern?

602, 607, 612, 617, ■, 627, ■

622, 632

7. What is the rule for the pattern?

41, 32, 23, 14, 5

Subtract 9.

8. Make a pattern using a 2-digit number that shows 2 added to each number. Write the first four numbers in the pattern.

Possible answer: 22, 24, 26, 28

Go On

Form B • Free Response

9. Make a pattern whose pattern unit uses 3 shapes and is repeated two times.
Possible answer:

○ △ □ ○ △ □

10. A bookshelf has 2 pictures on the first shelf, 5 pictures on the second shelf, and 8 pictures on the third shelf. If this pattern continues, how many pictures will be on the fifth shelf?

14 pictures

11. Zack wrote the following pattern.

135, 131, 127, 123, ■, 115, ■

What numbers are missing in Zack's pattern?

119, 111

12. Denise puts 3 yellow marbles, 4 blue marbles, 6 white marbles, and 1 black marble into a bag. What describes her chance of drawing the black marble from the bag?

unlikely

For 13–15, use the following information.

Sheli has a cube numbered 1, 2, 2, 2, 3, 4.

13. What possible outcomes should she include on her tally table?

1, 2, 3, and 4

14. Which outcomes are equally likely?

1, 3, and 4

15. What is the chance that she will roll a 2?

3 out of 6, or $\frac{1}{2}$

For 16–18, use this information about the bags of marbles used in an experiment.

Bag A—2 red, 2 white, 3 green

Bag B—1 yellow, 5 red, 3 blue

16. Is the following statement true or false? The chance of pulling a yellow marble from Bag B is 1 out of 10.

false

Go On

Form B • Free Response

17. For Bag A, which two outcomes are **equally likely**?

red and white

18. From which bag is it **impossible** to pull a green marble?

Bag B

For 19–20, use the line plot. It shows the results of pulling numbers from a bag.

```
              X
              X
X         X X
X   X X X X
X X X X X X
+---+---+---+---+---+
1   2   3   4   5   6
```
Numbers Pulled from a Bag

19. Predict which number is **unlikely** to be pulled from the bag.

2

20. Predict which number is **most likely** to be pulled from the bag.

4

21. June has 3 pairs of socks and 2 pairs of shoes. How many combinations of socks and shoes can she make, using 1 pair of socks and 1 pair of shoes in each?

6

22. Use the tree diagram to tell how many combinations of pizza are possible.

small ⟨ cheese / pepperoni

medium ⟨ cheese / pepperoni

large ⟨ cheese / pepperoni

6

For 23–24, use the information below.

Gina is making a code using the letters A, G, K, and M.

23. How many ways can Gina arrange the letters?

24

24. Which does NOT show how Gina can arrange the letters? Circle it.

AGKM   (AGAK)

KMAG   GKMA

Stop

Form B • Free Response

Name _____

Choose the correct answer.

1. Which fraction describes the shaded part of the figure?

   A $\frac{1}{2}$ C $\frac{2}{3}$
   (B) $\frac{1}{3}$ D $\frac{3}{3}$

2. What fraction names the point for the letter x on the number line?

   $\frac{0}{4}$ $\frac{1}{4}$ x $\frac{3}{4}$ $\frac{4}{4}$

   F $\frac{1}{4}$ H $\frac{3}{4}$
   (G) $\frac{2}{4}$ J $\frac{1}{5}$

For 3–5, choose the fraction that names the shaded part of the group.

3. △ △ △ △ △

   A $\frac{2}{5}$ B $\frac{1}{6}$ (C) $\frac{2}{6}$ D $\frac{3}{6}$

4.

   F $\frac{3}{5}$ G $\frac{1}{2}$ (H) $\frac{2}{5}$ J $\frac{1}{5}$

5.

   A $\frac{3}{6}$ (C) $\frac{6}{9}$
   B $\frac{3}{9}$ D $\frac{6}{6}$

6. Barb has 12 stickers. Of those stickers, $\frac{9}{12}$ are stars. The rest are hearts. How many heart stickers does she have?

   (F) 3   H 12
   G 9   J 21

For 7–8, find the missing numerator.

7.

   $\frac{1}{2} = \frac{\blacksquare}{10}$

   A 1   (C) 5
   B 2   D 10

8.

   $\frac{\blacksquare}{4} = \frac{6}{8}$

   F 1   H 4
   (G) 3   J 6

Go On

Form A • Multiple Choice   Assessment Guide **AG161**

Name _____

9. What group of fractions is in order from **least** to **greatest**?

   A $\frac{1}{2}, \frac{2}{3}, \frac{3}{4}$ C $\frac{1}{4}, \frac{2}{3}, \frac{1}{2}$
   (B) $\frac{1}{4}, \frac{2}{3}, \frac{2}{3}$ D $\frac{2}{3}, \frac{1}{2}, \frac{1}{4}$

10. Compare the fractions.

    $\frac{2}{4} \bullet \frac{3}{5}$

    (F) <   G >   H =

For 11–14, you may want to draw fraction bars to compare.

11. Which is true?

    A $\frac{1}{2} < \frac{1}{3}$ C $\frac{1}{2} > \frac{2}{3}$
    B $\frac{1}{2} > \frac{1}{3}$ (D) $\frac{1}{2} > \frac{1}{4}$

12. Which of these fractions is **greatest**?

    F $\frac{1}{2}$ (H) $\frac{3}{4}$
    G $\frac{2}{3}$ J $\frac{1}{5}$

13. Alan spent $\frac{1}{6}$ of his allowance on a pencil, $\frac{1}{10}$ on gum, $\frac{1}{3}$ on food, and $\frac{1}{5}$ on a book. On which item did he spend the **greatest** part of his allowance?

    A pencil   C book
    B gum   (D) food

14. Karry lives $\frac{4}{6}$ mile from school, Lynn lives $\frac{2}{3}$ mile from school, and Joe lives $\frac{1}{2}$ mile from school. Who lives the **greatest** distance from school?

    (F) Karry   H Mark
    G Joe   J Lynn

15. Choose the mixed number that names the shaded parts of the group.

    A $1\frac{1}{8}$ C $1\frac{2}{6}$
    B $1\frac{2}{8}$ (D) $1\frac{6}{8}$

16. Sam is making a model to show $2\frac{2}{3}$. How many thirds will he need for his model?

    F 10 thirds   H 6 thirds
    (G) 8 thirds   J 4 thirds

Stop

AG162 Assessment Guide   **Form A • Multiple Choice**

Name _____

Write the correct answer.

1. Write the fraction that names the shaded part of the figure.

   $\frac{1}{6}$

2. What fraction names the point for the letter x on the number line?

   $\frac{0}{3}$ $\frac{1}{3}$ x $\frac{3}{3}$

   $\frac{2}{3}$

For 3–5, write the fraction that names the shaded part of the group.

3.

   $\frac{2}{5}$

4.

   $\frac{5}{6}$

5.

   $\frac{3}{7}$

6. Maggie has 10 stuffed animals. Of the animals, $\frac{4}{10}$ are bears. The rest are dogs. How many stuffed dogs does she have?

   6

For 7–8, find the missing numerator.

7.

   $\frac{1}{4} = \frac{\blacksquare}{8}$

   2

8.

   $\frac{2}{3} = \frac{\blacksquare}{6}$

   4

Go On

Form B • Free Response   Assessment Guide **AG163**

Name _____

9. Write $\frac{1}{2}$, $\frac{3}{4}$, and $\frac{3}{5}$ in order from **least** to **greatest**.

   $\frac{1}{2}$, $\frac{3}{5}$, $\frac{3}{4}$

10. Compare. Write <, >, or = in the ○.

    $\frac{4}{5} (>) \frac{3}{4}$

For 11–14, draw fraction bars to help answer the question.

11. Circle the statement that is true.

    $\frac{1}{5} > \frac{1}{3}$ $\left(\frac{1}{2} < \frac{8}{10}\right)$

12. Circle the **greatest** fraction.

    $\frac{1}{2}$ $\left(\frac{3}{4}\right)$ $\frac{2}{5}$

13. Nathan spent $\frac{1}{6}$ of his allowance on food, $\frac{1}{2}$ on the movies, and $\frac{1}{3}$ on school supplies. On which item did he spend the **greatest** part of his allowance?

    movies

14. Susan walks $\frac{5}{6}$ of a mile on Monday, $\frac{1}{3}$ of a mile on Wednesday, and $\frac{1}{2}$ of a mile on Friday. On which day does she walk the **greatest** distance?

    Monday

15. Write the mixed number that names the shaded parts of the group.

    $2\frac{3}{5}$

16. Celine is making a model to show $3\frac{3}{8}$. How many eighths will she need for her model?

    31 eighths

Stop

AG164 Assessment Guide   **Form B • Free Response**

Assessment Guide   AG 249

Choose the correct answer.

For 1–5, use fraction bars to find the sum.

1. $\frac{2}{5} + \frac{1}{5} = \blacksquare$

A $\frac{2}{10}$ C $\frac{2}{5}$

B $\frac{3}{10}$ (D) $\frac{3}{5}$

2. $\frac{6}{8} + \frac{1}{8} = \blacksquare$

F $\frac{5}{16}$ H $\frac{5}{8}$

G $\frac{7}{16}$ (J) $\frac{7}{8}$

3. $\frac{1}{6} + \frac{2}{6} = \blacksquare$

(A) $\frac{3}{6}$ C $\frac{3}{12}$

B $\frac{4}{6}$ D $\frac{4}{12}$

4. Lamont has 3 dog stickers, 4 cat stickers, and 1 car sticker. What fraction of the stickers are animals?

F $\frac{1}{8}$ H $\frac{4}{8}$

G $\frac{3}{8}$ (J) $\frac{7}{8}$

5. Emily did $\frac{1}{4}$ of her homework before supper and $\frac{2}{4}$ after supper. What part of her homework did she do in all?

(A) $\frac{3}{4}$ C $\frac{3}{8}$

B $\frac{2}{4}$ D $\frac{1}{4}$

For 6–8, find the sum in simplest form. Use fraction bars if you wish.

6. $\frac{1}{4} + \frac{2}{4} = \blacksquare$

F $\frac{3}{8}$ H $\frac{2}{4}$

G $\frac{1}{4}$ (J) $\frac{3}{4}$

7. $\frac{3}{8} + \frac{2}{8} = \blacksquare$

A $\frac{1}{16}$ C $\frac{5}{16}$

B $\frac{1}{8}$ (D) $\frac{5}{8}$

8. $\frac{3}{10} + \frac{3}{10} = \blacksquare$

F $\frac{3}{20}$ H $\frac{9}{20}$

G $\frac{3}{10}$ (J) $\frac{3}{5}$

For 9–12, use fraction bars to find the difference.

9. $\frac{6}{8} - \frac{3}{8} = \blacksquare$

A $\frac{3}{1}$ (C) $\frac{3}{8}$

B $\frac{9}{16}$ D $\frac{3}{16}$

10. $\frac{5}{6} - \frac{1}{6} = \blacksquare$

F $\frac{4}{12}$ H $\frac{6}{6}$

(G) $\frac{4}{6}$ J $\frac{4}{4}$

Go On

---

11. Pablo has $\frac{3}{4}$ of a pizza to share. Amy and Tim eat $\frac{2}{4}$ of the pizza. How much of the pizza is left?

A $\frac{1}{8}$ C $\frac{5}{8}$

(B) $\frac{1}{4}$ D $\frac{2}{4}$

12. George shared a bag of raisins with Ellen. George ate $\frac{3}{5}$ of the bag and Ellen ate $\frac{1}{5}$. How much of the bag of raisins is left?

F $\frac{4}{5}$ (H) $\frac{1}{5}$

G $\frac{4}{10}$ J $\frac{1}{10}$

For 13–16, find the difference in simplest form. Use fraction bars if you wish.

13. $\frac{5}{10} - \frac{1}{10} = \blacksquare$

A $\frac{6}{20}$ (C) $\frac{2}{5}$

B $\frac{1}{2}$ D $\frac{6}{10}$

14. $\frac{2}{6} - \frac{1}{6} = \blacksquare$

F $\frac{1}{12}$ H $\frac{3}{12}$

(G) $\frac{1}{6}$ J $\frac{1}{3}$

15. $\frac{8}{10} - \frac{5}{10} = \blacksquare$

A $\frac{3}{20}$ C $\frac{13}{20}$

(B) $\frac{3}{10}$ D $\frac{8}{10}$

16. $\frac{5}{12} - \frac{1}{12} = \blacksquare$

F $\frac{1}{2}$ H $\frac{6}{24}$

(G) $\frac{1}{3}$ J $\frac{4}{24}$

17. Ryan finished $\frac{3}{4}$ of his homework at school. How much does he need to finish at home?

A $\frac{4}{4}$ (C) $\frac{1}{4}$

B $\frac{1}{3}$ D $\frac{1}{7}$

18. April's mother ate $\frac{1}{5}$ of a watermelon. April and some friends ate $\frac{3}{5}$ of the melon. How much of the melon is left?

F $\frac{1}{10}$ H $\frac{2}{5}$

(G) $\frac{1}{5}$ J $\frac{7}{10}$

19. Ashley read $\frac{1}{6}$ of a new book on Monday and $\frac{1}{6}$ on Tuesday. How much of the book does she have left to read?

(A) $\frac{2}{3}$ C $\frac{1}{6}$

B $\frac{1}{3}$ D $\frac{0}{6}$

20. Becky painted $\frac{1}{8}$ of her room. How much of the room does she still have to paint?

(F) $\frac{7}{8}$ H $\frac{1}{7}$

G $\frac{3}{8}$ J $\frac{1}{8}$

Stop

Write the correct answer.

For 1–5, use fraction bars to find the sum.

1. $\frac{4}{8} + \frac{3}{8} = \blacksquare$

_____ $\frac{7}{8}$

2. $\frac{2}{10} + \frac{5}{10} = \blacksquare$

_____ $\frac{7}{10}$

3. $\frac{3}{8} + \frac{1}{8} = \blacksquare$

_____ $\frac{4}{8}$, or $\frac{1}{2}$

4. Damon has a bag filled with 3 apples, 2 oranges, and 4 books. What fraction of the bag is filled with fruit?

_____ $\frac{5}{9}$ of the bag

5. Amy cleaned $\frac{1}{5}$ of her room in the morning and $\frac{2}{5}$ in the afternoon. How much of her room did she clean in all?

_____ $\frac{3}{5}$ of her room

For 6–8, find the sum. Write the answer in simplest form. Use fraction bars if you wish.

6. $\frac{1}{3} + \frac{1}{3}$

_____ $\frac{2}{3}$

7. $\frac{5}{8} + \frac{2}{8}$

_____ $\frac{7}{8}$

8. $\frac{2}{6} + \frac{1}{6}$

_____ $\frac{1}{2}$

For 9–12, use fraction bars to find the difference.

9. $\frac{5}{6} - \frac{4}{6} = \blacksquare$

_____ $\frac{1}{6}$

10. $\frac{3}{8} - \frac{1}{8} = \blacksquare$

_____ $\frac{2}{8}$, or $\frac{1}{4}$

11. Mary Jo has $\frac{2}{3}$ of an apple pie to share. She gives $\frac{1}{3}$ of the pie to Jamie. How much of the pie is left?

_____ $\frac{1}{3}$ of the pie

Go On

---

12. Erin shared a bag of popcorn with Patrick. Erin ate $\frac{3}{8}$ of the bag of popcorn and Patrick ate $\frac{2}{8}$. How much of the bag of popcorn is left?

_____ $\frac{3}{8}$ of the bag

For 13–16, find the difference. Write the answer in simplest form. Use fraction bars if you wish.

13. $\frac{5}{6} - \frac{3}{6}$

_____ $\frac{1}{3}$

14. $\frac{7}{8} - \frac{2}{8}$

_____ $\frac{5}{8}$

15. $\frac{7}{10} - \frac{4}{10}$

_____ $\frac{3}{10}$

16. $\frac{3}{4} - \frac{1}{4}$

_____ $\frac{1}{2}$

17. Todd cleaned $\frac{2}{5}$ of the basement before lunch. How much of the basement is left to clean after lunch?

_____ $\frac{3}{5}$ of the basement

18. Patty did $\frac{1}{6}$ of her homework at school. She came home and did $\frac{4}{6}$ of her homework before supper. How much of her homework is left to do?

_____ $\frac{1}{6}$ of her homework

19. Andrew did $\frac{2}{5}$ of an art project on Tuesday and $\frac{1}{5}$ on Thursday. How much of the art project does he have left to do?

_____ $\frac{2}{5}$ of the project

20. Peggy read $\frac{1}{4}$ of a book. How much of the book is left for her to read?

_____ $\frac{3}{4}$ of the book

Stop

Choose the correct answer.

1. What is the decimal for the shaded part?

   A 6
   (B) 0.6
   C 0.4
   D $\frac{6}{100}$

2. What is the decimal for the shaded part?

   F 10
   G 9
   (H) 0.9
   J 0.09

3. How is $\frac{5}{10}$ written as a decimal?

   A 510
   (C) 0.5
   B 5
   D 0.05

4. How is $\frac{3}{10}$ written as a decimal?

   F 0.13
   H 0.03
   G 0.31
   (J) 0.3

5. How is 0.9 written as a fraction?

   A $\frac{1}{9}$
   C $\frac{9}{90}$
   (B) $\frac{9}{10}$
   D $\frac{9}{100}$

6. Which of these names the same amount as $\frac{7}{100}$?

   F 710
   H 0.7
   G 7
   (J) 0.07

7. How is $\frac{29}{100}$ written as a decimal?

   A 29
   C 2.09
   B 2.9
   (D) 0.29

8. How is 0.15 written as a fraction?

   F $\frac{15}{10}$
   (H) $\frac{15}{100}$
   G $\frac{10}{15}$
   J $\frac{1}{5}$

9. How is 0.37 written as a fraction?

   A $\frac{3}{100}$
   C $\frac{3}{7}$
   (B) $\frac{37}{100}$
   D $\frac{37}{10}$

10. How is 4.76 written in expanded form?

    F 47 + 0.6
    (G) 4 + 0.7 + 0.06
    H 400 + 70 + 6
    J 476 + 100

11. What is the missing number?

    5.82 = 5 ones ■ tenths 2 hundredths

    A 2
    (C) 8
    B 5
    D 10

12. How is 2.09 written in word form?

    (F) 2 ones and nine hundredths
    G 2 ones and nine tenths
    H 2 tenths and nine hundredths
    J 2 tenths and nine ones

Go On

---

13. How is four ones and four hundredths written in standard form?

    A 404
    C 0.4
    B 4.4
    (D) 4.04

14. Compare these decimals.

    0.04 ● 0.05

    (F) <   G >   H =

For 15–18, identify problems with too little information. Solve problems with too much or the right amount of information.

15. Mrs. Barnard made cookies for her family. She gave 3 cookies to each member of her family. How many cookies did she bake?

    (A) too little information
    B 6
    C 9
    D 12

16. Harry bought 8 pencils, 10 markers, and 2 packages of paper at the store. He used 2 pencils at school. What fraction of the pencils were used?

    F too little information
    (G) $\frac{1}{4}$
    H $\frac{1}{2}$
    J $\frac{1}{8}$

17. At track practice, Kevin ran 2.9 miles, Louis ran 3.1 miles, and Jorge ran farther than both Kevin and Louis. How much farther did Jorge run than Kevin?

    (A) too little information
    B 0.2 miles
    C 1.2 miles
    D 6.0 miles

18. Janet spent $14 for dinner. She gave her waitress $20. How much change did Janet receive back?

    F too little information
    G $34
    (H) $6
    J $4

Use the number line for 19 and 20.

◄─┼─┼─┼─┼─┼─┼─┼─┼─┼─┼─►
  0 0.1 0.2 0.3 0.4 0.5 0.6 0.7 0.8 0.9 1.0

19. Which group of decimals is in order from **greatest** to **least**?

    A 0.2, 0.9, 0.5
    B 0.9, 0.2, 0.5
    C 0.2, 0.5, 0.9
    (D) 0.9, 0.5, 0.2

20. Pat bought 0.9 pound of cherries, 0.4 pound of grapes, and 0.6 pound of bananas. Which kind of fruit did she buy the most of?

    (F) cherries   H bananas
    G grapes   J oranges

Stop

Write the correct answer.

1. Write the decimal for the shaded part.

   _____0.3_____

2. Write the decimal for the shaded part.

   _____0.5_____

3. Write $\frac{7}{10}$ as a decimal.

   0.7

4. Write $\frac{2}{10}$ as a decimal.

   0.2

5. Write 0.9 as a fraction.

   $\frac{9}{10}$

6. Write $\frac{1}{100}$ as a decimal.

   .01

7. Write $\frac{18}{100}$ as a decimal.

   0.18

8. Write 0.19 as a fraction.

   $\frac{19}{100}$

9. Write 0.68 as a fraction.

   $\frac{68}{100}$

10. Write 6.24 in expanded form.

    6 + 0.2 + 0.04

Go On

---

11. Write the missing number.

    3.75 = 3 ones ___7___ tenths 5 hundredths

12. Write 9.32 in word form.

    nine and thirty-two hundredths

13. Write eight ones and eighty-eight hundredths in standard form.

    8.88

14. Compare. Write <, >, or = in the ○.

    0.06 (<) 0.5

For 15–18, identify problems with too little information. Solve problems with too much or the right amount of information.

15. Cody left for soccer practice at 4:30. When he arrived home he spent 45 minutes on homework. What time did he finish his homework?

    too little information

16. There are 18 players on the basketball team and 20 players on the soccer team. Half of the soccer team also plays basketball. How many soccer players also play basketball?

    10 players

17. Eve worked for 4.5 hours Saturday and 5 hours on Sunday every weekend. How many hours did she work during January?

    too little information

18. It cost Mr. Wendell $34 to have his dog groomed. If he gave the groomer $50, how much change did he receive?

    $16

Use the number line for 19 and 20.

◄─┼─┼─┼─┼─┼─┼─┼─┼─┼─┼─►
  0 0.1 0.2 0.3 0.4 0.5 0.6 0.7 0.8 0.9 1.0

19. Write the decimals 0.3, 0.6, and 0.1 in order from **greatest** to **least**.

    0.6 , 0.3 , 0.1

20. Jake bought 0.5 pound of oranges and 0.8 pound of apples. Which kind of fruit did he buy more of?

    apples

Stop

Assessment Guide AG 251

Choose the correct answer.

1. What fraction of a dollar is shown?

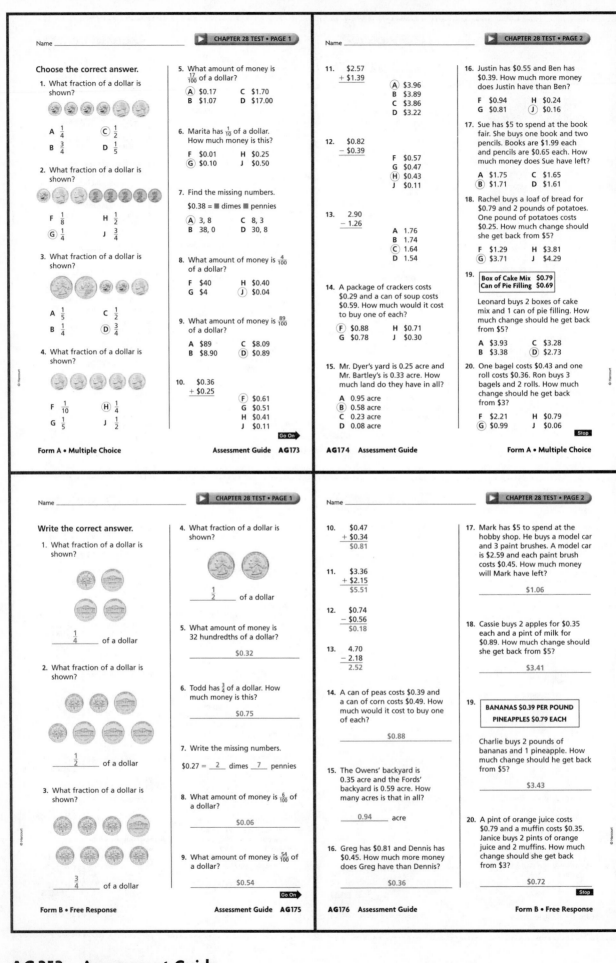

A $\frac{1}{4}$　　C $\frac{1}{2}$ (C circled)

B $\frac{3}{4}$　　D $\frac{1}{5}$

2. What fraction of a dollar is shown?

F $\frac{1}{8}$　　H $\frac{1}{2}$

G $\frac{1}{4}$ (G circled)　　J $\frac{3}{4}$

3. What fraction of a dollar is shown?

A $\frac{1}{5}$　　C $\frac{1}{2}$

B $\frac{1}{4}$　　D $\frac{3}{4}$ (D circled)

4. What fraction of a dollar is shown?

F $\frac{1}{10}$　　H $\frac{1}{4}$ (H circled)

G $\frac{1}{5}$　　J $\frac{1}{2}$

5. What amount of money is $\frac{17}{100}$ of a dollar?

A $0.17　　C $1.70

B $1.07　　D $17.00

6. Marita has $\frac{1}{10}$ of a dollar. How much money is this?

F $0.01　　H $0.25

G $0.10 (G circled)　　J $0.50

7. Find the missing numbers.

$0.38 = ■ dimes ■ pennies

A 3, 8 (A circled)　　C 8, 3

B 38, 0　　D 30, 8

8. What amount of money is $\frac{4}{100}$ of a dollar?

F $40　　H $0.40

G $4　　J $0.04 (J circled)

9. What amount of money is $\frac{89}{100}$ of a dollar?

A $89　　C $8.09

B $8.90　　D $0.89 (D circled)

10.　$0.36
　　+ $0.25

F $0.61 (F circled)
G $0.51
H $0.41
J $0.11

11.　$2.57
　　+ $1.39

A $3.96 (A circled)
B $3.89
C $3.86
D $3.22

12.　$0.82
　　− $0.39

F $0.57
G $0.47
H $0.43 (H circled)
J $0.11

13.　2.90
　　− 1.26

A 1.76
B 1.74
C 1.64 (C circled)
D 1.54

14. A package of crackers costs $0.29 and a can of soup costs $0.59. How much would it cost to buy one of each?

F $0.88 (F circled)　　H $0.71
G $0.78　　J $0.30

15. Mr. Dyer's yard is 0.25 acre and Mr. Bartley's is 0.33 acre. How much land do they have in all?

A 0.95 acre
B 0.58 acre (B circled)
C 0.23 acre
D 0.08 acre

16. Justin has $0.55 and Ben has $0.39. How much more money does Justin have than Ben?

F $0.94　　H $0.24
G $0.81　　J $0.16 (J circled)

17. Sue has $5 to spend at the book fair. She buys one book and two pencils. Books are $1.99 each and pencils are $0.65 each. How much money does Sue have left?

A $1.75　　C $1.65
B $1.71 (B circled)　　D $1.61

18. Rachel buys a loaf of bread for $0.79 and 2 pounds of potatoes. One pound of potatoes costs $0.25. How much change should she get back from $5?

F $1.29　　H $3.81
G $3.71 (G circled)　　J $4.29

19.

| Box of Cake Mix | $0.79 |
| Can of Pie Filling | $0.69 |

Leonard buys 2 boxes of cake mix and 1 can of pie filling. How much change should he get back from $5?

A $3.93　　C $3.28
B $3.38　　D $2.73 (D circled)

20. One bagel costs $0.43 and one roll costs $0.36. Ron buys 3 bagels and 2 rolls. How much change should he get back from $3?

F $2.21　　H $0.79
G $0.99 (G circled)　　J $0.06

Go On

Stop

Write the correct answer.

1. What fraction of a dollar is shown?

$\frac{1}{4}$ of a dollar

2. What fraction of a dollar is shown?

$\frac{1}{2}$ of a dollar

3. What fraction of a dollar is shown?

$\frac{3}{4}$ of a dollar

4. What fraction of a dollar is shown?

$\frac{1}{2}$ of a dollar

5. What amount of money is 32 hundredths of a dollar?

$0.32

6. Todd has $\frac{3}{4}$ of a dollar. How much money is this?

$0.75

7. Write the missing numbers.

$0.27 = _2_ dimes _7_ pennies

8. What amount of money is $\frac{6}{100}$ of a dollar?

$0.06

9. What amount of money is $\frac{54}{100}$ of a dollar?

$0.54

10.　$0.47
　　+ $0.34
　　$0.81

11.　$3.36
　　+ $2.15
　　$5.51

12.　$0.74
　　− $0.56
　　$0.18

13.　4.70
　　− 2.18
　　2.52

14. A can of peas costs $0.39 and a can of corn costs $0.49. How much would it cost to buy one of each?

$0.88

15. The Owens' backyard is 0.35 acre and the Fords' backyard is 0.59 acre. How many acres is that in all?

0.94 acre

16. Greg has $0.81 and Dennis has $0.45. How much more money does Greg have than Dennis?

$0.36

17. Mark has $5 to spend at the hobby shop. He buys a model car and 3 paint brushes. A model car is $2.59 and each paint brush costs $0.45. How much money will Mark have left?

$1.06

18. Cassie buys 2 apples for $0.35 each and a pint of milk for $0.89. How much change should she get back from $5?

$3.41

19.

| BANANAS $0.39 PER POUND |
| PINEAPPLES $0.79 EACH |

Charlie buys 2 pounds of bananas and 1 pineapple. How much change should he get back from $5?

$3.43

20. A pint of orange juice costs $0.79 and a muffin costs $0.35. Janice buys 2 pints of orange juice and 2 muffins. How much change should she get back from $3?

$0.72

Go On

Stop

Choose the correct answer.

1. What fraction names the point of the letter *x* on the number line?

$\frac{0}{6}$ $\frac{1}{6}$ $\frac{2}{6}$ $\frac{3}{6}$ *x* $\frac{5}{6}$ $\frac{6}{6}$
0   1.0

(A) $\frac{4}{6}$ B $\frac{3}{6}$ C $\frac{1}{2}$ D $\frac{1}{4}$

2. What fraction names the shaded part of the group?

F $\frac{1}{4}$ (G) $\frac{3}{4}$ H $\frac{2}{8}$ J $\frac{8}{8}$

3. Use the fraction bars. Find an equivalent fraction.

| 1 |
| $\frac{1}{6}$ $\frac{1}{6}$ $\frac{1}{6}$ |
| $\frac{1}{4}$ $\frac{1}{4}$ |

$\frac{3}{6} = \frac{\blacksquare}{4}$

A 4   B 3   (C) 2   D 1

4. 0.59
  + 0.33

F $0.86   (H) $0.92
G $0.82   J $1.26

5. Use the fraction bars. Find an equivalent fraction.

| 1 |
| $\frac{1}{5}$ $\frac{1}{5}$ |
| $\frac{1}{10}$ $\frac{1}{10}$ $\frac{1}{10}$ $\frac{1}{10}$ |

$\frac{2}{5} = \frac{\blacksquare}{10}$

A 10   (B) 4   C 2   D 1

6. Compare the fractions. Choose <, >, or =.

| $\frac{1}{6}$ $\frac{1}{6}$ |
| $\frac{1}{3}$ $\frac{1}{3}$ |

$\frac{2}{6}$ ● $\frac{2}{3}$

(F) <   G >   H =

7. Use the fraction bars to compare. Order $\frac{1}{3}$, $\frac{2}{5}$, and $\frac{1}{6}$ from least to greatest.

| $\frac{1}{5}$ $\frac{1}{5}$ |
| $\frac{1}{3}$ |
| $\frac{1}{6}$ |

A $\frac{1}{3}, \frac{2}{5}, \frac{1}{6}$ C $\frac{1}{3}, \frac{1}{6}, \frac{2}{5}$
(B) $\frac{1}{6}, \frac{1}{3}, \frac{2}{5}$ D $\frac{1}{6}, \frac{2}{5}, \frac{1}{3}$

8. 0.92
  − 0.56

(F) 0.36   H 0.46
G 0.38   J 0.55

Go On

Form A • Multiple Choice   Assessment Guide **AG177**

---

9. Use the model below to solve the problem. Jason ate $\frac{1}{2}$ of his sandwich. Jeff ate $\frac{3}{4}$ of his sandwich. Justin ate $\frac{2}{5}$ of his sandwich. Who ate the **greatest** part of his sandwich?

| $\frac{1}{5}$ $\frac{1}{5}$ |
| $\frac{1}{2}$ |
| $\frac{1}{4}$ $\frac{1}{4}$ $\frac{1}{4}$ |

(A) Jeff
B Jason
C Justin

10. Tasha has $5.00 to spend. She buys 2 muffins at $0.29 each and a carton of juice for $0.89. How much money will she have left?

F $4.63   H $3.82
G $4.53   (J) $3.53

11. Ron walked $\frac{2}{3}$ of a mile. Casey walked $\frac{6}{8}$ of a mile. Josie walked $\frac{3}{4}$ of a mile. Who walked the farthest?

| $\frac{1}{5}$ $\frac{1}{5}$ $\frac{1}{5}$ |
| $\frac{1}{3}$ $\frac{1}{3}$ |
| $\frac{1}{4}$ $\frac{1}{4}$ $\frac{1}{4}$ |

(A) Josie
B Casey
C Ron

12. What fraction names the shaded parts?

F $1\frac{1}{6}$ (H) $1\frac{4}{6}$
G $1\frac{3}{6}$ J $1\frac{5}{6}$

13. Use the fraction bars. Find the sum.

| $\frac{1}{8}$ $\frac{1}{8}$ $\frac{1}{8}$ $\frac{1}{8}$ $\frac{1}{8}$ $\frac{1}{8}$ |

$\frac{5}{8} + \frac{1}{8} = \blacksquare$

A $\frac{1}{2}$ B $\frac{5}{8}$ (C) $\frac{6}{8}$ D $\frac{5}{16}$

14. Danielle and Jimmy shared a granola bar. Danielle ate $\frac{2}{6}$ of the bar, and Jimmy ate $\frac{3}{6}$ of the bar. What fraction of the granola bar did they eat?

F $\frac{1}{2}$ G $\frac{1}{6}$ H $\frac{1}{4}$ (J) $\frac{5}{6}$

15. What is the sum in simplest form?

| $\frac{1}{6}$ $\frac{1}{6}$ $\frac{1}{6}$ |
| $\frac{1}{3}$ $\frac{1}{3}$ |

$\frac{2}{6} + \frac{2}{6} = \blacksquare$

A $\frac{1}{6}$ B $\frac{2}{6}$ C $\frac{1}{3}$ (D) $\frac{2}{3}$

Go On

AG178 Assessment Guide   **Form A • Multiple Choice**

---

16. Kevin rode his bike $\frac{2}{8}$ of a mile. Alan rode $\frac{4}{8}$ of a mile. How far did they ride their bikes altogether?

F $\frac{2}{16}$ of a mile H $\frac{6}{16}$ of a mile
(G) $\frac{3}{4}$ of a mile   J $\frac{1}{2}$ of a mile

17. Find the difference.

$\frac{6}{8} - \frac{3}{8} = \blacksquare$ | $\frac{1}{8}$ $\frac{1}{8}$ $\frac{1}{8}$ $\frac{1}{8}$ $\frac{1}{8}$ $\frac{1}{8}$ |

A $\frac{5}{8}$ B $\frac{4}{8}$ (C) $\frac{3}{8}$ D $\frac{2}{8}$

18. Jenny cut a loaf of bread into 8 equal slices. She ate 3 slices. What fraction shows how much of the loaf was left?

F $\frac{2}{3}$ G $\frac{3}{8}$ (H) $\frac{5}{8}$ J 5

19. What is the difference in simplest form?

$\frac{5}{6} - \frac{1}{6} = \blacksquare$

A $\frac{1}{6}$ (B) $\frac{2}{3}$ C $\frac{1}{3}$ D $\frac{1}{2}$

20. Jake ran $\frac{7}{10}$ of a mile. Denise ran $\frac{2}{10}$ of a mile. How much farther did Jake run than Denise?

F $\frac{9}{10}$ of a mile

G $\frac{9}{20}$ of a mile

H $\frac{1}{10}$ of a mile

(J) $\frac{1}{2}$ of a mile

21. Karen mowed $\frac{1}{7}$ of the grass in the morning and then $\frac{3}{7}$ of it in the afternoon. Her brother mowed the rest. How do you find the fraction of the grass that her brother mowed?

A Add $\frac{1}{7} + \frac{3}{7}$.

B Subtract $\frac{3}{7} - \frac{1}{7}$, and then subtract from $\frac{7}{7}$.

C Add $\frac{1}{7} + \frac{1}{7}$.

(D) Add $\frac{1}{7} + \frac{3}{7}$, and then subtract from $\frac{7}{7}$.

22. What is the decimal for the fraction $\frac{3}{10}$?

F 0.1 G 0.2 (H) 0.3 J 3.0

23. What is the decimal for the shaded part?

A 7.0   (C) 0.7
B 0.9   D 0.3

24. What is $\frac{8}{10}$ written as a decimal?

F 810   (H) 0.8
G 0.08 J 1.8

Go On

Form A • Multiple Choice   Assessment Guide **AG179**

---

25. What is 0.47 written as a fraction?

(A) $\frac{47}{100}$ C 47.00

B $\frac{47}{10}$ D $\frac{4}{7}$

26. What is 4.36 written in expanded form?

(F) 4.0 + 0.3 + 0.06
G 4.0 + 0.60 + 0.03
H 400 + 30 + 6
J 4 + 30 + 100

27. Which shows 0.8, 0.3, and 0.5 in order from **greatest** to **least**?

0 0.1 0.2 0.3 0.4 0.5 0.6 0.7 0.8 0.9 1.0

A 0.8, 0.3, 0.5
(B) 0.8, 0.5, 0.3
C 0.5, 0.3, 0.8
D 0.3, 0.5, 0.8

For 28–29, identify problems with too little information. Solve the problems with too much or the right amount of information.

28. Dylan ran after school. He ran 4 days each week. How far did Dylan run in 1 week?

(F) too little information
G 4 miles
H 10 miles
J 14 miles

29. Kendra bought 3 notebooks, 2 packs of pencils, and 1 package of markers. Each notebook cost $1.39. How much did Kendra spend on notebooks?

A too little information
(B) $4.17
C $4.71
D $6.95

30. What fraction of a dollar is shown?

F $\frac{1}{10}$ of a dollar

G $\frac{1}{5}$ of a dollar

(H) $\frac{1}{4}$ of a dollar

J $\frac{1}{2}$ of a dollar

31. What amount of money is $\frac{3}{4}$ of a dollar?

A $750   (C) $0.75
B $75   D $0.57

32. Find the missing numbers.

$0.42 = \blacksquare$ dimes $\blacksquare$ pennies

F 2, 4   H 4, 200
(G) 4, 2   J 2, 40

33. Larry has $5.00. He buys 2 pounds of apples at $0.39 a pound and a head of lettuce for $0.99. How much money is left?

A $4.33   C $3.62
B $4.23   (D) $3.23

Stop

AG180 Assessment Guide   **Form A • Multiple Choice**

Assessment Guide AG 253

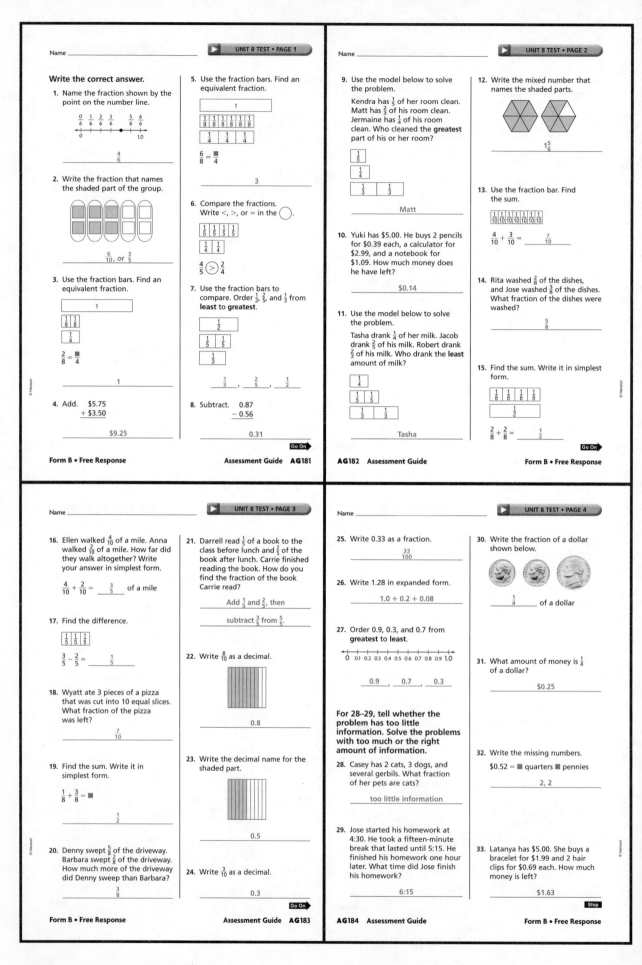

Name _____

Write the correct answer.

1. Name the fraction shown by the point on the number line.

$$\frac{0}{6}\ \frac{1}{6}\ \frac{2}{6}\ \frac{3}{6}\ \ \ \frac{5}{6}\ \frac{6}{6}$$

0 ————————•———————— 1.0

$$\frac{4}{6}$$

2. Write the fraction that names the shaded part of the group.

$$\frac{6}{10}, \text{ or } \frac{3}{5}$$

3. Use the fraction bars. Find an equivalent fraction.

1

| 1/8 | 1/8 |
| 1/4 |

$$\frac{2}{8} = \frac{\blacksquare}{4}$$

1

4. Add. $5.75
      + $3.50

$9.25

5. Use the fraction bars. Find an equivalent fraction.

1

| 1/8 | 1/8 | 1/8 | 1/8 | 1/8 | 1/8 |
| 1/4 | 1/4 | 1/4 |

$$\frac{6}{8} = \frac{\blacksquare}{4}$$

3

6. Compare the fractions. Write <, >, or = in the ○.

| 1/5 | 1/5 | 1/5 | 1/5 |
| 1/4 | 1/4 |

$$\frac{4}{5} \; \bigcirc\!\!> \; \frac{2}{4}$$

7. Use the fraction bars to compare. Order $\frac{1}{2}$, $\frac{2}{5}$, and $\frac{1}{3}$ from **least to greatest**.

| 1/2 |
| 1/5 | 1/5 |
| 1/3 |

$$\frac{1}{3}, \quad \frac{2}{5}, \quad \frac{1}{2}$$

8. Subtract.   0.87
        − 0.56

0.31

Go On

Form B • Free Response   **Assessment Guide   AG181**

Name _____

9. Use the model below to solve the problem.

Kendra has $\frac{1}{5}$ of her room clean. Matt has $\frac{2}{5}$ of his room clean. Jermaine has $\frac{1}{4}$ of his room clean. Who cleaned the **greatest** part of his or her room?

| 1/5 |
| 1/4 |
| 1/3 | 1/3 |

Matt

10. Yuki has $5.00. He buys 2 pencils for $0.39 each, a calculator for $2.99, and a notebook for $1.09. How much money does he have left?

$0.14

11. Use the model below to solve the problem.

Tasha drank $\frac{1}{4}$ of her milk. Jacob drank $\frac{2}{5}$ of his milk. Robert drank $\frac{2}{3}$ of his milk. Who drank the **least** amount of milk?

| 1/4 |
| 1/5 | 1/5 |
| 1/3 | 1/3 |

Tasha

12. Write the mixed number that names the shaded parts.

$$1\frac{5}{6}$$

13. Use the fraction bar. Find the sum.

| 1/10 | 1/10 | 1/10 | 1/10 | 1/10 | 1/10 | 1/10 |

$$\frac{4}{10} + \frac{3}{10} = \frac{7}{10}$$

14. Rita washed $\frac{2}{8}$ of the dishes, and Jose washed $\frac{3}{8}$ of the dishes. What fraction of the dishes were washed?

$$\frac{5}{8}$$

15. Find the sum. Write it in simplest form.

| 1/8 | 1/8 | 1/8 | 1/8 |
| 1/2 |

$$\frac{2}{8} + \frac{2}{8} = \frac{1}{2}$$

Go On

AG182   Assessment Guide   **Form B • Free Response**

Name _____

16. Ellen walked $\frac{4}{10}$ of a mile. Anna walked $\frac{2}{10}$ of a mile. How far did they walk altogether? Write your answer in simplest form.

$$\frac{4}{10} + \frac{2}{10} = \frac{3}{5} \text{ of a mile}$$

17. Find the difference.

| 1/5 | 1/5 | 1/5 |

$$\frac{3}{5} - \frac{2}{5} = \frac{1}{5}$$

18. Wyatt ate 3 pieces of a pizza that was cut into 10 equal slices. What fraction of the pizza was left?

$$\frac{7}{10}$$

19. Find the sum. Write it in simplest form.

$$\frac{1}{8} + \frac{3}{8} = \blacksquare$$

$$\frac{1}{2}$$

20. Denny swept $\frac{5}{8}$ of the driveway. Barbara swept $\frac{2}{8}$ of the driveway. How much more of the driveway did Denny sweep than Barbara?

$$\frac{3}{8}$$

21. Darrell read $\frac{1}{5}$ of a book to the class before lunch and $\frac{2}{5}$ of the book after lunch. Carrie finished reading the book. How do you find the fraction of the book Carrie read?

Add $\frac{1}{5}$ and $\frac{2}{5}$, then

subtract $\frac{3}{5}$ from $\frac{5}{5}$.

22. Write $\frac{8}{10}$ as a decimal.

0.8

23. Write the decimal name for the shaded part.

0.5

24. Write $\frac{3}{10}$ as a decimal.

0.3

Go On

Form B • Free Response   **Assessment Guide   AG183**

Name _____

25. Write 0.33 as a fraction.

$$\frac{33}{100}$$

26. Write 1.28 in expanded form.

1.0 + 0.2 + 0.08

27. Order 0.9, 0.3, and 0.7 from **greatest to least**.

0 0.1 0.2 0.3 0.4 0.5 0.6 0.7 0.8 0.9 1.0

0.9, 0.7, 0.3

For 28–29, tell whether the problem has too little information. Solve the problems with too much or the right amount of information.

28. Casey has 2 cats, 3 dogs, and several gerbils. What fraction of her pets are cats?

too little information

29. Jose started his homework at 4:30. He took a fifteen-minute break that lasted until 5:15. He finished his homework one hour later. What time did Jose finish his homework?

6:15

30. Write the fraction of a dollar shown below.

$$\frac{1}{4} \text{ of a dollar}$$

31. What amount of money is $\frac{1}{4}$ of a dollar?

$0.25

32. Write the missing numbers.

$0.52 = ■ quarters ■ pennies

2, 2

33. Latanya has $5.00. She buys a bracelet for $1.99 and 2 hair clips for $0.69 each. How much money is left?

$1.63

Stop

AG184   Assessment Guide   **Form B • Free Response**

Name _____

Choose the correct answer.

1. Complete the number pattern.

$7 \times 3 = 21$
$7 \times 30 = 210$
$7 \times \blacksquare = 2,100$

A 100   (C) 300
B 200   D 400

2. $7 \times 50 = \blacksquare$

F 35   H 500
(G) 350   J 750

3. $9 \times 10 = \blacksquare$

A 19   C 91
(B) 90   D 190

4. $8 \times 400 = \blacksquare$

F 320   (H) 3,200
G 480   J 4,800

5. $3 \times 70 = \blacksquare$

A 93   (C) 210
B 170   D 370

6. Use the base-ten blocks to find the product.

$2 \times 13 = \blacksquare$

F 62   (H) 26
G 46   J 13

7. Jon made an array of 3 rows of 15 tiles. Which multiplication sentence does his array show?

(A) $3 \times 15 = 45$
B $10 \times 5 = 50$
C $15 \times 10 = 150$
D $15 \times 15 = 225$

8. Use the base-ten blocks to find the product.

$3 \times 25 = \blacksquare$

(F) 75   H 50
G 65   J 25

9. Phil makes an array with 2 rows of 14 tiles. How many tiles are in his array?

A 14   C 42
(B) 28   D 56

10. Use the base-ten blocks to find the product.

$3 \times 14 = \blacksquare$

(F) 42   H 54
G 44   J 56

Go On

Form A • Multiple Choice

Name _____

11. Balloons cost 75¢ each. Which number sentence shows how to find the cost of 3 balloons?

A $75¢ + 3 = \blacksquare$
B $75¢ - 3 = \blacksquare$
(C) $3 \times 75¢ = \blacksquare$
D $75¢ \div 3 = \blacksquare$

12. Carolyn read 30 minutes on Monday and 50 minutes on Wednesday. Which could you use to find the number of minutes she read in all?

(F) addition   H multiplication
G subtraction   J division

13. Jerry has 45 model cars and Tom has 9. Which number sentence shows how to find how many more cars Jerry has than Tom?

A $45 \div 9 = \blacksquare$
(B) $45 - 9 = \blacksquare$
C $9 \times 45 = \blacksquare$
D $45 \div 5 = \blacksquare$

14. Jill paid $33 for 3 rosebushes. Which number sentence could you use to find the cost of one rosebush?

F $\$33 + 3 = \blacksquare$
(G) $\$33 \div 3 = \blacksquare$
H $\$33 \times 3 = \blacksquare$
J $\$33 - 3 = \blacksquare$

For 15–20, choose a method and solve.

15. $\begin{array}{r} 142 \\ \times\ 6 \\ \hline \end{array}$

A 856
(B) 852
C 582
D 148

16. $\begin{array}{r} 129 \\ \times\ 3 \\ \hline \end{array}$

F 497
G 487
(H) 387
J 307

17. $\begin{array}{r} 64 \\ \times\ 5 \\ \hline \end{array}$

A 80
B 160
C 240
(D) 320

18. $\begin{array}{r} 102 \\ \times\ 4 \\ \hline \end{array}$

F 308
G 388
(H) 408
J 418

19. Photos of local historic sites sell for $2 each. How much would 42 pictures cost?

(A) $84   B $64   C $44   D $21

20. An elementary school yearbook costs $5. How much would 30 yearbooks cost?

F $15   G $45   H $120   (J) $150

Stop

Form A • Multiple Choice

Name _____

Write the correct answer.

1. Complete the number pattern.

$8 \times 4 = 32$
$8 \times 40 = 320$
$8 \times \underline{400} = 3,200$

2. $8 \times 20 = \underline{160}$

3. $8 \times 10 = \underline{80}$

4. $7 \times 800 = \underline{5,600}$

5. $6 \times 700 = \underline{4,200}$

6. Use the array to find the product.

$3 \times 14 = \underline{42}$

7. Kristi made an array of 2 rows of 17 tiles. Write a multiplication sentence to show her array. You may draw a picture to help.

$2 \times 17 = 34$

8. Use the base-ten blocks to find the product.

$2 \times 26 = \underline{52}$

9. Tim makes an array with 5 rows of 16 tiles. How many tiles are in his array? You may draw a picture to help.

$\underline{80}$ tiles

10. Use the base-ten blocks to find the product.

$4 \times 23 = \underline{92}$

Go On

Form B • Free Response

Name _____

11. Wild animal stamps cost $0.33 each. Write a number sentence that shows how to find the cost of buying 6 stamps.

$6 \times \$0.33 = \$1.98$

12. Sheila jogged 40 minutes on Monday and 30 minutes on Tuesday. Write whether you would **add, subtract, multiply,** or **divide** to find the number of minutes she jogged in all.

add

13. Pete has 36 books and Rich has 19 books. Write a number sentence that shows how many more books Pete has than Rich.

$36 - 19 = 17$

14. Brandon has 24 stickers. He wants to put an equal number on each of 4 pages in a notebook. Write a number sentence that shows the number of stickers on each page.

$24 \div 4 = 6$

For 15–20, choose a method and solve.

15. $\begin{array}{r} 253 \\ \times\ 5 \\ \hline 1,265 \end{array}$

16. $\begin{array}{r} 103 \\ \times\ 6 \\ \hline 618 \end{array}$

17. $\begin{array}{r} 27 \\ \times\ 5 \\ \hline 135 \end{array}$

18. $\begin{array}{r} 114 \\ \times\ 3 \\ \hline 342 \end{array}$

19. Mike sold ticket packs for games at the school fair for $3 each. He sold 22 ticket packs. How much money did he make?

$66

20. The community center sells tickets to the talent show for $4 per ticket. They sold 45 tickets for the show. How much money did the community center make?

$180

Stop

Form B • Free Response

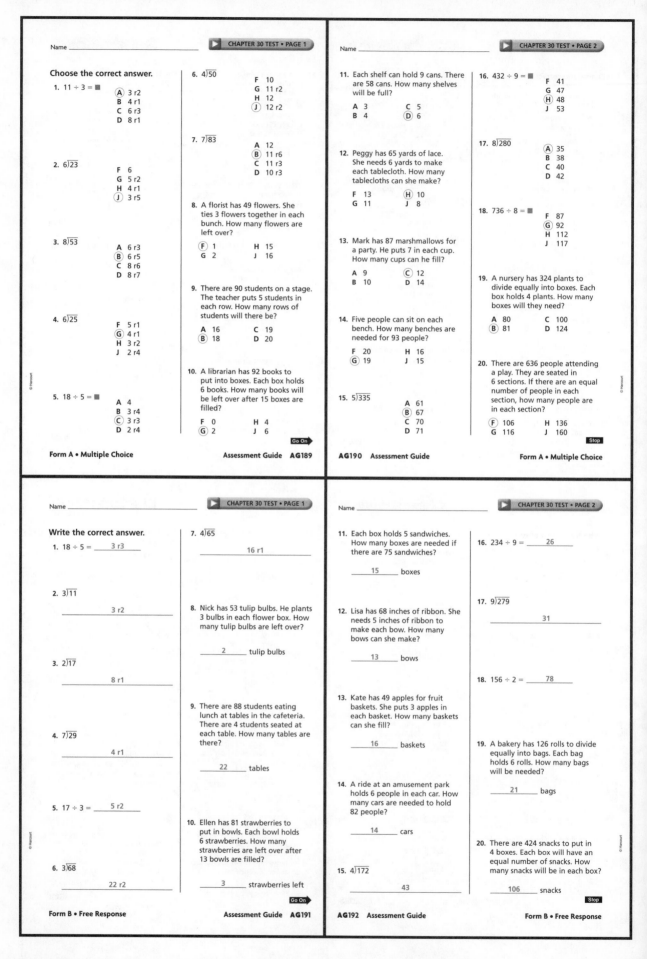

Choose the correct answer.

1. $11 \div 3 = \blacksquare$
   - Ⓐ 3 r2
   - B 4 r1
   - C 6 r3
   - D 8 r1

2. $6\overline{)23}$
   - F 6
   - G 5 r2
   - H 4 r1
   - Ⓙ 3 r5

3. $8\overline{)53}$
   - A 6 r3
   - Ⓑ 6 r5
   - C 8 r6
   - D 8 r7

4. $6\overline{)25}$
   - F 5 r1
   - Ⓖ 4 r1
   - H 3 r2
   - J 2 r4

5. $18 \div 5 = \blacksquare$
   - A 4
   - B 3 r4
   - Ⓒ 3 r3
   - D 2 r4

6. $4\overline{)50}$
   - F 10
   - G 11 r2
   - H 12
   - Ⓙ 12 r2

7. $7\overline{)83}$
   - A 12
   - Ⓑ 11 r6
   - C 11 r3
   - D 10 r3

8. A florist has 49 flowers. She ties 3 flowers together in each bunch. How many flowers are left over?
   - Ⓕ 1   H 15
   - G 2   J 16

9. There are 90 students on a stage. The teacher puts 5 students in each row. How many rows of students will there be?
   - A 16   C 19
   - Ⓑ 18   D 20

10. A librarian has 92 books to put into boxes. Each box holds 6 books. How many books will be left over after 15 boxes are filled?
    - F 0   H 4
    - Ⓖ 2   J 6

Go On

Form A • Multiple Choice   Assessment Guide   **AG189**

---

11. Each shelf can hold 9 cans. There are 58 cans. How many shelves will be full?
    - A 3   C 5
    - B 4   Ⓓ 6

12. Peggy has 65 yards of lace. She needs 6 yards to make each tablecloth. How many tablecloths can she make?
    - F 13   Ⓗ 10
    - G 11   J 8

13. Mark has 87 marshmallows for a party. He puts 7 in each cup. How many cups can he fill?
    - A 9   Ⓒ 12
    - B 10   D 14

14. Five people can sit on each bench. How many benches are needed for 93 people?
    - F 20   H 16
    - Ⓖ 19   J 15

15. $5\overline{)335}$
    - A 61
    - Ⓑ 67
    - C 70
    - D 71

16. $432 \div 9 = \blacksquare$
    - F 41
    - G 47
    - Ⓗ 48
    - J 53

17. $8\overline{)280}$
    - Ⓐ 35
    - B 38
    - C 40
    - D 42

18. $736 \div 8 = \blacksquare$
    - F 87
    - Ⓖ 92
    - H 112
    - J 117

19. A nursery has 324 plants to divide equally into boxes. Each box holds 4 plants. How many boxes will they need?
    - A 80   C 100
    - Ⓑ 81   D 124

20. There are 636 people attending a play. They are seated in 6 sections. If there are an equal number of people in each section, how many people are in each section?
    - Ⓕ 106   H 136
    - G 116   J 160

Stop

AG190   Assessment Guide   **Form A • Multiple Choice**

Write the correct answer.

1. $18 \div 5 =$ ___3 r3___

2. $3\overline{)11}$
   ___3 r2___

3. $2\overline{)17}$
   ___8 r1___

4. $7\overline{)29}$
   ___4 r1___

5. $17 \div 3 =$ ___5 r2___

6. $3\overline{)68}$
   ___22 r2___

7. $4\overline{)65}$
   ___16 r1___

8. Nick has 53 tulip bulbs. He plants 3 bulbs in each flower box. How many tulip bulbs are left over?
   ___2___ tulip bulbs

9. There are 88 students eating lunch at tables in the cafeteria. There are 4 students seated at each table. How many tables are there?
   ___22___ tables

10. Ellen has 81 strawberries to put in bowls. Each bowl holds 6 strawberries. How many strawberries are left over after 13 bowls are filled?
    ___3___ strawberries left

Go On

Form B • Free Response   Assessment Guide   **AG191**

---

11. Each box holds 5 sandwiches. How many boxes are needed if there are 75 sandwiches?
    ___15___ boxes

12. Lisa has 68 inches of ribbon. She needs 5 inches of ribbon to make each bow. How many bows can she make?
    ___13___ bows

13. Kate has 49 apples for fruit baskets. She puts 3 apples in each basket. How many baskets can she fill?
    ___16___ baskets

14. A ride at an amusement park holds 6 people in each car. How many cars are needed to hold 82 people?
    ___14___ cars

15. $4\overline{)172}$
    ___43___

16. $234 \div 9 =$ ___26___

17. $9\overline{)279}$
    ___31___

18. $156 \div 2 =$ ___78___

19. A bakery has 126 rolls to divide equally into bags. Each bag holds 6 rolls. How many bags will be needed?
    ___21___ bags

20. There are 424 snacks to put in 4 boxes. Each box will have an equal number of snacks. How many snacks will be in each box?
    ___106___ snacks

Stop

AG192   Assessment Guide   **Form B • Free Response**

AG256   Assessment Guide

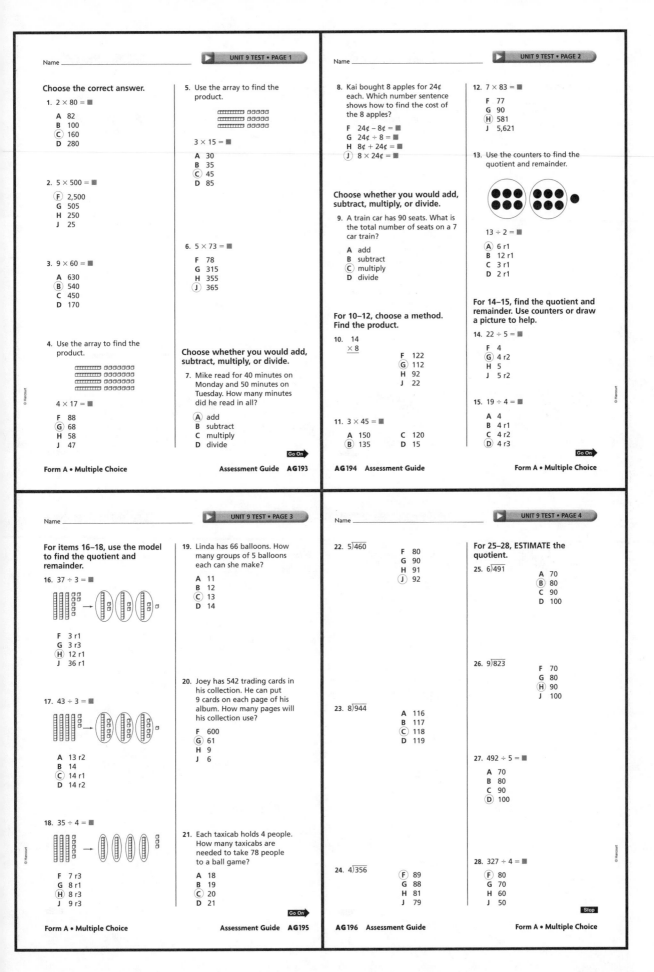

Choose the correct answer.

1. $2 \times 80 = \blacksquare$

   A 82
   B 100
   Ⓒ 160
   D 280

2. $5 \times 500 = \blacksquare$

   Ⓕ 2,500
   G 505
   H 250
   J 25

3. $9 \times 60 = \blacksquare$

   A 630
   Ⓑ 540
   C 450
   D 170

4. Use the array to find the product.

   $4 \times 17 = \blacksquare$

   F 88
   Ⓖ 68
   H 58
   J 47

5. Use the array to find the product.

   $3 \times 15 = \blacksquare$

   A 30
   B 35
   Ⓒ 45
   D 85

6. $5 \times 73 = \blacksquare$

   F 78
   G 315
   H 355
   Ⓙ 365

Choose whether you would add, subtract, multiply, or divide.

7. Mike read for 40 minutes on Monday and 50 minutes on Tuesday. How many minutes did he read in all?

   Ⓐ add
   B subtract
   C multiply
   D divide

Go On

8. Kai bought 8 apples for 24¢ each. Which number sentence shows how to find the cost of the 8 apples?

   F 24¢ − 8¢ = $\blacksquare$
   G 24¢ ÷ 8 = $\blacksquare$
   H 8¢ + 24¢ = $\blacksquare$
   Ⓙ 8 × 24¢ = $\blacksquare$

Choose whether you would add, subtract, multiply, or divide.

9. A train car has 90 seats. What is the total number of seats on a 7 car train?

   A add
   B subtract
   Ⓒ multiply
   D divide

For 10–12, choose a method. Find the product.

10. $\begin{array}{r} 14 \\ \times\ 8 \\ \hline \end{array}$

    F 122
    Ⓖ 112
    H 92
    J 22

11. $3 \times 45 = \blacksquare$

    A 150   C 120
    Ⓑ 135   D 15

12. $7 \times 83 = \blacksquare$

    F 77
    G 90
    Ⓗ 581
    J 5,621

13. Use the counters to find the quotient and remainder.

    $13 \div 2 = \blacksquare$

    Ⓐ 6 r1
    B 12 r1
    C 3 r1
    D 2 r1

For 14–15, find the quotient and remainder. Use counters or draw a picture to help.

14. $22 \div 5 = \blacksquare$

    F 4
    Ⓖ 4 r2
    H 5
    J 5 r2

15. $19 \div 4 = \blacksquare$

    A 4
    B 4 r1
    C 4 r2
    Ⓓ 4 r3

Go On

For items 16–18, use the model to find the quotient and remainder.

16. $37 \div 3 = \blacksquare$

    F 3 r1
    G 3 r3
    Ⓗ 12 r1
    J 36 r1

17. $43 \div 3 = \blacksquare$

    A 13 r2
    B 14
    Ⓒ 14 r1
    D 14 r2

18. $35 \div 4 = \blacksquare$

    F 7 r3
    G 8 r1
    Ⓗ 8 r3
    J 9 r3

19. Linda has 66 balloons. How many groups of 5 balloons each can she make?

    A 11
    B 12
    Ⓒ 13
    D 14

20. Joey has 542 trading cards in his collection. He can put 9 cards on each page of his album. How many pages will his collection use?

    F 600
    Ⓖ 61
    H 9
    J 6

21. Each taxicab holds 4 people. How many taxicabs are needed to take 78 people to a ball game?

    A 18
    B 19
    Ⓒ 20
    D 21

Go On

22. $5\overline{)460}$

    F 80
    G 90
    H 91
    Ⓙ 92

23. $8\overline{)944}$

    A 116
    B 117
    Ⓒ 118
    D 119

24. $4\overline{)356}$

    Ⓕ 89
    G 88
    H 81
    J 79

For 25–28, ESTIMATE the quotient.

25. $6\overline{)491}$

    A 70
    Ⓑ 80
    C 90
    D 100

26. $9\overline{)823}$

    F 70
    G 80
    Ⓗ 90
    J 100

27. $492 \div 5 = \blacksquare$

    A 70
    B 80
    C 90
    Ⓓ 100

28. $327 \div 4 = \blacksquare$

    Ⓕ 80
    G 70
    H 60
    J 50

Stop

Name _____

Write the correct answer.

For 1–3, use mental math and basic facts to find the product.

1. $4 \times 70 = \blacksquare$

   280

2. $3 \times 800 = \blacksquare$

   2,400

3. $4 \times 90 = \blacksquare$

   360

4. Use the array to find the product.

   $3 \times 16 = $ ___48___

5. Use the array to find the product.

   $4 \times 12 = $ ___48___

6. $4 \times 87 = $ ___348___

Choose whether you would add, subtract, multiply, or divide.

7. Carmen read for 25 minutes on Tuesday and 45 minutes on Thursday. How many minutes did she read in all?

   ___add___

8. Jason bought 6 pencils for $0.30 each. Write a number sentence that shows the cost of the 6 pencils.

   $6 \times \$0.30 = \$1.80$

Form B • Free Response

Name _____

Choose whether you would add, subtract, multiply, or divide.

9. There were 53 people on a bus. At the first stop, 37 people got off the bus. What is the number of people left on the bus?

   ___subtract___

For 10–12, choose a method. Find the product.

10. $\begin{array}{r} 24 \\ \times\ 3 \\ \hline 72 \end{array}$

11. $4 \times 36 = \blacksquare$

    144

12. $6 \times 29 = \blacksquare$

    174

13. Use the counters to find the quotient and remainder.

    $17 \div 3 = \blacksquare$

    5 r2

For 14–15, find the quotient and remainder. Use counters or draw a picture to help.

14. $19 \div 3 = \blacksquare$

    6 r1

15. $22 \div 4 = \blacksquare$

    5 r2

For 16–18, use the model to find the quotient and remainder.

16. Find the quotient and the remainder.

    $25 \div 4 = \blacksquare$

    6 r1

Form B • Free Response

Name _____

17. $32 \div 3 = \blacksquare$

    10 r2

18. $41 \div 3 = \blacksquare$

    13 r2

19. Chris has 74 marbles. He puts them into groups of 8. How many groups of marbles can he make?

    ___9___ groups

20. Jason has 245 shells in his collection. He can put 8 shells in each display box. How many display boxes does he need to hold his collection?

    ___31___ boxes

21. Each van holds 8 people. How many vans are needed to take 102 people to a park?

    ___13___ vans

22. $6\overline{)432}$ 72

23. $7\overline{)847}$ 121

24. $6\overline{)426}$ 71

Form B • Free Response

Name _____

For 25–28, ESTIMATE the quotient.

25. $7\overline{)647}$

    about 90

26. $8\overline{)812}$

    about 100

27. $631 \div 9 = \blacksquare$

    about 70

28. $137 \div 6 = \blacksquare$

    about 20

Form B • Free Response

AG 258   Assessment Guide

Choose the correct answer.

1. What is the value of the 5 in 5,307?

Ⓐ 5,000   C 50
B 500   D 5

2. Compare the numbers.

7,412 ● 7,413

Ⓕ <   G >   H =

3. Which operation symbol makes the number sentence true?

130 ● 15 = 115

A ÷   B ×   Ⓒ −   D +

4. 704
  − 88

F 516
G 612
H 606
Ⓙ 616

5. What amount is shown?

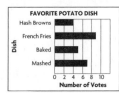

A $2.61   C $2.31
Ⓑ $2.56   D $2.16

6. $4.65
  −$2.90

F $7.65
G $2.75
H $1.95
Ⓙ $1.75

For 7, use the schedule.

MORNING CLASS SCHEDULE

Activity	Time
Reading	8:15 A.M. – 9:00 A.M.
Math	9:00 A.M. – 10:00 A.M.
Recess	10:00 A.M. – 10:20 A.M.
Art	10:20 A.M. – 11:00 A.M.
Spelling	11:00 A.M. – 11:35 A.M.

7. Which activity is the longest?

A reading   C spelling
Ⓑ math   D art

8. There are 8 oranges in each bag. Kyle buys 2 bags. How many oranges does he buy in all?

F 6   H 14
G 10   Ⓙ 16

9.   9
   × 3

A 36
Ⓑ 27
C 18
D 12

Go On ▶

Form A • Multiple Choice   Assessment Guide **AG201**

---

10. Compare. Choose <, >, or = for the ●.

0 × 8 ● 1 × 6

Ⓕ <   G >   H =

11. Luke buys 8 packages of balloons. Each package has 4 balloons in it. How many balloons does he buy in all?

A 40   C 24
Ⓑ 32   D 12

12. ■ = 10 × 8

F 18   Ⓗ 80
G 70   J 108

For 13, use the pictograph.

NEW LIBRARY BOOKS

Fiction	📘📘📘
Science	📘📘
History	📘📘
Art	📘📘📘

Key: Each 📘 = 4 books.

13. How many more new art books than science books are in the library?

A 1   C 4
Ⓑ 2   D 8

14. What is the rule for the table?

Chairs	1	2	3	4	5
Legs	4	8	12	16	20

Ⓕ Multiply chairs by 4.
G Divide chairs by 4.
H Add 1 to chairs.
J Add 2 to legs.

15. An adult's ticket costs $8. A child's ticket costs $4. How much would tickets cost for 3 adults and 7 children?

A $22   Ⓒ $52
B $24   D $53

16. Which number makes the number sentences true?

7 × ■ = 28   28 ÷ 7 = ■

F 2   Ⓗ 4
G 3   J 5

17. 42 ÷ 7 = ■

A 8   Ⓒ 6
B 7   D 5

18. What is the rule for the pattern?

345, 360, 375, 390, 405, 420

F Add 10.
Ⓖ Add 15.
H Add 25.
J Subtract 15.

Go On ▶

AG202 Assessment Guide   Form A • Multiple Choice

For 19–20, use the bar graph.

FAVORITE POTATO DISH

Dish: Hash Browns, French Fries, Baked, Mashed
Number of Votes: 0 2 4 6 8 10

19. Which potato dish got the **greatest** number of votes?

A hash browns
Ⓑ french fries
C baked
D mashed

20. How many more votes were for mashed than for baked potatoes?

Ⓕ 2   G 3   H 7   J 12

21. Which unit would you use to measure the length of your math book?

A mile   C foot
B yard   Ⓓ inch

22. Which word describes a triangle that has 3 equal sides?

F acute
G obtuse
H isosceles
Ⓙ equilateral

23. Which quadrilateral has only 1 pair of parallel sides?

A ▢   C ◇
Ⓑ ▱   D ▭

24. Which figure has 6 faces?

Ⓕ rectangular prism
G sphere
H cylinder
J cone

25. Judy has 16 feet of fencing to build a play area for her puppy. If she wants the **greatest** possible area, how long and wide should the sides of the play area be?

Ⓐ 4 feet long, 4 feet wide
B 5 feet long, 3 feet wide
C 8 feet long, 8 feet wide
D 16 feet long, 16 feet wide

26. What is the volume of the figure?

F 8 cubic units
Ⓖ 16 cubic units
H 24 cubic units
J 32 cubic units

Go On ▶

Form A • Multiple Choice   Assessment Guide **AG203**

---

27. Which color are you **most likely** to spin?

(spinner: Red, White, Red, Green, Blue, Red)

Ⓐ red   C green
B blue   D white

28. Lucy is arranging her vases on a shelf. She has a blue vase, a yellow vase, a red vase, and a purple vase. How many ways can she arrange her vases?

F 4   G 12   H 16   Ⓙ 24

29. Compare. Choose <, >, or =.

$\frac{1}{6}$	$\frac{1}{6}$	$\frac{1}{6}$

$\frac{1}{4}$	$\frac{1}{4}$	$\frac{1}{4}$

$\frac{3}{6}$ ● $\frac{3}{4}$

Ⓐ <   B >   C =

30. What is the sum in simplest form?

$\frac{3}{10} + \frac{2}{10} = ■$

Ⓕ $\frac{1}{2}$ G $\frac{2}{5}$ H $\frac{5}{20}$ J $\frac{1}{20}$

31. What is the difference in simplest form?

$\frac{7}{8} - \frac{5}{8} = ■$

A $\frac{2}{16}$ B $\frac{1}{2}$ Ⓒ $\frac{1}{4}$ D $\frac{1}{8}$

32. What is $\frac{9}{10}$ written as a decimal?

F 0.09   H 9.1
Ⓖ 0.9   J 910

33. Which shows the decimals in order from **least** to **greatest**?

A 0.4, 0.8, 0.6
B 0.8, 0.6, 0.4
Ⓒ 0.4, 0.6, 0.8
D 0.6, 0.4, 0.8

34.   0.17
   + 2.81

F 4.51   Ⓗ 2.98
G 3.15   J 2.64

35. Lauren exercises for 35 minutes each day. How many minutes does she exercise in 7 days?

A 42 minutes
B 56 minutes
C 215 minutes
Ⓓ 245 minutes

36. A group of 68 students is going to a museum. Each van can hold 8 students. How many vans do the students need?

F 7 vans
G 8 vans
Ⓗ 9 vans
J 10 vans

Stop

AG204 Assessment Guide   Form A • Multiple Choice

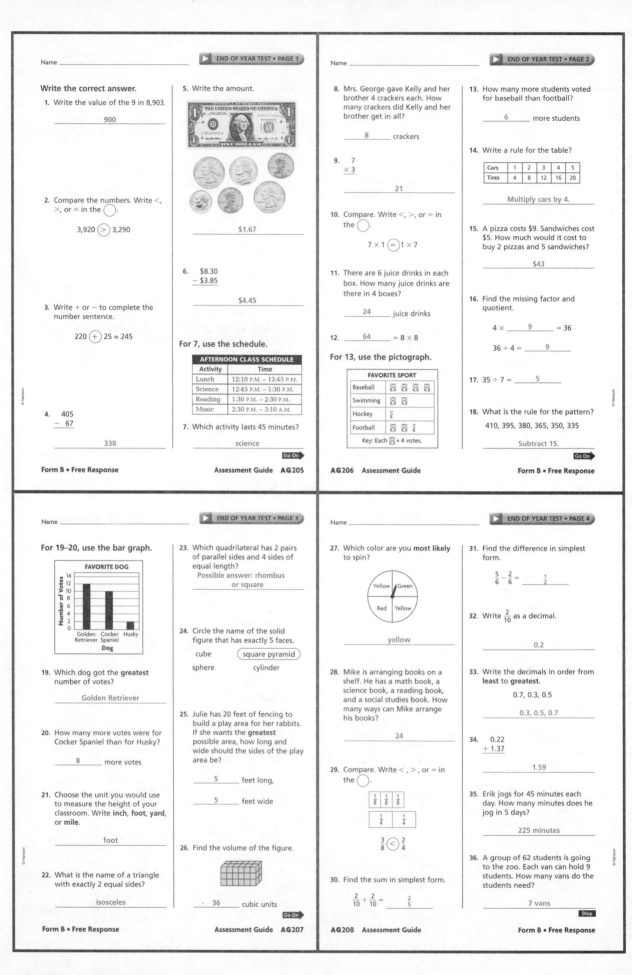

Name _____

Write the correct answer.

1. Write the value of the 9 in 8,903.

   _____900_____

2. Compare the numbers. Write <, >, or = in the ○.

   3,920 ⟨>⟩ 3,290

3. Write + or − to complete the number sentence.

   220 ⟨+⟩ 25 = 245

4. 405
   − 67
   _____338_____

5. Write the amount.

   $1.67

6. $8.30
   − $3.85
   _____$4.45_____

For 7, use the schedule.

AFTERNOON CLASS SCHEDULE	
Activity	**Time**
Lunch	12:10 P.M. − 12:45 P.M.
Science	12:45 P.M. − 1:30 P.M.
Reading	1:30 P.M. − 2:30 P.M.
Music	2:30 P.M. − 3:10 A.M.

7. Which activity lasts 45 minutes?

   science

Name _____

8. Mrs. George gave Kelly and her brother 4 crackers each. How many crackers did Kelly and her brother get in all?

   _____8_____ crackers

9. 7
   × 3
   _____21_____

10. Compare. Write <, >, or = in the ○.

    7×1 ⟨=⟩ 1×7

11. There are 6 juice drinks in each box. How many juice drinks are there in 4 boxes?

    _____24_____ juice drinks

12. _____64_____ = 8×8

For 13, use the pictograph.

FAVORITE SPORT	
Baseball	🏴🏴🏴🏴
Swimming	🏴🏴
Hockey	🏴
Football	🏴🏴🏴
Key: Each 🏴 = 4 votes.	

13. How many more students voted for baseball than football?

    _____6_____ more students

14. Write a rule for the table?

Cars	1	2	3	4	5
Tires	4	8	12	16	20

    Multiply cars by 4.

15. A pizza costs $9. Sandwiches cost $5. How much would it cost to buy 2 pizzas and 5 sandwiches?

    _____$43_____

16. Find the missing factor and quotient.

    $4 \times$ _____9_____ $= 36$

    $36 \div 4 =$ _____9_____

17. $35 \div 7 =$ _____5_____

18. What is the rule for the pattern?

    410, 395, 380, 365, 350, 335

    Subtract 15.

Name _____

For 19–20, use the bar graph.

FAVORITE DOG

19. Which dog got the **greatest** number of votes?

    Golden Retriever

20. How many more votes were for Cocker Spaniel than for Husky?

    _____8_____ more votes

21. Choose the unit you would use to measure the height of your classroom. Write **inch, foot, yard,** or **mile**.

    foot

22. What is the name of a triangle with exactly 2 equal sides?

    isosceles

23. Which quadrilateral has 2 pairs of parallel sides and 4 sides of equal length?

    Possible answer: rhombus or square

24. Circle the name of the solid figure that has exactly 5 faces.

    cube   ⟨square pyramid⟩

    sphere   cylinder

25. Julie has 20 feet of fencing to build a play area for her rabbits. If she wants the **greatest** possible area, how long and wide should the sides of the play area be?

    _____5_____ feet long,

    _____5_____ feet wide

26. Find the volume of the figure.

    ·   36   cubic units

Name _____

27. Which color are you **most likely** to spin?

    Yellow / Green
    Red / Yellow

    yellow

28. Mike is arranging books on a shelf. He has a math book, a science book, a reading book, and a social studies book. How many ways can Mike arrange his books?

    _____24_____

29. Compare. Write <, >, or = in the ○.

    | $\frac{1}{8}$ | $\frac{1}{8}$ | $\frac{1}{8}$ |
    | $\frac{1}{4}$ | $\frac{1}{4}$ | |

    $\frac{3}{8}$ ⟨<⟩ $\frac{2}{4}$

30. Find the sum in simplest form.

    $\frac{2}{10} + \frac{2}{10} =$ _____$\frac{2}{5}$_____

31. Find the difference in simplest form.

    $\frac{5}{6} - \frac{2}{6} =$ _____$\frac{1}{2}$_____

32. Write $\frac{2}{10}$ as a decimal.

    0.2

33. Write the decimals in order from **least** to **greatest**.

    0.7, 0.3, 0.5

    0.3, 0.5, 0.7

34. 0.22
    + 1.37
    _____1.59_____

35. Erik jogs for 45 minutes each day. How many minutes does he jog in 5 days?

    225 minutes

36. A group of 62 students is going to the zoo. Each van can hold 9 students. How many vans do the students need?

    7 vans